THE FINANCIAL TIMES

GUIDE TO

USING AND INTERPRETING COMPANY ACCOUNTS

THE FINANCIAL TIMES

GUIDE TO

USING AND INTERPRETING COMPANY ACCOUNTS

THIRD EDITION

WENDY MCKENZIE

FT Prentice Hall
FINANCIAL TIMES

An imprint of Pearson Education

London • New York • Toronto • Sydney • Tokyo • Singapore
Hong Kong • Cape Town • Madrid • Paris • Amsterdam • Munich • Milan

PEARSON EDUCATION LIMITED

Edinburgh Gate
Harlow, Essex CM20 2JE
Tel: +44 (0)1279 623623
Fax: +44 (0)1279 431059
Website: www.pearsoned.co.uk

First published in Great Britain in 2003

ISBN: 0 273 66312 7

British Library Cataloguing in Publication Data
A CIP catalogue record for this book can be obtained from the British Library

10 9 8 7 6 5 4

Typeset by Northern Phototypesetting Co Ltd, Bolton
Printed and bound in Great Britain by Biddles Ltd, King's Lynn, Norfolk

The Publishers' policy is to use paper manufactured from sustainable forests.

Contents

Preface

Everyone prepares accounts in one form or another. You have probably asked yourself questions like these:

> *'Can I afford to buy this house?'*
> *'Can I afford to buy a better car?'*
> *'How much am I worth?'*

If you have, you've prepared accounts. You've probably only done them mentally, and they wouldn't look anything like published accounts. Company accounts are not really very different to the ones that we prepare for ourselves, but their presentation and the words used make them look more complicated than they really are. Although most people prepare accounts, they believe that understanding company accounts is difficult, if not impossible. This book shows that once you have cut through the jargon and understood the presentation, anyone can use published accounts to assess a business's performance.

All senior managers need to be able to understand and analyse company accounts. This book shows you how to do it. It shows you the information found in a set of accounts and how to analyse this information so that you understand how well the company is performing. Although I'm primarily covering UK accounts, I'll also discuss some of the major differences that you'll find in overseas accounts.

The book is organised into three sections, each designed to answer different questions.

- The first section answers the question *'What information will I find in the accounts?'* This shows you:
  - what the financial statements look like;
  - what they tell you about a business;
  - the way they are prepared;
  - the judgements involved in preparing these statements;
  - the main differences between UK accounts and those prepared in other countries.
- The second section answers the question *'How do I analyse the accounts?'* and works through a set of published accounts, from the chemicals company Johnson Matthey, to show you:
  - how to approach and structure your analysis;
  - what ratios to use;
  - what the ratios do and don't tell you.

- The third section answers the question *'How can I use my analysis?'* by looking at four common uses for financial analysis:
  - analysing suppliers' accounts;
  - analysing customers' accounts;
  - analysing competitors' accounts;
  - identifying a company's acquisition potential.

Throughout the book I shall be using Johnson Matthey's accounts as a worked example. Now you may say 'Johnson Who?' and to be honest, I'd be surprised if you did know who they are, as they sell business to business. But:

- They're worth over £1.9 billion on the stock market, and this means that they are in the FTSE 100.
- You will have seen and used their products. Does your car have a catalytic converter? Or a tinted windscreen? Does your factory have an emissions control system? Do you have any gold, platinum or silver jewellery? Do you have any coloured tiles in your home? Have you ever taken a codeine-based medicine? If you've answered 'yes' to any of these questions, you probably have a Johnson Matthey product.

So let me tell you a bit more about this company . . .

Johnson Matthey has around 7,000 employees in 34 countries and is organised into four divisions:

- **Catalysts & Chemicals**: this division is helping to clean up and protect our environment. It is Johnson Matthey's largest division and consists of three separate business units:
  - *Catalytic Systems:* manufacturing catalysts controlling vehicle emissions and reducing emissions from industrial processes.
  - *Fuel Cells:* Johnson Matthey is the leading manufacturer of fuel cell catalysts and catalysed components that form the heart of a fuel cell. (A fuel cell converts hydrogen and air into heat and water, and has no dangerous emissions. There's currently no infrastructure for delivering hydrogen to our homes, and no acceptable way of storing hydrogen in cars, as it would mean there'd be no room for passengers. So fuel cell cars will initially use a catalytic reformer to generate hydrogen from a liquid fuel like methanol.) At the moment these are used for backup power and portable applications, but in a few years we'll see cars powered by Johnson Matthey's catalysts in their fuel cells.
  - *Chemicals:* manufacturing a variety of chemicals and catalysts used in a range of products including fuel cells and gas detectors. It also does the primary refining of platinum group metals, and recovers platinum and other materials from spent catalysts.
- **Precious Metals**: this division incorporates Johnson Matthey's worldwide precious metals operations and is organised into two global businesses – Platinum and Gold.
  - *Platinum:* marketing and fabricating platinum products. Johnson Matthey is the world's largest distributor of platinum.
  - *Gold and Silver:* refining gold and silver, including bullion.

- **Colours & Coatings**: this division is one of the leading suppliers of raw materials and decorative products for ceramics and glass. It manufactures a wide range of the chemicals and glazes used in the decoration of ceramic products – mainly tableware, glass and tiles. It is organised into three businesses, focusing on the division's key markets:
  - *Glass:* manufacturing decorative precious metal products and products for automotive glass.
  - *Structural Ceramics:* this business unit is primarily involved in manufacturing colours, glazes and ceramic adhesives called frits for sanitaryware industries.
  - *Speciality Coatings:* this division has two broad product ranges. The first focuses on developing and manufacturing colours, glazes and decorative precious metal products for fine china manufacturers throughout the world. The second develops and produces a range of inorganic pigments used in printing inks, automotive finishes, paints, woodstains and plastics.
- **Pharmaceutical Materials**: this division, created in 2002, is a global, integrated supplier of active pharmaceutical ingredients, mainly metal based, and controlled substances like opiates. It also supplies a range of services to pharmaceutical companies through all the stages in new product development.

So you can see that Johnson Matthey's products are part of our everyday lives, as they're incorporated into a range of products that we all use. They're a large, successful company that few people have heard of because they sell their products directly to other companies.

PART 1

What information will I find in the accounts?

1

An introduction to the accounts

- **The bases used to prepare accounts** – historical and current cost
- **The accounting principles** – the matching, or the accruals, principle; the prudence principle; the consistency principle; the going concern principle; substance over form; materiality
- **The accounts** – the chairman's statement; the directors' report; the profit and loss account; the statement of total recognised gains and losses; the balance sheet; the cash flow statement; the auditor's report; the notes to the accounts
- **Summary**

The amount of information that you'll find in the accounts and is publicly available depends on the type of company and its size. All companies registered in the UK have to file their annual accounts at Companies House, and all but very small companies must have their accounts audited by an independent accountant. This means that company accounts are in the public arena. However, small private companies prepare their accounts using a simpler set of rules and file very simple accounts. Medium-sized companies prepare the full financial statements but can file a simpler set at Companies House. Public companies and large private companies have to file their full annual accounts at Companies House, and consequently all of their accounts are in the public domain.

As a general rule the amount of information found in a set of accounts increases as ownership separates from control. Sole traders give very little external information, as they own, control, and take all the risks in their businesses. The other extreme is a public company listed on the Stock Exchange. Anyone can own a share in the business, and the directors of the company are unlikely to be its biggest shareholders. Consequently, listed companies have to comply with the Companies Act, the accounting rules (called accounting standards), and additional Stock Exchange listing requirements. They give a wide range of additional information to enable external investors to assess the investment risk more clearly.

The amount of detail disclosed in the accounts is influenced by four factors:

- the Companies Act;
- the accounting rules;
- a Stock Exchange listing;
- the company's size and ownership.

These four factors combine to determine the amount of detail required in the accounts.

The Companies Act

All companies have a legal requirement to prepare accounts that are 'true and fair' and, with the exception of very small companies, have been audited by an independent accountant. Until the implementation of the Fourth and Seventh EU Directives, in 1981 and 1989, there were no detailed rules on either accounting layout or measurement in British law. The Companies Act 1985 now identifies the minimum information that must be both disclosed in the accounts and subsequently filed at Companies House. It also requires that the accounts should include a director's report, a profit and loss account, a balance sheet, an auditor's report and that some additional disclosures are given in the notes to the accounts.

The accounting rules

These are called accounting standards and in the UK they are set by the Accounting Standards Board (ASB). Accounting rules issued before August 1990 are called Statements of Standard Accounting Practice (SSAPs); subsequently they have been called Financial Reporting Standards (FRSs). These rules cover things that are often set in law in other countries.

There are also international accounting standards that are becoming increasingly important, and most UK standards are broadly in line with the international view. By 2005 all companies within the EU that are listed on a Stock Exchange will have to use international accounting standards for their consolidated financial statements, and at the moment the Accounting Standards Board is revising UK accounting standards as part of the harmonisation process. This will probably affect all companies as the government has said that it may want to extend this to all companies in the future. To keep you up to date, I'll tell you about the ASB's current proposals (they're called Financial Reporting Exposure Drafts, or FREDs) to align UK accounting standards with the international standards.

The accounting rules clarify the way that profit should be measured and assets and liabilities valued, and require more information to be disclosed in the notes to the accounts. Whilst the accounting standards remain separate from the Companies Act, their legal position has been strengthened to ensure that the accounts show a true and fair view.

The accounting standards currently require most companies to publish three additional financial statements in their accounts:

- a cash flow statement;
- a note of historical cost profits and losses
- a statement of total recognised gains and losses.

A Stock Exchange listing

Companies listed on a Stock Exchange must disclose additional information concerned with the company's status, affairs and activities, directors, shares and shareholders, and loans and interest.

Company size and ownership

Until recently, the accounts prepared by small and large companies were broadly similar, although smaller private companies were exempt from some accounting standards. (For example, they did not have to prepare a cash flow statement.) However, since 1992 smaller companies have been increasingly allowed to prepare simpler accounts.

In 1992 an amendment to the Companies Act introduced substantial disclosure exemptions for small companies. The November 1993 budget continued the divergence between the accounting practices of small and larger companies. It modified the audit requirement for smaller companies. Companies with a turnover below £1,000,000 do not need to have their accounts audited, and the government is currently proposing to extend this requirement to larger companies with turnover of less than £4.8 million. Finally, in November 1997 the Accounting Standards Board issued its first Financial Reporting Standard for Smaller Entities (FRSSE). This increases the number of exemptions for smaller companies and simplifies the requirements of other accounting standards.

We are now seeing two different sets of generally accepted accounting practices evolving. Larger companies are required to comply with all statutory provisions and increasingly complex and detailed accounting standard requirements, whereas smaller private companies comply with a shorter, restricted set of rules that allow fewer disclosures in the accounts.

A private company's size is determined by its turnover, total assets, and its average employees. It is currently regarded as 'small' if two out of the three following conditions are met: its turnover must be less than £2.8 million, its total assets less than £1.4 million, and it has, on average, fewer than 50 employees. If it satisfies two of these conditions it qualifies for the Companies Act's small company disclosure exemptions, and its accounts may be based on the FRSSE.

The bases used to prepare accounts

In the UK, there are two fundamentally different ways in which accounts can be prepared:

- **historical cost:** based on the costs that the company has incurred;
- **current cost:** based on year end costs, and adjusted for the inflation that is being experienced in the business. Current cost accounts adjust the historical cost accounts to show the real profit, assets and liabilities for the year. It looks at the areas that are affected by inflation in the business, and adjusts the figures to reflect the inflation experienced by the business.

The accounts that you'll see are prepared using historical costs, with a few utilities using current cost accounting in their regulatory accounts.

The accounting principles

There are six accounting principles, or concepts, that influence the way that the accounts are prepared. The first four are incorporated into FRS 18 (*Accounting policies*) and the last two are reflected in many other accounting standards:

- matching/accruals;
- prudence;
- consistency;
- going concern;
- substance over form;
- materiality.

These provide the foundation for the preparation of the accounts, and consequently it's important to understand them.

The matching, or the accruals, principle

This requires companies to match their costs to the period's revenues. This means that the sales in the profit and loss account are the sales that have been legally made in the period, and the costs are those that relate to these sales, regardless of when they are paid. This means that the profit and loss account is unlikely to reflect the cash that has come in and gone out of the business.

Companies have to determine the costs that relate to the sales, and this means that judgements have to be made to identify the appropriate period. I'll discuss these judgements later in Chapter 2 – they are important as they can give companies the opportunity to engage in creative accounting.

The prudence principle

This is the most important principle. All other principles are subordinate to it. Prudence means you must take into the profit and loss account potential losses, but you can't take potential gains. Consequently companies must make provisions for items such as potential bad debts, but can't include increases in asset values in the profit and loss account as they haven't been realised.

The consistency principle

This requires items to be accounted for in a consistent manner, both within a period and from one period to the next, and ensures that the accounts are comparable.

The going concern principle

This assumes that the business will continue in existence for the foreseeable future.

Substance over form

This is one of the most important principles in UK accounting, and has protected us from the worst excesses of creative accounting recently uncovered in the USA. Accounts must reflect the commercial reality rather than the legal position. If a company has all the risks and rewards normally associated with owning something it should be shown in the accounts in the same way as if the company owned it. The way that long-term leases (called finance leases) are treated in the accounts is a good example of this. The company leasing the assets has all the benefits and risks that are associated with owning the assets. So although the leasing company legally owns the assets, they are shown in the company's accounts as fixed assets and depreciated in the usual way. The amount owed to the leasing company, over the life of the lease, is included in creditors.

One of the accounting standards, FRS 5 *(Reporting the substance of transactions),* is based on the principle of substance over form as it requires that the accounts should reflect commercial reality rather than the strict legal form.

Materiality

Accounts do not include items that are considered to be immaterial. But what is 'material'? Unfortunately there isn't a precise definition of what is and is not material. In some situations an error of less than 5% would be considered satisfactory, but in another situation any error would be unacceptable. For example, in a business with a billion pound turnover a £10,000 error in the materials cost is unlikely to be material. But a £10,000 error in the chairman's salary, which is subject to specific disclosure requirements, would be regarded as material.

Accountants tend to think something is material if there is a statutory requirement to disclose it accurately, or if knowing about it would influence your view about the company.

Let's summarise: accounts are prepared using six accounting principles. The accounting principles ensure that the accounts reflect an accountant's view of reality as:

- Profitable businesses can be liquidated, as cash transactions aren't necessarily reflected in the current period's profit and loss account.
- Companies have to make judgements to determine the costs that relate to the sales.
- The book value of a company is unlikely to be realised if it is liquidated.
- The accounts aren't totally accurate, as they contain approximations, and they may not reflect the legal position.

The accounts

The accounts found in larger companies follow the same format and will contain:

- a chairman's statement;
- a directors' report;
- a profit and loss account;
- a statement of total recognised gains and losses;
- a balance sheet;
- a cash flow statement;
- an auditor's report;
- some notes to the accounts.

Listed companies will also usually have a financial and an operating review.

I'll talk about some of these in later chapters, but I'll summarise each of them here.

The chairman's statement

The chairman's statement is a marketing document that some larger companies use to satisfy the legal requirement for a business review. It tries to present the company's performance in the best light and usually contains information on:

- the company's strategy and business plans;
- the general trading performance of the company within the context of the economic and competitive climate;

- their prospects for the next year;
- the performance of specific businesses within the company;
- any items of special interest during the year (for example, acquisitions).

The directors' report

This contains statutory information that may also be found elsewhere in the accounts. In the directors' report you'll find information about:

- the principal activities of the company and the business review, if this is not disclosed elsewhere in the accounts;
- the proposed dividend and the amount of profit that will be transferred to reserves if this is paid;
- any major changes in fixed assets and any significant difference between the market value and the book value of the assets;
- the directors, directors' interests and shareholdings, and any changes in the directors;
- employees, employee involvement in the running of the company, and their employment policies on equal opportunities and the employment of disabled persons;
- any political or charitable donations made during the year, above £200;
- any insurance taken out for directors or auditors against liabilities in relation to the company;
- the appointment of the auditors.

The profit and loss account

The profit and loss account tells you whether the company sold its goods and services for more, or less, than it costs it to deliver them to the customer. It takes the income from sales made in the period and then deducts the costs that relate to those sales.
When looking at a profit and loss account you must remember three things:

- **It is historical.** All profit and loss accounts will tell you what has happened, not what is happening now – they're out of date when you see them. A UK company's accounts are usually published three months after its year end. To reinforce the fact that they're historical, profit and loss accounts always say something like 'for the year ending . . ., for the six months ending . . ., for the period ending . . .'.
- **It does not include all of the capital expenditure.** The profit and loss account is concerned with the costs that relate to the period's sales. Businesses use fixed assets over a long period and spread the cost of these assets over their life through the depreciation charge. The depreciation charge reflects a percentage of the money that has been spent on the fixed assets. Consequently, a business can be profitable but run out of cash because of a capital expenditure programme. (Remember Railtrack?)
- **It is not concerned about whether the cash has been received from customers or paid to suppliers, just that the sale has been made and costs have been incurred.** If

I buy an apple for 5p and sell it for 8p, the profit and loss account records a profit of 3p. But I may have paid cash to buy the apple, and sold it on credit. The profit remains the same even though my cash is now at –5p. Consequently a business can be profitable but run out of cash if the customers haven't paid for the sales in the period.

This means that a business that is profitable in its latest accounts could be making losses today and profitable businesses can easily be bankrupt, as businesses can be profitable and still run out of cash.

The way a profit and loss account is laid out varies from one company to another. There are a number of different presentations that look at costs differently. The costs of materials, labour and overheads used in sales (the operating costs) can be calculated in two different ways:

- *You can look at what you have spent the money on:*
  - materials;
  - wages;
  - overheads;

or

- *You can look at why you have incurred the cost:*
  - cost of sales;
  - administration expenses;
  - selling and distribution expenses.

If the company has sold assets that have previously been revalued, the profit and loss account will be followed by a note of historical cost profits and losses. This shows what the profit would have been if there had been no revaluations, and I'll tell you about it in Chapter 6.

You'll find more information about the profit and loss account in Chapter 2.

The statement of total recognised gains and losses

This statement, which was introduced in June 1993, bridges the profit and loss account and the balance sheet. It combines all the gains and losses in the period regardless of whether they have been shown in the profit and loss account or the balance sheet. This enables the shareholders to identify clearly any gains, or losses, that the company has chosen to recognise in the period.

These gains and losses are analysed into those arising from:

- profits;
- revaluations of assets;
- currency translation differences.

It also discloses whether there have been any 'prior period adjustments' arising from changes in accounting policies or fundamental errors.

You'll find more information about the statement of total recognised gains and losses in Chapter 5.

The balance sheet

This is a 'snapshot' of the business on a certain day, identifying the company's assets and liabilities. It shows what the business is worth at the end of the year, given the set of assumptions that are detailed in the notes. Like any picture, there are a number of different views you can have of the company. A UK balance sheet identifies how much the business is worth to its shareholders; you'll find that other countries look at the business from a different point of view.

This is a very important snapshot as it is used to determine things like:

- the company's credit terms with its suppliers;
- the company's borrowing facilities;
- whether someone is going to invest their life savings in this company.

As a snapshot of the business on a certain day, it can be 'managed'. Companies will pick the best day in their year to take the snapshot, and you should always remember that they have 364 days' notice of that day arriving! It may well be as like the business for the rest of the year as your passport photographs represent true and fair views of you! Balance sheets should be read very carefully, and you should always remember to look for trends. Every year the company tries to show the best picture – is the best picture getting better, or worse?

You'll find more information about the balance sheet in Chapter 3.

The cash flow statement

This shows the movement of cash in the business during the past year. It identifies where the company's money has come from and where it has spent this money. Looking at the cash flow statement helps you see whether the company is living within its means.

It is probably the most important document of all; profit can be created, but you can't create cash. You either have cash or you don't. You can always spot a business engaging in creative accounting – it will be profitable but have no cash. Now this could happen quite legitimately if the company has a credit control problem, or high stock levels, and you'll see this on the cash flow statement.

You'll find more information about the cash flow statement in Chapter 4.

The auditor's report

With the exception of small companies, the accounts include a report from the auditors. The auditors are required to report to the shareholders whether, in their opinion, the financial statements:

- have been properly prepared in accordance with the Companies Act and the relevant accounting standards;
- give a true and fair view of the company's financial position and profit or loss.

To do this the auditor will check that proper accounting records have been kept and that the accounts reflect those accounting records.

The auditors' report is very important. Anyone looking at a set of accounts needs to be confident that those accounts are a true reflection of the company's performance. Auditors' reports must contain:

- a title specifying to whom the report is addressed;
- an introductory paragraph identifying the financial statements that have been audited;
- appropriately headed, separate sections discussing:
  - the respective responsibilities of the directors and the auditors;
  - the basis of the auditors' opinion;
  - the auditors' opinion on the financial statements.

The auditors report should be signed and dated.

The auditors may offer an unequivocal opinion that the accounts are true and fair, or that they're not. However it's not always that black and white, and in some situations they may need to qualify their opinion in some way. Consequently the audit report may contain a:

- **Fundamental uncertainty**: the auditors must draw attention to any inherent uncertainties that they believe to be fundamental to an understanding of the accounts. Perhaps the auditors are concerned about the continued support of the company's bankers, or the outcome of a major litigation.

  The fundamental uncertainty may, or may not, lead to the accounts being qualified. If the uncertainty has been properly disclosed and accounted for within the accounts, there will be no reason for the accounts to be qualified.
- **Qualification of the accounts**: there are some situations where the auditors may be unable to arrive at a definitive view on the accounts. Then they will qualify the accounts, by identifying the source of the problem. This will occur where:
  - There is inadequate, or insufficient, information available to the auditors; therefore they are unable to determine whether proper accounting records have been kept. This is referred to as a *limitation of scope*. This often happens in small companies, where there is often insufficient information to support some of the items shown in the accounts.
  - There is a disagreement about the accounting treatment, or disclosure, of information contained in the accounts. The auditors may disagree with the amounts, or the facts, disclosed in the accounts. (Perhaps the auditors are concerned about the level of provisioning.) Alternatively they could disagree with the way things have, or haven't, been disclosed in the accounts.
- **Disclaimer of opinion**: if an uncertainty, or lack of adequate information, could have a major impact on the accounts the auditors will give a 'disclaimer of opinion'. This is given when the auditors have been unable to obtain sufficient evidence to support an opinion on the financial statements. The audit report will clearly state that they are unable to form an opinion that the accounts are true and fair.
- **Adverse opinion**: this is the report you don't want to find in the accounts! This is given when the auditors believe that the information in the accounts is seriously misleading. They will then state that in their opinion the accounts do not give a true and fair view.

The notes to the accounts

My advice is to read these first. They tell you the accounting policies used in the preparation of the accounts and how all the numbers in the accounts have been calculated. Careful reading of the notes is essential if you want to spot creative accounting.

Summary

The accounts contain several financial statements, each showing different things about the company's performance:

- The profit and loss account is a historical document that shows whether the company has been selling its goods and services for more, or less, than it cost it to deliver them to its customers. As it is not concerned with the cash that has been received and paid during the year, profitable businesses can go bust.
- The balance sheet is a snapshot of the business at the year end, showing the company's assets and liabilities.
- The cash flow statement is concerned with the company's cash flows during the year, and helps you to understand whether the company is living within its means.
- The statement of total recognised gains and losses clearly identifies any gains and losses that the company has recognised during the year.

These documents should be read in conjunction with the auditor's report. This report will disclose if, in the auditor's opinion, the accounts are true and fair and if there are any qualifications to their opinion. The notes to the accounts will disclose the accounting policies and give additional information about the financial statements.

2

The profit and loss account

- **Capital costs and revenue costs**
- **What does the profit and loss account look like?** – turnover; operating costs; share of operating profits in associated undertakings and joint ventures; exceptional items; interest; extraordinary items; taxation; minority interests; dividends
- **The format of the profit and loss account** – a 'Format 1' presentation of the profit and loss account; a 'Format 2' presentation of the profit and loss account; a slight complication – acquisitions and disposals
- **The accounting judgements** – defining the costs that relate to the sales – provisions; accrued expenses; depreciation; stock; prepayments; currency adjustments
- **Profit and loss account summary**
- **Johnson Matthey's profit and loss account**

The profit and loss account shows you whether the company is managing to sell its products, or services, for more or less than it costs to deliver them to the customer. To do this, it starts with the sales that the company has made during the period, usually called the turnover, and then deducts the costs relating to those sales. The profit and loss account is not concerned with whether the cash has been received for the sales, or paid for the costs. This means that profit and loss accounts rarely reflect a company's cash position.

In this chapter I'm looking at the profit and loss account in detail and when you've finished this chapter you will understand:

- the difference between capital and revenue costs;
- the way the profit and loss account is presented in the accounts;
- the things you can expect to find in a profit and loss account;
- the judgements that have to be made to determine operating profit.

Capital costs and revenue costs

It is important you understand the way a company classifies costs, as it affects the business's reported profits and its asset values. Costs are classified as:

- **Capital costs:** these are the costs of buying, or improving, the business's assets. Consequently, these costs are charged to fixed assets.
- **Revenue costs:** these costs relate to the period's sales and are charged to the profit and loss account.

You might think about costs in this way too. Putting in an extra bathroom is a capital cost; you expect the extra bathroom to increase the value of your house. Even if you hate DIY you can usually be talked into a capital project! On the other hand, decorating a bedroom is a revenue cost that won't increase the value of your property.

The distinction is important in accounting, as only revenue costs are charged to the profit and loss account. Any capital costs are charged to the balance sheet. This means that it is possible for companies to improve profitability (and their apparent net worth) by capitalising costs. This was how the US telecom business WorldCom overstated its profits by over $7 billion in 2002 – by classifying operating expenses as capital expenditure. Both their profits and asset values improved! The opportunity for creative accounting arises because it is not always easy to work out what costs should be capitalised, even though both the Companies Act and the accounting standards define what should be shown as part of an asset's cost:

- **Company purchases the asset**
  If the company buys the asset it is relatively straightforward: it is the purchase cost plus 'any expenses incidental to its acquisition'.
- **Company builds the asset**
  This is where the problems start, as the company has to calculate the cost of production. The Companies Act defines the production cost as the price of raw materials and con-

sumables used, plus additional costs that are 'directly attributable to the production of the asset'. During the period of production companies may also include 'a reasonable proportion of the costs' . . . 'which are only indirectly attributable to the production of the asset'. This includes 'interest on capital borrowed to finance the production of the asset'.

The problem lies in the interpretation – what is reasonable? How do you calculate capitalised interest costs when the borrowings aren't necessarily specific to the construction of the asset? FRS 15 (*Tangible fixed assets*) clarifies the situation. It requires that all costs that have only been incurred following the construction, or installation, of an asset should be capitalised. (FRED 29 *Property, plant and equipment* and *Borrowing costs* is essentially the same – the borrowing costs that can be capitalised are those that 'would have been avoided had the expenditure . . . not been made'.) Interest costs may be capitalised during the construction period, but only if:

- they are 'directly attributable'; and
- it is the company's accounting policy and it is applied to all of its tangible fixed assets.

Once the asset is ready for use the capitalisation of costs should stop unless:

- the subsequent expenditure improves the performance of the asset;

or

- restores a fully depreciated asset.

What does the profit and loss account look like?

The profit and loss account can be presented in different ways, but broadly comprises a number of 'building blocks' that I've summarised in Figure 2.1. The profit and loss account starts with the business's 'turnover'.

Turnover

This represents the company's total sales in the period, excluding any VAT or similar taxes. Group accounts show only the third-party sales; any sales within the group are not shown on the profit and loss account, but may be disclosed in the notes.

Companies bring turnover into their profit and loss accounts in a number of different ways that can be broadly divided into two categories based on:

- An event that transfers the ownership of the goods, for example raising the invoice or shipping the product to the customer. Johnson Matthey's turnover is its invoiced sales.
- Time. This is used in long-term contracts, where the turnover shown in the profit and loss account is based on the completed percentage of the contract.

Any advance payments for sales are not shown in the profit and loss account until the sales are recognised as turnover. They are shown as *deferred income* and included with creditors on the balance sheet.

Fig. 2.1 The building blocks of profit

Sales

Less
- **Operating costs**

= **Operating profit**

Plus, or less
- Share of associated undertakings' profits
- Share of joint venture's profits
- Profits, or losses, on sale of fixed assets
- Profits, or losses, on sale of businesses
- Restructuring costs

= **Profit before interest**

Less
- Interest

= **Profit before tax**

Less
- Tax

= **Profit after tax**

Less
- Minority interests

= **Profit for the financial year**

Less
- Dividends

= **Retained profit**

Operating costs

These are the costs of materials, labour and overheads used in sales. In the first chapter I told you that there are two different ways that these can be shown in the profit and loss account. Following the introduction of FRS 3 (*Reporting financial performance*) in 1993, these operating costs will include most exceptional items. (Don't worry if you don't know what these are – I'll tell you about them later.)

Companies also include other operating income in their calculation of operating profit. Other operating income is income that doesn't fit into any other heading, like royalty income.

Share of operating profits in associated undertakings and joint ventures

Both associates and joint ventures are long-term investments, but the accounting treatment of their profits in the group profit and loss account will be slightly different.

Associates

Before we consider what an associate is, I'll explain the word 'undertaking'. It is a term straight from the Companies Act. It is all-embracing, covering companies, partnerships and associations that carry on a trade or a business. An undertaking doesn't have to have to be a company, or have a profit motive.

Both the Companies Act and the accounting standard, FRS 9 (*Associates and joint ventures*), refer to *participating interests*. This is where the company *can* influence the operational and the financial decisions in its investment. A 20%, or more, shareholding in a company is assumed to represent a participating interest. An associated undertaking is one where the company has participating interest in a long-term investment, and *does* exercise significant influence over the operating and financial policies of the associate. Once the investment is classed as an associate, the company will bring its share of the associate's operating profit, and all subsequent profit and loss account items, into its consolidated profit and loss account. This is called the *equity method* of accounting. (If the investment is not classed as an associate, or a subsidiary, only the income received from the investment will be shown in the profit and loss account as part of interest receivable and similar income.)

The investing company includes its share of the associate's following items in its profit and loss account:

- operating profit;
- profits, or losses, on sale or termination of subsidiaries;
- major restructuring and reorganisation costs;
- interest;
- tax.

As these aren't cash flows in the investing company, they have to be disclosed to enable you to understand the business's performance. Everything shown before profit before tax will be separately disclosed on the profit and loss account itself, whereas those items that are shown after tax can be disclosed in the notes to the accounts.

As this sounds complicated, I'll show you how it works in the following example.

EXAMPLE 2.1

Company A buys a 30% stake in Company B, and the investment is classed as an associate under the accounting rules. Before Company B's results are included in Company A's results, the two companies' profit and loss accounts were as shown in Table 2.1.

Table 2.1 Profit and loss accounts for Company A and Company B

	Company A	**Company B**
	£000	£000
Turnover	1,000	700
Operating costs	(750)	(520)
Operating profit	250	180
Interest payable	(50)	(30)
Profit before tax	200	150
Tax	(60)	(40)
Profit after tax	140	110
Dividend	(20)	(0)
Retained profit	120	110

Company A has to *consolidate* its investment in Company B. This means that it includes its 30% share of Company B's operating profits (£54,000), interest (£9,000), and tax charge (£12,000) into its consolidated profit and loss account (Table 2.2).

Table 2.2 Company A's consolidated profit and loss account

	£000	**£000**
Turnover		1,000
Operating costs		(750)
Operating profit		250
Share of associate's operating profits		54
Interest payable:		
Group	(50)	
Associate	(9)	(59)
Profit on ordinary activities before tax		245
Tax on profit on ordinary activities*		(72)
Profit after tax		173
Dividend		(20)
Retained profit for the group		153

* The notes would disclose that the tax charge comprises:

Parent and subsidiaries tax	(60)
Associate's tax	(12)

Whilst Company A's profits have grown its cash remains unchanged, as Company B is not paying dividends to its shareholders! However, this will be obvious when you look at its cash flow statement, as there will be no entry for dividends received from associates.

Johnson Matthey had four associates at the end of March 2002:

- Arora-Matthey Limited – based in India;
- Oximet SrL – based in Italy;
- Matthey Pharmaceutical Alkaloids LLC – based in the USA;
- Universal Pharma Technologies LLC – based in the USA.

They are relatively small in the context of the group, and unprofitable, with the group's share of their operating losses being just £100,000. (This compares to group operating profit of £168.5 million.)

Joint ventures

A joint venture is a long-term investment in an undertaking that:

- carries on a trade or business in its own right (the accounting standard refers to this as an *entity*);
- is jointly controlled by the reporting company and others under a contractual arrangement.

This means that joint marketing agreements aren't joint ventures under the accounting standard, as they don't trade in their own right and are just an agreement to share costs. A joint arrangement would be included in the group's activities.

The accounting for joint ventures is slightly different from that for associates, as the investing company's share of the joint venture turnover is also shown in the consolidated profit and loss account.

You can see how this works in Example 2.2. I'll use the same numbers I used in the first example, but this time I'll assume that Company B is a joint venture and that Company A has a 30% stake in it.

Significant associates and joint ventures

You've seen that associates and joint ventures can have an important effect on the reported profits, and only affect the business's cash flow if they pay dividends. In some industries associates and joint ventures can be an important element of a company's trading activities. This often happens in the construction industry where major projects are managed through joint ventures. FRS 9 requires companies to give more information where the investor's total share in its associates or joint ventures exceeds 15% of the investing group's:

- gross assets;
- gross liabilities;
- turnover;
- operating results (based on a three-year average).

EXAMPLE 2.2

The consolidated profit and loss account for Company A would then be as shown in Table 2.3.

Table 2.3 Consolidated profit and loss account for Company A

	£000	£000
Turnover: group and share of joint venture		1,210
Less: share of joint venture's turnover		(210)
Group turnover		1,000
Operating costs		(750)
Operating profit		250
Share of joint venture's operating profits		54
Interest payable:		
Group	(50)	
Joint venture	(9)	(59)
Profit on ordinary activities before tax		245
Tax on profit on ordinary activities*		(72)
Profit after tax		173
Dividend		(20)
Retained profit for the group		153

* Once again the notes would disclose additional information about the tax charge:

Parent and subsidiaries tax	(60)
Joint venture's tax	(12)

The company then has to disclose an associate's turnover, and give more information about some items on the balance sheet – I'll discuss these in the next chapter when I look at the balance sheet.

More information has to be given if an associate, or joint venture, exceeds 25% of any of the above. Then the investor's share of the following profit and loss account items is also disclosed:

- profit before tax;
- tax;
- profit after tax.

There are also more disclosures of balance sheet items.

Exceptional items

Exceptional items are things that you would expect to occur in the normal course of events, like bad debts, but their size, or their frequency, is so unusual that they have to be disclosed if the accounts are to show a true and fair view. FRS 3 (*Reporting financial performance*) requires that most exceptional items are included in the relevant operating cost heading, with the details disclosed in the notes to the accounts. The only exceptional items currently disclosed separately on the profit and loss account itself are:

- profits, or losses, on sale of fixed assets;
- profits, or losses, on sale or termination of subsidiaries;
- the costs of a major restructuring, or reorganisation, having a material effect on the business.

As most exceptional items don't have to be disclosed on the profit and loss account itself, you really have to read the notes if you want to understand the underlying trends in the company's profitability.

During its 2002 financial year Johnson Matthey's exceptional items comprised £18.1 million charged to operating profit and £5.6 million loss on disposal and closure of businesses. The exceptional items charged to operating profit were:

- £7.2 million profit on sale of unhedged palladium stock;
- £1.3 million cost of eliminating board and other costs at Meconic plc following its acquisition;
- £24 million cost of rationalising the Tableware sector of its Colours and Coatings division.

One of Johnson Matthey's associates, Metawave Video Systems Ltd, went into administration in 2001 and the further costs of £0.1 million incurred in 2002 were shown as an exceptional item. The £5.5 million loss on disposal of business arose from the sale of its loss-making French ceramic print business, part of Tableware, to its management. I'll now show you how this loss was calculated.

Profit on sale of fixed assets

Fixed assets are by definition things the business means to keep. But all businesses sell assets when they reach the end of their useful life. The sale of assets affects profitability if the company receives more or less than the asset value.

I'll show you how this works with an example. A company buys a machine for £15,000 and depreciates it by £10,000, so it's worth £5,000 on its books. If it then sells the asset for £6,000, it has made £1,000 profit on the sale of fixed assets. This is shown as a profit because the company has over-depreciated the machine. If it sold the machine for only £3,000, a loss of £2,000 will be shown on the profit and loss account. All assets have a value in the company's books. If they're sold for more than their book value the company reports the difference as a profit, if they're sold for less the difference shows as a loss.

This means that the profits, or losses, on sale of assets are determined by the asset's value in the accounts.

Profit on sale of subsidiaries

This is calculated in a similar way to the profit on sale of assets, but is slightly more complicated as it also has to take into account the price paid to acquire the subsidiary. You'll see the importance of this in the following example.

EXAMPLE 2.3

A predator decides to buy a company. This company is worth only £50,000 on paper (the company's assets less its liabilities), but last year it made £20,000 profit. When the predator buys this company it will have to pay more than £50,000. It's not just buying the assets; it's buying much more – the business's future profits, cash flows and customer base. If the predator pays £90,000 to acquire the company, it will have paid £40,000 more than the company's assets are worth. Accountants refer to this as 'goodwill' – it's simply the difference between the price paid and the acquired company's asset value. (I'll tell you a bit more about goodwill in the next chapter.)

I'll assume that the acquisition is consolidated into the predator's accounts at £50,000. (This isn't always the case, as you'll discover later.) The predator has paid £90,000 to buy a company that has a value in its accounts of £50,000. If the predator sells the company the following year for £70,000, has it made a profit or a loss? Common sense says that it has made a loss of £20,000, after all it paid £90,000 to buy it last year, and this should be shown on the profit and loss account. Fortunately, FRS 2 (*Accounting for subsidiary undertakings*) adopts this common sense approach. But it wasn't always the case; before the rules changed some companies reported a profit . . . as they had sold assets and liabilities worth £50,000 for £70,000, and had made a profit of £20,000!

Interest

This is the net interest figure, and the notes will disclose how much interest has been paid, received, and *capitalised* (remember this term means that it is charged to the balance sheet, not the profit and loss account). In Example 2.1 the interest shown on Company A's profit and loss account was £50,000; you'd have to look at the note about the interest to discover the various elements. The note might disclose:

	£
Interest paid	(80,000)
Interest received	20,000
Interest capitalised	10,000
Net interest paid	(50,000)

Of the £80,000 interest paid, only £70,000 is charged to the profit and loss account; £10,000 is charged to the balance sheet. You've already seen that FRS 15 (*Tangible fixed assets*) allows interest costs to be charged to fixed assets during the construction period if the interest is directly attributable and the company applies this accounting policy to all its tangible assets. But if you're analysing a business's performance you must remember that:

- The cash position isn't affected by where the interest is charged. The cash cost of interest is £60,000 (the £80,000 paid less the £20,000 received). A company could be having difficulties with its bankers, but on the profit and loss account the net interest may be only a small proportion of the profit as most of the interest has been charged to fixed assets.
- Different companies have different policies about capitalising interest, and this affects their reported performance.

Johnson Matthey doesn't capitalise interest and its note about interest discloses:

Net interest

	2002	2001
	£ million	£ million
Interest payable on bank loans and overdrafts	**(10.9)**	(6.8)
Interest payable on other loans	**(6.1)**	(5.6)
	(17.0)	(12.4)
Other interest receivable	**10.9**	17.7
Net interest	**(6.1)**	5.3

Extraordinary items

Whilst you'll find these in overseas accounts, you won't find them in the UK as they effectively disappeared when FRS 3 was implemented in 1993. It defines extraordinary items as 'extremely rare' items that relate to 'highly abnormal events or transactions that fall outside the ordinary activities . . . and are not expected to recur'. The accounting standard thinks they are so rare that it doesn't even give an example of them!

Taxation

This is shown on the profit and loss account as a total and if you want to know the components of the tax charge you'll have to look at the notes to the accounts. Apart from small companies, the notes will show you how the tax charge has been calculated. (Small companies only show the total tax charge, and don't disclose the components.)

The notes disclose:

- UK corporation tax;
- double taxation relief;
- UK income tax;
- overseas tax;
- the tax charge relating to associated undertakings and joint ventures;
- deferred tax.

Most of the tax note is self-explanatory; however, I'll discuss deferred tax and double taxation relief in more detail.

Deferred taxation

In the UK taxable profits aren't the same as the reported profit before tax. This means that you can't take the pre-tax profits, multiply them by the tax rate and arrive at the tax charge.

Consequently, UK companies prepare two sets of accounts: the published accounts that anyone can see, and the accounts prepared for the Inland Revenue. Some things that are charged to the published profit and loss account (e.g. entertaining clients) aren't allowed for tax purposes. Other things have different values in the tax accounts and the published accounts.

These differences between the two sets of accounts are called *timing differences*. They can be permanent, where they appear in one set of accounts, but not the other. Alternatively, they could show in the published accounts in a different year than they show in the tax accounts. Accountants talk about differences being either 'permanent' or 'timing'. Perhaps the best example of a timing difference is the different fixed asset values that are found in the two sets of accounts. Companies determine their depreciation charge, and the depreciation charged on the same asset could be different from one company to another. The Inland Revenue ignores the depreciation that the company has chosen, which varies from one company to another, and gives all companies a standard tax allowance. This is called a *capital allowance*. (Company tax allowances work essentially the same way as personal tax allowances, reducing the taxable profit.) Because the depreciation charge is different from the tax allowance, a timing difference arises. I'll explain this in the next example.

EXAMPLE 2.4

First, let's look at the published accounts.

A company buys a machine for £5,000 and plans to keep it for five years. At the end of the five years it believes that the machine will be worth nothing. To the company depreciation is a matter of simple arithmetic – it has £5,000 to write off over five years – £1,000 a year. (Most companies make an equal charge over the life of the asset, using a method of depreciation called the *straight line method*.) The depreciation charge is part of the operating costs in the profit and loss account.

Now the tax accounts.

The machine qualifies for a 25% capital allowance. Capital allowances are calculated differently from the way that most companies calculate depreciation. Capital allowances work on a *reducing balance*. In the first year the allowance would be 25% of £5,000 = £1,250, giving an asset value of £3,750. In the second it would be 25% of £3,750 (£5,000 – £1,250) = £938.

I've graphed the depreciation charge and capital allowance in Figure 2.2.

You can see that the depreciation charge differs from the capital allowance. In the early years depreciation would be lower than the tax allowance; in the later years it would be higher.

Fig. 2.2 Depreciation and capital allowances

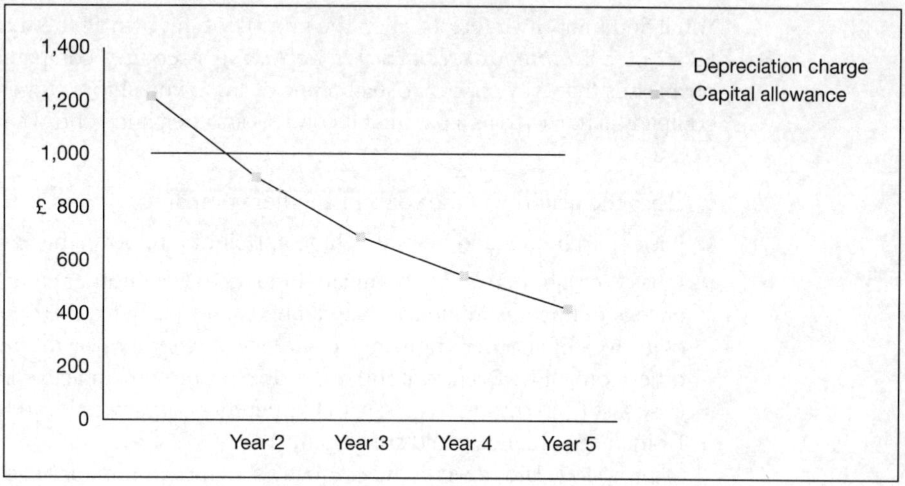

Deferred tax brings the tax accounts and the published accounts into line. It adjusts the tax charge to reflect the tax that would have been payable if the tax allowances had been the same as the depreciation charge. This has the effect of equalising the tax charged to the profit and loss account over the life of the asset. FRS 19 (*Deferred tax*) changed the accounting for deferred tax from 2002, as companies now have to provide for all short-term timing differences, rather than those that the company expects to have to pay. (However, a provision for deferred tax doesn't have to be made for differences arising from most asset revaluations.) This means that the tax charge now reflects the total possible tax charge, including tax that might never have to be paid. (Look at the graph – at the end of five years the difference between the two will be £1,187 – the residual value in the tax accounts.) However, this is in line with international practice and reduces the opportunities for 'massaging' the tax charge.

On the balance sheet deferred tax can be found in both the debtors and creditors. Deferred tax assets are likely to be small, as they can only be shown if they are recoverable. Most companies will have large deferred tax liabilities.

Double taxation relief

Most UK companies also pay tax overseas, and double taxation relief ensures that profits aren't taxed twice. However, the minimum tax rate should be the same as that in the UK. Consequently, agreements have been made with most countries to ensure that overseas profits are usually subject to UK tax only to the extent that UK tax is higher than the overseas tax paid. This ensures that any dividends paid to the parent company aren't taxed again, unless the overseas tax paid is lower than UK tax. Then the company will be liable to pay the difference.

Minority interests

You'll find minority interests when the group doesn't own all the shares in its subsidiaries. FRS 2 (*Accounting for subsidiary undertakings*) requires companies to consolidate any businesses that they control. Usually control and ownership go together, but not always. A company is regarded as a parent if it controls another, and control could arise from the following:

- It has the majority of the votes in another company.
- It is a shareholder and has the right to appoint, or remove, the majority of the directors.
- It has the right to exercise dominant influence over another company. (Dominant influence is defined as influence that can be used to achieve the operational and financial objectives of another company, regardless of whether it is in the best interests of the other company.) Dominant influence doesn't require an active intervention – it could arise just from setting targets, with the parent company only rarely directly intervening. Dominant influence could arise from:
  - provisions laid down in the company's Memorandum, or Articles of Association;
  - the two companies being managed as a single unit (FRS 2 refers to this as 'on a unified basis');
  - a contract. This is probably illegal in the UK, because of the rules on directors' obligations. (This provision comes from European Community law. Control contracts are common in Germany.)

This means that effectively there can be large minority interests where the company has been forced to consolidate because it has dominant influence over the subsidiary. It has the control, but does not own the shares. Whilst I've talked about companies, in fact the term you'll find is *undertakings* and you'll recall it is a much wider term. This effectively makes *off-balance-sheet funding* much more difficult. Enron held some of its debt (and some of its loss-making businesses) in partnerships where it had dominant influence. The fact that these were partnerships where it had limited ownership would have been regarded as irrelevant under UK accounting rules and it would have had to consolidate them into the group accounts.

Where one company controls another it must prepare *consolidated accounts* showing the results and financial position of both companies even though it doesn't own all of the shares in the company. If a company's results are consolidated, all its sales and costs will be taken into the group's profit and loss account and all its assets and liabilities will be taken into the group's balance sheet. Any of the profits, or net assets, that do not belong to the 'parent' company's shareholders will be shown as minority interests.

I'll show you how the consolidation process works in the next example.

EXAMPLE 2.5

I'll use the same profit and loss accounts I used in Example 2.1 to illustrate accounting for associates, but I'll assume that Company A now owns 60% of Company B. The two companies' profit and loss accounts before consolidation are shown in Table 2.4.

Table 2.4 The profit and loss accounts before consolidation of Companies A and B

	Company A	**Company B**
	£000	£000
Turnover	1,000	700
Operating costs	(750)	(520)
Operating profit	250	180
Interest payable	(50)	(30)
Profit before tax	200	150
Tax	(60)	(40)
Profit after tax	140	110
Dividend	(20)	(0)
Retained profit	120	110

The consolidated profit and loss account would then be as shown in Table 2.5.

Table 2.5 Consolidated profit and loss accounts for Companies A and B

	£000	
Turnover	1,700	
Operating costs	(1,270)	
Operating profit	430	
Interest payable	(80)	
Profit on ordinary activities before tax	350	
Tax on profit on ordinary activities	(100)	
Profit after tax	250	
Minority interests	(44)	*(110 × 40%)*
Profit for the financial year	206	
Dividend	(20)	
Retained profit for the group	186	

The £44,000 in my example represents the profit that has to be deducted from the consolidated profit and loss account to arrive at the profit available to the group's shareholders. Unfortunately, not all subsidiaries are profitable.

Johnson Matthey doesn't own all of its subsidiaries and in the year ending 30 March 2002 these subsidiaries had made a small loss. This means that it doesn't deduct its minority interests from the profit and loss account – it adds £300,000 back to arrive at the profit attributable to the group's shareholders.

Dividends

There are legal restrictions on the amount of dividends that companies are allowed to pay. Companies can only pay dividends if they have accumulated sufficient profits. This means that it is possible for companies to pay dividends when they have made a loss, but only if they have accumulated sufficient profits in the past to cover the dividend payment. I'll illustrate this in the following example.

EXAMPLE 2.6

A company has traded profitably for its first four years and has reinvested £24,000 in its business:

	Retained profits
	£
Year 1	10,000
Year 2	5,000
Year 3	7,000
Year 4	2,000
Total	24,000

The £24,000 accumulated profits are known in law as *distributable reserves*, and dividends can be paid until these reach zero. If the company makes a loss of £8,000 in the fifth year, but still wants to pay a dividend of £10,000, it would be able to do so. The retained loss for the year would be £18,000, which can be absorbed by the accumulated retained profits of £24,000. In fact the company could pay up to £16,000 in dividends (the accumulated retained profits on £24,000 less the £8,000 loss for the year).

Public companies have another restriction on the payment of dividends. They may only pay dividends when the value of their net assets (total assets less all liabilities, including provisions for liabilities and charges) is not less than the total of their share capital and undistributable reserves. (Undistributable reserves are all the other reserves I'll talk about in the next chapter; the revaluation reserve, the share premium account, the capital redemption reserve, and any other reserve where the distribution is prohibited by the company's articles.) This means that whilst private companies can pay dividends if they have sufficient realised profits available, public companies may only do so after they have provided for any unrealised losses.

Shareholders don't have to approve all dividend payments. As long as it is legal, directors can pay interim dividends without the shareholders' approval. However, the shareholders at the Annual General Meeting must approve the final dividend, and the directors will devote a lot of time to determining how much should be paid.

Only private companies like paying dividends, although they are likely to have taken money out of the business well before they reach dividends! Private company directors are generally paying dividends out to themselves, as in most private companies there are few shareholders who aren't also directors.

Public companies are different – the directors are proposing to pay dividends to strangers. The more the company pays as dividends, the less it can keep within the business for the next year's development and growth. Public companies use the same underlying principle for dividends as the one used to decide the level of salary increase for employees – they pay the least they can get away with! In fact the same things influence dividend decisions as influence salary decisions. It is a balance; they can't afford to disappoint the shareholders (they will vote with their feet and sell their shares). But neither can they afford to create unsustainable expectations (shareholders look for dividend growth; the dividend you pay this year creates an expectation about the size of the dividend that you will pay next year). To improve cash flow some companies offer a *scrip dividend*. A scrip dividend is where the shareholder receives extra shares instead of cash. This is often an attractive option for smaller shareholders as they can increase their stake in the company without paying dealing fees.

Most companies follow the Articles (the rules that govern the operation of the company) laid out in the Companies Act. If these Articles are followed, the only way the shareholders can change the dividend is to reduce it (probably about as likely as you asking for a reduction in the size of your next salary increase!).

The dividends that are charged to the profit and loss account are currently the dividends that have been paid and proposed for the year. The proposed dividend will show as part of 'Creditors: falling due within a year' in the balance sheet. However, the alignment proposal FRED 27 (*Events after the balance sheet date*) will only allow companies to show any dividend they have *paid* on their profit and loss account. The proposed dividend will then be disclosed in the notes.

The format of the profit and loss account

Having discovered the items that we might find in the profit and loss account, I'll now show you how it's laid out. Basically it follows the 'building blocks of profit' model that I showed you earlier, although the detailed layout of the profit and loss account varies slightly from one company to another. But one thing will be common to all companies reporting in the UK: the costs will be considered in a standard order and then deducted from turnover to arrive at different levels of profit. I've summarised these in Table 2.6.

Table 2.6 A summary of the profit and loss accounts

	Turnover
–	Operating costs
+	Other operating income
=	OPERATING PROFIT
+/–	Share of associates and joint ventures profits/losses
+/–	Profits and losses on sale of fixed assets or subsidiaries[1]
–	Major restructuring costs[1]
+/–	Interest[1]
=	PROFIT BEFORE TAX
+/–	Tax[2]
=	PROFIT AFTER TAX
+/–	Minority interests
=	PROFIT FOR THE FINANCIAL YEAR
–	Dividends
=	RETAINED PROFIT

You'll usually find this profit figure, and it's probably the most important, but it isn't actually required by the Companies Act! (→ OPERATING PROFIT)

Notes:

[1] The company's share of their associates' and joint ventures' costs will be shown on the profit and loss account.

[2] This includes associates' and joint ventures' tax, which is separately disclosed in the notes.

There are four different ways of presenting the profit and loss account within the EU, and these are reflected in the Companies Act. Only two formats are used in the UK, the others being more popular in continental Europe. The formats used in the UK present the profit and loss account vertically and differ only in their approach to calculating the operating costs:

Format 1 This is a functional presentation of operating costs answering the question *'Why have we spent the money?'*

Format 2 This is a factual presentation answering the question '*What have we spent the money on?*'

Formats 3 and 4 are essentially horizontal presentations of Formats 1 and 2.

A 'Format 1' presentation of the profit and loss account

This is the most commonly used presentation in the UK and classifies costs into:

- cost of sales;
- administrative expenses;
- distribution costs.

Unfortunately, these terms are not defined in the Companies Act. Some companies include their sales and marketing costs in distribution costs, others in administrative expenses. Some retailers define cost of sales as the cost of merchandise; others add distribution costs and store operating costs to the cost of merchandise. This means that it's not usually possible to compare the cost elements between companies, only within a company over time.

Table 2.7 shows a profit and loss account prepared in this presentation.

Table 2.7 Profit and loss account – Format 1

	£000	£000
Turnover		1,000
Cost of sales		(600)
Gross profit		400
Distribution costs		(140)
Administrative expenses		(70)
Other operating income		10
Operating profit		200
Share of associates' operating profits		20
Profit on sale of fixed assets		10
Interest receivable – group		10
Interest payable:		
Group	(50)	
Associate	(10)	
		(60)
Profit on ordinary activities before taxation		180
Tax on profit on ordinary activities		(40)
Profit on ordinary activities after taxation		140
Minority interests		(10)
Profit for the financial year		130
Dividend		(40)
Retained profit for the financial year		90

This is the first profit number that you can use when you're comparing companies (→ Operating profit)

A 'Format 2' presentation of the profit and loss account

This classifies costs as materials, staff costs (including social security and pension costs), other external costs, and depreciation. As these are the costs of *purchases* made in the period, two adjustments may have to be made to exclude:

- costs relating to stock – *changes in stock and work in progress*;
- staff costs spent on capital items – *own work capitalised*.

Table 2.8 shows the same profit and loss account in a Format 2 presentation.

Table 2.8 Profit and loss account – Format 2

	£000	£000
Turnover		1,000
Raw materials and consumables		(470)
Staff costs		(195)
Other external charges		(100)
Depreciation		(90)
Changes in stock and work in progress		20
Own work capitalised		25
Other operating income		10
Operating profit		200
Share of associates' operating profits		20
Profit on sale of fixed assets		10
Interest receivable – group		10
Interest payable:		
Group	(50)	
Associate	(10)	
		(60)
Profit on ordinary activities before taxation		180
Tax on profit on ordinary activities		(40)
Profit on ordinary activities after taxation		140
Minority interests		(10)
Profit for the financial year		130
Dividend		(40)
Retained profit for the financial year		90

A slight complication – acquisitions and disposals

FRS 3 (*Reporting financial performance*) requires acquisitive companies to show a more detailed profit and loss account, analysing profits between discontinued and continuing operations and clearly identifying, on the face of the profit and loss account, the contribution arising from acquisitions. I've illustrated this in Table 2.9.

It makes the profit and loss account appear very cluttered (and it gets even more complicated if the company has some exceptional items), but it does give you a lot of information. You can see that the business it's discontinuing loses money and that its acquisition made a major contribution to operating profits (over 40% of the continuing operation's profits came from the acquisition). You can see how this gives a much clearer idea of where the profits have been made this year and what they might be next year. You would expect turnover to fall next year but profits should rise.

Table 2.9 A more detailed profit and loss account

	Continuing operations	Acquisitions	Discontinued	Total
	£000	£000	£000	£000
Turnover	500	300	200	1,000
Cost of sales	(280)	(160)	(160)	(600)
Gross profit	220	140	40	400
Distribution costs	(70)	(40)	(30)	(140)
Administrative expenses	(35)	(15)	(20)	(70)
Other operating income	10			10
Operating profit	125	85	(10)	200
Share of associates' operating profits	20			20
Profit on sale of fixed assets	5	2	3	10
Profit before interest	150	87	(7)	230
Interest receivable – group				10
Interest payable:				
Group				(50)
Associate				(10)
Profit on ordinary activities before taxation				180
Taxation				(40)
Profit on ordinary activities after taxation				140
Minority interests				(10)
Profit for the financial year				130
Dividend				(40)
Retained profit for the financial year				90

The accounting judgements – defining the costs that relate to the sales

By now you know what the profit and loss account looks like, and that operating profit is the most important element. Now I'd like to spend some time showing you how operating profit is calculated, as it's as much a matter of judgement as measurement, and you'll find that managers are involved in making many of the judgements determining operating profit.

All companies make five major accounting adjustments to ensure that the costs charged to the profit and loss account are those that relate to the sales made in the period:

- Charges are made to the profit and loss account to include:
  - provisions for likely costs;
  - accrued expenses;
  - depreciation;
- and adjustments are made to exclude:
  - stock;
  - prepayments.

I've deliberately used the word 'charges' as they're nothing to do with cash

Companies involved in trading overseas have to make another adjustment, as they have to find a way to deal with exchange rates. I now want to show you how these adjustments affect both the profit and loss account and the balance sheet.

Provisions

Companies have to make provisions to cover the likely costs that will arise in the future from the sales they have made in this period. These include provisions made for:

- bad and doubtful debts;
- obsolete stock (this may not be obsolete in the literal sense, but stock must be shown on the balance sheet at the lower of its cost or net realisable value);

These two reduce asset values to their realisable amount

- warranty claims;
- litigation;
- rationalisation.

Whereas these are costs that will be paid in the future

You can see that I've categorised the provisions into two different types:

- those that are made to reduce an asset's value to the amount that the company expects to realise;
- those that are costs the business will incur in the future as a result of the sales (warranty), or decisions (rationalisation), that have been made in the period.

I've made this distinction because the accounting treatment is different for the two different types of provision.

I'll start by looking at the first category, illustrating this by considering doubtful debt provisions. These provisions can be:

- specific, where each debtor is considered individually;
- general, where the same level of provision is applied to all debtors; or
- a combination of the two, where perhaps large customers would be considered on an individual basis and smaller customers on a general basis.

I'll show you a general provision for doubtful debts.

EXAMPLE 2.7

A company's accounting policy is to make a general provision of 4% to cover doubtful debts. I'll show you how this policy would affect the accounts over a period of two years. You'll see it has a significant effect on the company's reported operating profit (Table 2.10).

Table 2.10 Profit and the effect of provision on debtors

	Year 1 £	Year 2 £	*Profit growth*
Outstanding invoices	100,000	110,000	
Less 4% provision	(4,000)	(4,400)	
Debtors on balance sheet	96,000	105,600	
Profit before provisions	110,000	115,500	5%

Two things affect the company's reported profit in the second year – its provisioning policy, and the cash it receives from its first year's debtors. I'll show you two possibilities:

1. The company collects £98,000 from its first year's debtors.
2. The company collects only £94,000.

In the first option it collects more than it expected to, and so it had *'over-provided'* £2,000 in the first year. This means that it only needs to charge £2,400 into the second period's profit and loss account to bring the provision to £4,400 (4% of £110,000). In the second option it had *under-provided* and has to increase the charge to the profit and loss account, to bring the provision to the 4% required. This means that its reported profit after provisions would be as shown in Table 2.11.

Table 2.11 The effect of over- and under-provision on reported profits

	Year 1 £	Year 2 £	*Profit growth*
Option 1	106,000	113,100	*6.7%*
Option 2	106,000	109,100	*2.9%*

Now I'll consider those provisions made to cover future costs. These are shown on the balance sheet under the heading of *Provisions for liabilities and charges.* You know that provisions are only the managers' best guesses and are unlikely to be a totally accurate reflection of what happens. They are approximations and can be used by companies to move profit from one year to the next, as an over-provision in one year could be written back later to boost profits when the cash is not needed. The accounting standard FRS 12 (*Provisions, contingent liabilities and contingent assets*) tightened up the provisioning rules in 1999. Provisions are only required when something has happened before the balance sheet date that gives rise to a measurable and clear obligation. The important words are:

- *before the balance sheet date* – so you can't account for something that happens after that date.

- *measurable and clear obligation* – so a board decision to restructure the business wouldn't justify the creation of a provision, as it's just a decision, not an obligation. The provision can only be made when the company has a detailed plan for the restructuring and there is a valid expectation that the plan will be implemented.

Provisions can only be made where there's a liability arising from a past event, and its probable future cash outflow can be measured. There are situations where the criteria for provisions won't be met. Perhaps there's only a possible obligation, or cash outflow that perhaps can't be measured. FRS 12 refers to these as *contingent liabilities* and they have to be disclosed in the notes to the accounts. Court cases are often disclosed as contingent liabilities, or could even be disclosed as a *contingent asset* in the notes to the accounts of the prosecuting company if it was probably going to win the case. I'll tell you more about these in Chapter 7.

Accrued expenses

These are outstanding invoices that relate to costs for items used in the period. You already know about accruals, even though you've probably never used the term. A lot of your personal costs are accrued ... gas, electricity, telephone. If they're not paid by direct debit they're paid quarterly in arrears. If you were trying to prepare a profit and loss account for the month of December you would have to identify the costs that relate to the period. This means that you would have to try to work out what proportion of your next gas bill etc. related to this period's sales. Companies do this to identify their accrued expenses – the costs of items they have used, but where they haven't yet received the invoice from their suppliers. Consequently, at the end of the financial year your accountants will send an e-mail to all cost centre managers asking for a list of their accrued expenses.

I'll show you how accruals affect the accounts in Example 2.8.

EXAMPLE 2.8

In the past two years a company has used and paid for electricity as shown in Table 2.12.

Table 2.12 Use of electricity

	Year 1 £	Year 2 £
Electricity used	80,000	84,000
Electricity invoiced and paid for	65,000	83,000
Charge to the profit and loss account	80,000	84,000
Accrued expenses *(These are included in creditors on the balance sheet)*	15,000	16,000

The profit and loss account is always charged with the costs *used*, not what has been paid for, as the cash flow is irrelevant. The accrued expenses in the second year are £16,000. £15,000 of the £83,000 paid during the second year related to the first year, so only £68,000 of this year's electricity has been paid for. Consequently, the outstanding invoices, relating to costs charged to the profit and loss account, were £84,000 – £68,000 = £16,000.

The balance sheet shows what the company owes at its year end and its creditors are analysed into those where the company has received an invoice (the trade creditors), and those where it hasn't (the accrued expenses).

Depreciation

Depreciation is something you know about. You buy something today, and it's not worth the same tomorrow. Some things depreciate more than others. Cars and computers generally depreciate faster than your other assets. Depreciation is a hidden business cost. The Companies Act requires companies to make a charge for depreciation to cover the cost of using their assets in the period. Once again, it's a *charge*, rather than a cost. (You don't pay depreciation in the same way that you pay rent – you physically pay depreciation when you trade the car in. That's when you find that it isn't worth what you paid for it.)

The charge to the profit and loss account should be based on an asset's:

- cost;
- life;
- net residual value (this just means its scrap value, at the end of its life).

The depreciation charge has to reflect the cost of using an asset in this period and FRS 15 (*Tangible fixed assets*) covers the depreciation of fixed assets. (This will be modified by the programme aligning UK accounting standards to the international ones.) I've already covered FRS 15's definition of an asset's cost. It also requires that:

- Some large assets have to be subdivided into smaller assets if different parts of the asset have different lives (for example, a furnace lining is unlikely to last as long as the furnace itself).
- Asset lives have to be reviewed annually, with the effects of any revision being spread over the asset's remaining life.
- Assets don't have to be depreciated if the depreciation charge would be immaterial or the asset has a long life of more than 50 years. In this case the company has to carry out an *annual impairment review* to check that the asset hasn't fallen in value. (This isn't required in the alignment proposal FRED 29 (*Property, plant and equipment* and *Borrowing costs*), so may not have to be done in the future.)
- The company's depreciation policy can only be changed if the new method gives a fairer view.

The alignment proposal, FRED 29 (*Property, plant and equipment* and *Borrowing costs*), also requires that any material residual values should be revised at each balance sheet date to reflect current prices. (This would be important in some industries, like shipping, where prices can change significantly from one year to the next.)

However, there are still a number of different methods that can be used to calculate the depreciation charged to the profit and loss account, and the resulting asset value shown on the balance sheet. I talked about some of them when I discussed deferred tax earlier in this chapter. I'll just run through the main methods, assuming the residual value remains unchanged, and their effect on the accounts in the next example.

EXAMPLE 2.9

A company buys a machine for £10,490, believes it will last for 5 years and will have a scrap value of £490 in 5 years' time.

Now I'll calculate the depreciation charge and the asset values over the life of the asset. I'll start with the straight line method, as it's the one that most companies use in the UK.

The straight line method

The company has £10,000 to depreciate over five years, and makes an annual depreciation charge to the profit and loss account of £2,000. It's called the straight line method of depreciation because both the depreciation charge and the asset value move in a straight line (Table 2.13).

Table 2.13 The straight line method of depreciation

	Depreciation charge	Asset value
1st year	£2,000	£8,490
2nd year	£2,000	£6,490
3rd year	£2,000	£4,490
4th year	£2,000	£2,490
5th year	£2,000	£490

The next most popular approach is the reducing balance method – you'll recall that this is the method the Inland Revenue uses to calculate capital allowances in the UK.

Reducing balance

This is sometimes also called the double declining balance method. It uses a fixed percentage each year and applies this to the reducing value of the asset to arrive at the net realisable value. The percentage is calculated using the following formula, which gives the chosen residual value at the end of the life.

$$1 - \sqrt[n]{\frac{\textit{residual value}}{\textit{cost}}}$$

(*n* is the expected asset life)

In my example, this formula gives an annual percentage of 45.8%. But please don't let the formula fool you – it isn't any more accurate. All it does is calculate the percentage based on my assumptions about the asset's life and the net residual value. Using the reducing balance method gives the depreciation charges and asset values shown in Table 2.14.

Table 2.14 The reducing balance method of depreciation

		Depreciation charge	**Asset value**
1st year	*£10,490 × 45.8%*	£4,805	£5,685
2nd year	*£5,685 × 45.8%*	£2,604	£3,081
3rd year	*£3,081 × 45.8%*	£1,411	£1,670
4th year	*£1,670 × 45.8%*	£765	£905
5th year	*£905 × 45.8%*	£414	£491

(there's a rounding error of 1)

Some companies prefer to use the reducing balance method, as they believe it gives a closer approximation to 'real' depreciation, which is usually higher in the earlier years.

Sum of the digits

This method is largely used by leasing companies in the UK, but it is widely used overseas, particularly in the USA. It gives a depreciation charge between the straight line method and the reducing balance method. The sum of the digits is simply the total of the number of years the asset is expected to last (1 + 2 + 3 + 4 + 5 = 15) and can be found quickly by using the formula:

$$\frac{n(n+1)}{2}$$

Once again, *n* is the anticipated life.

Having found the sum of the digits, the next step is to find the depreciation factor for each year. In the first year depreciation is calculated at 5/15 of £10,000, in the second 4/15 of £10,000, and so on (Table 2.15).

Table 2.15 Sum of the digits method of depreciation

		Depreciation charge	Asset values
1st year	*5/15 × £10,000*	£3,333	£7,157
2nd year	*4/15 × £10,000*	£2,667	£4,490
3rd year	*3/15 × £10,000*	£2,000	£2,490
4th year	*2/15 × £10,000*	£1,333	£1,157
5th year	*1/15 × £10,000*	£667	£490

Some companies prefer this method because it gives higher charges in the early years, but is less extreme than the reducing balance method.

Usage-based methods

Some companies use depreciation methods that are based on the asset's use, expressing its life in production units, or hours, rather than years. This method of depreciation is often used for machinery and aeroplanes. Continuing the example, if the company believed that the machine would last for 20,000 hours, the annual depreciation charge would be based on the usage at £0.50 for each hour the machine is used (£10,000 ÷ 20,000) (Table 2.16).

Table 2.16 The usage-based method of depreciation

	Hours used	Depreciation charge	Asset value
1st year	2,400	£1,200	£9,290
2nd year	3,600	£1,800	£7,490
3rd year	4,600	£2,300	£5,190
4th year	5,200	£2,600	£2,590
5th year	4,200	£2,100	£490

You can clearly see the effect that these different methods have on the depreciation charge, and therefore reported profitability and asset values, if you look at the chart shown in Figure 2.3.

In calculating the charge for depreciation, companies have four variables to consider:

- the cost;
- the asset's life;
- its net residual value;
- the depreciation method.

Any change in these will affect both profitability and asset values. Companies have to review asset lives annually, and can change the way they depreciate assets if they believe it provides a truer and fairer view.

Fig. 2.3 Depreciation charges using the different depreciation methods

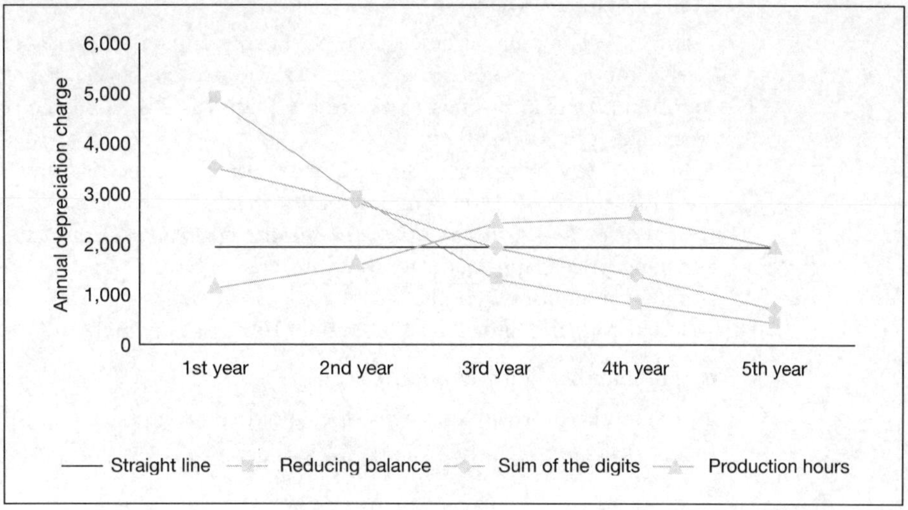

Stock

As stock hasn't been used, it isn't charged to the profit and loss account. This means that any costs that have been charged to stock are shown in the balance sheet rather than the profit and loss account. Consequently, stock valuation is an important determinant of the cost of sales.

Stock can be analysed into its component parts, starting with raw materials and adding labour and overhead costs as the materials move through the production process. It is shown on the balance sheet at the lower of cost and net realisable value. (Net realisable value is the selling price less any further costs to completion, sales, marketing and distribution costs. This is designed to limit the costs that can be charged to stock.)

To calculate the value of goods used in sales companies have to:

- measure the *volume* of units used in sales;
- calculate their *value*.

Measuring the volume of goods used in sales is theoretically very simple; all companies use some form of stocktaking:

	Opening stock	
Plus	Purchases	
Equals	Goods available	
Less	Closing stock ←	*This is shown on the balance sheet*
Equals	Goods used in sales	
	↑ *This is charged to the profit and loss account*	

Whilst the process is simple it's not necessarily accurate, as anyone who has been involved in stocktaking knows!

Once the company has measured how many units it has in stock, it has to value them. This is important, as small changes in stock values can have a disproportionate impact on reported profits in businesses where the materials cost is a large proportion of the total costs (like Johnson Matthey).

In practice, valuing stock can be difficult. Some guidance is given in the accounting standard *(SSAP 9 Stocks and long-term contracts)* and in the proposed standard FRED 28 (*Inventories* and *Construction and service contracts*). Companies have to cope with changing prices, and manufacturing businesses have to find a basis for valuing work in progress and finished goods.

To illustrate the difficulties I'll consider three different types of company:

- **a retailer** holding goods for resale;
- **a manufacturer** with materials stock, work in progress, and finished goods stock;
- **a construction company** with long-term contracts.

The retailer

It's easier for retailers to value their stock, as they only have one type of stock – the goods for resale. A number of retailers find it useful to show stock at resale value in their internal management accounts. When they publish their accounts they adjust this figure to arrive at 'cost' by deducting their expected gross margin. This means that if they had a dress that they would sell for £70.00, with a gross margin of 50%, the stock value of the dress would be £35.00. The accounting standard requires companies using the estimated margin method of valuing stock to test that this is a 'reasonable approximation of the actual cost'.

The company's accounting policy for stock is always disclosed – for example, Marks & Spencer discloses . . .

> **Stocks**
> Stocks are valued at the lower of cost and net realisable value using the retail method. All stocks are finished goods.

The manufacturer

Manufacturing businesses have more problems valuing their stock, as they have to cope with:

- **Different prices in the year**: manufacturers usually hold their stock for longer than retailers, and so they're more likely to have goods in stock that they have bought at different prices.
- **Complex valuation**: they have different types of stock – materials, work in progress, and finished goods stock. Labour and overhead costs have to be added to the value of the materials as they move through the production process, and are allocated to stock based on the business's normal activity levels.

To cope with these difficulties accountants have developed a number of different approaches to valuing stock. The most common methods are:

- first in first out (FIFO);
- weighted average cost;
- last in first out (LIFO).

I'll use the following example to show you the effect of using the three different methods:

EXAMPLE 2.10

Table 2.17 Establishing the value of closing stock

		Units	Unit cost £	Total cost £
1 January	Opening stock	1,500	1.00	1,500
28 February	Purchases	2,000	1.05	2,100
1 April	Purchases	1,500	1.06	1,590
30 June	Purchases	2,000	1.08	2,160
31 August	Purchases	2,200	1.10	2,420
30 November	Purchases	1,500	1.13	1,695
		10,700		11,465
31 December	Closing stock	1,000		

The company has bought units at different prices through the year, and has to determine the cost that will be charged to the profit and loss account. It does this by establishing the value of the closing stock.

First in first out

This applies the principle of stock rotation to stock valuation. The first goods into the warehouse are assumed to be the first sent to the customer, so the latest deliveries will be in stock.

The value of stock shown on the balance sheet using FIFO will be £1,130 (1,000 units times the latest price of £1.13) and the cost of sales charged to the profit and loss account will be £10,335 (11,465 – 1,130).

Weighted average cost

You have to use a weighted average, as a simple average isn't accurate enough. A simple average cost per unit would be:

$$\frac{£1.00 + £1.05 + £1.06 + £1.08 + £1.10 + £1.13}{6} = £1.07 \text{ per unit}$$

This means that £10,379 would be charged to the profit and loss account and the stocks would be £1,070. Unfortunately, this doesn't cover the total cost of purchases, £11,465. The stock and the cost of sales total £11,449, so you'd lose £6 in the calculation. This isn't a large number, but it could be, and to be exactly right you have to use a weighted average.

The weighted average cost per unit is:

$$\frac{(1{,}500 \times £1.00) + (2{,}000 \times £1.05) + (1{,}500 \times £1.06) + (2{,}000 \times £1.08) + (2{,}200 \times £1.10) + (1{,}500 \times £1.13)}{10{,}700}$$

$= £1.0714953.$

The extra decimal places guarantee the accuracy! The cost of sales will be £10,393.504 and the stock £1,071.4953.

Last in first out

Last in first out charges the most recent deliveries into the profit and loss account. This means that the closing stock on the balance sheet will be £1,000 and the cost of sales in the profit and loss account will be £10,465. Think about this for a minute – does this make sense? In the real world, do you send the newest stock to the customers before the oldest? The accounting standards agree with you; last in first out can only be used under SSAP 9 *(Stocks and long-term contracts)* if it is necessary to ensure the accounts show a true and fair view, and isn't an allowable method under FRED 28 (*Inventories* and *Construction and service contracts*). However, it is used in other countries and in some industries where it's the only way to show a true and fair view.

The other point worth making is that my example is far too simple; to operate LIFO properly companies have to calculate the last in each time they make a sale. This means that they would need a sophisticated accounting system to cope with the demands of operating LIFO.

The three methods of valuing stock give different profits and different stock values on the balance sheet (Table 2.18).

Table 2.18 Cost of sales and stock values using the three methods of valuing stock

	Cost of sales £	**Stock values** £
First in first out	10,335.00	1,130.00
Weighted average	10,393.50	1,071.50
Last in first out	10,465.00	1,000.00

Whilst these methods provide the basis for calculating the costs of goods used in sales, they don't cope with the problem of incorporating labour and production overhead costs into the value of work in progress and finished goods stock. Most companies' accounting procedures allow them to build in the cost of labour and production overheads as the materials move through the production process. But problems arise when production falls or rises dramatically, as the procedures assume 'normal' production levels.

Johnson Matthey's note is more complicated, reflecting the nature of its business.

> **Precious metal stocks:** Stocks of gold, silver and platinum group metals are valued according to the source from which the metal is obtained. Metal which has been purchased and committed to future sales to customers or hedged in metal markets is valued at the price at which it is contractually committed or hedged, adjusted for unexpired contango. Leased metal is valued at market prices at the balance sheet date. Other precious metal stocks owned by the group, which are unhedged, are valued at the lower of cost and net realisable value.
>
> **Other stocks:** These are valued at the lower of cost, including attributable overheads, and net realisable value.

Johnson Matthey is exposed to movements in precious metal prices, and has to decide how to minimise its risk exposure. This is just like insurance – you have to decide on the risks you're prepared to take and those you want to avoid. However, avoidance comes at a price – if you want to eliminate the risks completely it becomes very expensive. So you strike a balance, carrying some of the risks yourself, and minimising the others. Companies do this through a process called hedging, and I'll tell you more about this later in the book. Contango is a hedging term – it means that the price for delivering the metal in the future is greater than the current price (called the *spot* price).

The construction company

Construction companies have different problems, as large construction contracts often span a number of years. Normally, turnover and profit can only be shown in the profit and loss account once the full terms of the contract have been fulfilled. However, if a construction company waited until the project is finished before including a contract in the profit and loss account, the accounts would not reflect a 'true and fair' view of its financial performance. It might complete no contracts in one year and three in the following year. Consequently, there has to be a different way of accounting for long-term contracts, and this is known as *the percentage of completion method*. This allows construction companies to include in their profit and loss account an appropriate proportion of uncompleted profitable long-term contracts once the contract's outcome can be reliably estimated. If you're analysing a construction company you need to understand how it incorporates turnover and profit into its profit and loss account.

SSAP 9 (*Stocks and long-term contracts*) and the alignment proposal FRED 28 (*Inventories* and *Construction and service contracts*) have very similar requirements:

- If the company believes that the contract will make a loss, the full loss should be immediately taken into the profit and loss account.
- If the company can't reliably estimate the contract's outcome, no profit should be taken into the profit and loss account (although the company could show the relevant proportion of the turnover).

- If the contract is almost certainly profitable, the value of work completed is shown as turnover and the costs relating to the work done are charged to cost of sales. Then the 'attributable profit' is shown in the profit and loss account. (A lot of companies believe that profitability can be assessed with some certainty when more than 30% of the contract has been completed.)

However, identifying the turnover is only simple if the contract is a 'cost plus' one, or where the contract is divided into easily identifiable parts. A number of methods have evolved to identify the percentage of completion, and I've summarised the main three below, but unfortunately you'll find that each method has a potential downside.

Valuation by an independent surveyor

The surveyor certifies the percentage of the contract that has been completed. However, this certificate may pre-date the end of the financial year.

Valuation by the management

The management estimate the percentage of contract completion. This means that all of the relevant turnover can be included in the profit and loss account, but the valuation isn't independent.

Cost basis

Costs are easier to measure than revenues, so there are a number of different formulae based on cost. The appropriate percentage can be determined by taking:

$$\frac{\text{costs to date}}{\text{anticipated total costs}} \times \text{anticipated total contract value}$$

This method would only be appropriate if the costs were incurred evenly over the period of the contract and there is a direct relationship between the degree of completion and the level of the costs.

$$\frac{\text{labour costs to date}}{\text{anticipated total labour costs}} \times \text{anticipated total contract value}$$

This would only be appropriate if the labour costs were a fair reflection of the completion of the project.

Once the company has decided that the contract is reasonably certain to be profitable, it then decides how much profit should be shown in this period's profit and loss account. There are many different ways to calculate this, and auditors encourage companies to use methods that are similar to those used to calculate turnover.

Balfour Beatty's accounting policy is covered in two of its accounting policy notes, and I've italicised the part of the turnover note relating to construction contracts.

6 Turnover

Turnover represents amounts invoiced to outside customers, net of trade discounts, value added and similar sales-based taxes, *except in respect of contracting activities where turnover represents the value of work carried out during the year including amounts not invoiced.* Turnover is recognised on property developments when they are subject to substantially unconditional contracts for sale.

7 Profit recognition on contracting activities

Profit on individual contracts is taken only when their outcome can be foreseen with reasonable certainty, based on the lower of the percentage margin earned to date and that prudently forecast at completion, taking account of agreed claims. Full provision is made for all known or expected losses on individual contracts, taking a prudent view of future claims income, immediately such losses are foreseen. Profit for the year includes the benefit of claims settled on contracts completed in prior years.

Prepayments

This is an unusual accounting term as it actually means what it says! It's a payment made for goods that the business hasn't yet used. You're familiar with prepayments if you pay insurance and have a car. Insurance and road tax are both prepayments, you have to pay for them before you get any benefits.

As prepayments are payments in advance, they're not charged to the profit and loss account, as they do not relate to the sales made in the current period. I've illustrated this in the following example.

EXAMPLE 2.11

I'll assume that a company has a 31 March year end, but pays insurance premiums on 1 January.

On 1 January 2002 it paid £2,000 as an insurance premium. On 1 January 2003 the premium had risen to £2,800. The charge for insurance in the accounts for the year ending 31 March 2003 would be £2,200 (three-quarters of the payment made in 2002 – £1,500, and a quarter of the payment made in 2003 – £700). The balance of the 2003 payment (£2,100) would be charged to the 2004 profit and loss account. It would show on the 2003 balance sheet as a prepayment and is included with debtors (although in some countries you'll find that prepayments are shown separately on the balance sheet).

Currency adjustments

Any company exporting or importing goods, or that has a subsidiary or associate overseas, has to find a way of incorporating different currencies into its accounts. This can have a significant effect on a company's reported results; consequently, I'll show you how companies deal with exchange rates. You'll find that the accounting treatment is different in individual companies and groups.

Exchange rate accounting problems

Exchange rates pose two problems:

- Which rate do you use?
- How do you account for any exchange differences?

The problems facing companies aren't that different from the ones you face when you're on holiday abroad and buy souvenirs. When you're thinking about the cost, do you use the rate in the resort or the rate you're likely to get on your credit card? You've had personal experience of 'exchange differences' if you've found that the rate that you thought you would get is different from the rate that appears on your credit card bill. Just like companies, sometimes you win and sometimes you lose!

Exchange rates can have a significant effect on companies' reported profits, particularly in those businesses where the costs are incurred in one currency and revenues are earned in another. This is quite common in industries like shipping and oil, where revenues are earned in dollars, but a UK-based company could incur most of its costs in sterling.

I'll illustrate this by looking at the profitability of the following contract.

EXAMPLE 2.12

A company reports in sterling and has a contract that earns cash revenues of US$1,000 and has costs of £500. The reported sterling profit would vary widely according to the sterling:dollar exchange rate – I've used three rates ranging from parity to £1.00 = $2.00 (Table 2.19).

Table 2.19 The effect of exchange rates

	£1.00 = US$2.00	£1.00 = US$1.50	£1.00 = US$1.00
Sales	500	667	1,000
Operating costs	(500)	(500)	(500)
Operating profit	0	167	500

You've seen that the reported profit ranges from zero to £500, a 50% return on sales! Now I'm sure you realise that this example is far too simple; there are many more problems than this. What if the cash received from the sale came in at a different rate than the exchange rate on the day of the sale? What exchange rate should you use? Should you take the sale at the rate on the day the sale was made, or the rate actually received? (If you think about it, this is a fairly common problem, as most companies give credit.)

There are four possible exchange rates that could be used:

- **the closing rate**: the rate at the end of the financial year;
- **the average rate**: the weighted average exchange rate during the year;
- **the historical rate**: the rate on the date of the transaction;
- **the forward/contracted rate**: the rate that the company actually gets.

The accounting standard *(SSAP 20 Foreign currency translation)* gives some guidelines about accounting for foreign currencies, both the rates that should be used and the treatment of exchange differences. The rules are slightly different for individual companies and groups and will be modified as part of the process to align UK and international accounting standards. Two alignment proposals, FRED 24 (*The effect of changes in foreign exchange rates* and *Financial reporting in hyperinflationary economies*) and FRED 23 (Financial instruments: *Hedge accounting*), cover accounting for foreign currencies.

Handling exchange rates in individual companies

The profit and loss account

Items shown in the profit and loss account are translated at either the rate of exchange at the date of the transaction or, if there have been no significant fluctuations, average exchange rates. SSAP 20 allows, but does not require, forward rates to be used in trading transactions. Exchange differences may arise from the movement in exchange rates between the invoicing date and the payment date. These are charged to the profit and loss account and affect the reported profit. I've illustrated this in the following example.

EXAMPLE 2.13

A company sells $450,000 of goods to an American client on 12 February when £1.00 = $1.50, giving a turnover of £300,000. (The sales will be recorded using US$1.50, as this is the exchange rate at the date of the transaction.) The cost of the goods was £275,000, giving an apparent profit of £25,000 on the deal. However, the company was paid on 28 March when the exchange rate was £1.00 = US$1.55.

The profit and loss account will show turnover of £300,000 (450,000 ÷ 1.5), whereas the subsequent cash inflow will be only £290,323 (450,000 ÷ 1.55). The exchange loss of £9,677 will then be charged to the profit and loss account:

	£
Turnover	300,000
Cost of sales	(275,000)
Exchange loss	(9,677)
Profit	15,323

A 3.33% change in exchange rates has reduced profit by 39%!

When sterling is strengthening exporters lose both profit and cash; on the other hand, importers win!

The balance sheet

I'll cover this now, although the balance sheet is covered in the next chapter, as exchange rate differences affect both documents.

The accounting treatment for exchange differences depends on the type of asset or liability. SSAP 20 classifies assets and liabilities as:

- **Monetary assets and liabilities**: these include both money that is held by the company (e.g. deposits and loans) and amounts that will be received and paid in money (e.g. debtors and creditors). These are translated at the closing rate and any exchange differences are charged to the profit and loss account, unless the company has a forward contract for debtors and creditors. In this case the forward rate may be used.
- **Non-monetary assets**: these would include stocks and plant and machinery, and these are shown on the balance sheet at the exchange rate when they were acquired. This means that their value is unaffected by exchange rate movements.
- **Shares in foreign companies**: foreign equity investments are usually treated in the same way as any other non-monetary asset, with their value shown at the rate of exchange when the investment was made. The only exception to this is if the investment is financed by foreign borrowings. This is regarded as a *hedge* (a hedge is designed to minimise, or eliminate, a risk by moving in the opposite direction to the investment's value). In this case they may be translated at the closing (year end) rate. Any exchange differences are then taken to reserves, where any differences arising from the borrowings may be offset against them. The borrowings used to finance the investment don't have to be in the same currency as the investment. Companies have been tempted to designate loans as hedges, as the exchange differences move through the reserves rather than through the profit and loss account.

  The proposals in FRED 23 (Financial instruments: *Hedge accounting*) will change this. Firstly, hedge accounting can only be used where the hedging relationship has been pre-designated and meets hedge effectiveness tests that must be met both at the outset and continuously. These tests recognise that hedges aren't perfect and split the hedge into the effective and ineffective parts. (The definition of an effective hedge is that the value of the hedged item is offset by the hedge within a range of 80–125%.) The gain, or loss, on the effective portion should be taken to the statement of total recognised gains and losses and any ineffective part charged to the profit and loss account.

Once you've handled the exchange rates in the individual companies, they have to be consolidated to reflect the group position.

Handling exchange rates in groups

I have shown you how to account for transactions in foreign currencies in an individual company. I'll now move on to look at the other area where exchange rates affect the accounts – consolidating the results, assets and liabilities of a group's overseas subsidiaries.

The group financial statements should mirror the results, and the relationships, which are measured in the local currency before any consolidation. Consequently, groups would usually use the *closing rate method*, also known as the *net investment method,* for consolidating their subsidiaries, joint ventures and associates. This uses closing or average rates for the translation of profit and loss account items for most subsidiaries. (FRED 24 will not allow the use of the closing rate for profit and loss account items. This won't be a major change, as most companies use average rates, believing that this is more representative of the actual rates during the year. Any difference between the average rate and the closing rate is taken to the reserves.)

Balance sheet items are translated using closing rates. Any differences in the net investment (the parent's share of the capital and reserves) are taken to reserves.

Under SSAP 20, the only exception to this is where the subsidiary, or associate, isn't independent and its activities are interlinked with those of the parent. In this case the trade of the subsidiary is seen as a direct extension of the trade of the parent company. It is treated as though it were part of the parent, with historical or average rates being used. This is called the *temporal method.* (FRED 24 will simplify accounting in this area, as it proposes that integral foreign operations should be treated in the same way as other subsidiaries.)

Johnson Matthey's accounting policy for exchange rates is:

> **Foreign currencies:** Profit and loss accounts in foreign currencies and cash flows included in the cash flow statement are translated into sterling at average exchange rates for the year. Foreign currency assets and liabilities are translated into sterling at the rates of exchange at the balance sheet date. Gains or losses arising on the translation of the net assets of overseas subsidiaries and associated undertakings are taken to reserves, less exchange differences arising on related foreign currency borrowings. Other exchange differences are taken to the profit and loss account.

An important change proposed in FRED 24 (*The effect of changes in foreign exchange rates* and *Financial Reporting in hyperinflationary economies*)

Groups have always been required to present their accounts in the main currency of their business's operations and cash flow – their *functional currency*. FRED 24 requires companies to prepare accounts that are *measured* in this currency, but allows them to *report* their accounts in a different currency – the *presentation* currency. The International Accounting Standards Board have allowed this as:

- Increasing globalisation means that most large groups don't have a single functional currency. Instead they have a number of functional currencies that are used to monitor and control the group.
- In some countries, businesses are required to report in the local currency, regardless of the functional currency. Maintaining the requirement for reporting in the functional currency would require businesses to prepare two sets of accounts.

Profit and loss account summary

I've covered a lot of technical material, and I'd now like to summarise the key points that you need to remember in Table 2.20.

Table 2.20 Profit and loss account summary

Turnover	This is the cash sales in the period plus either the invoices raised, or the goods shipped during the period, depending on the company's accounting policy for recognising its revenue. Accounting for long-term contracts is different from normal accounting practice, as the turnover is recorded as the contract progresses and profit is recorded as it arises. Any payments in advance for sales in future periods will not be shown. They will be included in creditors and shown as *deferred income*.
Operating costs	This is the cost of goods used in sales. The numbers are adjusted to: ■ Include charges for: – Accrued expenses. These outstanding invoices will be included in creditors. – Depreciation. The company gets the benefit of using its fixed assets over a number of years. As the profit and loss account must match costs to revenues, the depreciation charge will represent this year's use of its fixed assets. There are different methods of depreciation, giving different charges to the profit and loss account and different asset values on the balance sheet. – Provisions for likely future costs relating to either sales, or decisions that have been made during the period (for example, restructuring). The provisions may reduce asset values (bad debts, stock write-downs) or relate to future costs. Unspent provisions relating to future costs will be included in provisions for liabilities and charges on the balance sheet. Provisions in the UK can only be made where there's a liability arising from a past event that has a measurable probable future cash outflow. ■ Exclude: – Prepayments. These advance payments to suppliers are included in debtors, and will be separately disclosed in the notes to the accounts. – Stock. This is shown on the balance sheet. There are different methods of valuing stock, giving different charges to the profit and loss account and different stock values on the balance sheet.

Exchange rates	Companies use either the actual exchange rate, or an average exchange rate, for profit and loss account items. However, exchange differences can arise from the movement in exchange rates between the invoicing date and the payment date, and these affect a company's reported profitability as they are charged to the profit and loss account.
Share of associated undertakings' profits or losses	An investment is classed as an associate when the investment is sizeable (usually 20–50% of the shares) and the company is involved in, but doesn't control, the decision making (*a participating interest*). The company brings into its profit and loss account the associate's operating profits (and subsequent costs excluding dividends) in proportion to its investment in the company (i.e. if the company holds 30% of the shares it incorporates 30% of the associate's operating profits (and subsequent costs, excluding dividends) into its profit and loss account). The associate's operating profit is separately disclosed. The accounting treatment for joint ventures is similar, with the joint venture's turnover being disclosed as well.
Sales, operating costs, and operating profits may be analysed between continuing and discontinued operations.	
Continuing operations	These are operations expected to continue next year. The sales, operating costs, and operating profit of any businesses acquired during the year are separately disclosed.
Discontinued operations	These are those operations that have been planned to be (or have already been) closed, discontinued, or sold during the year. Any provisions for losses are separately disclosed.
Exceptional costs	An exceptional cost relates to normal business trading but is disclosed because it is either very large or 'material'. The following exceptional costs are required to be disclosed separately after operating profit if they are significant: ■ profit, or losses, on disposal of fixed assets; ■ profit, or losses, on disposal of businesses; ■ restructuring costs.
Profit, or losses, on sale of fixed assets or businesses	All fixed assets have a 'book value'. If their sale proceeds are different from their book value, the difference shows on the profit and loss account as a profit or a loss. Profits, or losses, on sale of businesses are calculated in a similar way.

▶

Net interest payable	This is the interest payable, less any interest receivable or capitalised (charged to the balance sheet). This will not be the same as the interest paid and received shown on the cash flow statement, as interest (like all profit and loss accounts items) is accrued.
Taxation	This can't be calculated directly from the published profit and loss account in the UK, as profit for tax purposes is very different. It will also include an accrual for tax called *deferred taxation*. This is included in the provisions for liabilities and charges on the balance sheet.
Minority interests	This is shown when a company doesn't own all of its subsidiaries. The minority interests represent the proportion of a subsidiary's profits that do not belong to the group. For example, if a subsidiary makes £100 after-tax profits and the group owns 60% of its shares, the group's profit and loss account will show a deduction of £40 as minority interests, to reflect that proportion of the after-tax profits that belongs to shareholders outside of the group. (If a company controls another, the other company is classed as a subsidiary. All of its sales, costs, assets and liabilities are included in the accounts, and the other shareholders' share is shown as a single line adjustment.)

Johnson Matthey's profit and loss account

You'll find Johnson Matthey's profit and loss account on the next page. When you read it you notice that:

- The company made a number of acquisitions and disposals during 2002 and:
  - The acquisitions added £12.7 million to operating profits.
  - The discontinued operations made a small loss.
- Something called *goodwill amortisation* reduced its profits by £6.8 million in 2002. (I'm going to tell you about goodwill amortisation in the next chapter. You'll find it when a company has made an acquisition, and has paid more for the company than its assets are worth.)

Consolidated Profit and Loss Account

for the year ended 31 March 2002

	Notes	2002 Before exceptional items and goodwill amortisation £ million	2002 Exceptional items and goodwill amortisation £ million	2002 Total £ million	2001 Before exceptional items and goodwill amortisation restated £ million	2001 Total restated £ million
Turnover	1					
Continuing operations		**4,761.6**	–	**4,761.6**	5,899.5	5,899.5
Acquisitions		**67.3**	–	**67.3**	–	–
Total continuing operations		**4,828.9**	–	**4,828.9**	5,899.5	5,899.5
Discontinued operations		**1.2**	–	**1.2**	4.2	4.2
Group turnover		**4,830.1**	–	**4,830.1**	5,903.7	5,903.7
Operating profit	1					
Continuing operations		**181.2**	–	**181.2**	174.9	174.9
Acquisitions		**12.7**	–	**12.7**	–	–
Total continuing operations before goodwill amortisation		**193.9**	–	**193.9**	174.9	174.9
Goodwill amortisation		–	**(6.8)**	**(6.8)**	–	(0.3)
Continuing operations before exceptional items		**193.9**	**(6.8)**	**187.1**	174.9	174.6
Exceptional items	2	–	**(18.1)**	**(18.1)**	–	(0.6)
Total continuing operations		**193.9**	**(24.9)**	**169.0**	174.9	174.0
Discontinued operations	3	**(0.5)**	–	**(0.5)**	0.1	0.1
Group operating profit	5	**193.4**	**(24.9)**	**168.5**	175.0	174.1
Share of profit in associates – continuing		**(0.1)**	–	**(0.1)**	0.2	0.2
Share of profit in associates – discontinued	3	–	–	–	(0.2)	(0.2)
Total operating profit		**193.3**	**(24.9)**	**168.4**	175.0	174.1
Profit on sale/closure of discontinued operations						
Sale of French print business	2	–	**(5.5)**	**(5.5)**	–	–
Closure of Metawave Video Systems Ltd	2	–	**(0.1)**	**(0.1)**	–	(1.1)
Sale of Electronic Materials		–	–	–	–	3.4
Sale of Organic Pigments		–	–	–	–	(1.2)
Profit on ordinary activities before interest		**193.3**	**(30.5)**	**162.8**	175.0	175.2
Net interest		**(6.1)**	–	**(6.1)**	5.3	5.3
Profit on ordinary activities before taxation	6	**187.2**	**(30.5)**	**156.7**	180.3	180.5
Taxation	7	**(56.0)**	**5.8**	**(50.2)**	(54.1)	(54.2)
Profit after taxation		**131.2**	**(24.7)**	**106.5**	126.2	126.3
Equity minority interests		**0.3**	–	**0.3**	(0.6)	(0.6)
Profit attributable to shareholders		**131.5**	**(24.7)**	**106.8**	125.6	125.7
Dividends	8	**(53.2)**	–	**(53.2)**	(51.3)	(51.3)
Retained profit for the year	25	**78.3**	**(24.7)**	**53.6**	74.3	74.4

- Its exceptional items reduced operating profits by £18.1 million.
- Apart from the sale of its electronic materials business in 2001, it made losses on the businesses it sold.
- In 2002 it moved from being net interest receivers to net interest payers, but interest is still a relatively small cost.
- It doesn't own all of its subsidiaries.
- It pays out a large percentage of its profit as dividends – almost 50% of the available profit was paid in 2002, and almost 41% in 2001.

You'll also notice that it hasn't shown any analysis of its operating costs – it's actually shown in the notes to the profit and loss account. Many companies do this when their business has changed during the year, or they have a lot of exceptional items, as it makes the profit and loss account less cluttered and easier to read.

Here's Johnson Matthey's analysis of its operating costs, and it's quite interesting as it's not quite what you'd expect:

5 Group operating profit after exceptional items and goodwill amortisation

	2002 Continuing operations £ million	2002 Acquisitions £ million	2002 Total continuing operations £ million	2002 Discontinued operations £ million	2002 Total £ million	2001 Total £ million
Group turnover	4,761.6	67.3	4,828.9	1.2	4,830.1	5,903.7
Cost of materials sold	(4,156.8)	(28.3)	(4,185.1)	(0.6)	(4,185.7)	(5,330.6)
Net revenues	604.8	39.0	643.8	0.6	644.4	573.1
Other cost of sales	(310.1)	(20.0)	(330.1)	(0.5)	(330.6)	(265.6)
Gross profit	294.7	19.0	313.7	0.1	313.8	307.5
Distribution costs	(58.4)	(1.4)	(59.8)	(0.2)	(60.0)	(57.8)
Administrative expenses	(78.7)	(6.2)	(84.9)	(0.4)	(85.3)	(75.6)
Group operating profit	157.6	11.4	169.0	(0.5)	168.5	174.1

For continuing operations, exceptional credits of £4.6 million (2001 £ nil) are included in cost of materials sold, and exceptional charges of £18.4 million (2001 £0.6 million) are included in other cost of sales, £0.5 million (2001 £ nil) in distribution costs and £2.5 million (2001 £ nil) in administrative expenses. For acquisitions, exceptional charges of £1.3 million (2001 £ nil) are included in administrative expenses.

It has split its cost of sales into materials and other cost of sales. And you can see why when you look at how much of its turnover disappears in material costs – materials are almost 87% of its 2002 turnover! You know that the majority of its materials costs will be precious metals – and gold and platinum aren't cheap! This explains why its operating profit is a relatively low percentage of its turnover (just under 3.5%). Its net revenues line is really a measure of the value it has added to its materials.

3

The balance sheet

- **What is in a balance sheet?** – fixed assets; current assets; creditors falling due within a year; creditors falling due in more than a year; capital and reserves
- **The balance sheet in detail** – fixed assets; current assets; creditors: amounts falling due within a year; creditors falling due in more than a year; capital and reserves
- **Balance sheet formats**
- **Summary**
- **Johnson Matthey's balance sheets**

In this chapter I'll look at the balance sheet in detail, and when you've finished reading it you'll understand:

- *the things you'll find on a balance sheet* (I've summarised these below and discuss each one of them in detail later, so that you'll understand both the balance sheet and the wealth of information found in the notes to the balance sheet);
- *how balance sheet items are valued*;
- *the way the balance sheet is laid out in the accounts*.

The balance sheet is probably the only document that everyone regularly prepares, and yet it is the one that managers often find the hardest to understand! You've undoubtedly prepared a balance sheet, even though you didn't realise it.

Have you ever compared your lifestyle to someone else's? Perhaps you've looked at a friend and wondered how they can afford a flash car, or an exotic holiday? You wondered whether they have won the lottery, or maybe it's all on credit cards? If you have, then you have prepared a balance sheet; in fact you've probably created a balance sheet that's pretty similar to a UK company's balance sheet. You look at what your friends have, and deduct what you think they might owe, to find out what they are worth. That's a balance sheet!

Most people are much the same. I wonder if you have a group of friends that you think are intellectually similar, and work about as hard as you do. If they seem to be doing 'better' than you, you may well become dissatisfied and think about looking for another job. Most people mentally prepare their own balance sheets and compare them with their friends' balance sheets. Your parents can tell you how well off you are, but you don't believe them if all your friends have better standards of living and aren't up to their ears in debt. Some of your friends can have better houses and cars, but they probably have bigger mortgages and credit card bills. Everyone has a different level of debt that they feel comfortable with (that's why you end up having rows with your partner about money – their debt comfort level is different from yours). Companies are exactly the same.

A balance sheet shows you what the company has (its assets) and what it owes (its liabilities) on a certain day. It is a snapshot of the business and is a useful tool for looking at a company's financial health. If you know what the company has and what it owes, you can see whether it is likely to be able to pay its debts when they fall due. Company balance sheets do appear to be more complicated than the ones we prepare for ourselves, and sometimes these detailed differences can obscure the more obvious similarities.

There are three main differences between personal balance sheets and those prepared by companies:

- The layout is more complicated, with subtotals that are only useful once you understand what the balance sheet tells you.
- The jargon is unfamiliar, even though what it describes isn't.
- Companies have different types of loans and company treasurers are becoming increasingly innovative, often constructing debt to attract a specific type of lender or investor.

And then, to add to the complications, you'll usually find two balance sheets in the accounts. Most listed companies are not individual companies, but a group of companies. If you're looking at group accounts you'll find two balance sheets; a *consolidated balance sheet* for the whole group, and the *parent company's balance sheet* (sometimes the parent may be called the 'holding company', or just the 'company'). You have to imagine the group accounts like a family tree, but with a single parent at the top. Large businesses usually organise themselves into different divisions, and within these divisions there can be a number of operating companies. They then have a group structure like the one shown in Figure 3.1.

Fig. 3.1 Group structure

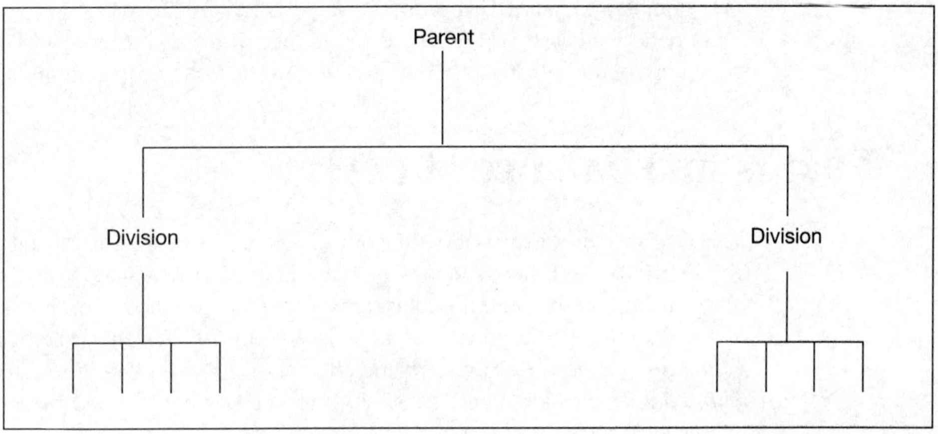

The consolidated balance sheet is the combined balance sheets of all the companies in the group. In the consolidation process some transactions cancel each other out (for example, a loan from one group company to another won't show on the consolidated balance sheet), so that the consolidated balance sheet reflects the group's position. (This is why the parent company often has more investments than the group. They're the shares it holds in the group companies and are cancelled out on consolidation with the group companies' share capital.) All of the companies in the group have to prepare their own accounts, except for the parent company which can choose to show just its own balance sheet with the group's accounts. The Companies Act requires the parent company to prepare consolidated group accounts and publish its balance sheet in the group accounts. It doesn't have to publish its own profit and loss account (although it still has to prepare it), as long as it discloses its profit for the financial year in the notes to the accounts. Most companies choose to do this and in the notes to its accounts Johnson Matthey discloses both its accounting policy and the parent company's profit for the financial year.

> **Basis of consolidation:** The consolidated accounts comprise the accounts of the parent company and all its subsidiary undertakings and include the group's interest in associates and joint ventures.
>
> The results of companies acquired or disposed of in the year are dealt with from or up to the effective date of acquisition or disposal respectively. The net assets of companies acquired are incorporated in the consolidated accounts at their fair values to the group at the date of acquisition.
>
> The parent company has not presented its own profit and loss account as permitted by section 230 of the Companies Act 1985.

Extract from **Note 25b**

> The parent company's profit for the financial year was £19.7 million (2001 restated £6.9 million).

(You'll find references to restated numbers in most companies' 2001 accounts as they had to implement a new accounting standard, FRS 19 (*Deferred tax*), and had to adjust their 2001 numbers to make the numbers comparable.)

In financial analysis you're interested in the *consolidated group* balance sheet, as all of the other documents in the accounts are consolidated group statements.

What is in a balance sheet?

A balance sheet is a snapshot of the company on a certain day, identifying its assets and liabilities. Both the assets and liabilities are sorted into short term and longer term (more than a year). The long-term assets are called *fixed assets* and the short-term assets are called *current assets*. Within the European Union the long-term liabilities are called *Creditors: amounts falling due in more than a year* and short-term liabilities *Creditors: amounts falling due within a year*. Outside the EU these short-term liabilities are called *current liabilities*. In the UK, a typical company balance sheet deducts these liabilities from the assets in order to show what the company is worth to the owners – adopting a 'net worth' presentation. This isn't the only way a balance sheet can be presented, and I'll tell you about the others later.

I'm going to discuss all balance sheet items in detail, but I'll start by summarising the balance sheet headings.

Fixed assets

The Companies Act defines fixed assets as those assets that the company intends to use on an ongoing basis. All other assets are regarded as current assets.

You'll find three different types of fixed asset balance sheets:

- **Intangible assets**: this term covers items like brands or patents that have an obvious value to the company, but it's more difficult to determine their value objectively. The difference between the price paid to buy a company and its net asset value (called *goodwill*) is also included in intangible assets.
- **Tangible assets**: within the EU this term is used to describe land and buildings, plant and machinery, and vehicles etc. Other countries may refer to these as 'property, plant and equipment', or simply 'fixed assets'.
- **Investments**: these are the long-term investments that the company intends to keep for more than a year.

Current assets

Current assets are all the other assets and include cash and any assets held for resale. Most companies' current assets would include:

- stock;
- debtors;
- investments;
- cash at bank and in hand.

Creditors falling due within a year

Most companies show this as a total figure on the balance sheet, detailing the individual items in the notes to the accounts. This heading would include anything that might represent cash, or services, expected to go out of the business in the next twelve months.

Creditors falling due in more than a year

These creditors are largely debt, but would also include other cash, or services, expected to leave the business after a year.

Capital and reserves

The capital and reserves represent the owners' stake in the business. It includes the cash received from the shareholders, the profits reinvested in the business, and any asset revaluations.

The balance sheet in detail

I'll now take you through each line of the balance sheet explaining how its value is determined.

Fixed assets

I'll start by looking at the three types of fixed assets shown on UK accounts and how they're valued.

Intangible assets

The Companies Act identifies the following categories of intangible fixed assets:

- development costs;
- concessions, patents, licences, trademarks and similar rights and assets;
- goodwill;
- payments on account.

The accounting standard FRS 10 (*Goodwill and intangible assets*) defines intangible assets and details the accounting treatment for them, apart from research and development. An intangible asset is a non-financial fixed asset that does not have physical substance, but is identifiable and controlled by the company through custody or legal rights. An 'identifiable' intangible asset is one that can be sold separately from the rest of the business. If it can only be sold by selling the whole business it has to be treated as goodwill.

Any intangible asset that the company has bought should be shown initially at its cost. Intangible assets that the business generates itself can only be capitalised if they have a 'readily ascertainable market value' and:

- belong to a uniform group of assets that are equivalent in all material respects (like licences);
- have an active market.

(This effectively means that most internally developed brand names and publishing titles can't be shown on the balance sheet, as they are essentially unique.)

All intangible assets should be *amortised* (in Europe we talk about amortising intangible assets and depreciating tangible ones). This is usually over a maximum of 20 years, unless the company can prove, in an annual impairment review, that their value has not diminished. Companies also have to have an impairment review at the end of the first full financial year following the acquisition of an intangible asset, and when events indicate an intangible asset's value might have fallen.

I'd now like to discuss three of the intangible assets you're likely to find on the balance sheet – development costs, goodwill, and brands.

Research and development

Whilst the Companies Act allows development costs to be shown as an intangible asset, it is rare to find them shown as an intangible asset in the UK. However, they are often found in other countries' accounts, as many other countries allow some, or most, research and development costs to be capitalised. Research and development is a problem for accountants. It's an investment in the long-term future of the business, but isn't always successful. In the UK prudence has won and most companies charge the revenue costs of research and development to the profit and loss account as they are incurred. The tangible fixed assets used for research and development are treated in the same way as any other tangible asset, and shown on the balance sheet. All *research* costs must be charged to the profit and loss account. However, the accounting standard (*SSAP 13 Accounting for research and development*) does allow *development* expenditure to be shown as an intangible fixed asset if all of the following criteria are met:

- There is a clearly defined project.
- The related expenditure is separately identifiable.
- It is reasonably certain that the project is both technically feasible and commercially viable.
- The project is expected to be profitable, having considered all current and future costs.
- The company has the resources to complete the project.

This means that very few development projects can be capitalised under UK accounting rules. If they are capitalised they don't have to meet FRS 10's requirements for an internally developed intangible asset. Any capitalised development costs are amortised over the periods that are expected to benefit from their use.

You'll always know whether a company is capitalising development costs, as they have to disclose their accounting policy for research and development in the notes to the accounts. Johnson Matthey discloses:

> **Research and development expenditure:** Charged against profits in the year incurred.

Goodwill

I mentioned goodwill in the last chapter, but now I'd like to explain it in more detail. Goodwill arises as companies usually pay more to acquire another company than the business is worth on its balance sheet. What would you pay for a company that has net assets worth £50 million, but is generating £10 million profit a year? I know you'd pay more than £50 million, as you're not just buying the assets, you should also have another £10 million profit every year. The difference between the purchase price and the value of the business shown in the accounts is called goodwill. It is simply the difference between the purchase price of a company and the value of the net assets acquired – effectively a premium paid to acquire the company's profits and cash flow.

I'll illustrate the accounting treatment for goodwill by using a simple example.

EXAMPLE 3.1

First, I need to tell you about my business – its net assets are currently £200 million, and I have agreed to buy the company I discussed earlier for £70 million in cash. My summarised balance sheet, before the acquisition, was as shown in Table 3.1.

Table 3.1 Summarised balance sheet before the acquisition

	£ million
Tangible fixed assets	200
Cash	120
Other current assets	130
Current liabilities	(150)
Long term loans	(100)
	200
Capital and reserves:	
Share capital	50
Profit and loss account	150
	200

I now have to consolidate my newly acquired subsidiary into my accounts. Following the acquisition my cash reduces by the £70 million I paid to acquire the business. In exchange I'll receive its £50 million net assets. Now look what happens when I try to add up the two balance sheets to prepare my new balance sheet (Table 3.2).

Table 3.2 My first attempt at consolidating my balance sheet

	My business £m	Acquisition cost	Acquisition £m	**Consolidated balance sheet £m**
Tangible fixed assets	200		30	**230**
Cash	120	(70)	0	**50**
Other current assets	130		50	**180**
Current liabilities	(150)		(20)	**(170)**
Long-term loans	(100)		(10)	**(110)**
	200		50	**180**
Capital and reserves:				
Share capital	50			**50**
Profit and loss account	150			**150**
	200			**200**

These two numbers should be the same!

Now there's one thing you probably already know about balance sheets – they're supposed to balance! The consolidated balance sheet's net assets of £180 million should be the same as the capital and reserves of £200 million! The balance sheet doesn't balance as I have paid more for the business than it was worth on its balance sheet – and that difference of £20 million is goodwill.

I can make the balance sheet balance in one of two ways:

- Reduce the capital and reserves, by reducing the profit and loss account. Before December 1998 UK companies did this.
- Increase the net assets, by creating an intangible asset. FRS 10 now requires all UK companies to do this.

I'll now show my consolidated balance sheet prepared under the old rules and the current rules (Table 3.3).

Table 3.3 Consolidated balance sheet prepared under the old and new rules

	Old accounting practice £m		Current accounting practice £m
Fixed assets	230		**230**
Intangible fixed asset – goodwill			**20**
Cash	50		**50**
Other current assets	180		**180**
Current liabilities	(170)		**(170)**
Long term loans	(110)		**(110)**
	180		**200**
Capital and reserves:			
Share capital	50		**50**
Profit and loss account	130	*(150 – 20)*	**150**
	180		**200**

Companies used to write goodwill off against *past* profits, whereas now they increase their assets and usually amortise goodwill against their *future* profits. The old accounting treatment overstated the returns on the investment, and made it harder to spot companies that had overpaid for their acquisitions. The current accounting treatment ensures that the management is held accountable for all aspects of the acquisition, and helps to identify whether the acquisition has added value for the shareholders.

However, FRS 10 only required companies to capitalise goodwill arising from acquisitions made *after* December 1998, when the standard became effective. Any goodwill previously written off through reserves can remain there until the companies they acquired are sold or terminated (when it is deducted to arrive at the profit, or loss, on disposal). This goodwill is disclosed in the notes to the accounts and some companies have sizeable amounts of goodwill written off through their reserves. (For example, as at 31 March 2002 Boots had capital and reserves of £2,017.6 million, but this is after writing off £743.6 million goodwill on acquisitions made before December 1998.) This means that you need to check the note on reserves before you calculate any ratios.

Johnson Matthey has £182.6 million goodwill shown on its balance sheet as an intangible asset and its note on the group's reserves discloses:

> At 31st March 2002, the cumulative amount of goodwill, net of goodwill relating to disposals, charged against the profit and loss account was £46.0 million (2001 £46.0 million).

So the group's total goodwill on 30 March 2002 was £228.6 million.

Unfortunately, my example was quite simple, as the value of the acquisition's assets didn't change when they were consolidated and the cost was simply the cash I paid to acquire the business. It's rarely that simple, as the Companies Act requires companies to consolidate the acquisition's assets and liabilities 'at their fair values as at the date of acquisition' and using the purchaser's accounting policies. FRS 7 (*Fair values in acquisition accounting*) identifies how the fair value for each asset and liability should be calculated.

Consequently, companies make two adjustments when consolidating acquisitions in the group accounts:

- aligning the acquisition's accounting policies with the group's;
- restating the values of the acquisition's assets and liabilities to fair values.

You can see this if you look at the information I've extracted from the notes to Johnson Matthey's 2002 accounts, which clearly illustrates these two adjustments and what is meant by 'fair values'. It acquired Meconic plc in 2002 for £154.1 million. (It also acquired other businesses in 2002.) Meconic's net assets on its accounts were £26.9 million, which reduced to £20.8 million on consolidation.

29 Acquisitions

Meconic plc

On 21st June 2001 the group announced that it had agreed terms for a recommended cash offer for Meconic plc, the quoted UK parent company of Macfarlan Smith, a manufacturer of active pharmaceutical ingredients and fine chemicals based in Edinburgh, Scotland. On 9th July 2001 the group announced that it had acquired over 50% of the company and hence the offer became unconditional. The results of Meconic plc since its acquisition on 9th July 2001 have been included in the results of Pharmaceutical Materials, and were turnover of £54.5 million and operating profit of £10.0 million. This has been accounted for by acquisition accounting. Meconic plc's profit after taxation and minority interests in its last financial year to 30th April 2001 was £6.6 million, and in the period from that date to the date of acquisition was £0.4 million.

The assets and liabilities acquired were:

	Book values immediately prior to acquisition	Fair value adjustments			Fair value at time of acquisition
		Revaluations	Consistency of accounting policies	Other	
	£ million	£ million	£ million	£ million	£ million
Goodwill	2.1	–	–	(2.1)	–
Tangible fixed assets	24.5	–	–	–	24.5
Stocks	21.0	(3.0)	–	–	18.0
Debtors and prepayments	14.5	(0.3)	–	–	14.2
Short term investments	0.1	–	–	–	0.1
Borrowings falling due within one year	(20.6)	–	–	–	(20.6)
Creditors falling due within one year	(11.3)	–	–	(0.6)	(11.9)
Provisions for liabilities and charges	(3.4)	–	(0.1)	–	(3.5)
Total net assets acquired	26.9	(3.3)	(0.1)	(2.7)	20.8
Goodwill on acquisition					133.3
					154.1

	£ million
Satisfied by:	
Purchase consideration – cash	128.7
Purchase consideration – loan notes	18.9
Purchase consideration – rollover of share options	0.7
Costs incurred – cash	5.7
Costs incurred – accrued	0.1
	154.1

> The revaluation fair value adjustments to stocks and debtors and prepayments reflect the write down to estimated realisable value. The fair value adjustment to achieve consistency of accounting policies in provisions for liabilities and charges is to provide for post-retirement medical benefits. The other fair value adjustment to goodwill is to write off goodwill previously capitalised, as it is not an identifiable asset. The other fair value adjustment to creditors falling due within one year is to include liabilities not previously fully recognised.
>
> Since acquisition Meconic plc has contributed £10.4 million to net cash inflow from operating activities, paid £0.3 million in respect of returns on investments and servicing of finance, paid £0.3 million of tax and £4.6 million in respect of capital expenditure and financial investment.

You can see that the notes give you a lot of information about an acquisition:

- The fair value adjustments bring the asset values to their realisable value. These can include assets and liabilities that weren't previously shown in the accounts. Goodwill has been excluded, as it is not *identifiable*. (I defined this for you in the initial discussion on intangible assets – intangible assets can only be shown if they can be sold separately from the rest of business.)
- You can see the composition and definition of 'cost', and that it includes any expenses directly incurred in making the acquisition.
- You can also see how Meconic has contributed to other aspects of the group's performance since its acquisition.

Now back to goodwill. It has to be reviewed at the end of the first full financial year to check that the premium that has been paid to acquire the company will be covered by the acquisition's future cash flows. The review is carried out in two stages. Initially the company compares the acquired company's first year performance with the pre-acquisition forecasts for the first year. It then has to do a full impairment review if there is evidence that the post-acquisition performance does not meet its pre-acquisition expectations. The impairment review compares the value of the acquisition with the present value of its future cash flows and ensures that if there has been an overpayment the loss is recognised immediately.

Sometimes it is possible to buy a company for less than its net asset value. In May 2000 BMW sold most of Rover Cars to the Phoenix Corporation for £10 – well below their asset value. In this case the goodwill is negative rather than positive. FRS 10 requires that negative goodwill should be shown separately from positive goodwill on the face of the balance sheet. It is subsequently written back into the profit and loss account over the periods expected to benefit.

Brand names

Although FRS 10 has made it difficult for companies to show internally developed brand names on the balance sheet, purchased brands are still shown and it is a common practice in some industries, like the food and drinks industry, where brand names are a large hidden asset. At 28 December 2001 Cadbury Schweppes had £2,764 million of brands it had acquired since 1985 shown as intangible assets on its balance sheet. To put this into context, its net assets were £3,183 million and it had borrowings of £2,094 million. As it has developed many of its brands itself, or acquired them before 1985, only a relatively small proportion of its brand value is shown on the balance sheet.

The accounting profession has yet to resolve the problem of brand accounting, although most companies have their brands valued independently by companies like Interbrand Group. The valuation is derived from applying a multiple (based on the brand's strength in certain areas) to the brand's earnings. Both components of the formula (the multiple and the future earnings) are subjective. The other alternative valuation method is to discount the present value of the future cash flows arising from the brand, using the company's after-tax weighted average cost of capital as the discount rate. The obvious problem with this method is the prediction of the future cash flows. But whatever method the company uses to value their brands, the assumptions used will make the valuation subjective, and open to debate.

The note on intangible assets

The intangible assets are usually shown as a total on the balance sheet, although some companies analyse them between goodwill and others. If you want to see the components of intangible assets you have to look in the notes, where all the details are shown. Johnson Matthey has only one intangible asset, goodwill, and its note for the group discloses:

12 Fixed assets – goodwill

	Group £ million
Cost	
At beginning of year	9.1
Additions (Note 29)	181.0
Disposals (Note 30)	(0.4)
Exchange adjustments	0.1
At end of year	189.8
Amortisation	
At beginning of year	0.5
Charge for the year	6.8
Exchange adjustments	(0.1)
At end of year	7.2
Net book value at 31st March 2002	**182.6**
Net book value at 31st March 2001	8.6

Goodwill amortisation of £0.5 million (2001 £0.2 million) arises in Catalysts & Chemicals, £0.1 million (2001 £nil) in Precious Metals, £0.2 million (2001 £0.1 million) in Colours & Coatings and £6.0 million (2001 £nil) in Pharmaceutical Materials. Geographically £5.2 million (2001 £nil) arises in Europe and £1.6 million (2001 £0.3 million) in North America.

You can see that most of the goodwill amortisation arose from the acquisitions made during the current financial year.

Tangible fixed assets

These assets are held by the business to use in generating sales, and aren't held for resale. (When the company decides to sell them they will be shown as current assets.)

When you are preparing personal balance sheets, you have a fair idea of what these assets are worth. Unfortunately, the *book value* of a company's assets may not reflect their market value. You need to remember two things when you're looking at the tangible assets on a balance sheet:

- The company may not own these assets.
- Their values are affected by the company's depreciation and revaluation policies.

Ownership of assets

In the introductory chapter I discussed the accounting principle of 'substance over form'. This says that if the company has the benefits, and risks, normally associated with owning an asset; the asset should be shown in the accounts, regardless of the legal position. This means that assets purchased under hire purchase agreements are included in tangible assets, even though the company doesn't own the asset until it has met certain conditions (normally when it has paid an agreed number of instalments).

Some leases also give companies most of the risks and rewards of ownership (*finance leases*), and these assets also appear as part of the tangible assets. Other leases don't have these risks and rewards (*operating leases*), and are treated like any other rental agreement. The accounting standard (*SSAP 21 Accounting for leases and hire purchase contracts*) defines these two types of leases and details the appropriate accounting treatment for them:

- **Finance leases**: the basic principle is that both the asset and the underlying liability should be shown on the balance sheet. Assets leased under finance leases are capitalised and depreciated over the shorter of the lease term and the anticipated useful life. The capital amount owed to the leasing company is included in creditors, split between creditors due within a year and more than a year. The subsequent lease rentals are then analysed into the capital element and the interest element. The capital repayment will reduce the amount owed to the leasing company, included in creditors, and the interest element of the lease rental is included in the interest charge on the profit and loss account.

  The allocation between capital and interest payments is not straightforward, as the standard requires companies to use present value techniques to determine the split.
- **Operating leases**: these are treated in the same way as any other short-term hire agreement. The assets don't show on the balance sheet and the lease rental is charged to the profit and loss account as an operating cost. The notes to the profit and loss account disclose the amount charged during the period, analysed between the hire of plant and machinery and other assets. As the leasing agreement represents a contingent liability, the notes also disclose the annual commitment for operating leases, analysed between leases expiring in:
  - one year;
  - between two and five years;
  - more than five years.

Johnson Matthey's notes on operating leases in the group disclose:

Extract from **Note 6 Profit on ordinary activities before taxation**

	2002	2001
	£ million	£ million
Operating lease rentals – on plant and machinery	**2.3**	2.1
– on other operating leases	**6.7**	6.4

Extract from **Note 26 Commitments, guarantees and contingent liabilities**

	2002	2001
	£ million	£ million
Annual commitments under operating leases		
Leases of land and buildings terminating		
Within one year	**0.5**	0.8
In one to five years	**3.4**	3.7
Over five years	**2.2**	2.1
Other leases terminating		
Within one year	**0.5**	0.4
In one to five years	**1.8**	1.4

Whether a lease is a finance lease or an operating lease is important, as it affects where it shows in the accounts. The accounting standard tries to define the differences between the two, but stresses that it can only be a matter of degree, not a fundamental difference. The standard recognises that it is often difficult to decide whether the lease is a finance or an operating lease, and this grey area historically allowed finance companies to develop finance leases that could be classified as operating leases under the standard. This gave companies a source of 'off-balance-sheet funding'. However, FRS 5 *(Reporting the substance of transactions)* reduced this flexibility, as it requires the company that has the risks and rewards associated with ownership to show the asset and the associated liability on its balance sheet.

Whilst I can't give a definitive definition of the difference between the two leases (the accounting standard defines an operating lease as 'a lease other than a finance lease'!), I've summarised the major differences in Table 3.4.

Table 3.4 Major differences between finance and operating leases

	Finance leases	Operating leases
Risks and rewards associated with ownership	Yes	No
Lease term is:	Similar to the asset's life.	Shorter than the asset's life.
Lease rental equivalent to:	At least 90% of fair value of asset when discounted to its present value.	The interest on, and the repayment of, the asset's depreciation.

There are proposals to change lease accounting in the future. In December 1999 the ASB issued a discussion paper developed by an international group of standard setters. The main proposals are:

- to bring operating leases onto the balance sheet;

- to extend the standard to some intangible assets, like exploration rights and licensing agreements.

Depreciation of assets

Most fixed assets are shown on the balance sheet at cost less depreciation, however there are some exceptions. Investment properties are the main one, as SSAP 19 (*Accounting for investment properties)* requires them to be shown at their market value. (They're shown at market value, as depreciating an asset that's used directly to generate income would be illogical.) UK accounting rules also relax the depreciation requirement for other assets if the depreciation charge would be immaterial. It could be immaterial because they have long lives (greater than 50 years), or because the estimated residual value is the same as the book value, or a combination of the two. If the company decides not to depreciate an asset, other than non-depreciable land, it must carry out an 'impairment test' each year to prove that depreciation is still immaterial. (However, this may change in the future as the alignment proposal FRED 29 (*Property, plant and equipment* and *Borrowing costs)* doesn't require an annual impairment test for tangible assets that aren't depreciated). Companies have to disclose, in the notes to the accounts, if they have any assets that aren't depreciated, as the Companies Act requires all fixed assets to be depreciated. Johnson Matthey doesn't depreciate all its fixed assets, as its note on depreciation discloses:

> **Depreciation:** Freehold land and certain office buildings are not depreciated. The depreciation charge and accumulated depreciation of these properties would be immaterial and they are reviewed for impairment annually. Other fixed assets are depreciated on a straight line basis at annual rates which vary according to the class of asset, but are typically; leasehold property 3.33% (or at higher rates based on the life of the lease), freehold buildings 3.33%, plant and equipment 10% – 33%.

You saw in the last chapter that depreciation can be somewhat subjective, and that it's possible that the market value of fixed assets could be different from the value in the accounts. However, FRS 11 (*Impairment of fixed assets and goodwill*) ensures that they are never shown *above* their market value. All fixed assets have to have an impairment review when circumstances suggest their values may have fallen. Impairment is measured by comparing an asset's book value to its 'recoverable amount'. The recoverable amount is the higher of its value:

- to the business by keeping and using it within the business;
- on the open market.

Most impairment losses are charged to the profit and loss account as soon as a loss is recognised. The only exception is previously revalued assets, where the loss is smaller than the previous revaluation. (I'll illustrate this in the section below on revaluing assets.) In this case companies have to identify *why* the asset's value has fallen, as this determines where the loss is shown in the accounts. The asset's value could have fallen because there has been a general fall in market prices – then the loss would be shown on the statement of total recognised gains and losses. On the other hand, if the asset's value has fallen because it has been damaged it would be charged to the profit and loss account.

Revaluation of assets

If you think about your own assets for a moment, they don't all depreciate. Property values have increased remarkably in recent years. You know that UK companies must show their investment properties at market value, and revalue these properties annually. However, most companies' properties are not held for investment purposes and, whilst they must disclose any significant differences between book values and market values, they *choose* whether to incorporate any surplus in the accounts. (The Companies Act requires most companies to disclose in the director's report any material difference between the book value and the market value of properties.)

You can always see if the company has chosen to revalue its assets, as it will have a 'revaluation reserve'. I'll show you how this works in the following example.

EXAMPLE 3.2

A company has tangible fixed assets of £100,000 and share capital of £100,000. The share capital has been used to buy the tangible assets, including a property costing £60,000. Property prices have been rising steeply; the company has had the property valued at £80,000 and decides to incorporate this value into its balance sheet. The revised balance sheet will be:

	£
Tangible fixed assets	120,000
Share capital	100,000
Revaluation reserve	20,000
	120,000

The revaluation reserve reflects the £20,000 increase in the property's value

There are three things I'd like to point out:

- Revaluation does not directly affect the profit and loss account, as it is not a realised gain (the principle of prudence means that it can only be shown in the profit and loss account when it is realised). However, it will affect the profit and loss account indirectly if it is depreciated, as the depreciation charge will now be based on £80,000, not the original cost of £60,000. (I'll cover depreciating revalued assets in more detail in Chapter 6.)
- The revaluation reserve is not a distributable reserve, which means it can't be used to pay dividends.
- The company's net worth has increased by £20,000. This will probably improve the company's borrowing powers and affects some of the ratios you'll use to analyse the company's performance. (I'll discuss these in detail in Chapter 11).

If the property subsequently falls in value (as commercial property did in the late 1980s and early 1990s), it should be recognised in the accounts. In my example, the company could absorb a fall of £20,000 on the balance sheet. So if a fall in property prices reduces the property's value to £65,000, the revaluation reserve would fall by £15,000 to £5,000 and the reduction in value, the *impairment*, would be shown in the statement of total recognised gains and losses. But if the value of the property fell to £50,000 a charge of £10,000 would have to be made to the profit and loss account.

Companies choosing to revalue assets must revalue all similar assets, and then keep the valuation up to date. The notes to the balance sheet will include disclosures about the:

- name and qualifications of the valuer, and whether they are internal or external valuers;
- basis of the valuation;
- dates and the amounts of the valuation.

The note on tangible assets

Once again, all the details are in the notes. They disclose their original cost, the accumulated depreciation to the balance sheet date, the assets' book value on the balance sheet date, and the amount of tangible assets held on finance leases. You can see this in the note to Johnson Matthey's group accounts.

12 Fixed assets – tangible assets

12a Group

	Freehold land & buildings £ million	Long & short leasehold £ million	Plant & machinery £ million	Total £ million
Cost				
At beginning of year	140.2	12.7	519.4	672.3
Purchases	13.4	0.9	119.5	133.8
Acquisitions	19.9	–	23.1	43.0
Disposals	(1.1)	–	(25.9)	(27.0)
Disposal of subsidiary	(1.0)	–	(1.6)	(2.6)
Exchange adjustments	(1.3)	(0.1)	(5.6)	(7.0)
At end of year	170.1	13.5	628.9	812.5
Depreciation				
At beginning of year	41.4	5.1	239.0	285.5
Charge for the year	5.2	0.7	42.4	48.3
Disposals	(0.1)	–	(13.1)	(13.2)
Disposal of subsidiary	(0.2)	–	(0.7)	(0.9)
Exchange adjustments	(0.3)	–	(2.0)	(2.3)
At end of year	46.0	5.8	265.6	317.4
Net book value at 31st March 2002	**124.1**	**7.7**	**363.3**	**495.1**
Net book value at 31st March 2001	98.8	7.6	280.4	386.8

The net book value of tangible fixed assets includes £5.8 million (2001 £1.8 million) in respect of assets held under finance leases.

Looking at this note you can see that Johnson Matthey has:

- has had a major capital expenditure programme in 2002, as the 2002 purchases represent 16.5% of the total cost of tangible assets (19% of the plant and machinery);
- owns most of its assets.

Investments

Investments are found in two places on the balance sheet – fixed assets or current assets. Their classification is determined by *why* the company is holding the investment, not the nature of the investment. An investment should be classed as a fixed asset if the company does not intend to, is not able to, or will not be required to sell it in the next year. Otherwise it is classed as a current asset investment.

Like all fixed assets, investments must be shown at cost less any necessary provisions. So if the net realisable value falls below the cost, or valuation, a provision is made to cover the 'diminution in value'.

You'll often find three different types of fixed asset investments:

- investments in subsidiaries;
- investment in associated undertakings, joint ventures, and other participating interests;
- other investments.

Subsidiaries

A subsidiary is an entity that is controlled by another, called the parent or the holding company. The parent consolidates the assets, liabilities, results and cash flows of its subsidiaries in the group accounts. This means that subsidiaries only show as a fixed asset investment in the parent company's balance sheet (usually published alongside the group balance sheet). They don't show as investments in the group's accounts as all their assets and liabilities will have been consolidated onto each line of the balance sheet.

Associated undertakings

Investments in associates are separately disclosed on the balance sheet. FRS 9 (*Associates and joint ventures*) requires that the investment in associated undertakings is valued using the 'equity method'. This is effectively a one-line consolidation. Rather than detailing all of the associate's assets and liabilities, the group determines its share of the associate's net assets (including any unamortised goodwill arising from the acquisition of the associate).

It sounds complicated, so I'll show you how the equity method values an associate. The investment is initially shown at cost. Then the subsequent value of the investment is adjusted for:

- any write-down of goodwill;
- asset write-downs in the associate;
- the investing company's share of the associate's retained profits since acquisition.

The balance sheet then shows the investor's share of the associate's net assets. Any goodwill is disclosed in the accounts, but is not included with the goodwill shown as an intangible asset.

You'll see this in the following example.

EXAMPLE 3.3

An investor buys 30% of another company for £20,000. The other company's total net assets at the date of acquisition were £50,000. The predator has £5,000 goodwill, as its share of the net assets is £15,000 (£20,000 – (£50,000 × 30%)). On the date of acquisition the investment will be shown at the cost of £20,000 and the goodwill of £5,000 will be disclosed in the accounts.

The investor's balance sheets are shown in Table 3.5.

Table 3.5 The investor's balance sheets

	Before the acquisition £000	After the acquisition £000	
Fixed assets:			
Tangible fixed assets	100	100	
Investments – associate		20	
		120	
Current assets:			
Stock	30	30	
Debtors	70	70	
Cash	100	80	*(100 – 20)*
	200	180	
Creditors: amounts falling due within a year:			
Creditors	(110)	(110)	
Net current assets	90	70	
Total assets less current liabilities	190	190	
Creditors: amounts falling due in more than a year:			
Loans	(30)	(30)	
	160	160	
Capital and reserves:			
Share capital	50	50	
Profit and loss account	110	110	
	160	160	

I'll keep it simple by assuming that the goodwill has not been amortised, and is not impaired at the end of the first year. The investor and the other company's profit and loss accounts for the year following the acquisition were as shown in Table 3.6.

Table 3.6 Investor's and other company's profit and loss accounts for the year following the acquisition

	Investor	The other company
	£000	**£000**
Turnover	1,000	300.00
Operating costs	(750)	(270.00)
Operating profit	250	30.00
Interest payable	(50)	(10.00)
Profit before tax	200	20.00
Tax	(60)	(6.67)
Profit after tax	140	13.33
Dividend	(20)	0
Retained profit	120	13.33

You saw, in the last chapter, that the investor has to include its 30% share of the other company's operating profits (£9,000), interest (£3,000), and tax charge (£2,001) into its consolidated profit and loss account (Table 3.7).

Table 3.7 Investor's consolidated profit and loss account

	£000	**£000**
Turnover		1,000
Operating costs		(750)
Operating profit		250
Share of associate's operating profits		9
Interest payable:		
Group	(50)	
Associate	(3)	(53)
Profit on ordinary activities before tax		206
Tax on profit on ordinary activities		(62)
Profit after tax		144
Dividend		(20)
Retained profit for the group and its share of associates		124

The investor's proportion of the other company's retained profit, less any dividends received, will be added to the value of the investment shown on the balance sheet. The value of the investment in the associate shown in the consolidated balance sheet rises to £24,000 – the £20,000 cost plus the associate's retained profit of £4,000 (13.33 × 30%). This ensures that the value of the investment increases to reflect both the cost and the investor's proportion of its associate's post-acquisition retained profit, or loss. The notes will disclose the components of the associate's balance sheet value; the predator's share of the victim's net assets (£15,000 net assets at acquisition + £4,000 post-acquisition profits = £19,000), and goodwill of £5,000.

If the other company had paid a dividend of £10,000, its retained profits would be £3,330 (£13,330 – £10,000 dividends paid). The investor would have received £3,000 cash from the dividend that wouldn't have shown on its profit and loss account, but affects the balance sheet as the cash increases. In this case, the investor would only increase the value of the associate on the balance sheet by £1,000 (£4,000 shown in the profit and loss account, less the £3,000 dividends received – 30% of the retained profits of £3,330). This reflects the investor's share in the other company's net worth. The value of the investment shown on the balance sheet would then be £21,000 – the cost plus the predator's share of the retained profits.

Joint ventures

A joint venture is a long-term investment in a business trading in its own right that is jointly controlled by the reporting company and others under a contractual arrangement. Investments in joint ventures are separately disclosed on the balance sheet using a variant of the equity method called the *gross equity method*. You have seen that the equity method is a one-line consolidation; the gross equity method is a three-line consolidation on the balance sheet showing the gross assets and liabilities underlying the net investment.

If the group's share of the joint venture's net assets was £24,000, comprising £40,000 gross assets and £16,000 gross liabilities, the investment is shown on the consolidated balance sheet as follows:

	£000	£000
Investments		
Investments in joint ventures:		
Share of gross assets	40	
Share of gross liabilities	(16)	24

Significant associates and joint ventures

Additional disclosures have to be made if a significant part of a company's business is conducted through associates or joint ventures. These disclosures are required when the associates or joint ventures exceed 15% of the investing group's:

- gross assets;
- gross liabilities;

- turnover;
- the operating result (based on a three-year average).

If these thresholds are exceeded the investing company gives more information about the gross assets and liabilities, disclosing:

- fixed assets;
- current assets;
- liabilities due within a year;
- liabilities due in more than a year;
- any other information that is necessary to understand the total amounts disclosed, for example the size of the debt and its maturity.

If an individual associate or joint venture exceeds 25% of the thresholds shown above, the same information is disclosed for the individual investment.

Other Investments

These are usually investments where the company owns less than 20%. If the company has investments of 20%, or more, and decides not to account for these as an associate, it must disclose the reason for its decision in the notes to the accounts. Investments in companies listed on a Stock Exchange are usually shown at cost, and the aggregate market value is disclosed if this is different. Unlisted investments should be shown at cost or valuation.

If a company has an investment that is 'significant' under the Companies Act it must disclose additional information. A significant investment is where the company holds 10% or more of the nominal value (this term is explained later in this chapter) of any class of shares, or where the investment represents more than 10% of the company's assets. In most situations companies have to disclose:

- the name of the investment;
- the country of incorporation;
- the size and nature of the investment.

It is possible that the DTI will exempt companies from the disclosure requirements if the directors believe that it will be prejudicial and the company trades overseas.

The note on investments

The notes analyse the total investment figure shown on the balance sheet. This is illustrated by Johnson Matthey's note on the group's investments. (Note 13b discloses the parent's investments.)

13 Fixed assets – investments

13a Group

	Investment in associates £ million	Investment listed on overseas stock exchanges £ million	Unlisted investments £ million	Other loans £ million	Total £ million
At beginning of year	0.7	–	0.2	0.1	1.0
Additions	–	–	–	1.0	1.0
Acquired with subsidiaries	–	1.0	0.3	–	1.3
Transfer on acquisition as subsidiary	–	–	(0.2)	(0.4)	(0.6)
Transferred to creditors	0.2	–	–	–	0.2
Losses retained for the year	(0.2)	–	–	–	(0.2)
At end of year	**0.7**	**1.0**	**0.3**	**0.7**	**2.7**

The market value of investments listed on overseas stock exchanges was £1.4 million (2001 £ nil).

13c Associates

	Issued share capital	Percentage holding of ordinary share capital %	Country of incorporation
Arora-Matthey Limited	INR 9,920,000	40	India
Oximet SrL	€312,000	33	Italy

Matthey Pharmaceutical Alkaloids, L.L.C., operating in the USA, of which the group has a 50% holding, has members' capital of US$395,000.

Universal Pharma Technologies, L.L.C., operating in the USA, of which the group has a 50% holding, has members' capital of US$4,700,000.

The group's cost of investment in associates amounted to £0.4 million (2001 £0.4 million).

Current assets

Current assets are the short-term assets, although not all current assets can be realised in a year.

Stocks

Companies usually show the total stock figure on the balance sheet, disclosing the detail in the notes. The accounting standard (*SSAP 9 Stocks and long-term contracts*) requires the sub-classification of stocks to be 'in a manner which is appropriate to the business and so as to indicate the amounts held in each of the main categories'. The Companies Act is stricter than the standard, requiring stocks to be analysed under the following sub-headings:

- raw materials and consumables;
- work in progress;
- finished goods and goods for resale;
- payments on account (these are payments made for items yet to be received).

Despite the lack of a clear definition of what constitutes stock, companies don't have any difficulty in determining what should be classed as stock. You'll also find other things included in stock, particularly assets, previously classed as fixed assets, that the company now wants to sell (for example, properties and brands).

When looking at stock you should understand:

- Not everything included in stock will be sold. Consumable stores are included in stock, but will be used within the business.
- Not all stock is tangible. For example, work in progress could currently include the cost of work on long-term contracts. (The alignment proposal, FRED 28 (*Inventories* and *Construction and service contracts*), is proposing to simplify long-term contract accounting.)
- A company may hold stocks that are subject to reservation of title clauses. The accounting principle of substance over form means that they will still show on the company's accounts, unless they are part of consignment stock.
- Consignment stock is treated slightly differently. Consignment stock is essentially the same as stock covered by a reservation of title clause. It is held by one party, but legally owned by another. Consignment stock is covered by one of the accounting rules (*FRS 5 Reporting the substance of transactions*). It shows on the accounts of the party who has the risks and rewards of ownership. To help companies decide who has the risks and rewards, the standard identifies four variables:
  - the manufacturer's right of return;
  - the customer's right of return;
  - the stock transfer price and deposits;
  - the customer's right to use the stock.

FRS 5 also covers accounting for sale and repurchase agreements (these are common in property companies and distilleries, where stock may be held for a number of years). Stock is shown on the balance sheet of the party who has all the risks, and benefits, normally associated with ownership.

I've covered how stock is valued in Chapter 2.

The note on stocks

Johnson Matthey's note on the group's stocks analyses stocks into their component parts:

15 Stocks

	Group 2002 £ million	2001 £ million
Raw materials and consumables	**47.7**	49.0
Work in progress – precious metals	**240.1**	120.3
– other	**28.6**	17.7
Finished goods and goods for resale	**97.9**	91.8
Total stocks	**414.3**	278.8

The group also holds customers' materials in the process of refining and fabrication and for other reasons.

Debtors

Debtors represent money that is owed to the business and are usually shown as a total on the balance sheet. They have to be analysed into those falling due within a year and more than a year. If the debtors due in more than a year are material, the analysis will be shown on the balance sheet. Otherwise the analysis is in the notes.

There are different types of debtor; some are identified in the Companies Act whereas others are determined by the accounting standards and the company's business practice. You're likely to find the following debtors in the notes to the accounts:

- **Trade debtors**: this is the money owed for sales that the company has made during the period.
- **Amounts recoverable on contracts**: this is the money owed for work done on long-term contracts. (These will disappear if the proposals in the alignment exposure draft FRED 28 (*Inventories* and *Construction and service contracts*) are adopted. It is proposed to simplify the analysis of long-term contract balances, showing only one heading 'Gross amounts due to/from customers for contract work'.)
- **Amounts owed by group undertakings**: (these are found in the notes to the parent company's balance sheet).
- **Amounts owed by undertakings in which the company has a participating interest**.
- **Other debtors**: these represent amounts owed to the company that are unrelated to the turnover. They may include amounts due from the sale of fixed assets and businesses, tax refunds and pension fund prepayments. (Johnson Matthey at 31 March 2002 had £108.8 million pension prepayment shown as a debtor falling due in more than a year.)
- **Unpaid called-up share capital**.
- **Prepayments and accrued income**: (it is possible to show this as a major heading, but this would be very unusual in the UK).

You may remember from Chapter 2 that the debtors are shown on the balance sheet net of any bad debt provisions. Companies in the UK don't usually disclose these provisions, although banks do (although they show 'advances' rather than debtors) and in some countries companies have to disclose their bad debt provisions.

Factoring

Having cash tied up in debtors can be a major problem in some companies, as profitable businesses can go bust if they can't get the money from their customers. It's a particular problem for small companies whose customers are often large companies seeking extended credit terms. Companies want to release the cash that's tied up in debtors, and factoring is an option used by many smaller companies.

So what is factoring? The company sells its invoices to a factoring company (they're usually part of a bank or an international factoring organisation), which advances them up to 85% of the invoice value. The balance will be paid (less the factor's fees) when the company's customer pays the invoice.

There are different types of factoring agreements and they may be:

- *Disclosed:* the customer deals with the factor, who manages the sales ledger.
- *Undisclosed:* the customer deals with the company, who manages its sales ledger in the normal way (this is also called *invoice discounting*).
- *With recourse:* if the customer does not pay (either in full, or by a certain date) the company repays the factor's advance.
- *Non-recourse:* the factor cannot force the company to repay the advance.
- *With partial recourse:* there are some non-refundable proceeds received by the company.

FRS 5 covers the accounting treatment of these different types of factoring agreements. If the factoring agreement gives any recourse back to the company, it has to disclose in the notes to the accounts:

- that it is factoring;
- the amount of factored debtors at the end of the year;
- the cost of factoring.

The accounting treatment depends on the degree of recourse specified in the agreement:

- *Non-recourse agreements:* neither the debtors nor the advance from the factor will show on the balance sheet. It is 'derecognised'. The cost of factoring is charged to the profit and loss account as an operating cost.
- *Limited recourse agreements:* the debtors are reduced by any non-recourse advances, to show a net debtor position. This is called a 'linked presentation', and is only used where the company selling the invoices can't be forced to re-acquire them in the future. The non-recourse advances could take several forms, including credit insurance, or a credit protection policy. The factoring cost is split between any administration cost and interest charges, each shown on the appropriate lines of the profit and loss account.
- *Full recourse agreements:* the gross debtors are shown on the balance sheet, less any provisions for bad debts. The advances from factors will show on a separate line within the notes to the creditors. This is called 'separate presentation'. The factoring cost is split between any administration costs and interest charges, which show on the appropriate lines of the profit and loss account.

Securitisation

Large companies often use their debtors as security for a loan in a process called securitisation. (You'll often see this term in the notes to large companies' accounts. It just refers to a loan that is backed by the collateral of future income streams arising from one of the business's assets. A range of assets have been used to collatarise loans, including credit card receivables, mortgages, car loans, film royalties and debtors.)

The note on debtors

Johnson Matthey's note on the group's debtors analyses them in detail. You'll see that there aren't any numbers shown for some of the entries, as they're entries that relate to the parent's accounts.

16 Debtors

	Group	
	2002	2001 restated
	£ million	£ million
Debtors: due within year		
Trade debtors	**303.9**	357.5
Amounts owed by subsidiary undertakings	**–**	–
Amounts owed by associates	**0.4**	–
Other debtors	**17.7**	39.1
Payment owed for disposals (note 30)	**1.0**	1.0
Current corporation tax	**–**	–
Deferred tax asset (note 23)	**0.6**	0.5
Prepaid pensions	**1.9**	–
Prepayments and accrued income	**19.7**	18.1
	345.2	416.2
Debtors: due after more than one year		
Prepaid pensions	**108.8**	103.9
Amounts owed by subsidiary undertakings	**–**	–
	108.8	103.9

Investments

Investments are shown at the lower of cost and net realisable value. The notes to the accounts will categorise the investments, with listed investments shown separately. You'll often find investment in 'own shares' shown as a current asset investment, and these are shares held by a separate trust for employee share options. UK accounting rules require these to be shown in the balance sheet if the sponsoring company has effective control of the trust, and has the risks and rewards of ownership.

Johnson Matthey's note for the group discloses:

17 Short term investments

	Group	
	2002	2001
	£ million	£ million
Interest in own shares	**14.9**	13.5
Investments listed on overseas stock exchanges	**1.7**	2.4
	16.6	15.9

The interest in own shares represents the cost of the shares held by the group's two Employee Share Ownership Trusts (ESOTs). The ESOTs currently hold 2,634,029 shares which were purchased in the open market, and are held in trust for employees participating in the group's executive share option schemes and long term incentive plan. The purchase of the shares was financed by a contribution of £511,100 and loans of £14,369,817 from the group. At 31st March 2002 the market value of the shares was £24,939,935. Mourant & Co., as trustees for the ESOTs, has waived its dividend entitlement.

The market value of investments listed on overseas stock exchanges was £4.8 million (2001 £25.2 million).

Cash

You'll often find that companies have large amounts of cash on their balance sheet. This doesn't necessarily mean that it's lying idle in a current account earning a notional interest. Cash also includes deposits repayable on demand, and in accounts that have up to seven days' notice, with banks, building societies and similar financial institutions. (The balance sheet uses a different definition of cash from the one used in the cash flow statement.)

Creditors: amounts falling due within a year

There are a number of these short-term creditors:

- bank loans and overdrafts;
- payments on account;
- trade creditors;
- bills of exchange payable;
- amounts owed to group undertakings (only on the parent company's balance sheet);
- amounts owed to undertakings in which the company has a participating interest;
- other creditors;
- corporation tax;
- other taxation and social security;
- accrued expenses and deferred income (it is possible to show this as a major heading, but this would be very unusual in a UK company);
- proposed dividend. (Most proposed dividends will no longer be shown once the proposals in the alignment exposure draft FRED 27 (*Events after the balance sheet date*)

are accepted. Only those dividends that are a liability at the balance sheet date would be recognised in the financial statements. Dividends declared after the balance sheet date would be disclosed in the notes to the accounts.)

Most of these are fairly self-explanatory, but you probably haven't come across *deferred income* before. Deferred income is money that has either been received by the company, or is due to it, but has yet to be earned. Any advance payments for sales, or government grants, would be included in deferred income. As it hasn't been earned, it can't be included in the profit and loss account. You might find it in both creditors due in a year and creditors in more than a year. For example, if a company is paid £5,000 for a five-year service agreement it brings it into the profit and loss account over the life of the agreement – £1,000 per year. Any remaining balance that has not been credited to the profit and loss account would show on the balance sheet as deferred income, split between that deferred for a year and more than a year.

Whilst the first classification is 'bank loans and overdrafts', if you look at the notes in a listed company's accounts you'll find a large variety of different types of debt detailed in the creditors. Company treasurers have become increasingly sophisticated and raise funds from the cheapest source matching their needs. They are innovative in their use of short-term debt instruments, often tailoring them to attract a specific investor.

Companies' short-term borrowings fall into two broad categories:

- overdrafts and short-term loans from banks and other financial institutions;
- issues of promissory notes (IOUs) and bills of exchange that can be held by anyone and are bought and sold.

I think you're probably familiar with bank overdrafts but may be less familiar with the second category of short-term debt. Some of the ones you'll often find are:

- bills of exchange;
- notes;
- commercial paper.

I'd now like to tell you what these are.

Bills of exchange

I wonder if you've ever written a post-dated cheque? Companies' post-dated cheques are called *bills of exchange*. Unfortunately, it's not quite as simple as that. Bills of exchange are different from post-dated cheques in two respects as they:

- are written by the supplier, and signed by the customer in an acknowledgement of the debt;
- can be sold. Bills of exchange are what lawyers call *negotiable instruments* – this just means that you can sell them!

Bills of exchange normally have a maturity of three months. If the supplier wants the cash today, rather than in three months' time, he sells the bill. These bills are bought by discount houses. (Discount houses are specialist banks that borrow short-term money from commercial banks, and use the cash to buy various forms of short-term IOUs like bills of exchange.) If the buyer of the bill has to wait three months for his money, he won't pay £100 today for a bill that gives him £100 in three months' time. He'll be losing three months' interest. Bills of exchange are *discounted*; effectively the interest is paid in advance, with the discount reflecting the three months' interest that has been lost by the purchaser. This type of bill is called a *trade bill*; there is another kind called a *bank acceptance*.

An acceptance is similar to a post-dated cheque, but now has the equivalent of a cheque card number on the back. A bank guarantees payment, and then the acceptance can be sold. Once a bank puts its name on the bill it's guaranteeing payment, even if the company defaults. An acceptance sells at the lowest interest rates because the payment of the bill is certain.

Bills of exchange have been around for centuries, and have always been normal trade practice in import and export businesses. However, treasurers often use acceptances as part of their short-term financing programmes, and a marked increase in acceptances could indicate a cash shortage.

Notes

Notes are unsecured IOUs. They are negotiable instruments and can have a maturity of up to 10 years, although most have a much shorter maturity and may even be repayable at the option of the holders.

Commercial paper

Commercial paper has been widely used overseas since its creation in America in the nineteenth century. The commercial paper market started in 1986 in the UK, and commercial paper is another form of short-term unsecured borrowing in the form of a negotiable instrument. It is only available to high quality borrowers and in some markets (for example, the USA) companies must have their commercial paper credit rated. Large companies use commercial paper as an alternative to bank overdrafts, as they are very cheap to establish, and are often cheaper than bank overdrafts. Whilst commercial paper maturities can be as long as five years, most issues tend to be very short dated (it is not unusual for commercial paper to have a three-week maturity). It is issued at a discount to the face value, and is often 'rolled over' – with one tranche being repaid by the issue of another.

Creditors falling due in more than a year

This covers all the money owed by the business that has to be repaid in more than a year. This includes:

- bank loans;
- finance leases;
- convertible debt;
- payments on account;
- trade creditors;

- amounts owed to group undertakings (this is only found on the parent company's balance sheet);
- amounts owed to undertakings in which the company has a participating interest;
- other creditors;
- accrued expenses and deferred income.

Most of the long-term creditors will be borrowings of one sort or another, and you'll find a lot of information about the loans in the notes to the accounts. They're shown as a total and then analysed in detail. The analysis includes details of each specific material loan, its repayment date, currency, and even the rate of interest, if it is fixed. The notes also tell you how much of the borrowing is secured and unsecured, and you'll find a loan repayment schedule identifying how much has to be repaid:

- in one to two years;
- in two to five years;
- after five years.

Companies' long-term loans fall into two broad categories, similar to their short-term debt:

- loans from banks and other financial institutions;
- issues of debentures and other forms of loan stock which are offered to investors, and therefore can be held by the general public. They are bought and sold in the same way as shares.

I'd now like to tell you about:

- the type of security offered for loans;
- traditional long-term bank loans;
- debentures and bonds;
- Eurobonds.

Security for loans

Loans can be secured in one of two ways:

- **A fixed charge**: when you have a mortgage the lender has a fixed charge on your house. This gives them a legal right to your house if you don't pay your mortgage, and you can't sell your house without the lender's permission. Fixed charges on a company's assets work in exactly the same way. The lender has the legal right to specified assets and the company can't dispose of them without the lender's permission. Fixed charges tend to be given on long-term fixed assets like land, properties and ships. If the company falls into arrears or defaults on the agreement the lender can either:
  - repossess and sell the assets, giving any surplus to the company (this is also called *foreclosure*); or
  - appoint a receiver to receive any income from the asset (for example, property rents).
- **A floating charge**: this is a general charge on the company's assets. Floating charges are usually taken on short-term fixed assets (like plant and machinery and vehicles) and

current assets. Whilst the lender has the legal right to a group of assets, the company continues to manage those assets in the normal course of business. (After all, the company has to be able to sell its stock – otherwise it couldn't trade!)

Some loans may be secured, but rank after all the other borrowings in the event of a liquidation. These are called *subordinated loans*. It is also common for a lending bank to require a company to seek the bank's permission before giving security to anyone else – this is called a *negative pledge*.

Long-term bank loans

A traditional long-term loan is rather like an endowment mortgage, but without the endowment policy. All the company has to do on a day-to-day basis is pay interest; the loan is repaid either in full at the end of the term, or in stages. It is also possible to take the loan in stages; if the company doesn't want all the money at once, it can draw it down in specified tranches. The loan could be either with one bank, or syndicated amongst a number of banks.

In some industries (like shipping) companies repay some of the capital as well as interest. Most of the loan is repaid in a final payment at the end of the loan.

Debentures and bonds

There is no real difference between a debenture and a bond; both are formally recognised in a written instrument, sold to the general public and may be secured or unsecured.

A debenture is a negotiable instrument that is usually, but not always, secured and is covered by either a debenture deed or a trust deed:

- A debenture deed places a fixed or floating charge on the company's assets.
- A trust deed contains all the details of the debenture and may include clauses (called *covenants*) that restrict the company's operations in some way. (If these are important they are disclosed in the notes to the accounts.)

Bonds are also negotiable instruments offered to the general public that may, or may not, be secured on the company's assets. They are covered by a trust deed. A bondholder is entitled to receive a stream of interest payments, and the repayment of the principal at maturity.

Before a company has a bond issue it will have the debt credit rated. There are two types of rating agencies looking at companies:

- agencies that look at the company from a supplier's point of view (like Dun and Bradstreet) and help to answer the question 'Will I get paid if I supply goods to this company?';
- agencies that look at the company from the investor's point of view (like Standard and Poor, Moody) to help to answer the question 'Will I lose all my money if I invest in this company?'.

The latter rate corporate debt and the best quality corporate debt is rated triple A. The rating is very important as it affects both the ability to sell the bonds (as ratings affect who can buy the bonds) and the rate of interest that the company will have to pay to be able to sell the bond. The higher the rating, the lower the risk; the lower the risk, the lower the interest! Bond interest is called the 'coupon' and is expressed as a percentage of the face value of the bond. The face value of the bond is unlikely to be the same as the current bond price. Bond prices are influenced by two factors:

- Relative interest rates: if current interest rates are 6% and the bond is paying 10% investors will pay a premium to buy the bond.
- The current credit rating of the company: if the credit rating has fallen, the interest may not reflect the current level of risk so the bond price falls.

Bonds are a flexible form of finance and you'll find many different types of bonds in company accounts. Banks and companies have been very innovative, custom-designing bonds to attract specific investors. They are an ideal vehicle for financial innovation, as there are four variables that can be modified:

- **The security given for the bond**: for example, banks issue bonds that have our mortgages and credit card balances as collateral. Companies may securitise their debtors.
- **The coupon paid**: for example, some bonds are issued that don't pay interest, and are called *Zeroes*. They are issued at a discount. For example, a £10 million five-year bond may be issued for £6.209 million. This has an implied interest rate of 10% and the value of the bond would increase by 10% a year. All other things being equal, at the end of the first year the bond would be worth £6.83 million, at the end of the second £7.513 million, and so on until the end of the fifth year when the investors would receive the £10 million.

  Some bonds increase the interest over the life of the bond (*step-up bonds*), whereas others reduce it (*step-down bonds*).
- **The repayment of the principal amount borrowed**: for example, the repayment of the principal in some bond issues is index linked. In others, the bond may be issued in one currency and repaid in another (*dual currency bonds*).
- **The bond maturity**: for example, a bond can have two maturity options – it might have a maturity of 30 years, with an option to reduce this to 10 years (*a retractable bond*), or a maturity of 10 years with an option to extend it to 30 years (*an extendible bond*).

Eurobonds

Large companies often issue Eurobonds. The first thing you need to know is what the term 'Euro' means, because it's very confusing as we now spend the euro in parts of Europe. In this context, a currency goes 'Euro' when it is traded outside of the country of origin and its banking regulations. Japanese yen on deposit in London are Euroyen, American dollars deposited in Tokyo are Eurodollars. Euro does not mean European, and isn't always the name of a currency.

A Eurobond is simply a bond issued outside the country of its currency that has few restrictions on its issue and trading. Companies never keep a register of Eurobond holders (whereas they may for a domestic or foreign bond). The bond is sold in 'bearer' form (this means that whoever holds the bond claims the interest and repayment of the principal). As Eurobond interest is paid gross, they are very attractive to investors who wish to keep their affairs secret from the tax authorities!

Eurobonds are available to large, internationally known, high quality borrowers.

The note on creditors

Johnson Matthey shows the details of its creditors falling due within a year and more than a year in two notes to the accounts: borrowings and finance leases, and other creditors. The group's notes on loans and other creditors discloses:

18 Borrowings and finance leases

	Group	
	2002	2001
	£ million	£ million
Borrowings and finance leases falling due after more than one year		
Bank and other loans repayable by instalments		
From two to five years	**0.8**	0.4
From one to two years	**0.1**	0.1
Bank and other loans repayable otherwise than by instalments		
6.36% US Dollar Bonds 2006	**70.2**	70.3
Other after five years	**6.0**	6.0
Other from two to five years	**104.6**	–
Finance leases repayable		
After five years	**3.2**	–
From two to five years	**0.7**	0.5
From one to two years	**0.2**	0.4
Borrowings and finance leases falling due after more than one year	**185.8**	77.7
Borrowings and finance leases falling due within one year		
Bank and other loans	**64.5**	19.4
Finance leases	**1.3**	0.4
Borrowings and finance leases falling due within one year	**65.8**	19.8
Total borrowings and finance leases	**251.6**	97.5
Less cash and deposits	**92.6**	237.4
Net borrowings/(cash) and finance leases	**159.0**	(139.9)

The loans are denominated in various currencies and bear interest at commercial rates.

21 Other creditors

	Group	
	2002	2001
	£ million	£ million
Amounts falling due within one year		
Trade creditors	**167.5**	145.3
Amounts owed to subsidiary undertakings	**–**	–
Current corporation tax	**32.9**	51.2
Other taxes and social security costs	**8.1**	7.1
Other creditors	**39.7**	40.2
Accruals and deferred income	**74.0**	88.1
Dividends	**37.0**	35.9
Total other creditors falling due within one year	**359.2**	367.8

Amounts falling due after more than one year		
Amounts owed to subsidiary undertakings	–	–
Other creditors	**0.4**	1.0
Total other creditors falling due after more than one year	**0.4**	1.0

Provisions for liabilities and charges

When I discussed provisions in Chapter 2, I pointed out that some provisions reduced the value of assets (like bad debt provisions), whereas others related to likely costs that the business would incur in the future (like restructuring costs). The provisions for likely future costs are shown under this heading and include:

- deferred tax provisions;
- unfunded pension obligations (in some countries it is normal to provide for pensions in this way);
- rationalisation provisions;
- litigation settlement provisions.

These may be simply shown as 'deferred tax' and 'other provisions'; the degree of detail is determined by the need for a true and fair view.

The note on provisions

Johnson Matthey details the provisions in the notes and discloses:

22 Provisions for liabilities and charges

22a Group

	Rationalisation provisions £ million	Retirement benefits (note 10c) £ million	Other provisions 3 million	Deferred taxation (note 23) £ million	Total £ million
At beginning of year (restated)	–	25.5	4.0	49.7	79.2
Charge for year	25.3	3.4	1.2	13.3	43.2
Acquisitions	–	0.1	–	3.5	3.6
Utilised	(16.4)	(12.2)	(1.4)	–	(30.0)
Credit to recognised gains and losses	–	–	–	(0.2)	(0.2)
Transferred between provisions	–	(1.4)	1.4	–	–
Transferred to prepayments	–	2.6	–	–	2.6
Exchange adjustments	–	(0.1)	–	(0.2)	(0.3)
At end of year	**8.9**	**17.9**	**5.2**	**66.1**	**98.1**

The rationalisation provisions relate to Colours & Coatings and Meconic plc (note 2) and are expected to be fully spent in 2002/03.

Capital and reserves

This represents the owners' stake in the business, and shows the business's share capital and its reserves. Reserves can come from a variety of sources:

- The premium paid, above the nominal value, for the shares issued by the company – this is called the *share premium account*.
- The cumulative retained profit, less any losses, since the business started – this reserve is called the *profit and loss account* and is the only distributable reserve.
- The revaluation of the businesses' assets – this is called the *revaluation reserve*.
- The reserve arising from the cancellation, or redemption, of shares – this reserve is called the *capital redemption reserve*. This is now very common, as companies rationalise their capital structure through share buy-backs.
- If a company merges with another company, the accounting treatment is different to an acquisition. There is no goodwill and the companies are treated as though they have always been combined. This often means that the merged company will have a *merger reserve*.

You might also find other reserves on the balance sheet, especially in other countries where statutory reserves are common. These are undistributable reserves made for the protection of creditors. They are established by transferring a percentage of the dividends, or profit, each year to the reserve until it equals a predetermined percentage of the share capital.

I'll now take you through the main components of the capital and reserves.

Share capital

I'll tell you about:

- authorised and issued share capital;
- share issues;
- the different types of shares found in company accounts.

Authorised and issued share capital

You'll find two share capital numbers in the notes to the accounts: the *authorised* share capital and the *issued* share capital. The authorised share capital is the amount that the company can issue at the moment. If the directors of the company want to issue more shares they have to seek approval from their shareholders. This normally just requires the passing of a resolution by a majority of the shareholders.

The issued share capital on the balance sheet is the total number of shares currently in issue at their original value (this is called the *nominal* or the *par* value). All UK shares must have a par value that is determined when the company is started. Shares have to be issued for at least this amount, as they can't be issued at a discount to their par value. (This is not always true overseas – for example, in some American states you'll find shares with no par value and shares can be issued for any price.) The notes to the accounts usually describe the issued shares as *allotted* (the company has decided who is going to hold the shares), *called up* (they have asked for the money) and *fully paid* (they've received it).

Share issues

Two things affect a company's ability to issue more shares:

- Their authorised share capital.
- The Companies Act: this limits the amount of shares that can be placed with new investors, forcing companies to have major new issues in the form of a *rights issue*. (Private companies can amend their articles to avoid this.)

  In a rights issue, a company offers its existing shareholders the opportunity to buy new shares, in proportion to their existing holding, at a discounted price. The shareholders then have three alternatives:
  - They can exercise their right to buy the share.
  - They can sell their rights to buy the share (in practice, this option is only available to large shareholders in listed companies; the smaller shareholders' profit will be wiped out by dealing fees).
  - They can do nothing. Usually, if shareholders do nothing, a listed company sells the shares on their behalf and sends them the proceeds.

Most share issues are *underwritten*. Underwriting is a form of insurance, provided by banks and financial institutions, where the underwriters agree to buy the shares if no one else wants them. This ensures that the company receives some cash from the rights issue.

Not all share issues raise cash. Companies can have *scrip*, *bonus* or *capitalisation* issues – they all mean the same thing! In these issues the company converts some of its reserves into share capital. The share price falls after the issue, as the company's market value hasn't changed and it is now spread over an increased number of shares. Companies usually do this when they believe their share price is too high.

Another way of reducing the share price, without capitalising reserves, is to have a share split. This reduces the nominal value of each share in issue. Barclays had a share split in 2002; its shares had a nominal value of £1.00, and each share was split into four 25p shares.

Both bonus issues and share splits reduce share prices. In a bonus issue shareholders receive additional shares. In a share split shareholders receive new shares in place of the old share.

Classes of share

You'll find different types of shares found in company accounts, including:

- deferred shares;
- ordinary shares;
- preference shares;
- associated depository receipts.

Companies may also issue warrants to allow people to subscribe for shares at some future date.

Deferred shares

These are often the founders' shares and are rarely seen now in company accounts. They either:

- do not receive a dividend until some future date, usually several years after issue; or
- only receive a dividend after ordinary shareholders' dividends have reached a predetermined level.

The shipping company P&O has deferred shares rather than ordinary shares. This dates from the time it became a limited company following the granting of a royal charter in 1840.

Ordinary shares

These are the commonest form of shares, but they're not necessarily all the same. Companies can have more than one type of ordinary shares with differences in:

- voting rights;
- entitlement to dividend;
- ranking if the company is liquidated.

Preference shares

Preference shares have a fixed dividend that must be paid *before* other dividends can be paid. There are a number of different types of preference share, and they can include one, or more, of the features outlined below:

- **Cumulative**: if a company doesn't pay a dividend to a cumulative preference shareholder this year, the dividend is carried over into the following year and accumulates. This means that it's only postponing the payment. The preference dividend is referred to as 'in arrears' (which must be noted in the accounts) and no other dividend can be paid until all the preference dividend arrears have been paid.
- **Redeemable**: these shares are redeemed (repaid) at a fixed date. This makes them fundamentally the same as debt, but with the dividend being paid out of after-tax profits. They are common in two situations; management buyouts and bank rescues (the bank undertakes a debt equity conversion, turning loans into redeemable preference shares).
- **Participating**: shareholders may receive two dividends: a fixed dividend and a variable dividend (usually a proportion of the ordinary dividend).
- **Convertible**: preference shareholders have the right to convert into ordinary shares at a predetermined rate, at some future date.

Preference shares are shown in UK accounts as 'non-equity' shares. FRS 4 (*Capital instruments*) categorises shares as either *equity* or *non-equity shares*. Non-equity shares are those that have any of the following characteristics:

- **Fixed dividend**: the dividend payment isn't dependent on the company's financial performance, or the dividends paid to other shareholders.

- **Limited rights in a liquidation**: there are limited rights to share in any 'winding-up surplus' if the company is liquidated.
- **Redeemable**: they have to be repaid at some future date.

If a share has none of these characteristics it would be regarded as an equity share. Most ordinary shares are equity shares and most preference shares are non-equity shares.

Companies are required to disclose the following information about their non-equity shares:

- the dividends, and the dividend rights;
- the redemption date, and the amount to be paid on redemption;
- their priority, and the amounts receivable, on a winding up of the company;
- their voting rights.

The proposals in the alignment proposal, FRED 30 (*Financial instruments: disclosure and presentation* and *Recognition and measurement*), will change the accounting treatment for many preference shares in listed companies. It proposes that shares should be classified on the basis of their substance. If a preference share pays a fixed dividend and is redeemable it is effectively the same as debt. Consequently, it will be classified as debt. This also means that the preference dividend would be included in interest.

American depository receipts

You may find reference in some accounts to American Depository Receipts (ADRs), and although they aren't another type of share I'm discussing them here. An ADR is a mechanism used in the USA to simplify the procedures for holding shares in foreign companies. The shares are bought, on behalf of the American investor, and deposited in a bank outside the USA. An American bank then issues ADR certificates to the American shareholder. The custodian bank then processes the payment of dividends, rights issues etc. ADRs may be traded on American Stock Exchanges if the company is registered with the Securities Exchange Commission and complies with their requirements (they are then called *sponsored ADRs*).

The note on share capital

You can see that Johnson Matthey has purchased some of its own shares in 2002, and there was a small increase in the share capital as executive share options were exercised. Its note on share capital discloses:

24 Called up share capital

	Authorised		Allotted, called up and fully paid	
	Number	£ million	Number	£ million
Ordinary shares of £1 each				
At beginning of year	291,550,000	291.6	222,511,587	222.5
Purchase of own shares	–	–	(4,931,000)	(4.9)
Executive share option schemes – options exercised	–	–	1,115,076	1.1
At end of year	291,550,000	291.6	218,695,663	218.7

At 30th May 2002 there were 4,919,025 options outstanding under the company's executive share option schemes, exercisable at various times up to the year 2011 at prices from 410.39 pence per share to 1083.00 pence per share.

At 30th May 2002 three allocations had been made under the company's long term incentive plan which had yet to mature. The 1999 allocation of 412,356 shares, the 2000 allocation of 317,600 shares and the 2001 allocation of 385,551 shares will mature at the end of their respective three year performance periods in July 2002, July 2003 and July 2004. Should the performance conditions be satisfied, the number of shares allocated, or a proportion thereof, will be released to the participants.

The company has no non-equity share capital.

Reserves

You'll find that there are a number of reserves in company accounts. They can be classified into those that are *distributable* (this means that they can be used to pay dividends), and those that are *undistributable*. The only distributable reserve is the *profit and loss account*.

You'll usually find the following reserves on a balance sheet.

The profit and loss account

This is the accumulated profits and losses made since the company started, adjusted by two factors: goodwill written off before 23 December 1998, and some currency adjustments. (I discussed these in the last chapter.) In some countries this called a *revenue* reserve.

The revaluation reserve

This represents the accumulated revaluations of fixed assets. When previously revalued assets are sold, and the revaluation is realised, the revaluation is transferred from the revaluation reserve to the profit and loss account.

Whilst the revaluation reserve is not a distributable reserve, it can be used for a bonus issue.

The share premium account

Shares are usually issued at a premium to their nominal value, and this premium is shown in the share premium account. The only exception to this rule is when shares are issued for an acquisition. (The company may then qualify for statutory share premium relief under Section 131 of the Companies Act. This allows companies, meeting certain criteria, to write off any goodwill arising on consolidation through the share premium account, via a merger reserve.)

Once a share premium has been created it is legally treated as part of the company's share capital, and is not a distributable reserve. It may, however, be used for:

- writing off any expenses, commissions, or discounts relating to share or debenture issues;
- writing off the company's preliminary expenses;
- providing for any premium repayable on the redemption of debentures;
- a bonus issue.

The capital redemption reserve

Shares can generally only be bought out of distributable profits, or from the proceeds of a new share issue. A company creates a capital redemption reserve if it buys back, or redeems, its shares. These shares are then cancelled, and the issued share capital reduced accordingly. The authorised share capital is unaffected by the buy-back.

The accounting for share buy-backs and redemptions is as follows:

- **Share capital**: this is reduced by the nominal value of the shares purchased, or redeemed, and the amount is then transferred to a *capital redemption reserve*. This is a non-distributable reserve of the company, which is separately disclosed on the balance sheet. (The principle underlying the Companies Act's requirements is that the total of the share capital and the undistributable reserves should remain unchanged following the repayment of share capital. This is achieved by transferring the nominal value of the shares bought, or redeemed, from issued share capital to the capital redemption reserve.)
- **Profit and loss account**: when shares are purchased from distributable profits, rather than a share issue, this reserve is reduced by the total cost of the purchase. If the shares are purchased through another share issue, the profit and loss account is only reduced if the buy-back cost more than the cash the company received when the shares were issued. The profit and loss account is then reduced by the difference between the cash received when the shares were issued and the cash paid to buy the shares.

You'll see this when you look at Johnson Matthey's note on reserves below.

The merger reserve

You'll only find this when companies have merged and it reflects any:

- differences between the nominal value of the shares that have been issued and the nominal value of the shares received;
- existing balances on the new 'subsidiary's' share premium account and capital redemption reserve.

The note on reserves

Johnson Matthey's note on reserves discloses:

25 Reserves

25a Group

	Share premium account £ million	Capital redemption reserve £ million	Associates' reserves £ million	Profit & loss account £ million
At beginning of year (restated)	123.2	–	–	461.0
Exchange adjustments	–	–	–	(7.5)
Purchase of own shares	–	4.9	–	(45.9)
Premium on shares issued	5.0	–	–	–
Rollover of share options on acquisitions	–	–	–	0.7
Retained profit/(loss) for the year	–	–	(0.2)	53.8
At end of year	**128.2**	**4.9**	**(0.2)**	**462.1**

At 31st March 2002, the cumulative amount of goodwill, net of goodwill relating to disposals, charged against profit and loss account was £46.0 million (2001 £46.0 million).

In the group accounts, £1.6 million of net exchange gains (2001 £14.7 million losses) on foreign currency borrowings have been offset in reserves against exchange losses (2001 gains) on the translation of the related net investment in overseas subsidiaries.

Debt equity hybrids

There are an increasing number of instruments that are neither debt nor equity, but have the features of both. I'll discuss three that are commonly found in company accounts.

Convertible bonds

Holders of convertible bonds have the option of having a cash repayment, or converting the bond into a fixed number of ordinary shares. Convertibles have two advantages for the issuing company:

- The interest rate is lower as the conversion option has a value.
- The company may not have to repay the loan, just issue additional shares (they will need shareholder permission to do this in the UK).

These bonds show as part of the company's debt, as FRS 4 (*Capital instruments*) doesn't allow companies to anticipate the debt conversion.

The proposals in the alignment proposal FRED 30 (*Financial instruments: disclosure and presentation* and *Recognition and measurement*) will complicate the accounting for convertible bonds. You'll remember that FRED 30 classifies financial instruments by their substance. A convertible bond has two elements:

- a financial liability to repay the bondholder;
- a conversion option for a fixed number of shares.

The bond will have to be split between these two elements. The financial liability will be shown as debt, with its value being the present value of the bond discounted by the interest rate of a similar bond without the benefit of a conversion option. The conversion option will be shown as part of the equity, with its value being the difference between the financial liability and the proceeds from the bond issue.

Redeemable preference shares

Redeemable preference shares are a form of equity that is repaid at a fixed date, normally at their nominal value. They usually pay a fixed dividend, often linked to interest rates. FRS 4 requires that these should be disclosed in the shareholders' funds as 'non-equity shares'. FRED 30 will classify them as debt.

Mezzanine finance

The financial press often refers to something called 'mezzanine finance'. It is another example of a debt equity hybrid that tends to be used in young companies or management buyouts and buy-ins. Companies in these situations often find it difficult to raise finance.

Mezzanine finance is a subordinated loan (ranking behind the other loans) that has a higher rate of interest than the other debt (to reflect the increased risk) and is convertible into shares via:

- an option to convert all, or part, of the loan into equity;
- a warrant to subscribe for equity (a warrant gives the holder the right to subscribe at some future date for shares at a fixed price).

Mezzanine finance is treated in the accounts in the same way as convertible bonds.

Balance sheet formats

You can take a picture from different perspectives. The European Union allows two presentations for the balance sheet's 'snapshot'. Whilst the presentations may be different, the content of the balance sheet is the same – only the perspective has changed. You may find that the degree of detail and the basis for valuations varies in other countries, but the information on the balance sheet remains broadly the same.

Most UK companies prepare the balance sheet from the shareholders' point of view, but this is a British perspective. Most other countries total their assets and liabilities, looking at the business from the point of view of everyone who has put money into the business, whether directly or indirectly.

I've used the same numbers for these different balance sheet presentations (Tables 3.8 and 3.9). They're called Format One and Format Two in the Companies Act.

Table 3.8 Format 1 presentation of the balance sheet

	£000
Fixed assets	
Intangible assets	50
Tangible assets	200
Investments	75
	325
Current assets	
Stocks	80
Debtors	270
Investments	40
Cash	10
	400
Creditors: Amounts falling due within one year	(300)
Net current assets	100
Total assets less current liabilities	425
Creditors: Amounts falling due after more than one year	(100)
Provisions for liabilities and charges	(15)
Minority interests[1]	(25)
	285
Capital and reserves	
Share capital	50
Profit and loss account	175
Revaluation reserve	40
Share premium account	20
	285

[1] Minority interests can be shown on either side of the balance sheet. I have shown them as a negative on the 'net assets' side. The alternative would be to report net assets of £310,000 that would balance with the capital and reserves of £285,000 plus the minority interests of £25,000, giving £310,000.

Now I'd like you to compare this with the assets and liabilities presentation in Table 3.9.

I've presented assets and liabilities in the order you'd find them in the UK, but not all countries start with their long-term assets. An American balance sheet would reverse the order, starting with cash and then going through the current assets. I've also presented it vertically, whereas many countries use a horizontal presentation with assets on one side and liabilities on the other (Table 3.10).

Table 3.9 Format 2 presentation of the balance sheet

	£000
Fixed assets	
Intangible assets	50
Tangible assets	200
Investments	75
	325
Current assets	
Stocks	80
Debtors	270
Investments	40
Cash	10
	400
	725
Capital and reserves	
Share capital	50
Profit and loss account	175
Revaluation reserve	40
Share premium account	20
	285
Minority interests[1]	25
Provisions for liabilities and charges	15
Creditors	400
	725

[1] A Format 2 balance sheet shows creditors as a single item. Each component of the creditors will be analysed in the notes between those falling due within a year and in more than a year. The totals should also be given.

Table 3.10 Horizontal presentations

	£000		£000
Fixed assets		**Capital and reserves**	
Intangible assets	50	Share capital	50
Tangible assets	200	Profit and loss account	175
Investments	75	Revaluation reserve	40
	325	Share premium account	20
Current assets			285
Stocks	80	**Minority interests**	25
Debtors	270	Provisions for liabilities and charges	15
Investments	40	Creditors	400
Cash	10		725
	400		
	725		

Summary

I've covered a lot of technical material, and I'd now like to summarise the key points that you need to remember.

The balance sheet is a snapshot of the company on a certain day, and like most snapshots it can be presented from different perspectives. Globally, the most popular presentation groups assets and liabilities, whereas UK balance sheets usually look at the business from the shareholders' point of view.

You'll usually find two balance sheets in group accounts: one for the parent (sometimes called the *company*), and one for the group (sometimes referred to as the *consolidated* balance sheet). You are interested in the group balance sheet, as this relates to the profit and loss account and cash flow statement found in the accounts.

The parent's balance sheet is included in the group balance sheet, with its investment in the group companies cancelled out by the group companies' share capital.

I've summarised the important points about each balance sheet item in Table 3.11.

Table 3.11 Balance sheet summary

Fixed assets	These are assets that the business intends to use on a continuing basis.
Intangible assets	These can include brand names, patents and goodwill (see below). They must be able to be sold separately, and have a market value that can be easily determined. Intangible assets are *amortised*.
Goodwill	This represents the difference between the cost of acquiring a company and the fair value of its assets. (The acquiring company will probably change the value of the assets. It modifies them to reflect the market values at the date of the acquisition and aligns the accounting policies to those of the group.) Only *purchased goodwill*, in other words that arising from an acquisition, can be shown on the balance sheet.
Tangible assets	These are usually depreciated, ensuring that the cost of acquiring the asset is charged to the profit and loss account over its life. (The only exceptions are investment properties, which are shown at their market value, and where the depreciation charge is immaterial.) A permanent drop in the asset's value, a *permanent diminution*, should be charged to the profit and loss account immediately. Companies have the option of revaluing assets to reflect current market values. If they choose to do this, the valuation must be professional and has to be kept up to date. If the company has revalued its assets, a revaluation reserve will be shown in the capital and reserves.

Investments	The investments shown as fixed assets are long-term investments. Investments in associates and joint ventures are shown separately on the balance sheet. Associates are valued using the *equity method*, showing the investor's share of the associate's net assets in a single line on the balance sheet. Joint ventures are valued using the *gross equity method,* where the company's share of the joint venture's gross liabilities is deducted from its gross assets to arrive at the balance sheet value.
Current assets	In the UK not all current assets are short term, as they are simply those assets not satisfying the fixed asset definition. Debtors due in more than a year are included as current assets. These are often pension fund prepayments.
Stocks	Stocks must be shown at the lower of cost and market value. All companies not classed as small private companies will analyse stock into its component parts in the notes to the accounts.
Debtors	Not all debtors represent a future cash inflow to the business, as prepayments are included in debtors. The notes to the group balance sheet will disclose trade debtors (the amount owed by customers), other debtors, unpaid called-up share capital, prepayments and accrued income.
Investments	This represents short-term deposits, loans to other organisations like banks and building societies, marketable shares and other securities.
Cash	This includes short-term deposits with a notice period of seven days or less. This represents a different definition of cash to that used in the cash flow statement (24 hours).
Creditors: amounts falling due within a year	The notes to the accounts will analyse these into bank loans and over drafts, payments received on account, trade creditors, other creditors, and accruals and deferred income. The company's borrowings can be a mixture of loans from banks and investors. Loans from investors are usually *negotiable instruments* (can be bought and sold). All loans may be either secured on the company's assets, or unsecured.
Creditors: amounts falling due in more than a year	These are longer-term versions of the short-term creditors, and are analysed in the same way.
Convertible debt	This debt has the option to be converted into shares at a predetermined rate. The terms are disclosed in the accounting notes.
Provisions for liabilities and charges	This represents unspent provisions, which have been charged to the profit and loss account, for future costs relating to the past period's sales. This will include an accrual for tax called deferred tax.

Called up share capital	These are the shares in issue at the end of the financial year, shown at their *nominal,* or *par,* value. Any unpaid share capital is shown as debtors.
Non-equity shares	Most preference shares are classed as non-equity shares. A non-equity share is one that has any of the following characteristics: ■ entitled to a fixed dividend; ■ limited rights in a liquidation; ■ is redeemable.
Share premium account	This represents the amount above the par value received by the company for its shares. For example, the par value of a share is £1 and the company receives £5. The share capital would increase by £1, and the share premium account by £4.
Profit and loss account	This represents the accumulated profits and losses reinvested in the business since it started. It may be adjusted by: ■ the write-off of goodwill arising from acquisitions made before 31 December 1998; ■ exchange adjustments arising from the consolidation of overseas assets and liabilities.
Revaluation reserve	This arises from the revaluation of fixed assets.
Capital redemption reserve	This is created following a share 'buy-back'.

Johnson Matthey's balance sheets

Now it's time to look at a 'real' balance sheet, and Johnson Matthey's consolidated and parent company balance sheets are on the next page. You'll see that they follow the Format 1 presentation you saw earlier but:

- The 2001 balance sheet has been restated, following the implementation of FRS 19 (*Deferred tax*), which required companies to make a full provision for deferred taxation.
- Johnson Matthey has another short-term creditor – precious metal leases, which are a way of financing their precious metals stocks. Note 20 to their accounts explains them:

> Precious metal leases are rental and consignment stock arrangements under which banks provide the group with precious metals for a specified period and for which the group pays a fee. The group holds sufficient precious metal stocks to meet all the obligations under these lease arrangements as they come due.

Now you've covered all of the notes, you can see the totals shown in the balance sheet. Remember that when you're analysing a business's performance you're only interested in the consolidated accounts.

Consolidated and Parent Company Balance Sheets

as at 31st March 2002

		Group		Parent company	
		2002	2001 restated	**2002**	2001 restated
	Notes	**£ million**	£ million	**£ million**	£ million
Fixed assets					
Goodwill	11	**182.6**	8.6	**0.2**	0.2
Tangible fixed assets	12	**495.1**	386.8	**155.3**	137.1
Investments	13	**2.7**	1.0	**390.0**	210.0
		680.4	396.4	**545.5**	347.3
Current assets					
Stocks	15	**414.3**	278.8	**246.7**	117.3
Debtors: due within one year	16	**345.2**	416.2	**646.9**	736.8
Debtors: due after more than one year	16	**108.8**	103.9	**264.5**	246.5
Short term investments	17	**16.6**	15.9	**13.9**	12.2
Cash at bank and in hand	18	**92.6**	237.4	**3.6**	159.1
		977.5	1,052.2	**1,175.6**	1,271.9
Creditors: Amounts falling due within one year					
Borrowings and finance leases	18	**(65.8)**	(19.8)	**(45.4)**	–
Precious metal leases	20	**(131.0)**	(91.8)	**(139.2)**	(111.0)
Other creditors	21	**(359.2)**	(367.8)	**(754.4)**	(747.8)
Net current assets		**421.5**	572.8	**236.6**	413.1
Total assets less current liabilities		**1,101.9**	969.2	**782.1**	760.4
Creditors: Amounts falling due after more than one year					
Borrowings and finance leases	18	**(185.8)**	(77.7)	**(178.7)**	(70.3)
Other creditors	21	**(0.4)**	(1.0)	**(0.2)**	(24.5)
Provisions for liabilities and charges	22	**(98.1)**	(79.2)	**(50.3)**	(40.1)
Net assets		**817.6**	811.3	**552.9**	625.5
Capital and reserves					
Called up share capital	24	**218.7**	222.5	**218.7**	222.5
Share premium account	28	**128.2**	123.2	**128.2**	123.2
Capital redemption reserve	28	**4.9**	–	**4.9**	–
Associates' reserves	25	**(0.2)**	–	**–**	–
Profit and loss account	25	**462.1**	461.0	**201.1**	279.8
Shareholders' funds		**813.7**	806.7	**552.9**	625.5
Equity minority interests		**3.9**	4.6	**–**	–
		817.6	811.3	**552.9**	625.5

The accounts were approved by the Board of Directors on 30th May 2002 and signed on its behalf by:

C R N Clark **Directors**

J N Sheldrick

4

The cash flow statement

- **What is in a cash flow statement?**
- **The cash flow statement in detail** – operating activities; dividends received from associated undertakings and joint ventures; returns on investment and servicing of finance; taxation; capital expenditure and financial investment; acquisitions and disposals; equity dividends paid; management of liquid resources; financing; cash
- **The cash flow statement**
- **Johnson Matthey's cash flow statement**

The success and survival of every organisation depends on its ability to generate and acquire cash. We all understand the importance of cash flow. Companies survive when they have cash, and fail when they don't. This means that you have to understand a company's cash flow and you will be interested in a company's ability to generate cash for itself, and acquire it from other sources. You can clearly see this in the cash flow statement.

There isn't a legal requirement for companies to prepare a cash flow statement. However, the accounting standard FRS 1 (*Cash flow statements*) requires all companies, other than those shown below, to prepare a cash flow statement. Most companies have to prepare cash flow statements, and only the following companies are exempt:

- small private companies (I gave you the definition of a small private company in Chapter 1);
- subsidiary companies where more than 90% of the voting rights are controlled within the group, providing that the group's consolidated accounts are publicly available;
- mutual life assurance companies owned by their policyholders;
- pension schemes;
- open-ended investment funds meeting certain conditions.

The cash flow statement identifies the cash movement within the business during the period. It shows where the cash came from and where the cash was spent. It is purely concerned with the movement of cash, so the accounting adjustments found in the other financial statements don't affect the cash flow statement. The cash the business has received is shown as a cash *inflow* and that paid as a cash *outflow*. I think it's the most important financial statement, as cash is the one thing that cannot be created – the company either has cash or it hasn't! By looking at the movement of cash, you get a much clearer idea of the company's financial stability and viability.

What is in a cash flow statement?

The cash flow statement summarises the company's cash flows during the year. It classifies the cash flows into nine headings showing the cash flows from:

- **Trading:** these cash flows are shown under the heading '*Operating activities*'.
- **Dividends from joint ventures and associates.**
- **Interest, dividends received and any dividends paid to 'non-equity' shares and minority interests:** these are shown under the heading '*Returns on investment and servicing of finance*'.
- **Tax:** these are shown under the heading '*Taxation*'.
- **Buying and selling fixed assets:** these are shown under the heading of '*Capital expenditure and financial investment*'. (This heading can be shortened to capital expenditure, if the company hasn't bought or sold any fixed asset investments during the period. It then reflects the actual cash flow.)

- **Buying and selling businesses and trades**: these are shown under the heading '*Acquisitions and disposals*'.
- **Dividends paid to ordinary shareholders**: these are shown as '*Equity dividends paid*'.
- **Short-term investments shown as current asset investments**: these investments are used to manage a company's net debt, or net funds, position rather than for their investment potential. Any deposits maturing in more than 24 hours will be included under the heading '*Management of liquid resources*'.
- **Shares and loans**: these are shown under the heading '*Financing*'.

The first seven headings must be in the order above, and companies can take subtotals at any point.

The cash flow statement then finishes with the increase, or decrease, in cash. The definition of cash includes short-term deposits and other investments with less than 24 hours' maturity minus any borrowings repayable on demand.

You'll also find reconciliations to:

- net debt – linking the cash flow statement to the balance sheet;
- operating profit – linking the cash flow statement to the profit and loss account.

These reconciliations may either follow the cash flow statement or be shown in the notes.

The cash flow statement in detail

I'll now look at the items shown in the cash flow statement in more detail, and illustrate it with a simple cash flow statement. First, I'll show you the cash flows you will find under each heading, and then the cash flow statement as it appears in the accounts.

All the cash flows exclude any recoverable VAT, and similar sales taxes. Foreign currencies are translated at the same rate used in the profit and loss account, unless the actual rate is used. The actual rate can be used for cash flows within the group to ensure that these cancel out in the consolidated cash flow statement.

Operating activities

The cash flow statement starts by looking at the cash flows from operating activities. I've mentioned that all companies have to reconcile their operating profit to the cash flow from operating activities. Companies can also choose to add information that shows the operating cash flow presented in a slightly different way. I'm going to start with this option first, as I think that you'll find it easier to understand. It shows the period's cash receipts and payments for operating items (Table 4.1).

Table 4.1 Cash flow from operating activities

	£000
Cash received from customers	910
Cash paid to suppliers	(530)
Cash paid to, and on behalf of, employees	(200)
Other cash paid	(100)
Net cash inflow from operating activities	80

Whilst this approach is straightforward and easier to follow, very few companies use it. So I'll now show you the reconciliation of operating profit to operating cash flow (Table 4.2). Everyone has to prepare this, although it shouldn't be shown as part of the cash flow statement.

It starts with the operating profit and then adds back any paper charges (primarily depreciation) that have been made in arriving at the profit, to show the cash that *will* be generated from this period's trading. This is then adjusted for any changes in the working capital, to arrive at the cash generated from operations during the year.

Table 4.2 Reconciliation of operating profit to operating cash flow

	£000
Operating profit	80
Depreciation	40
Less Increase in stocks	(20)
Less Increase in debtors	(90)
Plus Increase in creditors	70
Net cash inflow from operating activities	80

The £120,000 operating profit plus depreciation is the cash the business *will* receive from the period's trading. But they've only received £80,000 as an additional £40,000 had to be invested in working capital

The first approach tells you *what* the operating cash flow is; the second tells you *why* it's £80,000.

Dividends received from associated undertakings and joint ventures

This isn't necessarily just dividends as described by the heading. Joint ventures and associates, particularly if they're based overseas in countries with remittance restrictions, are frequently financed by loan capital rather than equity. In this situation, interest received would be regarded as part of the investor's return and would be shown under this heading.

Returns on investment and servicing of finance

These are the cash flows from dividends and interest, excluding any dividends paid to ordinary shareholders and dividends received from associated undertakings, as these are shown under separate headings. You'll see this in Example 4.1.

EXAMPLE 4.1

During the past year a company has had the following cash flows. Only those marked ✓ will show as part of returns on investment and servicing of finance:

	£000	
Interest received	30	✓
Interest paid	70	✓
Interest element of finance lease rentals	10	✓
Dividends received from associate	10	✗
Dividends paid:		
to ordinary shareholders	30	✗
to preference shareholders	5	✓
to minority interests	5	✓

The entries for returns on investment and servicing of finance would be as shown in Table 4.3.

Table 4.3 Returns on investment and servicing of finance

	£000
Interest received	30
Interest paid	(70)
Dividends paid to minority interests in subsidiary undertakings	(5)
Dividends paid to non-equity shareholders	(5)
Interest element of finance lease rentals	(10)
Net cash outflow from returns on investment and servicing of finance	(60)

Taxation

This is the net cash payment for tax. So if the company in my example paid £15,000 to the tax authorities during the period, and received a cheque for £5,000 for a previous overpayment, the cash flow from taxation would be an outflow of £10,000.

Capital expenditure and financial investment

You'll only find this heading in the UK. In other countries' cash flow statements there's a heading called *investing activities*, combining capital expenditure and financial investment with acquisitions and disposals.

Capital expenditure and financial investment covers the cash flows from most of the company's fixed assets. However, the fixed asset investments exclude investments in a business that is a joint venture, associate, or subsidiary, as these are shown as acquisitions and disposals.

If the company in my example has the following cash flows during the year, those marked ✓ would appear as part of capital expenditure and financial investment, whereas those marked ✗ would be included in acquisitions and disposals:

	£000	
Purchase of new machinery	90	✓
Purchase of motor vehicles	40	✓
Purchase of fixed asset investments		
(other than associates and joint ventures)	20	✓
Investment in an associated undertaking	10	✗
Proceeds from sale of machinery	20	✓
Proceeds from sale of motor vehicles	5	✓
Purchase of subsidiary undertaking	200	✗

The cash flow statement would then show the cash flows for capital expenditure and financial investments given in Table 4.4.

Table 4.4 Capital expenditure and financial investment

	£000
Purchase of tangible fixed assets	(130)
Disposal of tangible fixed assets	25
Purchase of fixed asset investments	(20)
Net cash outflow from capital expenditure and financial investment	(125)

Acquisitions and disposals

This shows the other cash flows from my example.

	£000
Purchase of subsidiary undertaking	(200)
Investment in an associated undertaking	(10)
Net cash outflow from acquisitions and disposals	(210)

Equity dividends paid

These would be the £30,000 dividends paid to ordinary shareholders. The other dividends paid have been included in returns on investment and servicing of finance.

Management of liquid resources

Most companies don't keep their cash in a petty cash tin. They invest it, and have become increasingly sophisticated in the vehicles used as part of their treasury activities. Large companies don't just invest surplus cash in deposit accounts; they invest wherever they feel they will get the best return. Consequently, they invest in gilts, money markets, and even shares. They don't intend to hold these investments on a long-term basis; they are just short-term 'liquid' investments that are shown as part of current assets.

If these investments:

- are able to be sold without harming the business;
- can be easily converted into cash either at the amount shown in the accounts, or very close to it;
- are traded in an active market;

they are included in management of liquid resources.

I'll assume that the company in my example has sold £50,000 government gilts.

Financing

These are either receipts from, or repayments to, the external providers of finance. The receipts could arise from share issues and additional long-term borrowings. The payments could include purchases of own shares, the redemption of bonds, and loan repayments.

In my example the company had the financing cash flows shown in Table 4.5.

Table 4.5 Financing

	£000
Proceeds from share issue	250
Increase in short-term borrowings	50
Long-term loan repayment	(20)
Capital element of finance lease rental payments	(40)
Net cash inflow from financing	240

Cash

This covers cash, any deposits that are repayable on demand, together with bank overdrafts and other loans that are repayable on demand. (Deposits are regarded as being repayable on demand if they are repayable without notice and penalty, or the agreed notice period is 24 hours or less.)

The company in my example had opening cash balances of £100,000 and closing cash balances of £45,000. This means that the cash flow statement would show a decrease in cash of £55,000.

The cash flow statement

The cash flow statement follows the order I've used in my example, although companies can combine the management of liquid resources with financing as long as the cash flows relating to each are shown separately. (This is allowed to reflect the commercial reality in large companies that manage their treasury operations in an integrated way.)

There is also some flexibility in the *reporting* of the cash flows. Whilst the detailed cash flows must be shown in the accounts, companies may decide to report net cash flows on the statement itself; disclosing the detailed cash flows in the notes.

As I've worked through the detailed cash flows, I'll show you how the cash flow statement would look if it used the net cash flows on the statement (Table 4.6).

Table 4.6 Cash flow statement

	£000
Cash flow from operating activities	80
Dividends received from joint ventures and associates	10
Returns on investment and servicing of finance	(60)
Taxation	(10)
Capital expenditure and financial investment	(125)
Acquisitions and disposals	(210)
Equity dividends paid	(30)
Net cash flow before management of liquid resources and financing	**(345)**
Management of liquid resources	50
Financing:	
Proceeds of share issue	250
Reduction in debt	(10)
Net cash flow from financing	240
Decrease in cash for the period	**(55)**

The cash flow statement is then followed by a note, reconciling the change in the cash to the movement in the net debt. In my example the note might look like the one shown in Table 4.7.

Table 4.7 Reconciliation of net cash flow to movement in net debt

	£000
Decrease in cash for the period	**(55)**
Cash used to repay debt and finance leases	10
Cash inflow from decrease in liquid resources	(50)
Change in net debt resulting from cash flows	(95)
Loans acquired with subsidiary	(25)
New finance leases	(20)
Translation difference	(15)
Movement in net debt in the period	(155)
Net debt at 1/1/200x	(500)
Net debt at 1/1/200y	(655)

These have increased the net debt, but they haven't shown on the cash flow statement, as they aren't a cash inflow.

This cash flow statement shows a business whose operating cash flows just cover the interest paid on loans and finance leases. It is not generating sufficient cash from the current year's trading to meet its interest, tax and dividend payments, and has had to dip into its existing cash balances. The capital expenditure, acquisitions, and investment in associates had to be partly funded from the share issue and the sale of the gilts, with the balance coming from the company's cash.

The note reconciling the cash movement to that in net debt shows how the net debt of the company has increased significantly during the year. However, not all of the increase in net debt gave rise to cash flows; some was acquired with subsidiaries, some arose from finance leases, and exchange rate movements adversely affected the reported debt. The increase in net debt would cause concern as:

- the operational cash flow only just covered the interest on the debt this year;
- the reduction in the cash balances and the redemption of the gilts will reduce any interest received.

Johnson Matthey's cash flow statement

Johnson Matthey shows its gross cash flows, and the detailed cash flows are shown in the notes to the accounts. The cash flow statement is on the next page and the detailed cash flows are shown in the following pages.

If you look at Johnson Matthey's cash flow statement you'll notice the following:

- Reconciliation of operating profit to operating cash flow: you can see that the cash flow from operating profit and depreciation has grown slightly between the two years – £223.6 million in 2002, compared with £215.2 million in 2001. The bulk of the increase in the operating cash flow has come from the change in working capital. In 2001 it increased by £58 million, reducing the cash flow from operating activities, whereas in 2002 it decreased by £1.9 million, and this turnaround in the working capital requirements was the main reason for the increased operating cash flow.
- It has significantly increased cash flows in 2002 for:
  - taxation;
  - capital expenditure and financial investment – this ties in with the increase in tangible assets shown on the balance sheet;
  - acquisitions and disposals – this isn't surprising, as you've already learnt about its acquisition of Meconic, which was only one of its acquisitions.
- There were also smaller movements in interest (the company moved from a net interest-receiving position to a net interest-paying one) and dividends (where the cash payment increased by more than 12%).
- Consequently, its cash outflow before management of liquid resources and financing increased to £165.3 million.
- Whilst there were small inflows from financing and management of liquid resources, the majority of the funding came from the group's cash resources.

Consolidated Cash Flow Statement

Annual Report and Accounts 2002

for the year ended 31st March 2002

	Notes	2002 £ million	2001 £ million
Reconciliation of operating profit to net cash inflow from operating activities			
Operating profit		**168.5**	174.1
Depreciation and amortisation charges		**55.1**	41.1
Profit on disposal of tangible fixed assets and investments		**(1.4)**	(0.7)
(Increase)/decrease in owned stocks		**(83.6)**	15.0
Decrease/(increase) in debtors		**73.9**	(82.0)
Increase in creditors and provisions		**11.6**	9.0
Net cash inflow from operating activities		**224.1**	156.5

Cash Flow Statement

	Notes	2002 £ million	2001 £ million
Net cash inflow from operating activities		**224.1**	156.5
Dividends received from associates		**0.1**	0.1
Returns on investments and servicing of finance	27	**(4.9)**	5.8
Taxation		**(55.8)**	(38.2)
Capital expenditure and financial investment	27	**(131.0)**	(94.7)
Acquisitions and disposals			
Acquisitions	27	**(143.5)**	(6.2)
Disposals	27	**(2.2)**	0.6
Net cash outflow for acquisitions and disposals		**(145.7)**	(5.6)
Equity dividends paid		**(52.1)**	(46.5)
Net cash outflow before use of liquid resources and financing		**(165.3)**	(22.6)
Management of liquid resources	27	**0.2**	157.8
Financing			
Issue and purchase of share capital	27	**(44.1)**	7.9
Increase/(decrease) in borrowings and finance leases	27	**57.5**	(12.1)
Net cash inflow/(outflow) from financing		**13.4**	(4.2)
(Decrease)/increase in cash in the period		**(151.7)**	131.0

Reconciliation of net cash flow to movement in net debt

	Notes	2002 £ million	2001 £ million
(Decrease)/increase in cash in the period		**(151.7)**	131.0
Cash (inflow)/outflow from movement in borrowings and finance leases	28	**(57.5)**	12.1
Cash inflow from term deposits included in liquid resources		**(0.2)**	(157.8)
Change in net funds/debt resulting from cash flows		**(209.4)**	(14.7)
Borrowings acquired with subsidiaries		**(46.8)**	(1.3)
Loan notes issued to acquire subsidiaries		**(40.6)**	–
New finance leases		**(4.3)**	–
Translation difference	28	**2.2**	(9.9)
Movement in net funds/debt in year		**(298.9)**	(25.9)
Net funds at beginning of year	28	**139.9**	165.8
Net (debt)/funds at end of year	28	**(159.0)**	139.9

27 Gross cash flows

27a Returns on investments and servicing of finance

	2002	2001
	£ million	£ million
Interest received	**11.0**	18.0
Interest paid	**(15.9)**	(12.0)
Dividends paid to minority shareholders	**–**	(0.2)
Net cash flow for returns on investments and servicing of finance	**(4.9)**	5.8

27b Capital expenditure and financial investment

	2002		2001	
	£ million	**£ million**	£ million	£ million
Purchase of tangible fixed assets		**(134.1)**		(98.8)
Purchase of long term investments		**(1.0)**		(0.1)
		(135.1)		(98.9)
Sale of tangible fixed assets	**0.6**		0.9	
Sale of short term investments	**3.5**		3.3	
		4.1		4.2
Net cash outflow for capital expenditure and financial investment		**(131.0)**		(94.7)

27c Cash flows on acquisitions and disposals

	2002		2001	
	£ million	**£ million**	£ million	£ million
Investment in subsidiary undertakings (note 29)		**(142.5)**		(3.4)
Cash and overdrafts acquired with subsidiary undertakings (note 29)		**(1.0)**		0.3
Purchase of businesses		**–**		(3.1)
		(143.5)		(6.2)
Disposal of French print business (note 30)	**(1.0)**		–	
Cash disposed of with French print business (note 30)	**(1.1)**		–	
Closure of Metawave Video Systems Ltd (note 2)	**(0.1)**		–	
Disposal of Electronic Materials	**–**		2.5	
Disposal of Organic Pigments	**–**		(1.9)	
		(2.2)		0.6
Net cash flow for acquisitions and disposals		**(145.7)**		**(5.6)**

27d Management of liquid resources

	2002 £ million	2001 £ million
Cash paid into term deposits of less than one year	**(0.2)**	(13.9)
Cash withdrawn from term deposits of less than one year	**0.4**	171.7
Net cash flow from management of liquid resources	**0.2**	157.8

27e Financing

	2002 £ million	2002 £ million	2001 £ million	2001 £ million
Issue of ordinary share capital		**6.1**		7.9
Purchase of own shares		**(50.2)**		–
		(44.1)		7.9
Decrease in borrowings falling due within one year	**(45.7)**		(10.5)	
Increase/(decrease) in borrowings falling due after more than one year	**103.4**		(1.2)	
Capital element of finance lease rental payments	**(0.2)**		(0.4)	
		57.5		(12.1)
Net cash flow from financing		**13.4**		(4.2)

28 Analysis of net debt

	Cash at bank and in hand £ million	Borrowings due within one year – overdrafts £ million	Borrowings due within one year – other £ million	Borrowings due after more than one year £ million	Finance Leases £ million	Total £ million
At beginning of year	237.4	(1.5)	(17.9)	(76.8)	(1.3)	139.9
Cash flow						
From cash and overdrafts	(142.5)	(9.2)	–	–	–	(151.7)
From borrowings and finance leases	–	–	45.7	(103.4)	0.2	(57.5)
From term deposits	(0.2)	–	–	–	–	(0.2)
Net cash flow	(142.7)	(9.2)	45.7	(103.4)	0.2	(209.4)
Acquired with subsidiaries	–	–	(46.6)	(0.2)	–	(46.8)
Loan notes issued to acquire subsidiaries	–	–	(38.9)	(1.7)	–	(40.6)
Other non cash changes	–	–	(0.1)	0.1	(4.3)	(4.3)
Effect of foreign exchange rate changes	(2.1)	0.7	3.3	0.3	–	2.2
At end of year	**92.6**	**(10.0)**	**(54.5)**	**(181.7)**	**(5.4)**	**(159.0)**

5

The statement of total recognised gains and losses

- **What's in a statement of total recognised gains and losses?** – reconciliation of movements in shareholders' funds
- **Johnson Matthey's statement of total recognised gains and losses**

This is a relatively new primary statement (primary means it can't be relegated to the notes) and was introduced in June 1993, as part of FRS 3 *(Reporting financial performance)*. The statement of total recognised gains and losses (often abbreviated to the STRGL) shows all the movements in the shareholders' funds that the owners haven't either contributed to (like a share issue) or benefited from (like dividends or a buy-back). You now know that only recognised gains are shown on the profit and loss account. Other gains, like asset revaluations, are shown on the balance sheet until they are realised. So some transactions are shown immediately in the profit and loss account, whereas others are shown in reserves. This statement brings all these gains, or losses, together – showing any gain that the company has recognised during the year. As such, it bridges the profit and loss account and the balance sheet, taking information from both statements.

The information found in the statement has always been in the accounts, as it is also disclosed in the note on the reserves – but I wonder how many people read it? This statement enables you to see at a glance all of the gains and losses recognised during the year, showing you:

- *the profit for the financial year;*
- *any adjustments to asset valuations;*
- *any differences in the net investments in overseas businesses arising from changes in exchange rates;*
- *any prior year adjustments* (these could arise from changes in accounting policies or fundamental errors);
- *any tax associated with items shown on the STRGL.* (This has only been shown on the STRGL since March 2000, following the implementation of FRS 16 (*Current tax*).

What's in a statement of total recognised gains and losses?

Basically, all the gains, and losses, the company has recognised in the period. It won't show all the increases and decreases in the shareholders' funds, as some of them (like changes in the share capital) are neither gains, nor losses, to the company. Consequently, companies have to show a reconciliation to the movements in the shareholders' funds to complete the picture.

I'll show you how this works in Example 5.1.

EXAMPLE 5.1

During the year a company has:

- changed its accounting policies following the introduction of a new accounting standard (conforming to this new standard reduces the profits it previously reported by £20 million);
- revalued properties upward by £10 million;
- sold some fixed assets for £5 million (these had been revalued from the cost of £3 million to £4 million; consequently, it reported a profit on sale of fixed assets of £1 million);
- written £2 million off an investment, reflecting a fall in the market value after a valuation (the value of the investment is still above the original cost);
- issued shares with a nominal value of £5 million for £7 million;
- written off through reserves an £11 million exchange loss on overseas net investments.

You'll see these transactions reflected in the profit and loss account (Table 5.1) and balance sheets (table 5.2), where I've shaded the relevant entries.

Table 5.1 Profit and loss account

	This year £ million
Turnover	**1,000**
Cost of sales	**(650)**
Gross profit	**350**
Administration expenses	**(100)**
Distribution costs	**(150)**
Operating profit	**100**
Profit on sale of fixed assets	**1**
Net interest payable	**(11)**
Profit before tax	**90**
Tax	**(30)**
Profit for the financial year	**60**
Dividends	**(20)**
Retained profits	**40**

Table 5.2 Balance sheets

	This year £ million	Last year £ million
Fixed assets		
Tangible assets	**520**	500
Investments	**8**	10
	528	510
Current assets		
Stock	**200**	150
Debtors	**300**	200
Cash	**36**	100
	536	450
Creditors: Amounts falling due within a year		
Creditors	**(350)**	(300)
Net current assets	**186**	150
Total assets less current liabilities	**714**	660
Creditors: Amounts falling due in more than a year		
Loans	**(200)**	(200)
Provisions for liabilities and charges	**(70)**	(60)
	444	400
Capital and reserves		
Share capital	**55**	50
Share premium account	**52**	50
Profit and loss account	**280**	250
Revaluation reserve	**57**	50
	444	400

Note on Reserves extracted from the notes to the balance sheet:

	Share premium account £ million	Revaluation reserve £ million	Profit and loss account £ million	Total £ million
At beginning of year as previously stated	50	50	270	370
Prior year adjustment			(20)	(20)
At beginning of year as restated	50	50	250	350
Premium on issue of shares	2			2
Transfer from profit and loss account of the year			40	40
Transfer of realised profits		(1)	1	0
Decrease in value of investment		(2)		(2)
Currency translation differences on foreign currency net investments			(11)	(11)
Surplus on property revaluations		10		10
At the end of the year	**52**	**57**	**280**	**389**

I can now construct a statement of total recognised gains and losses.

The statement follows a standard format. It starts with the profit for the financial year, then you'll find asset revaluations, and finally currency adjustments. Some companies show a subtotal before currency adjustments, showing the recognised gains and losses before changes in exchange rates.

The statement using my example, showing a subtotal before currency adjustments, is shown in Table 5.3. The statement clearly shows the relative importance of profit, revaluations, and currency adjustments to the company. It also highlights the fact that the company has adjusted its previously reported profits.

Table 5.3 Statement of total recognised gains and losses

	£ million
Profit for the financial year	60
Unrealised surplus on revaluation of properties	10
Unrealised loss on investment	(2)
	68
Currency translation differences on foreign currency net investments	(11)
Total recognised gains and losses for the year	57
Prior year adjustment	(20)
Total gains and losses recognised since last annual report	37

Now I'd like to look at each item on the statement in more detail:

- Profit for the financial year. This is always the profit before dividend payments, not the retained profits that are transferred to the reserves.
- The revaluations are not netted off, and surpluses and deficits have to be separately disclosed. This means that the recognised gains are different to those you'll see by looking at the movement on the revaluation reserve. It has increased by seven million on the balance sheet, not the net eight million that has been recognised on the STRGL. This is because one million was transferred from the revaluation reserve to the profit and loss account on the sale of assets, as the gain is now realised.
- Currency translation differences are clearly shown in the body of the accounts. Whilst they have always been disclosed in the note to the reserves, historically an average reader of accounts would have been unaware how exposed the company's net worth was to exchange rate movements.
- Prior year adjustments. Companies have to restate all the comparative figures if they make a prior year adjustment. The total *cumulative* adjustment has to be shown in the STRGL, not just the amount relating to the previous year. This enables you to see the effect that the adjustment has on the business's net worth in the year that it's made. (Prior year adjustments are important, as they could have arisen from a fundamental error. You could miss this if you had to read through all the notes to find it. Now as soon as you see 'prior year adjustment' you can look to find out what it is.)

The profit and loss account and the statement of total recognised gains and losses are important measures of the company's financial performance during the year. However, it is important that you understand why this may not reflect the changes in the shareholders' funds – the business's net worth. This is shown in the 'reconciliation of movements in shareholders' funds', which may be found either in the notes, or following the statement of total recognised gains and losses.

Reconciliation of movements in shareholders' funds

There are two ways that the recognised gains can be reconciled to the movement in the shareholders' funds. The first starts with the total recognised gains in the period (Table 5.4).

Table 5.4 First reconciliation option

	£ million
Total recognised gains	57
Dividends	(20)
New share capital subscribed	7
Net addition to shareholders' funds	44
Opening shareholders' funds (originally £420 million, before deducting prior year adjustment of £20 million)	400
Closing shareholders' funds	444

The other alternative starts with the profit for the financial year, rather than the recognised gains and losses (Table 5.5). This is the presentation illustrated in the accounting standard, but is less 'user friendly' than the first, as it is more difficult to identify the total recognised gains. To do this you have to add the profit for the financial year of £60 million to the other recognised gains and losses of –£3 million. This gives the £57 million gains recognised during the year.

Table 5.5 Second reconciliation option

	£ million
Profit for the financial year	60
Dividends	(20)
Other recognised gains and losses relating to the year (net)	(3)
New share capital subscribed	7
Net addition to shareholders' funds	44
Opening shareholders' funds (originally £420 million, before deducting prior year adjustment of £20 million)	400
Closing shareholders' funds	444

Johnson Matthey's statement of total recognised gains and losses

You'll see Johnson Matthey's STRGL below. It clearly shows that profit is the most important element of its recognised gains in both years. You'll also see that it has exchange differences on foreign currency net investments and loans and a related tax credit (or charge).

Total Recognised Gains and Losses

for the year ended 31st March 2002

	2002 £ million	2001 restated £ million
Profit attributable to shareholders	106.8	125.7
Currency translation differences on foreign currency net investments and related loans	(8.0)	9.5
Taxation on translation differences on foreign currency loans	0.5	(9.7)
Total recognised gains and losses relating to the year	99.3	125.5
Prior year adjustment	(44.3)	
Total recognised gains and losses recognised since last annual report	55.0	

Movement in Shareholders' Funds

for the year ended 31st March 2002

	2002 £ million	2001 restated £ million
Profit attributable to shareholders	106.8	125.7
Dividends	(53.2)	(51.3)
Retained profit for the year	53.6	74.4
Other recognised gains and losses relating to the year	(7.5)	(0.2)
New share capital subscribed	6.1	7.9
Rollover of share options on acquisitions	0.7	–
Purchase of own shares	(45.9)	–
Net movement in shareholders' funds	7.0	82.1
Opening shareholders' funds (originally £851.0 million before prior year adjustment of £44.3 million)	806.7	724.6
Closing shareholders' funds	813.7	806.7

6

The note of historical cost profits and losses

- What does a note of historical cost profits and losses look like?
- Johnson Matthey's note of historical cost profits and losses

Now I'd like to give you a little test. You and I buy identical plots of land for £100,000, but I decide to revalue my land to £120,000 at the end of the first year. The following year, we both sell our land for £150,000. *What is our reported profit on the deal?* We both have £50,000 more cash in our pockets than we started with, but our reported profit will be very different. You'll report £50,000, whereas I'll only show £30,000 profit, as I revalued my land and the profit is the difference between the book value and the cash received. You'll appear more profitable than me, but really our profitability is the same. The note on historical cost profits and losses resolves this problem, as it brings my profit into line with yours – £50,000.

You know that, in the UK, revaluation is optional. You also know that revaluation can affect profit in two ways:

- Firstly, it affects the profit, or loss, on disposal of the asset.
- Secondly, it could increase the depreciation charge if the revalued asset is depreciable.

The note on historical cost profits and losses was introduced to improve the comparability of reported profits. It tells you what the profit would have been had there been no asset revaluations, eliminating the distortions arising from different revaluation policies. It is only concerned with revaluation, and ignores the effect of different depreciation policies. It shows you what the profit before tax and the retained profit would have been if the company hadn't revalued.

What does a note of historical cost profits and losses look like?

You'll see how this works if you read through Example 6.1, which is based on a depreciated asset to show you how the additional depreciation charge affects the balance sheet, and how it is shown in the note.

EXAMPLE 6.1

Two companies, A and B, each buy a fixed asset for £1,000 at the start of the first year, and sell them for £750 on the last day of the third year. I'll keep it really simple by making cash their only other asset. Both companies have identical profits throughout the three years of £4,000 before depreciation. They both depreciate the asset on a straight line basis over five years (20% a year). Company B revalues its asset to £1,200 at the start of the second year, whereas Company B doesn't. The asset's life remains five years.

You know that the revaluation affects both the profit and loss account and the balance sheet.

First, I'll look at Company A's profit and loss account for the three years (Table 6.1). Its profit after depreciation will be £3,800 each year (£4,000 less £200 depreciation). Its depreciation charge is £200 a year, so by the end of the third year its fixed asset has a book value of £400 (£1,000 – (3 × £200)). When it's sold for £750, the company reports a profit on sale of fixed assets of £350. When you look at its balance sheet in Table 6.2, you'll see that the asset's value reduces by £200 each year and cash increases by the profit before depreciation, plus the cash received from the asset's sale in the third year. (Remember depreciation is only a paper charge, not a real annual cash cost.)

Table 6.1 Company A – profit and loss accounts

	Year 1 £	Year 2 £	Year 3 £
Turnover	10,000	10,000	10,000
Profit before depreciation	4,000	4,000	4,000
Depreciation	(200)	(200)	(200)
Operating profit	3,800	3,800	3,800
Profit on sale of fixed assets	0	0	350
Retained profit	3,800	3,800	4,150

Table 6.2 Company A – balance sheets

	Year 1 £	Year 2 £	Year 3 £
Fixed asset	800	600	0
Cash	4,000	8,000	12,750
	4,800	8,600	12,750
Share capital	1,000	1,000	1,000
Profit and loss account	3,800	7,600	11,750
	4,800	8,600	12,750

Now Company B revalues its asset, and this complicates its accounts. Firstly, its depreciation charge isn't so straightforward (Table 6.3). It will be £200 in the first year, but at the start of the second year the asset's value increases to £1,200. This creates a revaluation reserve of £400 on the balance sheet (1,200 less the book value of £800). The £1,200 then has to be written off over the remaining four years of the asset's life, increasing the annual depreciation charge to £300. When the asset is sold at the end of the third year its book value will be £600 (its value, £1,200, at the start of the second year less two years' depreciation of £300), and the profit on sale of the asset will be £150.

Table 6.3 Company B – profit and loss accounts

	Year 1 £	Year 2 £	Year 3 £
Turnover	10,000	10,000	10,000
Profit before depreciation	4,000	4,000	4,000
Depreciation	(200)	(300)	(300)
Operating profit	3,800	3,700	3,700
Profit on sale of fixed assets	0	0	150
Retained profit	3,800	3,700	3,850

Now I'll look at Company B's balance sheets (Table 6.4). But before I do, I'll ask you a question. Now you learnt in Chapter 2 that companies can pay dividends when they're loss making as long as they have sufficient distributable reserves. In Chapter 3 you learnt that the profit and loss account is a company's only distributable reserve. Now the question – *Should Company B's distributable reserves be lower than Company A's just because it's revalued its asset?* (You can see that its retained profit is lower than Company A's for the last two years.) The accounting rules say no – the distributable reserves should remain the same. To do this, the additional depreciation each year is transferred from the revaluation reserve to the profit and loss account.

Table 6.4 Company B – balance sheets

	Year 1 £	Year 2 £	Year 3 £
Fixed asset	800	900	0
Cash	4,000	8,000	12,750
	4,800	8,900	12,750
Share capital	1,000	1,000	1,000
Revaluation reserve		300	0
Profit and loss account	3,800	7,600	11,750
	4,800	8,900	12,750

The revaluation reserve falls to £300, as the £100 additional depreciation is transferred to the profit and loss account to maintain the distributable reserve

The balance on the revaluation reserve is transferred to the profit and loss account once the revaluation is realised

In the third year the net worth of the two companies is the same for the first time since the assets were revalued, as the asset has been sold and the revaluation realised.

You need the note on historical cost profit and losses, as if you just looked at the profit and loss account Company A is more profitable than Company B. This is reflected in the common performance measures I've calculated for the third year (Table 6.5).

Table 6.5 Performance measures

	Company A	Company B
Operating margin	$\frac{3,800}{10,000} = 38\%$	$\frac{3,700}{10,000} = 37.0\%$
Return on capital	$\frac{4,150}{12,750} = 32.6\%$	$\frac{3,850}{12,750} = 30.2\%$

It appears that Company A outperforms Company B, but you know that both businesses are, in reality, identical! Company B would follow its profit and loss account with a note of historical cost profits and losses that makes this obvious (Table 6.6). Company B's profits are now the same as Company A's.

Table 6.6 Note of historical cost profits and losses Company B – Year 3

	Year 3 £	Year 2 £
Reported profit	**3,850**	3,700
Realisation of revaluation gains of previous years	**200**	
Difference between the historical cost depreciation charge and the actual depreciation charge of the year calculated on the revalued amount	**100**	100
Historical cost profit	**4,150**	3,800

Once again, I've used a simple example. My reported profit is the retained profit; however, a published note of historical cost profits and losses starts with the profit before tax (in my example it's the same as the retained profit). It then shows you the historical cost profit before taxation and the historical cost retained profits. This note is useful if you are comparing the profits of two companies in the same sector, who have different policies on revaluation.

Johnson Matthey's note of historical cost profits and losses

You may remember that Johnson Matthey doesn't revalue, consequently it doesn't have a detailed note. Between the statement of total recognised gains and losses and their reconciliation to shareholders' funds it discloses:

> There were no material differences between reported profits and losses and historical cost profits and losses on ordinary activities before tax for 2002 and 2001.

7

Other information found in the accounts

- **Segmental analysis** – what information will I find?
- **Accounting for pensions** – different types of company pension scheme; accounting for final salary schemes under SSAP24; accounting for final salary schemes under FRS 17; FRS 17 and the international accounting standards – IAS 19; pension accounting and financial analysis
- **Contingent liabilities**
- **Capital commitments**
- **Post balance sheet events**
- **Related party transactions**
- **Disclosure of risk management, derivatives and other financial instruments**
- **The operating and financial reviews**

You'll find that there's other information in the accounts that provides you with some useful insights into a company's financial performance. Its turnover, operating profit and operating assets are analysed between its different businesses and geographical locations. You'll also find information about its:

- accounting for pensions;
- contingent liabilities;
- capital commitments;
- post balance sheet events;
- transactions with related parties;
- financial risk management;
- operating review;
- financial review.

Reading, and understanding, this information improves your understanding of the company's financial performance, as it enables you to see:

- how well the company has performed in specific areas;
- if it could face problems in the future;
- whether, and how, the company has changed between the date of the accounts and their publication.

Segmental analysis

You know that a lot of the accounts you see are consolidated group accounts. Companies like Johnson Matthey have different businesses, and trade throughout the world. The group accounts show you the total picture, but how useful is it? When you're trying to understand a business's performance you want to know *where* the company is making its profits, and *where* it's trading. Unless you know that, how can you make a realistic assessment of the risks facing the business and its long-term prospects? You have to have more detailed information about the company's activities and its performance in different markets. You'll find this information in the notes to the profit and loss account. You'll find turnover, profits, and net assets analysed into the different businesses, and, if it's appropriate, geographically. This analysis is called *segmental reporting*.

Most companies have to disclose this information in the notes to their accounts. The Companies Act requires that all companies disclose their turnover and profit, or loss, before tax for each class of business and each geographical market that differs substantially from one another. All public and large private companies are required to give more information by SSAP 25 (*Segmental reporting*) and the Stock Exchange has additional requirements for listed companies. (For segmental reporting purposes a large company is defined as one that has ten times the medium-sized company criteria. They would currently need to exceed two out of the following three criteria: turnover £112 million, total assets £56 million, 2,500 employees.) However, companies don't have to give this information if their directors believe its disclosure would be 'seriously prejudicial'.

Companies analyse their performance between their different business segments and classes of business. So how do business segments differ from classes of business? The accounting standard defines business segments as those having different:

- returns on investment;
- degrees of risk;
- growth rates;
- potential.

Whereas a class of business is where part of the company provides different products or services.

The accounting standard requires companies to disclose both different classes of business and geographical segments where the turnover, or the profit and loss, or the net assets are 10%, or more, of the total. (This analysis only has to be given for associated undertakings, when their profit and loss or their net assets are 20%, or more, of the total.)

What information will I find?

Companies disclose their turnover, profits (or losses) before tax, and operating assets by class of business and geographical segment. I'll now tell you how each of these is defined.

- *Turnover:* there are two possible ways to identify geographical segments. You could look at either where the company's operations are located, or where its goods and services are sold. The standard refers to these as 'origin' (where it's made) and 'destination' (where it's sold). The accounting standard requires all companies to disclose their turnover by origin, and exporting companies also have to disclose the destination of their sales. (All companies have to disclose the origin of their turnover, as this is the basis that's used for determining the profits and the operating assets.)
- *Profit:* this is usually the profit before interest, tax, minority interests and any extraordinary items. However, some companies include interest. (The accounting standard only allows this if 'all, or part, of the entity's business is to earn and/or incur interest . . . or where interest income/expense is central to the business'.) You may also find that some companies apportion their central costs between the segments.
- *Operating assets:* these are the assets and liabilities used by the business. Consequently they are the non-interest-bearing assets (fixed assets, stocks and debtors) less the non-interest-bearing liabilities (creditors).

Whilst segmental information is very useful you can't always rely on being able to use this information in your analysis, as companies change their reporting to reflect changes in their business. You'll see that this happened in Johnson Matthey in 2002, when it created a new segment for Pharmaceutical Materials. It restated its 2001 figures, but this won't help if you're analysing its business over a number of years.

Johnson Matthey's note on segmental analysis

1 Segmental information

	Turnover		Operating profit		Net operating assets	
	2002	2001 restated	**2002**	2001 restated	**2002**	2001 restated
	£ million	£ million	**£ million**	£ million	**£ million**	£ million
Activity analysis						
Catalysts & Chemicals	**1,302.6**	1,467.6	**94.7**	80.9	**446.4**	413.4
Precious Metals	**3,167.4**	4,145.7	**55.9**	57.4	**82.0**	38.8
Colours & Coatings	**253.4**	251.0	**25.5**	32.1	**200.7**	193.4
Pharmaceutical Materials	**105.5**	35.2	**31.3**	18.0	**268.4**	39.4
Corporate	**–**	–	**(13.6)**	(13.3)	**(20.9)**	(16.3)
	4,828.9	5,899.5	**193.8**	175.1	**976.6**	668.7
Discontinued operations	**1.2**	4.2	**(0.5)**	(0.1)	**-**	2.7
Total turnover	**4,830.1**	5,903.7				
Goodwill amortisation (note 11)			**(6.8)**	(0.3)		
Exceptional items included in total operating profit (note 2)			**(18.1)**	(0.6)		
			168.4	174.1	**976.6**	671.4
Profit on sale/closure of discontinued operations (note 2)			**(5.6)**	1.1		
Net interest			**(6.1)**	5.3		
Profit on ordinary activities before taxation			**156.7**	180.5		
Net (borrowings and finance leases)/cash					**(159.0)**	139.9
Net assets					**817.6**	811.3

	Turnover		Operating profit		Net operating assets	
	2002	2001 restated	**2002**	2001 restated	**2002**	2001 restated
	£ million	£ million	**£ million**	£ million	**£ million**	£ million
Geographical analysis by origin						
Europe	**3,304.1**	4,111.8	**75.3**	66.9	**625.0**	421.0
North America	**1,280.1**	1,585.2	**84.6**	81.4	**245.1**	158.4
Asia	**955.5**	1,094.4	**13.3**	13.8	**48.7**	65.7
Rest of the World	**271.3**	307.7	**20.6**	13.0	**57.8**	23.6
	5,811.0	7,099.1	**193.8**	175.1	**976.6**	668.7
Discontinued operations	**2.0**	5.0	**(0.5)**	(0.1)	**-**	2.7
	5,813.0	7,104.1				
Less inter-segment sales	**(982.9)**	(1,200.4)				
Total turnover	**4,830.1**	5,903.7				

Goodwill amortisation (note 11)	**(6.8)**	(0.3)		
Exceptional items included in				
total operating profit (note 2)	**(18.1)**	(0.6)		
	168.4	174.1	**976.6**	671.4
Profit on sale/closure of discontinued operations (note 2)	**(5.6)**	1.1		
Net interest	**(6.1)**	5.3		
Profit on ordinary activities before taxation	**156.7**	180.5		
Net (borrowings and finance leases)/cash			**(159.0)**	139.9
Net assets			**817.6**	811.3

	2002 **£ million**	2001 £ million
External turnover by geographical destination		
Europe	**2,070.0**	2,459.0
North America	**1,356.4**	1,858.8
Asia	**1,112.8**	1,293.2
Rest of the World	**290.9**	292.7
Total turnover	**4,830.1**	5,903.7

Turnover by destination relating to the United Kingdom amounted to £1,277.5 million (2001 £1,568.2 million).

The activity analyses have been restated to show Pharmaceutical Materials as a new segment. This was previously included within Catalysts & Chemicals but is now shown separately as a result of its increased size. The group sold its French print business (part of Colours & Coatings) during the year and its results are now reported in discontinued operations (note 3).

- This tells you that:
- *Turnover:* this grew in all divisions apart from Precious Metals and Catalysts & Chemicals. (But don't forget that this is where its refinery operations are based and these divisions are most exposed to precious metal prices, which fell during the period. You'll find more useful information about this towards the end of the chapter, in the company's financial review.) The new Pharmaceutical Materials Division showed the most growth, but this was largely through acquisitions. (I'd like to remind you that the two largest acquisitions in 2002, Meconic and Pharm-Eco Laboratories, were in this division and contributed £66.2 million to the division's turnover, and £11.9 million to its operating profit.) Most of the company's turnover in 2002, almost 66%, came from its Precious Metals division.
- *Operating profit:* almost 46% of its continuing operating profit before exceptional items and group costs came from Catalysts & Chemicals. However, Pharmaceutical Materials Division has the best operating margin – 29.67% in 2002, and an amazing 51.14% in 2001.

- *Operating assets:* Precious Metals Division has very low operating assets, both in relation to its sales and to its operating profit. You can see in the note that this figure comprises all the assets and liabilities used in the division apart from net debt. This gives an extraordinary return on assets (operating profit ÷ operating assets) of 68.17% in 2002, and 147.94% in 2001. Exposure to precious metal prices would encourage the business to keep working capital low, and in its financial review (shown at the end of this chapter) it discloses that 'The value of the precious metals included in sales is generally separately invoiced and payment made within a few days.' This could well explain such a low operating asset figure, although it may be that the fixed asset figure is also low. This can arise if the company is leasing most of the assets on operating leases, or if the assets are almost fully depreciated.
- *The importance of Europe:* most of the company's sales are made in Europe (almost 57%), and this is its largest market, accounting for almost 43% of its sales.

Accounting for pensions

Whilst pensions accounting can appear very esoteric, the way a UK company accounts for pensions has a significant effect on its reported financial performance. This effect will increase as companies implement FRS 17 (*Retirement benefits*). This means that you have to understand some of the more important principles of pensions accounting if you want to interpret a set of accounts.

Different types of company pension scheme

Pension schemes can be classified in two ways:

- Firstly, by where the assets and liabilities are held. Most UK pension schemes are 'funded', as companies make payments to a separate pension fund holding the fund's assets. However, many overseas pension schemes are 'unfunded'. This means that the company has a large pension provision in its accounts, as it doesn't make any payments to a separate fund.
- Secondly, by the type of pension offered. Pension schemes can be classified as:
  - A *money purchase,* or *defined contributions,* scheme. The contributions are invested and the employee's pension is determined by the scheme's investment performance. If the investment performance is poor, the employee's pension is poor – the employee has the risks of adequate pension provision.
  - A *final salary,* or *defined benefits,* scheme. The employee is entitled to receive a proportion of his or her salary on retirement that is totally unrelated to the scheme's investment performance. If the scheme under-performs, the company has to make additional contributions to honour its obligations to the employee. The recent poor performance in the stock market, coupled with past 'pension holidays', has led to many companies either closing these schemes to new employees, or converting them into money purchase schemes. The risk in a final salary scheme lies with the employer.

Now just think about money purchase schemes and defined benefit schemes for a moment. Pension costs are staff costs and have to be charged to the profit and loss account as the employee earns the benefits. Now, accounting for money purchase schemes is simple – the employer's contributions in the period are charged to the profit and loss account.

But it's difficult to work out the employer's cost in final salary schemes, as they have so many variables that interrelate with one another . . . including:

- the employee's final, or average salary – this determines the size of the pension they'll receive in the future;
- their remaining lifetime as a pensioner – this determines how long the pension will be paid;
- the returns that will be made on the fund's investments – this determines the balance between the payments to the fund and the fund's eventual value.

If you think about it, the pension costs in a final salary scheme can only be accurately determined when the scheme is wound up. But that's not an acceptable accounting option – companies have to make a charge to the profit and loss account for the cost of providing pensions as they're benefiting from the employee's services. So companies have to find a way to predict both the pension benefits and the investment returns. This is calculated by an actuarial valuation, usually done every three years. The actuarial valuation:

- determines the size of the fund needed to meet its obligations;
- assesses whether the fund is in surplus or deficit;
- accounts for the surplus, or the deficit, in calculating the pension cost for the period;
- determines the scheme's contribution rate.

I'll take you through these in more detail later. Now, once actuaries have found a way to spread the cost of providing the pension over the working lives of the employees, the pension cost can be charged to the profit and loss account. But what should you do if the fund is in deficit? In a final salary scheme, the employer guarantees a pension regardless of the fund's investment performance. If the fund can't meet its obligations the employer has to make up the shortfall. This means that the employer is ultimately responsible for the employee's pension. So should a pension fund deficit show on the employer's balance sheet as a liability? After all, the employer will have to make additional contributions to eliminate the deficit. And if the deficit docs appear on the balance sheet – when should it be shown? As soon as the actuaries decide that, on their current assumptions, the fund's assets aren't sufficient to meet its liabilities – in other words, immediately the fund is in deficit? Or when the deficit reaches a certain size?

These questions are being discussed as I write, and the implementation of a new UK accounting standard (FRS 17 *Retirement benefits*) has been delayed to allow further discussions with the International Accounting Standards Board. This means that pension accounting is in a period of flux. Currently UK accounts are being prepared using the old accounting rule (SSAP 24 *Accounting for pension costs*), with additional disclosures in the notes based on FRS 17. Listed UK companies will have to prepare their accounts using international accounting standards by 2005, and FRS 17 has a number of fundamental differences to its international counterpart. So I'll now tell you about:

- how final salary pension costs are currently calculated, and charged to the profit and loss account;
- the changes in FRS 17;
- the main differences between FRS 17 and the current international standard.

Accounting for final salary schemes under SSAP 24

The first thing you should know is that the charge for pensions in the profit and loss account may well be different from the cash the employer contributes to the scheme. SSAP 24's objective is to have a regular pension cost that is, as far as possible, a *level percentage* of the current, and future, pensionable payroll using the current actuarial assumptions.

The first thing the actuaries have to do is to determine the size of the fund that's needed to meet the fund's obligations.

The size of the fund

It's actually quite complicated to determine this, as you have to start by making some assumptions based on the answers to the following questions:

- How many staff will stay with the scheme until they retire?
- When will they retire?
- What will they be earning when they retire?
- How will the fund perform until they retire?
- How long will the employees live after they've retired?
- Will the fund's return be large enough to cover its liabilities?

Actuaries then carry out valuations, usually every three years, to determine the size of the fund needed to meet the pension liabilities. The accounts disclose their actuarial assumptions, which are usually very conservative (tending to overestimate salary increases and underestimate fund performance). You can see this in the extract from Johnson Matthey's disclosures on its UK group pensions scheme:

> . . . The financial assumptions applicable to the last actuarial valuation at 1st April 2000 were: long term rate of investment return 6.75%, dividend increase rate 4%, general salary and wage inflation rate 5% and pension increase rate 3%. . . .

The notes also tell you whether the fund is in surplus or deficit. A surplus arises when the fund's value is greater than the amount it needs to satisfy its liabilities. Given the conservatism of the actuarial assumptions, in the past it was relatively easy for a pension fund to be in surplus. During the 1980s and 1990s investment returns easily outpaced wage inflation. Unfortunately, this trend has now reversed and many companies' pension funds are moving into deficit, as recent poor investment returns are shrinking fund values at a time when many staff have elected to take early retirement options in restructuring programmes. In 2002 Johnson Matthey's fund is still in surplus, as the following extract from its note on its UK group pensions scheme discloses:

> **10c Retirement benefits**
>
> **(i) United Kingdom pension schemes**
>
> The group's principal UK pension scheme is of the defined benefit type which requires contributions to be made to a separately administered fund. At 1st April 2000, the date of the latest actuarial valuation, the market value of the UK scheme's assets was £633.0 million, the actuarial value of which represented 141% of the liability for benefits that had accrued to that date, making full allowance for future salary and pension increases. This represents an actuarial surplus of £164.2 million which, following actuarial recommendations, has permitted the company to suspend contributions for the foreseeable future. A surplus cannot be refunded to the company except by dissolution of the scheme in accordance with the rules of the scheme and relevant legislation.

Three important things are disclosed in this note:

- On 1 April 2000, its fund represented 141% of its liabilities and had a surplus of £164.2 million.
- This surplus can only be refunded to the company if the fund is dissolved.
- The company is not making any contributions for the foreseeable future – it's having a 'pension holiday'.

Although Johnson Matthey is not making any payments to the UK fund, it still makes a charge in its profit and loss account. SSAP 24 requires companies to match the pension costs charged to the profit and loss account to working lives of their employees. This means that the profit and loss account is being charged with the cost of providing pensions over the period that the company is benefiting from the employees' services (following the accruals principle). Consequently, the accounting charge for pensions can be very different from the cash cost of funding the pension schemes. The pension charge is analysed in the notes into three components:

- The regular pension cost: this is the charge based on the actuarial assumptions.
- The variation from the regular cost: this variation arises if the scheme's performance is different to the actuarial assumptions; or there are changes in the actuarial assumptions; or changes in benefits or membership conditions (like admitting part-time employees to the scheme).
- Interest: if the scheme is in surplus or deficit, it generates income, or costs, that are recognised as interest. It is shown as part of the pension cost, as it's part of the pension cost's actuarial assessment.

So let's have a look at how companies account for a surplus, as this is a variation that also generates interest.

Accounting for a surplus

The surplus has to be spread over the remaining service life of employees. The next part of Johnson Matthey's note discloses this:

> In accordance with the applicable accounting standard, the surplus on the group's principal UK pension fund has been spread over the average of the expected remaining service lives of current employees (12 years) as a variation from regular cost. The regular pension cost is assessed using the projected unit method.

As the surplus is spread over the remaining expected service lives, it is possible for the current year's share of the surplus to be greater than the normal cost of the company's contributions. This gives rise to a 'negative cost' (effectively a credit) to the profit and loss account that is reflected by a prepayment asset in the balance sheet. So, if the normal cost of providing the pension in the future (the regular cost) is £10 million, and the surplus allocated to the current period is £12 million (the variation from the regular cost), the profit and loss account would be credited with £2 million. This means that it would not be charged with any pension cost, showing a positive £2 million instead (this is only disclosed in the notes, not on the profit and loss account itself). And a £2 million pension fund prepayment would be shown on the balance sheet, as part of debtors, to reflect this credit. However, this prepayment is not one of the company's liquid assets (remember Johnson Matthey's earlier note – the surplus can only be refunded if the scheme is dissolved). Now consider what happens if, in the following year, the fund moves out of surplus . . . the company's profits appear to collapse. It now has to charge the £10 million regular cost, when compared to the £2 million credit in the previous year, and its profits have fallen by £12 million! The problem is that today's surplus can become tomorrow's deficit.

The size of a surplus is a matter of judgement, as SSAP 24 allows actuaries to use a number of different methods (FRS 17 only allows one method, the projected unit method that Johnson Matthey already uses). However, you don't have to be concerned about the effect of different actuarial methods. All you need to understand is that any apportioned surplus reduces the charge to the profit and loss account, and affects the reported profitability.

It is further complicated by the fact that SSAP 24 allows the company to charge a notional interest, where the difference between the charge to the profit and loss account and the cash cost gives rise to a prepayment asset. (This reflects the money that the prepayment is earning as part of the fund.) The logic may be sound, but remember there is no cash flowing into the company. It just represents the interest that is notionally earned on the surplus.

You know that one of the ways that a pension prepayment can be created is when the normal cost is less than the proportion of the surplus relating to the year. However, not all pension prepayment assets are accumulated 'negative costs'; they may reflect the pension fund surplus itself. When SSAP 24 was issued, companies were allowed to either:

- spread the surplus as I've discussed above;
- incorporate the pension fund surplus, or deficit, onto the balance sheet by making a prior year adjustment.

FRS 7 (*Fair values in acquisition accounting*) requires pension fund surpluses of acquired businesses to be treated as an asset, and deficits to be shown as a liability, although it does stress that companies should only recognise the amount that is likely to be realised.

The note on pensions details the effect of providing pensions on the profit and loss account and the balance sheet. You can see this in the following extract from the note to Johnson Matthey's group accounts:

(iv) Profit and loss account and balance sheet impact of providing retirement benefits

The effect of providing pensions and other retirement benefits on operating profit was as follows:

	2002 £ million	2001 £ million
United Kingdom		
Regular pension cost	**(12.5)**	(10.7)
Variation from regular cost	**8.2**	10.1
Interest on prepayment	**7.0**	6.6
Cost of post-retirement medical benefits	**(0.4)**	(0.3)
	2.3	5.7
Overseas		
Cost of foreign pension schemes	**(4.5)**	(3.6)
Cost of post-retirement medical benefits	**(0.8)**	(0.6)
	(3.0)	1.5

The following prepayments and provisions relating to pension schemes and other post-retirement benefits are included in the group and parent company's balance sheets:

	Group		Parent company	
	2002 £ million	2001 £ million	**2002 £ million**	2001 £ million
Prepaid pension costs in the UK	**107.7**	103.9	**107.7**	103.9
Prepaid pension costs overseas	**3.0**	–	**–**	–
Provision for foreign pensions	**1.0**	9.0	**–**	–
Provision for post-retirement medical benefits – UK	**4.2**	3.9	**4.1**	3.9
Provision for post-retirement medical benefits – overseas	**12.7**	12.2	**–**	–
Provision for other post-retirement benefits – overseas	**–**	0.4	**–**	–

You can see that the UK pension fund's surplus resulted in a credit to the company's profit and loss account in both years. However, its overseas pension schemes have costs that are being charged to the profit and loss account. This meant that the group moved from a net credit of £1.5 million in 2001 to a charge of £3 million in 2002. (Whilst this is worth noting, it's not significant in the context of an operating profit of over £168 million.)

Its pension prepayment of £110.7 million is included in debtors, with £1.9 million due within a year and the balance of £108.8 million falling due in more than a year. The £17.9 million provisions for foreign pensions and post-retirement health benefits are included in provisions for liabilities and charges on the balance sheet.

Accounting for final salary schemes under FRS 17

FRS 17 is one of the few accounting standards that non-financial managers in the UK have heard of, and I'm often asked to explain it on 'Finance for the non-financial manager' courses. People have heard of it because it has been blamed, quite wrongly, for the closure of final salary schemes. (The timing of FRS 17's introduction has been unfortunate, coinciding with a collapse in the markets and the subsequent movement in company schemes from large surpluses to deficits. Final salary schemes are closing because they're becoming too expensive to provide when stock markets are falling and volatile – not because of the way that these schemes are shown in the accounts.)

FRS 17 has three objectives:

- The employer's financial statements should reflect the assets and liabilities arising from pension fund obligations and related funding, measured at fair values (market value). *This means that they will be valued at their market value every year and some of a surplus, or all of a deficit, will appear on the company's balance sheet.*
- The operating costs of providing pension benefits are recognised in the period when the benefits are earned by employees, and finance costs and any other changes in the value of assets and liabilities are recognised in the periods they arise. *This means that only some of the pension costs will be charged to operating profit, others will be shown alongside interest.*
- There should be adequate disclosure in the accounts.

FRS 17 brings the net assets and liabilities of companies' pension funds onto their balance sheets for the first time. It uses present value techniques to value the fund and requires that:

- The scheme's assets are valued at fair values at the balance sheet date.
- The scheme's liabilities are valued using the projected unit method and discounted by the AA corporate bond rate in the same currency and with the same term. (This discount rate is likely to be lower than the return on the scheme's assets.) There doesn't have to be a full actuarial valuation each year, but the assumptions may need to be updated.
- A surplus can only be recognised to the extent that the employer benefits from either reduced future contributions, or a refund from the scheme. Any overpaid or unpaid contributions are shown as a debtor, or creditor, due in a year. (The surplus or the deficit is the difference between the present value of the scheme's assets and liabilities. The reduction in future contributions is the present value of the liability arising from future service of employees less the present value of the future employee contributions.)

The net pension asset or liability is shown on the balance sheet. Its position depends on the presentation used:

- Format 1 – shown after net assets on the balance sheet.
- Format 2 – shown after total assets, or liabilities, as appropriate.

FRS 17 also affects the profit and loss account and the statement of total recognised gains and losses. The charge to the profit and loss account will be split between:

- operating costs, which will include:
  - current service cost;

  - past service costs (these arise if the company improves benefits);
  - any previously recognised surplus deducted from past service costs;
  - gains or losses on curtailment (this could arise from a redundancy programme), or settlement (this could arise from buying out the employees' rights);
  - any previously recognised surplus deducted from curtailment, or settlement;
- exceptional costs required to be shown after operating profit under FRS 3 – if any of the curtailment gains and losses relate to exceptional restructuring costs;
- financing costs (these will be shown next to interest):
  - interest cost (the expected increase in the present value of the scheme's liabilities because you're now one period closer to settlement; this is also called 'the unwinding of the discount');
  - the expected return on the scheme's assets.

You've seen Johnson Matthey's actuarial assumptions . . . now do you think that this is what will actually happen? Perhaps not. If the assumptions differ from what actually happens there will be different surpluses and deficits, and the assumptions may have to be changed in the light of changing circumstances. These differences and the effects of changed actuarial assumptions are referred to as 'actuarial gains and losses'. Once you know the total gain or loss, you have to calculate how much of it belongs to this period by dividing it by the expected working lives of the employees in the scheme. This is then shown in the statement of total recognised gains and losses, as it's the amount 'recognised' in the period.

FRS 17 has a lengthy implementation period, and companies don't have to comply fully until June 2005 (although they're encouraged to comply earlier). Currently, companies only have to disclose some of the information required by FRS 17 in the notes to their accounts. To illustrate this I'll show you the note to Johnson Matthey's accounts.

(v) FRS 17 – 'Retirement Benefits' disclosures

The group operates defined benefit pension schemes in the UK and the US. Full actuarial valuations were carried out at 1st April 2000 for the principal UK scheme, 31st December 1999 for the Meconic defined benefits scheme and 30th June 2001 for the US schemes and updated to 31st March 2002 by qualified independent actuaries. For the principal UK scheme the company made no contributions in the year and the company has suspended contributions for the foreseeable future. The contribution to the Meconic defined benefits scheme amounted to £0.6 million (at a rate of 17%) and to the US schemes £11.3 million. The Meconic defined benefits scheme closed to new members on 31st December 1998 and under the projected unit method the current service cost would increase as the members of the scheme approach retirement. The group operates a number of other small schemes around the world which are not material and their net liabilities of £0.4 million are included in the balance sheet.

The main assumptions at 31st March 2002 were:

	UK schemes %	US schemes %
Rate of increase in salaries	**4.75**	**4.50**
Rate of increase in pensions in payment	**2.75**	**–**
Discount rate	**5.80**	**7.25**
Inflation	**2.75**	**3.50**
Current medical benefits cost trend rate	**5.50**	**10.00**
Ultimate medical benefits cost trend rate	**5.50**	**5.00**

The assets in the schemes and the expected rates of return at 31st March 2002 were:

	UK pension schemes Expected long term rate of return	Value	UK post-retirement medical benefits schemes value	US pension schemes Expected long term rate of return	Value	US post-retirement medical benefits scheme value
	%	£ million	£ million	%	£ million	£ million
Equities	8.0	416.1	–	9.0	33.5	–
Bonds	5.3	144.7	–	5.5	22.4	–
Property	6.8	33.7	–		–	–
Total market value of assets		594.5	–		55.9	–
Present value of scheme liabilities		(483.7)	(4.7)		(60.0)	(10.9)
Surplus/(deficit) in scheme		110.8	(4.7)		(4.1)	(10.9)
Related deferred tax (liability)/asset		(33.2)	1.4		1.6	4.1
Net retirement benefits asset/(liability)		77.6	(3.3)		(2.5)	(6.8)

If the above amounts had been recognised in the accounts, the group's net assets and profit and loss reserves at 31st March 2002 would be:

		Group	Parent company
		£ million	£ million
Net assets excluding retirement benefits asset/liability		751.9	480.4
Retirement benefits asset/(liability)	– UK pensions	77.6	78.9
	– US pensions	(2.5)	–
	– Medical benefits	(10.1)	(3.2)
	– Other schemes	(0.4)	–
Net assets including retirement benefits asset/liability		816.5	556.1
Profit and loss account reserve excluding retirement benefits reserve		396.4	128.6
Retirement benefits reserve	– UK pensions	77.6	78.9
	– US pensions	(2.5)	–
	– Medical benefits	(10.1)	(3.2)
	– Other schemes	(0.4)	–
Profit and loss account reserve		461.0	204.3

If the profit and loss account for the year ended 31st March 2002 had been restated for FRS 17 the impact would not have been material.

You can see that both the assumptions, and the resulting surplus, are slightly different using FRS 17 from those you saw earlier using the old accounting rule.

FRS 17 and the international accounting standard – IAS 19

The main difference between FRS 17 and the international standard is its requirement for the immediate recognition of *all* the period's actuarial gains and losses in the *statement of total recognised gains and losses*. The international accounting standard allows companies to take only *some* of these into the *profit and loss account*.

I need to tell you what I mean by 'some'. The international standard takes the view that, in the long term, actuarial gains and losses could offset one another. Consequently, it uses a range around the best estimate of the company's pension obligation. As long as the actuarial gains and losses remain within 10% they don't have to show in the profit and loss account. However, when they are above 10% they are shown in the profit and loss account – but only to the extent that they are greater than 10%. (This means that if this period's actuarial loss was 12%, only 2% would have to be charged to the profit and loss account – although the company could, if it wanted to, charge the whole 12%!)

Pension accounting and financial analysis

Pension accounting has a significant effect on financial analysis and it will become more important in the future. Currently:

- Profitability is affected by the performance of the company's pension fund, as this determines the pension charge. For example, in its 2002 accounts BT disclosed that its pension fund was in deficit based on its last actuarial valuation in 1999. Its disclosure on its pension charge was:

> In the year ended 31 March 2002, the group made regular contributions of £303 million (2001 – £308 million, 2000 – £253 million) and additional special and deficiency contributions of £600 million (2001 – £300 million, 2000 – £230 million). The group will continue to make employer's contributions at a rate of 11.6% of pensionable pay in the year ending 31 March 2003 and an annual deficiency payment of £200 million. It will also pay a special contribution in the year ended 31 March 2003 which is expected to amount to approximately £130 million in respect of redundancies and early leavers in the year ended 31 December 2001.

  You can see that the deficit has almost tripled the pension charge, as its additional contribution was almost twice that of the regular cost. And it looks like it'll get worse before it gets better – in its FRS 17 disclosures its fund's asset value was almost 9.6% smaller than that under SSAP 24, suggesting that its charge will have to increase after the next actuarial valuation.

Under FRS 17 financial analysis will be affected further as:

- not all of the pension costs will be charged to operating profit – the financing costs of the fund will be shown next to interest;
- the pension fund will affect the company's net assets, and its distributable reserves (thus affecting possible dividend payments). Some ratios will have to be adjusted to take account of this.

Contingent liabilities

I briefly mentioned contingencies when I talked about provisions in the earlier chapters covering the profit and loss account and the balance sheet. A contingency is a gain or liability that hasn't happened by the balance sheet's date. FRS 12 (*Provisions, contingent liabilities and contingent assets*) covers the accounting treatment for contingent assets and contingent liabilities. Whilst all provisions are effectively contingent, under FRS 12 a contingency differs as it:

- Requires the occurrence of one, or more, events that aren't totally within the business's control to confirm its existence.
- Is unable to be classified as a provision under FRS 12, as either it isn't probable that it will happen, or its cash outflow can't be reliably measured.

I've summarised the accounting treatment for contingent assets and liabilities in the table below.

Table 7.1 SSAP 18 requirements for contingent gains and losses

Probability	Asset	Liability
Probable	Note in the financial statements, but don't anticipate a profit that may not be realised.	If the cash outflow is also measurable, the company must make a provision. Otherwise it is noted in the accounts.
Possible	Ignore	Doesn't have to be included in the financial statements, but it should be noted in the accounts.
Unlikely	Ignore	Ignore

You can see that FRS 12 doesn't allow contingent assets to be shown in the accounts. However, accounting for contingent gains is different if the company has made an acquisition. FRS 7 (*Fair values in acquisition accounting*) requires that both contingent assets and liabilities are valued on the basis of reasonable estimates of their outcome. This means that contingent assets, arising from contingent gains, are shown in the accounts if they existed when the company acquired the subsidiary.

You'll find that companies regularly disclose some contingencies (like bank guarantees, discounted bills, performance bonds), whereas they're reluctant to disclose others. A good example is contingent liabilities arising from court cases. Most companies don't like disclosing them, as they feel that it might jeopardise their position – implying that they believe they'll lose the case. Companies are also unwilling to show the financial effect of a breach of the law, although the disclosure would probably result in it not being seen as a contingency, but as a liability.

Capital commitments

You'll find a note on capital commitments disclosing the capital expenditure for the following year that has already been approved. It is sorted out into two categories of expenditure where:

- The contracts have been placed.
- It has been approved, but contracts have not been placed at the balance sheet date.

This is often a useful note to refer to, as it gives some indication of the company's expansion plans and future cash flows.

Johnson Matthey's note on capital commitments, guarantees and contingent liabilities

26 Commitments, guarantees and contingent liabilities

	Group		Parent company	
	2002	2001	**2002**	2001
	£ million	£ million	**£ million**	£ million
Commitments				
Future capital expenditure contracted but not provided	**13.5**	8.1	**8.9**	5.3
Annual commitments under operating leases				
Leases of land and buildings terminating				
Within one year	**0.5**	0.8	**–**	–
In one to five years	**3.4**	3.7	**1.7**	1.7
Over five years	**2.2**	2.1	**1.2**	1.2
Other leases terminating				
Within one year	**0.5**	0.4	**0.3**	0.3
In one to five years	**1.8**	1.4	**0.8**	0.4
Guarantees				
Guarantees of subsidiary undertakings' borrowings	**–**	–	**17.7**	24.4
Other guarantees	**6.1**	0.5	**5.9**	0.5

Post balance sheet events

The accounts tell you about the company on its balance sheet date, but a lot could have happened in the company during the months between taking the snapshot and publishing the accounts. These are called post balance sheet events and are covered by SSAP 17 (*Accounting for post balance sheet events*). It divides post balance sheet events into two types:

- *Adjusting events:* these give you extra information about conditions that were known about on the balance sheet date. The extra information allows the company to adjust its figures to show a more accurate view. For example, perhaps the company has made a bad debt provision for a customer's account. If the customer goes into receivership a month after the date of the balance sheet, the company's view is confirmed. The total amount outstanding would be written off, but it would only be disclosed if it was so large that its disclosure was necessary for the accounts to show a true and fair view.

- *Non-adjusting events:* these occurred after the balance sheet date. They would include acquisitions, disposals, resignation of directors and share issues. They have to be separately disclosed in the notes to the accounts and the company gives an estimation of their financial impact, where it's possible.

The only major change arising from the alignment proposal FRED 27 (*Events after the balance sheet date*) is to exclude proposed dividends from adjusting events. This means that they won't appear on the profit and loss account, as they aren't a liability at the balance sheet date.

Related party transactions

Relationships between related parties are a normal part of business life. However, dealings between related parties can have a material effect on a company's performance and its financial position. There could be an asset sale, or trading between companies that are controlled by the same group. When these have been made at arm's length and at fair value there's no cause for concern. Unfortunately, this isn't always the case. If there is any possibility that transactions have not been fairly conducted, the shareholders have a right to know. The financial statements have to contain sufficient disclosures to make readers aware of the possibility that the company's reported financial position, and its profitability, might have been affected by transactions with related parties.

There are statutory and Stock Exchange requirements covering some of the potential concerns, such as loans made to directors, and the accounting standard (FRS 8 *Related party disclosures*) goes much further. It has a wider definition of related parties and requires most transactions to be disclosed if they are material to either party. The accounting standard identifies both related parties and those presumed to be related parties. A related party is anyone who:

- controls, or influences, another party;
- is subject to common control, or common influence, by another party.

The standard also presumes the following to be related parties, unless it can be proved otherwise:

- the key management of the company, its parent and its subsidiaries;
- any business that manages, or is managed by, the company under a management contract;
- anyone owning or controlling directly, or indirectly, 20% or more of the company's voting rights;
- concert party members who could exercise control or influence;
- a related party's family members, or a member of the same household: these are the related party's close family (this extends both the statutory and Stock Exchange's definitions);
- businesses that are controlled by related parties, or their close families.

FRS 8 requires that all companies should disclose the name of the party controlling the reporting company, together with the name of the ultimate controlling party, if it is different. These have to be disclosed whether or not any transactions have taken place.

Most material transactions are disclosed in the notes to the accounts. (The accounting standard offers some exemptions for some intra-group transactions, pension contributions, payments for services as an employee of the company, and any disclosure that would represent a breach of a legal duty of confidentiality.)

The alignment proposal, FRED 25 (*Related party disclosures*), contains a number of differences in the definition of related parties, the required disclosures, and the exemptions from disclosure. I've summarised these below:

- The related parties are broadly the same, but would no longer include:
  - concert party members who could exercise control or influence;
  - any business that manages, or is managed by, the company under a management contract.
- There is no requirement to disclose the names of the related parties.
- Pension contributions, and disclosures representing a breach of a legal duty of confidentiality, would not be exempt from disclosures (although the names of the related parties don't have to be disclosed).

Johnson Matthey's note on related party transactions

14 Transactions with related parties

The group's related parties are its associates described in note 13c.

During the year the group supplied thermocouple products to a value of £20,000 to Arora-Matthey Limited (2001 £ nil).

During the year the group purchased £43,000 (2001 £145,000) of raw materials from Oximet SrL. Total balances payable to Oximet SrL at 31st March 2002 were £4,000 (2001 £13,000).

There were no transactions with Matthey Pharmaceutical Alkaloids, L.L.C. during the year (2001 £ nil).

From 20th April 2001 (when Universal Pharma Technologies, L.L.C. was acquired as part of the acquisition of Pharm-Eco Laboratories, Inc.) to 31st March 2002 the group paid royalties of £55,000 and made service charges of £311,000 to Universal Pharma Technologies, L.L.C. Total balances receivable from Universal Pharma Technologies, L.L.C. at 31st March 2002 were £1.4 million, against which a provision of £1.0 million has been made.

Disclosure of risk management, derivatives and other financial instruments

In Chapter 2 you came across the term 'hedging', as Johnson Matthey hedged some of its precious metal stocks, and most companies hedge their exposure to exchange rate movements. You discovered that hedging is designed to minimise, or eliminate, a risk by moving in the opposite direction to the investment's value. Companies are exposed to a range of risks, including commodity price changes, interest rate movements, and movements in exchange rates. A number of hedging products have been developed to help protect companies against these risks, and a number of these are commonly referred to in the accounts. You'll often find references to:

- *Forward rate agreements:* these are usually used to hedge exchange and interest rate movements. They lock the company into a fixed rate and it receives this rate regardless of what happens in the market. Forward rate agreements provide certainty.
- *Options:* this gives the right, but not an obligation, to buy or sell something at a fixed price for a fixed period of time. If the company can get a better rate it doesn't have to exercise the option. This gives flexibility, but the company has to pay for this flexibility and options are more expensive than forward rate agreements.
- *Swaps:* a swap is an agreement between two parties to exchange cash flows over a period of time. The commonest swap is an interest rate swap, where companies exchange fixed rates for floating rates. Exchange rate swaps are usually used to finance overseas subsidiaries, and associates. Loans are normally raised in the currency of the parent and then this loan is swapped into the preferred currency.

Now hedging is just like insurance – you can protect yourself against most things for a price! Hedging just passes the risk to someone else, so the cost increases with probability. If something's likely to happen, it's probably too expensive to cover yourself.

When you're analysing a company you're interested in the risks it's facing and how it manages them. You'll find a range of disclosures in the accounts explaining some of the risks facing the company.

Firstly, the company's objectives, policies, and strategies for managing risk are usually disclosed in the financial review. The notes to the balance sheet give also some numerical disclosures in four tables disclosing the:

- interest rate risk profile of financial assets and liabilities, analysed between fixed and variable rates in the company's main currencies;
- currency exposures;
- fair values of financial assets and liabilities;
- gains and losses on hedging agreements.

As Johnson Matthey's disclosures cover four pages in its accounts I've not shown them, but you can read them in its accounts on the web.

I mentioned the operating and financial review and I'd now like to tell you what these are.

The operating and financial reviews

Since 1993 listed companies have published an operating review and a financial review in their accounts. The Accounting Standards Board developed this as a 'statement of voluntary best practice' for public companies and other large companies 'where there is a legitimate public interest in their financial statements'.

If you want to understand the company you should always read the operating review, as it identifies:

- the main factors underlying the business;
- the way that these have varied in the past, and are expected to vary in the future.

It also gives you:

- a full discussion on the operating results and the business's dynamics, including the main risks and uncertainties facing the business.

The content of the financial review has changed since the ASB's statement was originally issued, as the implementation of FRS 13 (*Derivatives and other financial instruments: Disclosure*) has meant that the numerical disclosures are now found in the notes to the accounts. (They're the ones I discussed earlier.) But you'll still find the financial review particularly interesting, as it will disclose:

- the operational cash flows and the factors that have affected them;
- the business's current liquidity, including:
  - its year end borrowings;
  - any seasonality in its borrowing requirements;
  - the maturity profiles of its borrowings;
- that the business is a going concern;
- a commentary on any assets or resources that aren't fully reflected on the balance sheet.

It's also very useful if you prefer words to numbers, as it discusses the financial statements. This is where you'll find out about how the metal prices have affected the business in the year. There's a lot of information in Johnson Matthey's Financial Review:

Financial Review

Review of Results

In the year 31st March 2002 turnover fell by 18% to £4.8 billion reflecting significantly lower average platinum and palladium prices. The average platinum price fell by 13% while palladium was 39% lower. Sales excluding the value of precious metals rose by 12% to £1.1 billion. Operating profit before exceptional items and goodwill amortisation rose by 10% to £193.3 million.

Divisional results are discussed in the Chief Executive's Statement on pages 4 to 7, and in the individual divisional reports on pages 12 to 19.

Profit before tax, exceptional items and goodwill amortisation for the group rose by 4% to £187.2 million. Earnings per share, before exceptional items and goodwill amortisation rose by 6% to 60.4 pence. The board is recommending to shareholders a final dividend of 17.1 pence, making a total dividend for the year of 24.6 pence, an increase of 6%. The dividend would be covered 2.5 times by earnings.

Sales and Margins

Johnson Matthey's turnover is heavily impacted by the high value of precious metals sold by the group particularly in the Precious Metals Division (PMD). The total value of sales each year varies according to the mix of metals sold and level of trading activity. The value of the precious metals included in sales is generally separately invoiced and payment made within a few days. Consequently, although return on sales (operating profit/total external sales) for the precious metals businesses is low, profit growth has been relatively stable and return on investment is high.

To provide a more useful measure of return on sales, the adjacent table shows sales by division excluding the value of precious metals. Total sales excluding precious metals were £1,093 million which was 12% up on last year and return on sales averaged 17.7% compared with 17.9% in 2000/01. The group's target for each of its divisions is to achieve a return on sales excluding precious metals in excess of 10%. All four divisions were ahead of that target in 2001/02.

Catalysts & Chemicals achieved 11% growth in sales excluding precious metals and improved margins despite additional research and development expenditure on fuel cells. PMD's sales excluding precious metals fell, partly reflecting the impact of lower metal prices on commissions, and partly following the exit from low margin product manufacturing in Canada which improved return on sales.

Colours & Coatings' sales were slightly up but margins fell, particularly in the Tableware sector. Urgent action has been taken to reduce costs. Pharmaceutical Materials' sales and margins show the impact of the acquisitions made in the year.

	Sales excluding Precious Metals		Return on Sales	
	2001	**2002**	2001	**2002**
	£ million	**£ million**	%	**%**
Catalysts & Chemicals	535	**597**	15.1	**15.9**
Precious Metals	162	**143**	35.5	**39.1**
Colours & Coatings	246	**251**	13.1	**10.2**
Pharmaceutical Materials	30	**101**	60.2	**30.9**
Discontinued	4	**1**	n/m	**n/m**
	977	**1,093**	17.9	**17.7**

Return on Investment

We set a target of 20% for the pre-tax return on assets (ROA) for all our businesses. For the group as a whole ROA was 22.2% (see pages 66 and 67) compared with 26.4% in 2000/01. The decline in the overall return reflects the more difficult trading conditions experienced in the year and the impact of the acquisitions made which are expected to take a few years to meet the group's target.

On a post-tax basis the return on invested capital was 15.6% which was well above the estimated weighted average cost of capital (WACC) for the group of 9%. The margin above the cost of capital for the year was 6.6%, which was below last year's figure of 8.5% but still very healthy.

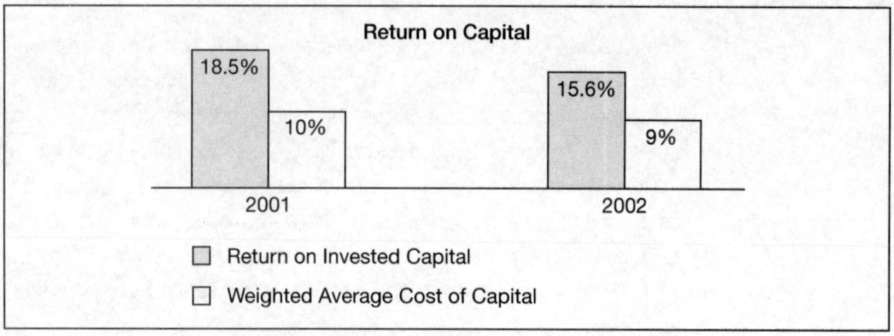

Exceptional Items and Goodwill Amortisation

Exceptional items included in operating profit gave rise to a net charge of £18.1 million. They comprised the cost of rationalising production in the Tableware sector of Colours & Coatings (£24.0 million); the cost of eliminating board and other related costs at Meconic plc following its acquisition (£1.3 million); partly offset by a gain on disposal of some of the group's holding of unhedged palladium stock (£7.2 million).

In addition, in early September 2001 we sold our loss-making French ceramic print business (part of Tableware). This sale gave rise to an exceptional book loss of £5.5 million shown in sale of discontinued operations.

Goodwill amortisation increased to £6.8 million following the acquisitions of Meconic plc, Pharm-Eco Laboratories, Inc., and Avocado Research Chemicals Limited.

Interest and Exchange Rates

The group had a net interest charge of £6.1 million for the year compared with a net credit of £5.3 million last year. The change reflects the funding cost of the major investments and share buybacks undertaken in the period. Interest payable on gold and silver leases rose to £3.5 million in the year, compared with £1.4 million last year. This rise reflects higher average holdings and also high lease rates, particularly for silver in the second half of the year.

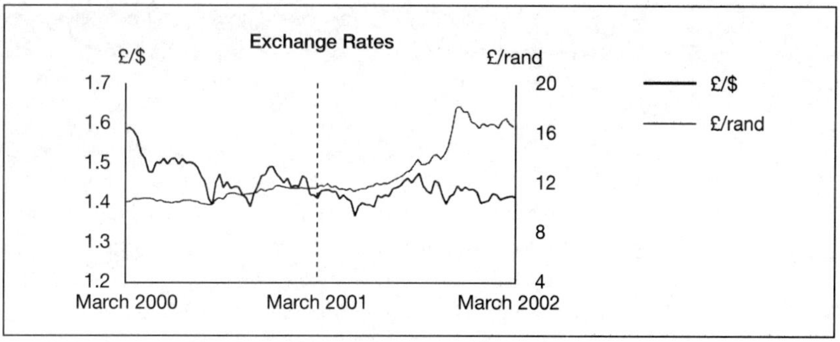

Exchange translation reduced the group's profits by £2.1 million compared with 2000/01. The group benefited from the stronger US dollar which averaged $1.43/£ compared with $1.48/£ for our last financial year. However, this benefit was more than offset by the impact of other currencies, particularly the South African rand which averaged R13.7/£ compared with R10.8/£ in 2000/01. To some extent the group was able to mitigate this weakness by linking the prices of products manufactured in South Africa to the Euro or US dollar, which produced higher profits in rands.

Taxation

This year the group has adopted FRS 19, a new accounting standard requiring companies to provide fully for deferred tax. Last year's results have been restated accordingly. The effect of the new standard is to increase the group's average tax rate by about 1%, and to increase the net deferred tax liability included in the balance sheet by £44.3 million.

Compared with last year's restated figure, the group's total tax charge fell by £4.0 million, as a result of the inclusion of tax credits on the exceptional charges. Excluding these credits, tax was £1.9 million higher than last year, reflecting the growth in profit before tax.

Before exceptional items and goodwill amortisation the average tax rate for the year was 29.9%, which was very similar to last year.

Cash Flow

Johnson Matthey's net cash inflow from operations rose by 43% to £224.1 million. Working capital showed a small net inflow of £1.9 million. A significant reduction in debtors was achieved, benefiting in part from the fall in the palladium price. Inventories rose significantly at year end, part of which should be temporary, as metal holdings have been increased during the major upgrading of the pgm refinery at Royston.

Capital expenditure rose to £133.8 million, which was nearly £30 million higher than last year and represents about 2.8 times depreciation. Capital expenditure in 2002/03 is budgeted to be somewhat lower, at around 2 times depreciation. As a consequence of the high level of capital expenditure in 2001/02, free cash flow for the group (after interest, tax and dividends but before acquisitions and share buy-backs) was negative at £19.6 million.

The group spent a total of £230.9 million on acquisitions, which included £46.8 million of debt acquired and £40.6 million of loan notes issued as part of the purchase price. We also bought back 4.9 million shares in the year for a cash cost of £45.9 million (an average price of £9.32 per share), which has improved the financial efficiency of the balance sheet, and was earnings enhancing. As a consequence of this expenditure the group moved from a net cash position of £139.9 million at 31st March 2001 to a net borrowing position of £159.0 million at 31st March 2002. Johnson Matthey's balance sheet remains very strong, with shareholders' funds of £813.7 million and gearing (net borrowings/shareholders' funds and minority interests) of 19%.

Pensions

In the accounts for the year ended 31st March 2002 the group is adopting the transitional arrangements for reporting under FRS 17, the new accounting standard on retirement benefits. Under these arrangements the surplus or deficit arising on the group's pension funds calculated in accordance with FRS 17 is shown as a note on the accounts on pages 46 and 47.

The group operates significant defined benefit pension schemes in the UK and in the US. At 31st March 2002 the group had a net surplus before tax on these schemes of £106.7 million calculated using FRS 17. Reported earnings for 2001/02 would not have been materially different under the new standard.

Financial Risk Management

We use financial instruments, in particular forward currency contracts and currency swaps, to manage the financial risks associated with our underlying business activities and the financing of those activities. The group does not undertake any trading activity in financial instruments. Our Treasury department is run as a service centre rather than a profit centre.

Interest Rate Risk

At 31st March 2002 the group had net borrowings of £159.0 million. This included £70.2 million (US $100 million) of long term fixed rate borrowings in the form of an issue of US dollar bonds, which carry an interest coupon of 6.36%. The remaining 56% of the group's net borrowings are funded on a floating rate basis, mainly in the form of loans under committed bank facilities. A 1% change in all interest rates would have a 0.6% impact on group profit before tax. This is well within the range the board regards as acceptable.

Liquidity Policy

Our policy on funding capacity is to ensure that we always have sufficient long term funding and committed bank facilities in place to meet foreseeable peak borrowing requirements. The group has committed bank facilities of £255 million. Borrowings drawn under these facilities at 31st March 2002 amounted to £107.5 million. The group also has a number of uncommitted facilities and overdraft lines.

Foreign Currency Risk

Johnson Matthey's operations are global in nature with the majority of the group's operating profits earned outside the UK. The group has operations in 34 countries with the largest single investment being in the USA. In order to protect the group's sterling balance sheet and reduce cash flow risk, we finance most of our US investment by US dollar borrowings. Although most of this funding is obtained by directly borrowing US dollars, some is achieved by using currency swaps to reduce costs and credit exposure. We also use local currency borrowings to fund our operations in other countries (see page 52).

We use forward exchange contracts to hedge foreign exchange exposures arising on forecast receipts and payments in foreign currencies. Currency options are occasionally used to hedge foreign exchange exposures, usually when the forecast receipt or payment amounts are uncertain. Details of the contracts outstanding on 31st March 2002 are shown on page 55.

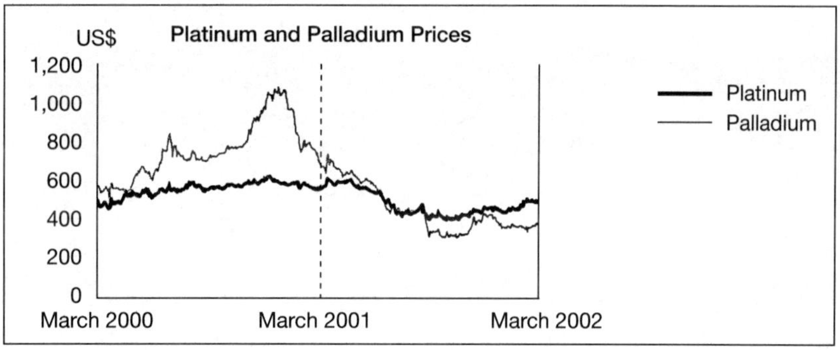

Precious Metal Prices

Fluctuations in precious metal prices can have a significant impact on Johnson Matthey's financial results. Our policy for all our manufacturing businesses is to limit this exposure by hedging against future price changes where such hedging can be done at acceptable cost. The group does not take material exposures on metal trading.

All the group's stocks of gold and silver are fully hedged by leasing or forward sales. Currently the majority of the group's platinum group metal stocks are unhedged because of the lack of liquidity in the platinum metal markets.

There are some interesting disclosures in its financial review, including:

- Precious metal prices have a significant effect on turnover
- The two key exchange rates are the US dollar and the South African rand.
- A 1% movement in interest rates affects profit before tax by 0.6%.

8

Accounts in other countries

- **United States of America** – introduction; the income statement (sometimes called the statement of earnings); the balance sheet (sometimes called the statement of financial position); the cash flow statement; comprehensive income; American accounts
- **France** – introduction; the profit and loss account (Compe de résultat); balance sheet (Bilan); cash flow statement (Tableau des flux de trésorerie); French accounts
- **Germany** – introduction; profit and loss account (Gewinn-und Verlustrechnung); balance sheet (Bilanz); cash flow statement (Kapitalflussrechnung bewegungsbilanz); German accounts
- **Japan** – introduction; profit and loss account; balance sheet; cash flow statement; Japanese accounts

There are a number of pressures for the standardisation of accounting practices and the way accounts are presented. This harmonisation process gained pace following the spread of the Asian financial and economic crisis in 1998. This prompted the G7 Finance Ministers and Central Bank Governors to press countries operating in global stock markets to use internationally agreed standards. In June 2002 the European Union agreed that most European companies listed on a Stock Exchange would use international accounting standards (IAS) by January 2005, and all by 2007. Member states have the option to extend IAS to unlisted companies, and it's likely that most countries will choose to do this. In June 2002 seven member states already allowed listed companies to prepare their accounts using the international standards (Austria, Belgium, Finland, France, Germany, Italy and Luxembourg). This move to international standards is not just a European phenomenon; Australia has recently announced its intention to use them. In the future international accounting standards are likely to be the basis of accounting in most countries, with only the USA seeing a role for locally established standards.

However, there are still a number of important differences in European accounting practices, as whilst the international standards provide agreed underlying principles they usually allow a number of methods to be used. And currently the European harmonisation process is incomplete. I'll summarise the main differences between the accounting and presentation in the UK and that of the USA, France, Germany and Japan in September 2002. However, the speed of the European harmonisation process may mean that some of the differences I've highlighted between French, German and UK accounting practices could have disappeared by the time you read this book.

Listed companies in these countries prepare similar financial statements to those found in the UK, including a profit and loss account, balance sheet and cash flow statement, whereas private companies usually provide less information than their UK counterparts.

The presentation of the profit and loss accounts and balance sheets in the European countries is similar to our own, as they are derived from European Union directives. But even within EU countries there are considerable differences. There were two balance sheet formats and four profit and loss account formats in the fourth directive. The preferred format, and the way that these formats have been adhered to, varies widely across Europe.

United States of America

Introduction

America and Britain have the reputation of being separated by a common language, and this is as true in accounting as in any other area of life. You may find the terminology used in American accounts unfamiliar, and so I've given you a 'translation' of the main terms in Table 8.1.

Table 8.1 UK and US accounting terms

UK	USA
Associated undertaking	*Affiliated enterprise*
Balance sheet	*Balance sheet*
	Statement of financial position
Creditors	*Payables*
	Accounts payable
Earnings per share	*Net income per share*
	Net earnings per share
Debtors	*Receivables*
	Accounts receivable
Financial review	*Management's discussion of financial resources and liquidity*
Financial year	*Fiscal year*
Operating review	*Management's discussion of operations*
Ordinary shares	*Common stock*
Own shares (as in buy-backs)	*Treasury stock*
Profit and loss account	*Income statement*
	Statement of earnings
Profit and loss account reserve	*Retained earnings*
Provisions	*Accounting for loss contingencies*
	Reserves
Scrip dividend	*Stock dividend*
Share premium account	*Paid in surplus*
Shares	*Stock*
Stock	*Inventory*
Tangible fixed assets	*Property, plant and equipment*
Total recognised gains and losses	*Comprehensive income*
Turnover	*Revenue/sales*

You'll often find American terms used in English translations of overseas accounts. For example, Japanese accounts are always translated into American English.

Only listed companies have to follow a standard format, and I'll cover the listed company presentation in this chapter. American companies will publish a profit and loss account, a balance sheet and a cash flow statement. Public companies publish quarterly interim statements, which tend to be more detailed than the ones prepared in the UK.

The income statement (sometimes called the statement of earnings)

The profit and loss account is known as the income statement, or statement of earnings. There are two possible presentations:

- The commonest presentation is similar to a UK Format 1 profit and loss account. Cost of sales is deducted from sales to show gross profit, then other income and costs are deducted to show operating income and income before and after tax.
- The alternative is a 'single-step' format where all of the costs and expenses, subdivided either by function or business segment, are deducted from the total income. Income taxes may be shown either as the last expense item or as a separate item after a subtotal 'income before income taxes'.

These formats are not always followed, as different industries have adapted these presentations. (For example, in the finance sector, the income statement differentiates net interest income before, and after, provision for loan losses. Its presentation is more complex, showing the sources of income on the face of the profit and loss account, and disclosing a number of income figures.)

Major differences

Some of the main differences are:

Capitalisation of interest

Interest must be capitalised if:

- The company has built the assets for its own use.
- The assets are constructed in distinct projects and will be sold, or leased (e.g. ships).
- The company has to spend additional money to start operations in an investment in order to start trading. This investment must be accounted for using the equity method.

Extraordinary items

Extraordinary items are still common in American accounts. Extraordinary items are defined as a transaction that is distinguished by its unusual nature and infrequency of its occurrence.

Dividends

Dividends are not shown on the accounts until they are formally declared, when they are shown as a liability and a deduction from retained earnings. The only dividends shown on the profit and loss account are those paid during the year.

Earnings per share

All public companies show a number of earnings per share figures, calculated using:

- profit before extraordinary items;
- profit from continuing operations;

- profit from discontinued operations;
- any cumulative effect of a change in accounting policies.

Comparatives

Three years' profit and loss accounts are shown in the accounts.

The balance sheet (sometimes called the statement of financial position)

Balance sheets are prepared using an assets and liabilities format and they generally show assets and liabilities in decreasing order of liquidity. (This means that cash is the first asset shown, and fixed assets the last. This is the opposite of the UK practice of showing assets and liabilities in reverse order of liquidity with fixed assets first and cash last.)

Major differences

Some of the main differences are:

Goodwill

Goodwill is capitalised and, since December 2001, does not have to be amortised. It is reassessed annually to see if there has been any impairment in value. Any impairment is then charged to the profit and loss account.

Fixed assets

Property, plant and equipment must be shown at historical cost and depreciated. Companies can only revalue assets when they acquire another company, as the assets of the acquired company have to be restated to fair values.

Debtors

Debtors due after a year are shown separately and aren't included in current assets, as all current assets must be realisable within a year.

Shares

State laws govern the issue of shares, and in some states they can be issued with, or without, a par value.

Comparatives

Two years' balance sheets are shown in the accounts.

The cash flow statement

The cash flow statement is similar to that found in the UK, with fewer cash flow classifications:

- *Operating activities:* these include the cash flows from interest and taxation.
- *Investing activities:* this covers both capital expenditure and financial investment and acquisitions and disposals.
- *Financing activities.*
- *Cash and cash equivalents:* a 'cash equivalent' is a short-term investment, or loan, that usually has an original maturity of less than three months.

Comparatives

Three years' cash flow statements are shown in the accounts.

Comprehensive income

This is effectively the same as the UK's total recognised gains and losses. It may be presented:

- as a separate statement and starting with net income;
- below net income on the income statement;
- in a statement of the changes in equity.

American accounts

Examples of the commonest presentation of the profit and loss account, balance sheet and cash flow statement used by American companies are shown in Tables 8.2, 8.3 and 8.4.

Table 8.2 American income statement

Revenues and other income
Sales and operating revenue
Income from equity affiliates
Other income
Total revenues and other income
Cost of goods sold
Selling, general and administrative expenses
Other income (expenses)
Investment income
Gain on sale of investment
Interest expense
Minority interest
Total costs and expenses
Income (loss) from continuing operations before taxes, discontinued operations, and extraordinary charge
Provision (benefit) for income taxes
Income (loss) from continuing operations before discontinued operations and extraordinary charge
Discontinued operation, net of taxes:
Income from discontinued operation
Gain (loss) on sale of discontinued operation
Income before extraordinary charge
Extraordinary charge
Net income
Other comprehensive income, net of tax:
Foreign currency translation adjustments
Unrealised gains on securities net of reclassification adjustment
Minimum pension liability adjustment
Other comprehensive income
Comprehensive income
Basic earnings per share:
Continuing operations
Discontinued operations
Extraordinary charge
Basic earnings per share
Diluted earnings per share:
Continuing operations
Discontinued operations
Extraordinary charge
Diluted earnings per share

Table 8.3 American balance sheet

ASSETS
Current assets:
Cash and cash equivalents
Marketable securities
Total cash and marketable securities
Accounts and notes receivable, less allowances
Inventories, less allowances
Other current assets
Total current assets
Investments and other assets:
Investments in and advances to jointly owned companies
Other investments
Total investments and other assets
Property plant and equipment:
Land
Buildings
Machinery and equipment
Construction in progress
Less accumulated depreciation
Plant, property and equipment – net
Intangible assets
Deferred income taxes
Other assets
Net assets of discontinued operations
TOTAL ASSETS
LIABILITIES & STOCKHOLDERS' EQUITY
Current liabilities:
Accounts payable
Payable to affiliated companies
Loans payable
Accrued expenses
Taxes
Other current liabilities
Total current liabilities
Long-term debt
Deferred income and other non-current obligations
Reserves for employee benefit plans
Other non-current liabilities
Minority interests
Total liabilities
Stockholders' equity
Preferred stock
Common stock
Additional paid in capital
Retained earnings
Sub-total
Accumulated foreign currency translation adjustments
Net unrealised gain on securities
Accumulated other comprehensive loss
Total stockholders' equity
TOTAL LIABILITIES AND STOCKHOLDERS' EQUITY

Table 8.4 American cash flow statement

Cash flows from operating activities:
Net income
Adjustments to reconcile net income to net cash provided by operating activities:

Depreciation and amortisation
Provision for losses on accounts receivable
Loss on sale of investment
(Gain)/loss on sale of discontinued operation
Deferred income taxes
Minority interest
Change in assets and liabilities net of effects from acquired companies:
Increase in accounts receivable
Increase in inventory
(Increase)/decrease in prepaid expenses
Increase (decrease) in checks outstanding
Increase in accounts payable and accrued expenses
Decrease in income taxes payable
Net cash provided by operating activities

Cash flows from investing activities:
Proceeds from sale of investment
Proceeds from sale of discontinued operation
Capital expenditures
Net assets of acquired companies, net of cash acquired
Other assets
Net cash used in investing activities

Cash flows from financing activities:
Proceeds from issuance of long-term debt
Sale of common stock under option plans and ESOP
Cash dividends paid
Net cash provided by financing activities

Net increase in cash and cash equivalents
Cash and cash equivalents at beginning of year
Cash and cash equivalents at end of year

Supplemental cash flow information:
Interest (net of amount capitalised)
Income taxes

France

Introduction

Accounting standards are part of French business law and all businesses have to comply with them. There are a number of different sources of law, and in April 1998, an official accounting body was created, the *Comité de la Réglementation Comptable* (CRC), which is responsible for approving new accounting standards. It was created as, historically, French accounting standards:

- could be interpreted in several ways – the CRC's standards are designed to be more specific and to improve the transparency of the financial statements;
- had been set by several sources, and there was a need to provide more consistency to the standard-setting process.

French accounting is largely encapsulated in the accounting plan (Plan Comptable Général). This is prepared by a government committee and has the force of law. It is very prescriptive, making French accounts very easy to read, as everything is shown in the same place in the accounts and is calculated in a similar manner.

The French Code de Commerce allows companies listed on the French Stock Exchange to prepare financial statements using International Accounting Standards (IAS). However, the CRC has not yet endorsed the requirements for adopting this option, and French companies still have to produce their primary financial statements under French GAAP. However, by 2005 all French listed companies will be preparing accounts using international accounting standards.

Small and medium-sized companies are allowed to prepare abbreviated accounts. These accounts would disclose similar information to those prepared by UK companies, with medium-sized companies making fewer disclosures in the notes to the accounts.

There are different rules for consolidated accounts and individual companies' statutory accounts. Individual companies' accounts are strongly influenced by the tax rules. Fiscal considerations often appear to override the need for a true and fair view, even though the true and fair view is supposed to be the overriding legal principle. This is still affecting French reporting, as the individual company's accounts tend to reflect the tax accounts, whereas the consolidated accounts are based on the true and fair view. For example, in June 2002, depreciation could still be calculated differently in the individual and consolidated financial statements. This means that the individual company accounts can't really be used for comparative purposes, as they're prepared on a different basis.

French companies do not have to publish a statement similar to the statement of total recognised gains and losses.

The profit and loss account (Compte de résultat)

Whilst the law allows the profit and loss account to be prepared either horizontally or vertically, most French profit and loss accounts are presented vertically using a similar presentation to Format 2 in the UK. The main presentational difference is that there is no requirement to analyse turnover and profit between continuing and discontinued operations on the face of the profit and loss account.

Major differences

Some of the main differences are:

Depreciation

In the consolidated accounts, the depreciation charge reflects the economic depreciation and is usually calculated using the straight line method.

However, to qualify for tax deduction, depreciation is charged using the standard rates accepted by tax authorities in the individual company's accounts. This means that other methods are often used in the statutory accounts where the depreciation charge is based on advantageous tax rules and options. Consequently, French companies usually have to restate their depreciation charge in their consolidated accounts.

Provisions

Large French companies disclose more information about their provisions than their British counterparts. French companies show the different types of provisions, analysing those relating to asset write-downs (with provisions relating to fixed assets and current assets disclosed separately) and those relating to potential liabilities and losses. However, many provisions are tax deductible, and the provisions often bear little resemblance to the commercial reality in individual companies' accounts that would seem to be consistent with the true and fair view. The provisions that have been made for tax purposes are 'corrected' in the consolidated accounts, which consequently show deferred tax provisions.

From 1 January 2002 the basis for recognising provisions became broadly similar to the UK's. (The old rules did not allow provisions for general risks, and provisions could be recognised even if they couldn't be reliably measured.)

Associates

Only the share of the associate's profit after tax is disclosed.

Extraordinary items

Extraordinary items are called 'exceptionnel' in France. They cover items that would be considered both extraordinary and exceptional in the UK. They include all items outside normal trading activities, and would include things like profits or losses from the sale of fixed assets and restructuring costs. In their consolidated accounts, companies can show exceptional and extraordinary items separately, and include most of their exceptional items in operating income (or loss).

Dividends

Dividends paid and proposed are not shown on the profit and loss account for the year, but are deducted from reserves in the year they're paid. It's less common for listed companies to pay interim dividends.

Research and development

Research and development costs are usually written off as incurred, but the company can make exceptions if a project is technically feasible and commercially viable. Once it has been capitalised, it should be written off as soon as possible, usually within five years. If the project subsequently is found to be unviable, the costs have to be written off immediately. Whilst the research and development is capitalised, dividends can only be paid if the reserves are sufficient to cover the research and development asset.

Balance sheet (Bilan)

Balance sheets are prepared on an assets and liabilities (actif et passif) format, with assets and liabilities being shown in reverse order of liquidity. They are prepared horizontally, with assets shown on one side and liabilities on the other. The liabilities are not split between current and long-term amounts.

At first glance the French balance sheet appears more detailed than a UK balance sheet. However, the degree of detail shown in both countries is similar; the difference lies in *where* the detail is found. In France the detailed information is usually shown on the balance sheet itself, rather than in the notes.

Major differences

Some of the main differences are:

Fixed assets

Balance sheet valuations are unlikely to reflect market values. Fixed assets are largely based on historical cost, with revaluations occasionally allowed by the Ministry of the Economy and Finance. Fixed assets were revalued as a result of the 1978 fiscal laws in accordance with certain inflation-based ratios; previous revaluations were conducted in 1959 and 1945. Any other revaluations are subject to tax, and consequently are rarely made. The revaluations must not exceed the market values of the assets. There is no requirement to keep revaluations up to date.

French law requires a general impairment review every 12 months. This means that if the net book value of an asset appears to be overstated, the asset is written off to its estimated recoverable amount by a 'provision'. This provision can subsequently be reversed if the asset's value increases.

Companies don't have to capitalise finance leases, although this is the preferred accounting treatment.

Investment properties

As there are no specific rules for investment properties, they are treated in the same way as any other property.

Joint ventures

Joint ventures are proportionally consolidated into the accounts.

Legal reserves

These are non-distributable reserves that are designed to increase the company's undistributable capital base and provide more protection for creditors. In the statutory accounts, a minimum of 5% of retained profits must be transferred to a designated legal reserve (*réserve légale*) each year until it equals 10% of the issued share capital. A company's articles of association may require an additional element of profit to be transferred to non-distributable statutory or contractual reserves, called *reserves statutaires*.

Cash flow statement (Tableau des flux de trésorerie)

A cash flow statement is recommended by the Plan Comptable, and all companies preparing consolidated financial statements must now publish one. The French cash flow statement has been influenced by the international standard, as it:

- reports gross cash receipts and gross cash payments arising from:
  - operating activities;
  - investing activities;
  - financing activities;
- shows a reconciliation of the changes in the balance of cash and cash equivalents for the period.

The cash flows arising from acquisitions and disposals of subsidiaries are disclosed as a separate item under financing activities, and include the amount of cash and cash equivalents in the subsidiary either acquired or disposed of.

French accounts

Examples of the presentation of the profit and loss account, balance sheet and cash flow statement usually used by French companies are shown in Tables 8.5, 8.6 and 8.7.

Table 8.5 French profit and loss account

Turnover
Other operating income
Purchases used in sales
Staff costs
Other operating charges
Taxes other than income taxes
Depreciation and amortisation
Operating income (loss)
Net interest income (expense)
Other income (expense)
Income (loss) before tax of fully consolidated undertakings
Income taxes
Net income (loss) of fully consolidated undertakings
Share of the net income (loss) of associated undertakings
Goodwill amortisation
Net income (loss) before minority interests
Minority interests
Net income (loss)
Earnings per share
Diluted earnings per share

Table 8.6 French balance sheet

Assets	Liabilities and shareholders' equity
Fixed assets	**Shareholders' equity**
Goodwill	Share capital
Intangible fixed assets	Share premium account
Tangible fixed assets	Profit and loss account
Investments	Other reserves
Investments accounted for using the equity method	Total shareholders' equity
Total fixed assets	
	Minority interests
Current assets	
Stocks and work in progress	**Provisions for liabilities and charges**
Trade debtors and related accounts	
Other debtors and prepayments	**Creditors:**
Short-term investments	Borrowings and other financial liabilities
Cash at bank and in hand	Trade creditors and related accounts
Total current assets	Other creditors and accruals
	Total creditors
Total assets	**Total liabilities and shareholders' equity**

Table 8.7 French cash flow statement

Net income of fully consolidated undertakings
Adjustments to reconcile net income to net cash provided by operations
Depreciation and provisions
Changes in deferred taxes
(Gains) or losses on disposal of fixed assets
Cash flow from operating activities of fully consolidated undertakings
Dividends received from associated undertakings
Changes in working capital:
(Increase) decrease in stocks
(Increase) decrease in debtors
Increase (decrease) in creditors
Net cash provided by operating activities
Cash flow from investing activities
Purchase of fixed assets
Sale of fixed assets, net of taxes
Purchase of businesses
Sale of businesses
Net cash flow from investing activities
Cash flow from financing activities
Dividends paid:
Dividends paid to ordinary shareholders
Dividends paid to minority interests
Issue of share capital
Purchase of own shares
Increase in loans
Repayments of loans
Net cash from financing activities
Change in cash
Cash at the beginning of the year
Effects of exchange rate fluctuations
Cash at the end of the year

Germany

Introduction

German accounting was historically noted for its uniformity and was based on the historical accounting rules found in their Commercial Code (Handelsgesetzbuch – abbreviated to HGB). German accounts were determined by the tax rules, and one of the major elements of German accounting law was 'Massgeblichkeitsprinzip' (literally translated as the principle of bindingness). This meant that the tax accounts were prepared on the same basis as those prepared for the shareholders, and many tax allowances could only be taken if they were reflected in the accounts. The effect of this is that in Germany there were relatively few differences between tax and financial accounts. However, recent legislation, both commercial and taxation, is changing this relationship.

The changes started in 1998 when:

- Listed companies were allowed to prepare their consolidated financial statements according to International Accounting Standards (IAS) or US Generally Accepted Accounting Principles (US GAAP) rather than according to German GAAP (companies currently using US GAAP have until 2007 to change to IAS).
- The government established the German Accounting Standards Committee (Deutsches Rechnungslegungs Standards Committee or DRSC). Part of its brief was to develop accounting standards for listed companies' consolidated financial statements and to liaise with international standard setters. The DRSC is currently aligning its accounting standards with IAS.

Four new laws have come into force since 1998 that have significantly changed the Commercial Code and contributed towards convergence of German accounting principles with international accounting practice. In February 2002 the harmonisation process continued with:

- The publication of a German Corporate Governance Codex. Whilst compliance will be voluntary it has recommended that:
  - consolidated financial statements and interim statements are prepared under internationally accepted accounting rules;
  - companies extend their disclosures. This includes the compensation of Management Board members and details of their share options.
- A reform of the Commercial Code and the Stock Corporation law. These amendments will align the code and the law with international practices and further erode the relationship between the consolidated financial statements and the tax regulations.

However, there are still considerable differences in the presentation of individual (statutory) accounts and the consolidated accounts. In Germany, profit distributions are assessed and taxed on the basis of the companies' individual accounts. This meant that in the past the individual accounts were viewed as the most important, with the consolidated financial statements having little significance. This is now changing, with the consolidated financial statements becoming the main focus of public interest.

All companies are required to prepare a balance sheet, profit and loss account and notes to the accounts, which must present a true and fair view. A cash flow statement doesn't have to be included in individual companies (statutory) financial statements. But all listed companies have to include a statement of cash flows in the notes to their consolidated financial statements. Companies also have to prepare a management report ('Lagebericht') that is consistent with the information in the financial statements. There is no requirement to prepare a statement that is similar to the statement of total recognised gains and losses.

Profit and loss account (Gewinn-und Verlustrechnung)

The profit and loss account must be presented vertically, using similar presentations to those found in the UK.

Major differences

Some of the main differences are:

Discontinued operations

There are no rules requiring the separate disclosure of discontinued operations.

Provisions

Provisions are only created where obligations to third parties exist, but there is a more extensive recognition of provisions than that found in the UK.

Dividends

Any dividends shown on the profit and loss account are the dividends paid, or those for which a formal shareholders' resolution exists. Most companies pay dividends annually.

Research and development

Development costs are more likely to be shown as an intangible asset.

Long-term contracts

The 'percentage of completion' method can only be used in exceptional circumstances. This means that most long-term contracts are not shown in the profit and loss account until they are substantially finished. An alignment proposal was issued in 2002 covering construction contracts.

Balance sheet (Bilanz)

Balance sheets are prepared on an assets and liabilities format, with assets and liabilities being shown in reverse order of liquidity. They're usually presented in a horizontal format, with assets on one side and liabilities on the other. However, in Germany liabilities don't have to be analysed between current and long term on the balance sheet; this disclosure can be given in the notes to the accounts.

Major differences

Some of the main differences are:

Fixed assets

The revaluation of assets is not allowed. Whilst the German Commercial Code requires finance leases to be capitalised, there are fewer finance leases in Germany largely because of the unfavourable tax treatment. Most leases are designed to qualify as operating leases in order to avoid capitalisation.

Stocks

Stocks are valued at the lower of cost and either of:

- net realisable value;
- market value;
- replacement value.

Long-term contract work in progress must be valued at cost, as the percentage of completion basis is generally not allowed.

Reserves

To protect creditors, companies are required to transfer 5% of their annual profits into a legal reserve until it reaches 10% of the issued share capital.

Shareholders' funds

Shareholders' funds and minority interests are not analysed between equity and non-equity.

Cash flow statement (Kapitalflussrechnung bewegungsbilanz)

On 31 May 2000 the standard on the cash flow statement (DRS 2) was published and its requirements are broadly similar to FRS 1 in the UK, with fewer classifications of cash flows. The German accounting standard recommends that cash flows are classified under the following headings:

- current business activities;
- investment activities (including disposals);
- financing activities.

Listed companies must prepare a cash flow statement.

German accounts

Examples of the presentation of the profit and loss account, balance sheet and cash flow statement usually prepared by German companies as shown in Tables 8.8, 8.9 and 8.10.

Table 8.8 German profit and loss account

Sales
Cost of sales
Gross profit on sales
Selling expenses
General administration expenses
Other operating income
Other operating expenses
Operating profit
Share of profits and losses of companies accounted for using the equity method
Income from other investments and financial assets
Other interest and similar income
Interest and similar expenses
Financial result
Results from ordinary activities
Extraordinary income
Extraordinary expenses
Extraordinary result
Profit before tax
Taxes on income
Profit after tax
Minority interests
Net profit (loss) for the year attributable to ordinary shareholders
Earnings per ordinary share
Diluted earnings per ordinary share

Table 8.9 German balance sheet

Assets	Equity and liabilities
Non-current assets	**Capital and reserves**
Intangible fixed assets	Subscribed capital
Tangible fixed assets	Capital reserve (Share premium account)
Investments accounted for using the equity method	Revenue reserves (includes statutory reserves and the capital redemption reserve)
Other financial assets	Accumulated profits
Total non-current assets	Total capital and reserves
Current assets	Minority interests
Stocks and work in progress	Provisions for liabilities and charges
Trade debtors	Deferred tax liabilities
Other debtors and assets	
Marketable securities	**Liabilities**:
Cash at bank and in hand	Non current borrowings
Total current assets	Current borrowings
	Trade creditors
Deferred tax assets	Other creditors
Prepayments and deferred charges	Total liabilities
	Deferred income
Total assets	**Total equity and liabilities**

Table 8.10 German cash flow statement

Operating activities
Net profit
Adjustments to reconcile net income to net cash provided by operations:
  Depreciation and amortisation
  Change in provisions
  Changes in deferred taxes
  (Gains) or losses on disposal of fixed assets
  Share of retained earnings of companies accounted for using the equity method
  Other (income) or expenses not affecting cash flow
Changes in working capital:
  (Increase) decrease in stocks
  (Increase) decrease in debtors
  Increase (decrease) in creditors
Net cash flows from operating activities

Cash flow from investing activities
Purchase of fixed assets
Sale of fixed assets, net of taxes
Purchase of businesses
Sale of businesses
Net cash flow from investing activities

Cash flow from financing activities
Dividends paid:
  Dividends paid to ordinary shareholders
  Dividends paid to minority interests
Issue of share capital
Purchase of own shares
Increase in loans
Repayments of loans
Net cash from financing activities

Change in cash and cash equivalents
Effects of exchange rate fluctuations
Cash at the beginning of the year
Cash at the end of the year

Japan

Introduction

Traditional Japanese accounting evolved from three major influences:

- a local, medieval tradition of double entry bookkeeping;
- the adoption of the Prussian commercial legal code in the nineteenth century, reflected in the commercial code;
- the post-war influence of American practices reflected in the securities and exchange law.

Historically, Japan didn't have a tradition of accounting disclosure, largely as a result of the structure of its share ownership. Both suppliers and customers are likely to be shareholders in Japanese companies, with investment decisions being influenced more by the possibility of long-term sales growth than any short-term profit maximisation. This cross-ownership of companies and emphasis on long-term decision making made the interpretation of Japanese accounts difficult. However, the Asian financial crisis hastened the process of international harmonisation. In November 1996 Japan embarked on a change process that has dramatically improved the international comparability of its financial statements.

Between 1997 and 2002 it has:

- moved the responsibility for standard setting from the government to an independent standard setting authority;
- more closely aligned its reporting with international and US accounting standards;
- developed new auditing standards that become effective in 2002;
- allowed companies that were also registered with the US SEC and submitting form 20F to prepare their accounts using US GAAP. (The regulation doesn't allow IAS consolidated financial statements to substitute for Japanese GAAP, only those prepared using US GAAP.) This happened in 2002.

Under Japanese rules, it's possible that not all of the subsidiaries consolidated in the accounts use the same accounting policies. Overseas subsidiaries can use different policies if they conform to those used in the country where they're located.

You'll find that the current year's results are also shown in US dollars, usually based on year end exchange rates. (This information is provided to help readers who are unfamiliar with the value of the Japanese yen.) It doesn't represent the amount obtained if the yen has been, or could be, converted into US dollars.

Profit and loss account

The Japanese statement of income is similar to the UK's Format 1 profit and loss account.

Major differences

Some of the main differences are:

Provisions

There is a wider definition of provisions, and they can be based on directors' decisions before an obligation arises.

Extraordinary items

These are widely defined and are shown before tax. They include both exceptional and extraordinary items, some of which would not be regarded as material in the UK.

Other income and expenses

This usually includes profits and losses on sale of assets, exceptional and extraordinary costs.

Balance sheet

Balance sheets are prepared using the assets and liabilities format, showing both in decreasing order of liquidity.

Major differences

Some of the main differences are:

Fixed assets

Fixed assets are usually shown at historical cost less depreciation, although there is a temporary regulation allowing land to be revalued. (This revaluation doesn't have to be kept up to date.) The definition of leases is different, as leases, apart from those transferring ownership to the lessee, can be treated as operating leases. Finance leases may be, but don't have to be, capitalised, and capitalising finance leases is very rare because of the tax implications. Leased assets are disclosed in the notes to the accounts.

Stocks

Stocks are generally shown at cost, not the lower of cost and net realisable value. The Commercial Code does not require companies to make provisions for any falls in value.

Reserves

You may find three types of reserves shown in Japanese accounts:

- **Capital reserve**: this includes the share premium account.
- **Legal earned reserve**: this is designed to protect creditors, and is similar to that found in many European countries. Companies must build up the legal reserve to 25% of share capital, by allocating at least 10% of dividends until the required amount is reached.
- **Other surpluses**: this is undistributed profits and proposed dividends.

Cash flow statement

The Japanese cash flow statement is similar to the US one.

Japanese accounts

Examples of the presentation of the profit and loss account, balance sheet and cash flow statement usually prepared by Japanese companies following Japanese accounting rules are shown in Tables 8.11, 8.12 and 8.13. (Some of the larger Japanese companies prepare their accounts using American accounting rules.)

Table 8.11 Japanese profit and loss account

Net sales
Cost of sales
Gross profit
Selling, general and administrative expenses
Other operating income
Other operating expenses
Operating income
Interest and dividend income
Interest expense
Other income
Other expenses
Income before income taxes and minority interests
Income taxes:
Current
Deferred
Minority interests
Net income
Per share of common stock:
Basic
Diluted
Dividends

Table 8.12 Japanese balance sheet

Assets	Liabilities, minority interests and stockholders' equity
Current assets:	**Current liabilities:**
Cash and cash equivalents	Trade notes and accounts payable
Trade notes and accounts receivable	Short-term borrowings
Marketable securities	Current portion of long-term debt
Inventories	Accrued income taxes
Short-term loans	Other current liabilities
Deferred tax assets	Total current liabilities
Prepaid expenses and other current assets	
Allowance for doubtful receivables	**Long-term liabilities:**
Total current assets	Long-term debt
	Deferred tax liabilities
Property, plant and equipment, net	Accrued retirement benefits
	Other
Intangible assets	Total liabilities
Investments and other assets:	**Minority interests**
Investments	
Long-term loans	**Stockholders' equity:**
Deferred tax assets	Common stock:
Long-term prepaid expenses and other	Authorised: ______ shares
Allowance for doubtful receivables	Issued and outstanding: ____ shares in ___
Investments and other assets, net	Capital surplus (also called additional paid in capital)
	Retained earnings
Translation adjustments	Unrealised holding gain on securities
	Translation adjustments
	Total stockholders' equity
	Contingent liabilities
Total assets	**Total liabilities, minority interests and stockholders' equity**

Table 8.13 Japanese cash flow statement

Operating activities
Net income
Adjustments to reconcile net loss to net cash provided by operating activities:
  Depreciation and amortisation
  Allowance for doubtful receivables, net of reversal
  Accrued retirement benefits, net of reversal
  Gain on sales of marketable securities, net
  Gain on sales of investment in securities, net
  Loss on revaluation of marketable securities
  Loss (gain) on sales and disposal of property, plant and equipment, net
  Equity in income of affiliates
  Deferred income taxes
  Minority interests
  Changes in operating assets and liabilities:
    Trade notes and accounts receivable
    Inventories
    Other assets
    Trade notes and accounts payable
    Other liabilities
  Other
Net cash provided by operating activities

Investing activities
Decrease in short-term investments
Purchase of property, plant and equipment
Proceeds from sales of property, plant and equipment
Decrease (increase) in investments in securities
Loans made
Collection of loans receivable
Changes in scope of consolidation
Other
Net cash used in investing activities

Financing activities
Decrease in short-term borrowings
Proceeds from issuance of long-term debt
Repayment or redemption of long-term debt
Issuance of common stock
Other
Net cash flow from financing activities

Effect of exchange rate changes on cash and cash equivalents
Net changes in cash and cash equivalents
Cash and cash equivalents at beginning of year
Adjustments to beginning balance for inclusion of subsidiaries in consolidation
Supplemental disclosures of cash flow information: (usually shown in the notes)
  Interest and income taxes paid for the year ended March 31, 200x amounted to ¥____ million ($____thousand) and ¥_____ million ($____thousand), respectively.

PART 2

How do I analyse the accounts?

9

How do I analyse the accounts?

- **Where to start the analysis** – the profit and loss account; the balance sheet
- **And now, a few words about ratios . . .**
- **What's in this part of the book?**

Welcome to the world of the amateur detective! You're now entering the part in the book where you start to understand what the accounts do (and don't) tell you about a company's financial performance. Like any good detective, you'll probably have as many questions as answers, but you should be able to make sense of what is going on. Interpretation starts with understanding – it's only after you've understood the wealth of information you'll find in the accounts that you can start to analyse and interpret it.

I'm now going to show you how to do this in a structured way. You've already looked at the accounts, and reading through them is the starting point for financial analysis. You'll now move on to:

- identify the components of a business's financial performance;
- complete a financial analysis;
- interpret your analysis.

You'll discover the main elements of a business's performance, how they're measured, and develop a structured approach for analysing any company's accounts. The subsequent interpretation involves taking this analysis of isolated factors and bringing it together into a coherent whole. All the factors interact with one another to reveal the company's financial performance.

Where to start the analysis

Analysis doesn't start with ratios – it starts with *understanding*. You have to think before you calculate! The first thing that you need to do is read the company accounts, and to start to understand what's been happening in the company in the period. Once you've done this, look at the financial statements, starting with the sales shown in the profit and loss account. I then move line by line through the profit and loss account and the balance sheet, trying to think about *why* things might have changed.

Why start with turnover? Well, if you think about it, sales drive some of the costs and some of the assets on the balance sheet.

The profit and loss account

Sales, costs and profit

I'll start with costs. Some costs move in line with sales – the more you sell, the bigger the cost. Materials' cost is the best example of this. The more platinum Johnson Matthey refines, the bigger the platinum cost charged to the profit and loss account. Rent, on the other hand, is a different type of cost. The company has to pay rent regardless of the level of production, whereas most material costs are only incurred when another unit is produced. Some costs move with sales and others don't, and consequently costs can be described as being variable or fixed. Fixed costs are those that don't increase proportionally with volume, whereas variable costs do – the more you make, and sell, the bigger the cost. This doesn't mean that fixed costs are constant. They increase over time, and will also increase when the business's volumes increase. Sometimes, if the company has an additional order it needs to run another shift, or move to a larger factory. Fixed costs increase in 'steps', and are only fixed within certain levels of volume and certain periods of time. I've illustrated this in Figure 9.1, where the fixed costs are £1m until sales reach 800 units, when they increase to £1.3 million.

Fig. 9.1 Fixed and variable costs

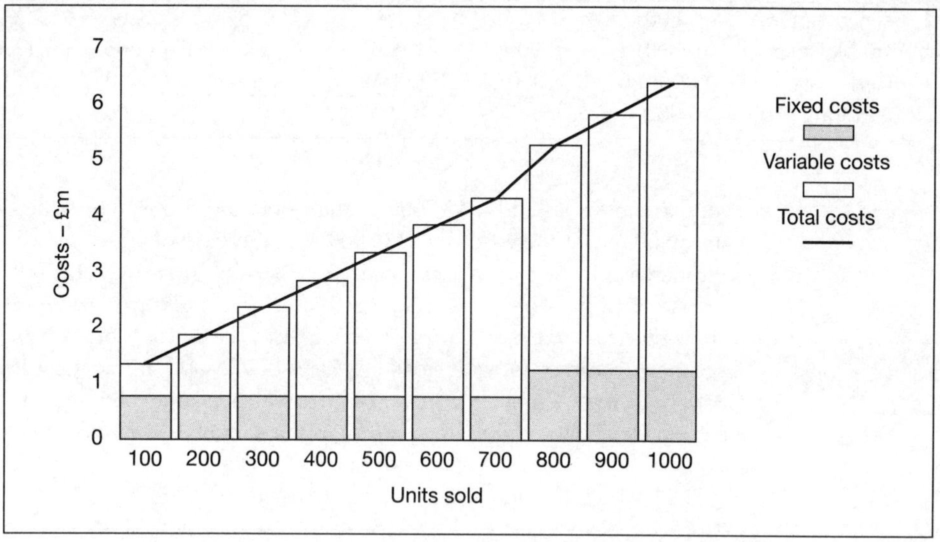

Fixed costs aren't necessarily constant, but they don't increase *proportionately*. Now I'll show you how this affects a company's profitability by adding sales to the graph, but I'll keep the units sold below 800 to keep the graph simple (Figure 9.2).

Fig. 9.2 Turnover, costs, and profit

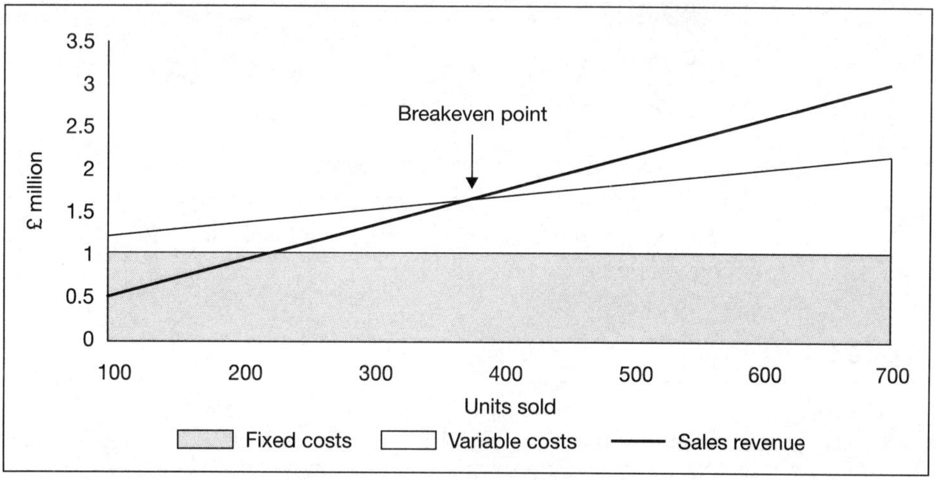

You can see that the company has to sell 400 units before it covers all of its costs, and breaks even. It only starts to makes a profit when it sells 401 units, and the more it sells the bigger the profit. But the percentage profit growth isn't constant – just look at Table 9.1.

Table 9.1 Profit growth

Units sold	400	450	500	550	600	650	700
	£ million	£ million	£ million	£ million	£ million	£ million	£ million
Sales revenue	1.800	2.025	2.250	2.475	2.700	2.925	3.150
Variable costs	(0.800)	(0.900)	(1.000)	(1.100)	(1.200)	(1.300)	(1.400)
Fixed costs	(1.000)	(1.000)	(1.000)	(1.000)	(1.000)	(1.000)	(1.000)
Operating profit	0.000	0.125	0.250	0.375	0.500	0.625	0.750

Every 50 units sold adds £125,000 to the operating profit. When the units increase from 450 to 500, profit increases by £125,000 – an increase of 100%. However, when the units sold increase from 650 to 700, profit increases by the same £125,000, but the reported increase is now only 20% (Figure 9.3). *Profit volatility increases as a company approaches its breakeven point*. If a company is close to its breakeven point it can report large increases in profit with small increases in sales, but it's actually a riskier company. (It works both ways – small falls in its volumes will give large falls in its profits.) The reported sales increase follows the same pattern, but it's much less marked.

Fig. 9.3 Reported increase as the units sold increase by 500

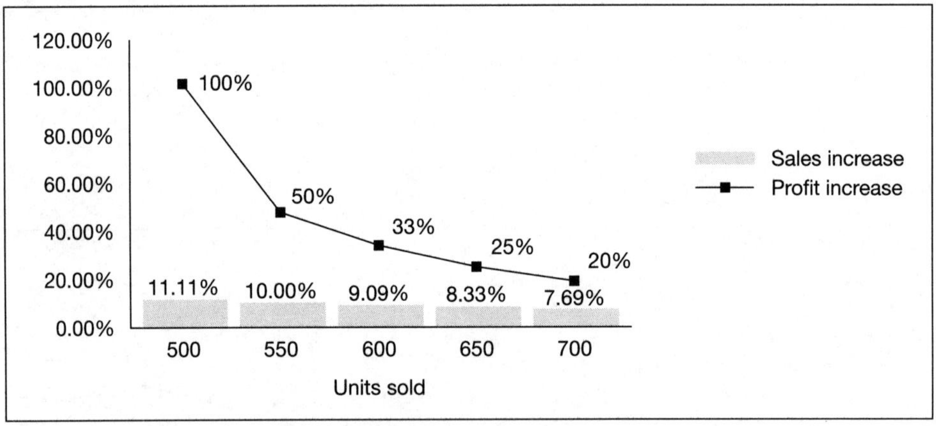

Now look at the effect that the relatively smaller increase in sales has on the company's reported profit margin (Table 9.2).

Table 9.2 Profit margin

Units sold	400	450	500	550	600	650	700
Operating profit margin	0.00%	6.17%	11.11%	15.15%	18.52%	21.37%	23.81%

Unfortunately, in their published accounts, companies don't analyse their costs into fixed and variable costs, so you can't work out their breakeven point. But I hope that you now understand that:

- *some costs move with sales;*
- *profit moves disproportionally, as not all costs are variable;*
- *the percentage change in profits, and profit margins, increases the closer the company gets to its breakeven point.*

Sales and assets

If a company doubles its sales, what do you think would happen to its stocks, trade debtors and trade creditors? Assuming that the company was operating at optimum efficiency, you wouldn't be surprised if these doubled too. Working capital tends to move in line with sales. Fixed assets, on the other hand, tend to behave in the same way as fixed costs. They have a capacity constraint; once this 'trigger point' is reached, the company has to invest more in fixed assets. These additional fixed assets could then be used to support higher levels of sales. This means that you expect:

- *working capital to move in line with sales;*
- *fixed assets to move in 'steps', increasing when the company hits a capacity ceiling.*

Now that you understand this, I'd like to run through the key items in the profit and loss account, and think about why they might have changed. You'll see that it's common sense, not rocket science, but approaching the analysis in this way is useful as it:

- helps you understand the company's performance and interpret the data;
- identifies the appropriate ratios to use.

Turnover

The turnover is the number of units sold times the selling price. Now just think about *why* the company's turnover could change . . .

It could change because of changes in:

- *prices;*
- *volume;*
- *mix;*
- *exchange rate movements (this could affect exporting companies);*
- *a combination of a number of these factors.*

Now in the operating and financial review, you'll find information about which of these could have affected the turnover. (You may remember that Johnson Matthey, in its financial review, disclosed that in 2002 its turnover fell by 18%, whereas its sales, excluding the value of precious metals, rose by 12%. The fall in precious metal prices had masked a real increase in sales.)

Materials costs

These aren't disclosed in every company's accounts, but some companies (like Johnson Matthey) disclose them. Materials cost, as a percentage of turnover, could have changed if:

- *The company has had to pay more for its materials.*
- *The company is using more materials. This could have arisen from:*
  - *the company's selling different products, or a different mix of products;*
  - *manufacturing difficulties leading to increased scrap levels.*
- *Adverse exchange rates have increased the material costs.*
- *There could be a combination of a number of these factors.*

Staff costs

These are always disclosed in the notes to the accounts and could change if:

- *The company is paying higher salaries.*
- *The company has changed the type of staff it employs, and is employing more expensive staff.*
- *The company is employing more staff.*
- *There could be a combination of a number of these factors.*

The common theme in all the explanations for changes in turnover, materials, and staff costs is changes in the volume, price, mix, or a combination of these. However, there's another possibility that would explain some of the changes, linked to mix. The company's acquisitions, or disposals, could have changed the business's turnover and profitability. You can see this if you look at the disclosures about acquisitions and disposals.

Other costs

The other costs could change if:

- *The company's volume caused the fixed costs to move up, or down, a 'step'.*
- *The company is paying more, or less, for some of its costs.*

Interest

There are two things you should remember about interest:

- *Interest received relates to average cash balances and interest paid relates to average borrowings.*
- *If the company both receives and pays interest, the business may be seasonal.*

The financial review will give you additional information about peak, and average, borrowings if the business is seasonal.

The balance sheet

Again I recommend that you adopt a line-by-line approach in understanding the balance sheet. I'm always interested to see where the company has spent its money, and at this stage in the analysis I focus on the business's assets.

Intangible assets

Intangible assets will have changed if:

- *They've fallen because the company has amortised them. This will be disclosed in the profit and loss account and the notes.*
- *The company has:*
  - *bought, or sold, intangible assets – this will be shown on the cash flow statement;*
  - *acquired, or sold, another company resulting in changes in goodwill – this will be disclosed in the notes.*
- *The company has developed intangible assets. This capitalisation of costs will be disclosed in the notes to the accounts.*

Tangible assets

There are a number of reasons why tangible asset values could have fallen:

- *Firstly, you should expect tangible asset values to fall, as most of them have to be depreciated. The depreciation charge is disclosed in the notes to the accounts.*
- *The company has capitalised some costs – charged them to tangible assets. In the UK this is usually disclosed in the notes to the accounts on staff costs. WorldCom did disclose that it was capitalising costs on page 89 of its 2001 accounts:*

  > We construct certain of our own transmission systems and related facilities. Internal costs directly related to the construction of such facilities, including interest and salaries of certain employees, are capitalized. Such internal costs were $625 million ($339 million in interest), $842 million ($495 million in interest) and $858 million ($498 million in interest) in 1999, 2000 and 2001, respectively.'

  This meant that it had disclosed that it had charged $286 million staff costs to transmission systems in 2001, $347 million in 2000, and $360 million in 1999, making a total of $993 million – a long way short of the over $7 billion subsequently revealed!
- *The company has bought, or sold, some tangible assets – this will be shown in the cash flow statement and the notes to the accounts.*
- *The company has revalued its assets. Go to the statement of total recognised gains and losses to discover this. (There will be a corresponding movement in the revaluation reserve in the balance sheet, but you'll have to check this in the notes as an upward revaluation could be eliminated on the balance sheet if the company had sold some previously revalued assets.)*

A common theme is emerging . . . all fixed assets can change if the company has bought some, sold some, or is recognising a different value. In a multinational business, their values will also change if the year end exchange rate used to consolidate them into the group accounts differs from the rate used the previous year. This will be disclosed in the statement of total recognised gains and losses and the notes to the reserves.

If the company has bought or sold fixed assets, you need to think about why it's doing so. It could be replacing existing assets, upgrading technology, or manufacturing new products requiring different machinery. Or it may simply be that the fixed assets were bought, or sold, when the company bought or sold a business. (This will be disclosed in the notes about acquisitions and disposals.)

Now I'll consider working capital, and you would expect this to move in line with sales. Consequently, I'm looking at changes in working capital in relation to changes in turnover. However, the change could arise from the variables affecting the company's turnover, and have nothing at all to do with its control of working capital. So you should also bear in mind the possible reasons for turnover changes I summarised earlier.

Stocks change by a different percentage to the turnover

Stocks need to be analysed into their component parts, as different things can cause their changes. Price, mix and volume could all cause stock differences. I'll start by looking at raw materials, which could have changed for a number of reasons, including:

- *a change in the price paid for materials;*
- *a change in the volume of stock held;*
- *a change in the mix of stock held;*
- *a combination of the above.*

Work in progress is partly manufactured orders, and changes in the value of work in progress could also be caused by two factors in addition to those shown above:

- *an increase, or decrease, in orders;*
- *a manufacturing problem;*
- *a change in the price paid for materials and/or labour;*
- *a change in the mix of stock held;*
- *a combination of the above.*

And changes in the finished goods stock could be caused by another two new factors:

- *A fall, or increase, in orders towards the end of the year. (This may also be reflected by changes in raw materials stock.)*

- *The company has developed a new product, and initially is building up its stocks prior to the product launch. The following year stocks will fall, as the new product is launched.*
- *A change in the price paid for materials and/or labour.*
- *A change in the mix of stock held.*
- *A combination of the above.*

Trade debtors change by a different percentage to the turnover

You must use trade debtors, not the total debtors shown on the balance sheet, as only trade debtors relate to turnover. Changes in trade debtors could have arisen for a number of reasons, including:

- *A change in the quality of the company's credit control procedures.*
- *An increase, or decrease, in the sales towards the end of the year.*
- *A change in the company's payment terms.*
- *A change in the type, or location, of the company's customers. (Different industries, and countries, have different standard payment terms.)*
- *There could be a change in the number of queries on the company's invoices – increasing queries is a common indication of administration problems and new computer systems.*
- *If debtors are rising, it could indicate that one of the company's major customers has a cash flow problem.*
- *If debtors are rising, it could indicate that customers are unwilling to pay because of poor product quality, or late deliveries.*

Trade creditors change by a different percentage to the turnover

- *There could have been an increase, or a fall, in the purchases towards the end of the year. This should be reflected by a corresponding change in stock.*
- *A change in the suppliers' payment terms.*
- *A change in the type, or location, of the company's suppliers.*
- *A change in the mix of the company's purchases.*
- *If the supplier has administration problems, the company may be querying the accuracy of the invoice. Its creditors will rise, until the company has an accurate invoice. When the problem is resolved, the creditors will fall, as the company will be prepared to pay once the invoice is correct.*
- *If creditors are rising, it could indicate that the company is unwilling to pay because of poor product quality, or late deliveries. This could have a 'knock-on' effect on the company's own business.*
- *The company has a cash flow problem.*

I've given you some possible reasons for year on year changes, and they could reflect good news (stocks are increasing because the company is about to launch a new product), or bad news (stocks are increasing because customers don't want to buy the company's products). You'll find some answers when you read through the accounts. Other factors may combine to offer you a plausible scenario, but don't be surprised if you still have as many questions as answers.

And now, a few words about ratios . . .

In this part of the book I'll introduce you to the ways that a company's financial performance is measured, and you'll find that means I'll use lots of ratios. However, you already know that the most important tool in financial analysis isn't in this book. It's one you already have – your common sense! Your common sense will help you identify creative accounting, and assess the company's financial performance. Financial performance is only *measured* by using financial ratios. And you'll find that most ratios only quantify what you can already see. They measure it to six decimal places, and give you a feeling of comfort as they tell you that you were right in the first place! Ratios are reassuring, but they're not the only way to understand a business's performance. In interpretation workshops I've been known to divide the group into two; one with calculators who are allowed to calculate ratios, the other group having no calculators and asked not to calculate any ratios. (I tend to rely on the fact that most of us couldn't calculate ratios without a calculator.) The quality of the interpretation is largely the same, and often the 'ratio free' group have a better understanding of the company's performance! Whilst I'm going to introduce you to lots of ratios, I'm not actually a great ratio fan. There's a tendency for people who are just starting financial analysis to become overly obsessed with them. They are only a means to an end, and it's so easy to lose sight of what the ratios are actually telling you. There is no need to calculate every ratio I've illustrated in this book; I don't. You'll use the ratios that help you understand the company's performance in specific areas. The ratios you choose will be determined by the things you spotted when you read through the accounts, and why you wanted to look at the company's financial performance in the first place.

When you start your analysis you will find that ratios are not as easy to calculate as you first thought. Most people want to see nice standard formulas that they can program into a spreadsheet, input the accounts, press the return key, and get the ratios. Sadly, it isn't quite that simple. (If it were, you wouldn't need financial analysts in the City; computers would do the job for less money!) You have to think about which numbers should be included in the ratios.

Take the return on capital employed (sometimes called the return on assets) – this is a ratio that most managers have heard about. It tells you the return the company is making on the capital it uses. It's an important measure, as it allows you to rank companies' financial performance, and identifies whether their return is good enough to compensate for the investment risk. It's often calculated by using the following formula (I'll explain why in Chapter 11):

$$\frac{\text{Profit before tax and interest}}{\text{Capital employed}}$$

But is that the best profit figure to use? The profit before tax includes operating profit, profit (or losses) on sale of fixed assets, and profit (or losses) on sale of subsidiaries. If the company has sold a sizeable subsidiary during the year (as Johnson Matthey did in 2000) it could have a considerable effect on the reported profits for the year. Should this be included? It will distort the ratio. Should you only include profit made on the businesses it still has?

And what about the capital employed? Traditionally, this is the long-term capital tied up in the business – the capital and reserves plus any long-term loans. But company treasurers may decide to fund the business using short-term debt – should this be included? Should you include provisions for liabilities and charges? It would certainly make calculating the ratios easier. In UK accounts you could just lift the number off the balance sheet from the total assets less current liabilities line. Some of the provisions will have been made to 'smooth' profits. If they hadn't been made the profits would have been larger and that would be reflected in the capital and reserves. Should you take account of the different policies that different companies have in accounting for goodwill and revaluation of assets? You'll need to read Chapter 11 to find the resolution to this debate!

You have to decide what should be included in the ratios, and different people will have different views. If you read analysts' reports, you'll find that different analysts often report different returns on capital for the same company. Why? Their definitions are slightly different, some making considerable adjustments to improve the comparability of the company's numbers, and others just using the numbers from the published accounts. Different views about how to calculate the ratios could give you different views about the company's financial performance. So the ratios aren't always what they appear to be. Most managers like ratios because they think they are an objective measure of the company's performance. Unfortunately, they aren't. Reporting ratios to six decimal places is confusing precision with accuracy. You have to decide how to calculate them, and you must always remember that they are based on numbers that represent the 'best' picture that the company could present. Ratios give you a feel for what is going on in the company. In isolation they are meaningless, and you always need to look at trends. Ideally you would need to look at the company's performance over a number of years, and within the context of its sector.

And remember you need to have a consistent approach when you're analysing different companies, otherwise you introduce another variable – yourself!

What's in this part of the book?

In this section of the book I'll cover analysing a business's:

- *Solvency – can the business pay its debts when they fall due?* This is obviously the crucial question – insolvent businesses go bust, not unprofitable ones. You have to be able to identify whether the company is likely to have any problems with its bank, or its suppliers. If it does have problems, is it likely to be able to resolve them? This chapter will help you identify if the company has any current, or potential, solvency problems.
- *Profitability – is the business profitable?* This chapter helps you identify if the prof-

itability of the company has changed, why it's changed, and whether any improvement is likely to be sustainable. The profitability of the company needs to be considered in detail to find out:
 - if the company is more or less profitable than it used to be;
 - if it's more or less profitable than its competitors;
 - why?

- *Cash – is the business managing its cash in the most effective way?* The cash flow statement is your starting point for looking at the way the company manages its cash. You need to know where the company is getting its money from, and what it is spending its money on. Is it tapping the right sources of funds, considering the type of expenditure? Is it living within its means? What is the company's approach to managing its cash resources? Is it conservative or innovative? There are different risks and opportunities associated with different strategies.
- *Investment performance – is it satisfying its shareholders?* In most financial analysis you look at the business from the investor's point of view. It gives you information about the company's ability to have a rights issue, or to make an acquisition. You will be able to tell whether it is under-performing the market and is a possible takeover target. Understanding the stock market perspective is an important management skill. Sometimes the market undervalues companies – why? Does it matter?
- *Interpreting the data – what does it all mean?* Analysing the information is only the first step in conducting the analysis. We must tie all the information together to understand what is really going on in the company. This chapter will integrate the analysis to form a view of the financial performance of Johnson Matthey over the last three years.

In each chapter I'll identify the key issues, the principal ratios, and what they tell you. I'll also calculate each ratio twice; first using the simple accounts shown in Tables 9.3, 9.4 and 9.5, and then using Johnson Matthey's 2002 accounts. So, by the time you've read this section of the book you will be able to analyse and interpret a set of company accounts.

You'll find it useful to look at the simple accounts, shown in Tables 9.3, 9.4 and 9.5, before moving on to the next chapter.

Table 9.3 Profit and loss account

Turnover	100,000
Cost of sales	(60,000)
Gross profit	40,000
Administration expenses	(20,000)
Distribution costs	(10,000)
Operating profit	10,000
Interest	(6,000)
Profit before tax	4,000
Tax	(2,000)
Profit after tax	2,000
Dividends	(1,000)
Retained profit	1,000

Table 9.4 Balance sheet

Tangible fixed assets	100,000
Current assets:	
Stock	10,000
Trade debtors	25,000
Cash	5,000
	40,000
Creditors: amounts falling due in a year:	
Trade creditors	(15,000)
Other creditors	(5,000)
Bank overdraft	(10,000)
	(30,000)
Net current assets	10,000
Total assets less current liabilities	110,000
Creditors: amounts falling due in more than a year:	
Loan (at 10% interest)	(60,000)
Net assets	50,000
Capital and reserves:	
Share capital (nominal value 1.00 each)	20,000
Profit and loss account	30,000
	50,000

Table 9.5 Cash flow statement

Net cash inflow from operating activities	*7,000*
Returns on investment and servicing of finance:	
Interest received	1,000
Interest paid	(7,000)
Net cash outflow from returns on investment and servicing of finance	*(6,000)*
Taxation:	
Tax paid	(1,500)
Net cash outflow from taxation	*(1,500)*
Capital expenditure:	
Purchase of fixed assets	(15,000)
Disposal of fixed assets	2,000
Net cash outflow from capital expenditure	*(13,000)*
Equity dividends paid	*(1,000)*
Net cash outflow before financing	*(14,500)*
Financing:	
Issue of ordinary share capital	5,000
Loan	5,000
Net cash inflow from financing	*10,000*
Decrease in cash	*(4,500)*

10

Solvency

- **Immediate solvency/liquidity**
- **Short-term solvency**
- **Long- and medium-term solvency** – net worth; gearing; interest cover; the loan repayment schedule
- **Summary of the solvency ratios and analysis**
- **Johnson Matthey's solvency** – immediate solvency/liquidity; short-term solvency; long- and medium-term solvency; what have we learnt?

When you're analysing a company, your first concern has to be whether the company is still going to be trading next year. What are the chances of it going into receivership? If it looks likely, then doing any further analysis seems a waste of time! So you start by looking at a company's solvency, as this gives you an indication of whether the company has a long-term future.

A business is solvent when:

- Its assets exceed its total liabilities (this means that it has a positive net worth).
- It can pay its debts when they fall due.

I'll look at solvency on three timescales:

'Could the company pay all of its short-term liabilities immediately?'
'Will the company be able to meet its short-term obligations?'
'Will the company be able to meet its long- and medium-term obligations?'

When you're looking at a company's solvency you'll find that most of the information is on the balance sheet, as it is this snapshot that shows you the business's assets and liabilities.

Immediate solvency/liquidity

Immediate solvency is the same as *liquidity*, as liquidity is the term used to describe the company's ability to pay its short-term liabilities on time. The question that this analysis answers is 'Could the company pay all its short-term creditors if they all wanted to be paid today?' It is the most pessimistic view of solvency, as you are imagining that all of the company's creditors falling due within a year demand immediate payment. To answer the question you have to identify the assets that the business could turn into cash within a day. You know these assets are going to be found in the current asset section of the balance sheet, as it would take more than a day to sell fixed assets. So look at the current assets in my example, and try to identify the ones that you think could be realised in a day:

Current assets:	
Stock	10,000
Debtors	25,000
Cash	5,000
	40,000

Not as easy as it sounds, is it? It does depend on the type of company that you're analysing. Most manufacturers would be unable to sell their stock in a day, particularly as part of it would be in work in progress (although Johnson Matthey could possibly sell some of its precious metals stock, but it may not be its to sell – you may recall that it leased some of its metal). However, some retailers could sell their stock that quickly. You need to understand the company to be able to accurately determine its 'liquid assets' – those that could be sold quickly to generate cash. Retailers would normally be able to realise all of their current assets; most manufacturers would only be able to realise debtors due in a year (remember factoring?), short-term investments and cash. This is the standard definition of liquid assets used in accounting textbooks, as it covers most companies. If I use this definition, my liquid assets are 30,000 – the total current assets of 40,000 less the stock of 10,000. These are then compared to the creditors falling due in a year of 30,000.

$$\frac{\textit{Liquid assets}}{\textit{Creditors falling due in a year}} = \frac{30{,}000}{30{,}000} = \mathbf{1.00}$$

This means that the company has £1.00 in liquid assets for every £1.00 it owes. So it's unlikely to have an immediate liquidity problem. As long as a large customer doesn't go into receivership, the company shouldn't have any difficulties. This ratio of liquid assets to short-term liabilities has three names – it can be called the:

- *quick ratio;*
- *liquid ratio;*
- *acid test.*

Now, you know that this is a pessimistic measure, but is it appropriate? That largely depends on whether you think that everyone is likely to ask for their money back immediately. To find this out, you need to find out if the company is likely to be having difficulties with its suppliers or the bank. How long is it taking to pay its suppliers? Well, there are two ways to find this out. UK companies have to disclose their policy for paying their creditors and should disclose their creditor days in their directors' report. However, many companies don't disclose their creditor days and just tell you something like 'the group pays its creditors on a timely basis', and so you may well have to work out the payment period for yourself. This company has trade creditors of 15,000 at the end of the year, and if you knew its purchases in the period you could calculate how long the company is taking to pay its suppliers.

Unfortunately, you'll only find purchases disclosed on the least popular profit and loss account presentation, so you're unlikely to be able to calculate an accurate figure. Some analysts use cost of sales as an approximation to purchases, but this can mean different things to different companies. Consequently, if you want to compare companies with different profit and loss account presentations, or definitions of their cost of sales, you have to find a different basis. Most analysts compare trade creditors in relation to the turnover, and although it's wrong, it's consistently wrong and enables you to compare one company with another! (You should remember that you are only trying to identify whether the company may have a problem, not quantify it exactly. You're unlikely to be able to quantify it exactly anyway, as the balance sheet only shows you the year end 'best view'.) You do not need to have a Mensa-sized intellect to know that if turnover is at £3 million, and trade creditors are at £1.5 million, the company has a problem.

Whichever way you choose to calculate it you should still get the same trend (unless the profit margins have fluctuated wildly during the period), although not the same answer! So let me show you how to work out, roughly, how long a company takes to pay its suppliers. Firstly, I need some information from the profit and loss account:

Turnover	100,000
Cost of sales	(60,000)
Gross profit	40,000
Administration expenses	(20,000)
Distribution costs	(10,000)
Operating profit	10,000

And then I need to know the trade creditors. I've shown them on the balance sheet, but you'll usually find them in the notes.

Creditors: amounts falling due in a year:	
Trade creditors	(15,000)
Other creditors	(5,000)

I'm only interested in the *trade* creditors, as they're the ones that relate to expenses charged to the profit and loss account. I can now calculate the *creditor days,* or the *payment period*.

Firstly, I'll base the calculation on turnover:

$$\frac{\textit{Trade creditors}}{\textit{Turnover}} \times 365 = \frac{15{,}000}{100{,}000} \times 365 = \mathbf{54.75\ days}$$

Now when I base the calculation on cost of sales the payment period increases to over 91 days:

$$\frac{\textit{Trade creditors}}{\textit{Cost of sales}} \times 365 = \frac{15{,}000}{60{,}000} \times 365 = \mathbf{91.25\ days}$$

(I'm multiplying by 365 in both calculations, as the trade creditors represent the money owed on a given day and both the turnover and the cost of sales are for the whole year.)

You can see that using turnover as the denominator has the effect of understating creditor days. Even assuming the worst view, the company is taking three months to pay its suppliers. So, they are unlikely to be threatening liquidation – yet!

When you're looking at liquidity, you're taking a pessimistic view. You are assuming that all the creditors falling due in a year have to be repaid today. This is only likely to happen if someone is going to petition to have the company liquidated. The payment period is a good indicator of whether the company is having difficulties paying suppliers.

Short-term solvency

Now I'd like to extend the settlement period and look at short-term solvency. Here you're trying to see if the company can meet all its short-term liabilities. You do this by looking at the relationship between the current assets and the creditors falling due within a year. So I'm now assuming that the company has sufficient time to sell its stock. I've extracted the relevant information from the balance sheet in my example:

Current assets:	
Stock	10,000
Debtors	25,000
Cash	5,000
	40,000
Creditors: amounts falling due in a year:	
Trade creditors	(15,000)
Other creditors	(5,000)
Bank overdraft	(10,000)
	(30,000)
Net current assets	10,000

The company has net current assets, so it has more than a pound for every pound it owes

The company has 1.33 in short-term assets, for every 1.00 in short-term liabilities. This ratio is called the *current ratio*:

$$\frac{\textit{Current assets}}{\textit{Creditors falling due in a year}} = \frac{40{,}000}{30{,}000} = \mathbf{1.33}$$

Whether a current ratio of 1.33 is good, or bad, depends on a number of things that are largely determined by the company you're analysing. For example, consider:

- **Grocers**: when you look at grocers' accounts you will find that they tend to have net current *liabilities*, as their short-term liabilities are greater than their short-term assets. If you look at Tesco's 2002 accounts you find that it has total current assets of £2,053 million and total creditors due in a year of £4,809 million, giving a current ratio of just under 0.43. Tesco has 43 pence for every pound it owes! Now does this mean that Tesco's is on the brink of insolvency? Of course not – just think about its business . . . It doesn't carry much stock, only gives credit via credit cards, but has the usual credit terms with its suppliers. The very nature of its business allows it to have negative working capital. People shop there almost every day and so it is fairly safe in not having its short-term liabilities covered by its short-term assets.
- **Manufacturing companies**: manufacturers have more current assets than retailers. They have more stock – there's raw materials, work in progress and finished goods stock. They're often carrying retailers' stock, giving retailers normal corporate credit

terms and having the same terms with their suppliers. Consequently, you can see that a manufacturer should have a higher current ratio than a retailer. How large the current ratio needs to be depends on the type of manufacturing business. It really depends on how long it takes it to convert its materials back into cash. The longer it takes to turn its raw materials back into cash, the more it needs, and should have, in current assets to cover its creditors. A heavy engineering company, which may have a nine-month production cycle, may need as much as 2.5; whereas for a confectioner a current ratio of 1.4 may be acceptable.

This means that current ratios can't be viewed in isolation – they have to be considered in the light of the company's business and over a period of time. The size of the current ratio is determined by the interrelationship of two factors:

- how long does it take the company to convert its materials into cash – the shorter the period, the lower the ratio;
- how frequently do people buy the product – the greater the frequency, the lower the ratio.

Long- and medium-term solvency

Now I'm taking a longer-term view and there are a number of different indicators of a business's longer-term solvency:

- positive net worth;
- gearing (also referred to as *leverage*);
- interest cover;
- the loan repayment schedule.

When you're looking at the company's ability to meet its long-term obligations you have to find out whether:

- its assets cover its liabilities;
- it has borrowed too much money:
  - Can it afford the loans it has?
  - Can it repay the loans when they're due?

I'll start by looking at whether the company's assets cover its liabilities.

Net worth

The first thing that you can check is that the company's total assets exceed its total liabilities, and by how much. The bottom line on a UK company's balance sheet shows us this instantly, as the net worth is the same as the net assets. If you look at the balance sheet extract below you'll see that the company in my example has a net worth of 50,000.

Net assets	50,000
Capital and reserves:	
Share capital	20,000
Profit and loss account	30,000
	50,000

The net worth is the same as the net assets and the total capital and reserves

Unfortunately, it's not always that simple, as the net worth on the balance sheet can be influenced by a number of factors:

- **Revaluation of assets**: revaluing assets increases a company's net worth. Now this may not be important unless you're comparing companies. Only some companies revalue their assets, and you've seen that in some countries revaluation is not allowed. So it is often difficult to make realistic comparisons of companies' net worth.
- **Exchange rate movements**: the value of overseas investments moves in line with exchange rates, and most of these adjustments are shown on the statement of total recognised gains and losses. The net worth of multinational companies with overseas subsidiaries will be exposed to exchange rate movements and their net worth may be more volatile. However, the statement of total recognised gains and losses discloses this, as it tells you the effect of exchange rate movements on the company's net worth.
- **Goodwill write-offs**: you've already seen that UK companies can have sizeable amounts of goodwill written off through their reserves for acquisitions made before the implementation of FRS 10. This will have reduced their net worth when compared to a company overseas where goodwill may always have been shown as an intangible asset.
- **Provisions for liabilities and charges**: you've learnt that UK companies can make provisions when they have a measurable obligation, but in other countries provisions are based on directors' decisions. Provisions are charged against profits and either reduce asset values or are shown as a liability. Either way they reduce the company's net worth.
- **FRS 17**: final salary pension fund surpluses and deficits will affect both the net assets and the capital and reserves when FRS 17 is fully implemented.

Gearing

Now I'd like to move on to look at gearing, which measures the amount of debt a company has. But before I show you how to calculate it, I'll show you *why* it might be important. I'm now going to show you two balance sheets (Table 10.1). I'm comparing the company in my example with another company in the same sector. They both have the same amount of capital invested in their business, and the same profits, but a different balance of debt to their shareholders' investment.

Table 10.1 Two balance sheets

	My company	A competitor
Fixed assets	100,000	100,000
Current assets:		
Stock	10,000	10,000
Debtors	25,000	25,000
Cash	5,000	5,000
	40,000	40,000
Creditors: amounts falling due in a year:		
Trade creditors	(15,000)	(15,000)
Other creditors	(5,000)	(5,000)
Bank overdraft	(10,000)	(10,000)
	(30,000)	(30,000)
Net current assets	10,000	10,000
Total assets less current liabilities	110,000	110,000
Creditors: amounts falling due in more than a year:		
Loan (at 10% interest)	(60,000)	0
Net assets	50,000	110,000
Capital and reserves:		
Share capital	20,000	80,000
Profit and loss account	30,000	30,000
	50,000	110,000

You can see that they both have the same amount of capital invested in the business, but all of the competitor's capital has come from its shareholders. The competitor's business would be safer in a recession. My company has to pay interest regardless of its profitability and at some time the loan will have to be repaid. The competitor doesn't have a legal obligation to pay dividends, only interest; if times are bad it can reduce, or waive, its dividend. But in boom times my company would offer investors the best return. My identical profit could be shared amongst fewer shareholders, and I would have the opportunity to pay four times my competitors' dividend.

It's obvious that my company has borrowed more than the competitor, but I have to find a way of measuring this – hence the gearing ratios. Gearing measures the proportion of borrowed money, either to the total capital (the traditional way of calculating gearing in the UK), or to the shareholders' stake in the business (the City's and banks' approach). I'll now show you how to calculate all three.

The gearing ratios

I'll calculate the gearing ratios using the example shown in 'my company', starting with the traditional approach.

Traditional gearing calculation

This traditional way of calculating gearing expresses the loans as a percentage of the capital invested in the business. This capital invested, also called the *capital employed*, is all the loans (the lenders' investment) and the capital and reserves (the shareholders' investment). It shows how much of the capital invested has been borrowed.

$$\frac{\textit{Loans}}{\textit{Capital employed}} = \frac{10{,}000 + 60{,}000}{110{,}000} = \mathbf{63.64\%}$$

If you calculate gearing in this way it will always be less than 100%, but now look at what happens when I calculate it using the investors' approach.

Investors' gearing

This looks at the relationship between debt and the shareholders' stake in the business, often called the *equity*. This ratio is usually called the *debt to equity ratio* and there are three different ways that this can be calculated, each using a slightly different debt figure:

- long-term debt;
- all debt;
- net debt.

I'll show you how to calculate all three.

Long-term debt to equity ratio

$$\frac{\textit{Long-term loans}}{\textit{Capital and reserves}} = \frac{60{,}000}{50{,}000} = \mathbf{120\%}$$

This adds the overdraft to the long-term loan and tells you that the company's long-term loans are 20% greater than its equity.

All debt to equity ratio

This is a measure that is often used by banks and credit rating agencies. It is also a more appropriate measure when looking at smaller private companies, which have limited access to long-term loans.

$$\frac{\textit{Total debt}}{\textit{Capital and reserves}} = \frac{70{,}000}{50{,}000} = \mathbf{140\%}$$

The total debt is 40% greater than the equity.

Net debt

This is the commonest way of calculating gearing. It deducts any cash and short-term deposits from the total debt and looks at the business's net debt in relation to its equity. It tends to be a better measure when looking at multinational companies who may have both cash balances and bank overdrafts. This would arise if there are early redemption penalties attached to the debt (just like your mortgage). But often the cash balances and the borrowings are in different countries, with the cash balances in one country and bank overdrafts in another. There are three reasons why this could occur:

- The business could be seasonal, and the company only has this amount of cash at its year end.
- It is very difficult to take cash out of some countries, as they have *remittance restrictions*. Consequently, companies may have an overall cash surplus, but are reluctant to use it to repay loans in a country with remittance restrictions.
- Some companies take advantage of interest rate differentials, borrowing money in countries with low interest rates and depositing in countries with high interest rates. However, whilst this may flatter profits in the short term, it can create problems in the long term. Countries paying higher interest rates aren't doing so because they feel generous towards investors! Their economy is viewed as being a less attractive one to invest in, so they have to pay higher rates to attract investors. Currently, companies can avoid this affecting their reported profits if the foreign currency borrowings have been used to hedge against, or finance, foreign equity investments. (In this case, the exchange differences are written off through reserves. They can defer the capital loss until the loan has to be repaid. They then incur the loss, in cash terms, but it doesn't show on their profit and loss account.) However, the proposals in FRED 23 (*Financial instruments: Hedge accounting*) will change this as it requires documentary evidence of the hedging relationship at the inception of the hedge, and any ineffective part of the hedge will have to be charged to the profit and loss account.

Whatever the reason for maintaining both cash balances and debt, a number of companies could pay off their loans and are described as having *negative gearing*. (This just means that their cash and short-term deposits at the year end are greater than their loans.) This has made net gearing the most popular way of calculating gearing.

$$\frac{\textit{All debt – cash and short-term deposits}}{\textit{Capital and reserves}} = \frac{65{,}000}{50{,}000} = \mathbf{130\%}$$

Whilst this is the commonest way of calculating gearing, you should choose the definition of gearing that seems the most appropriate for the company you are analysing.

How you calculate gearing is largely irrelevant as long as you're consistent, although gearing based on long-term debt is inappropriate if the company has changed the maturity of its debt during the period of analysis. (A move from long-term to short-term debt would reduce the apparent gearing.) It is important that you calculate your own gearing figures, and don't rely on the ones chosen in the company accounts. If borrowing becomes a problem, finance directors will always pick the most flattering definition and sometimes it changes from one set of accounts to the next!

You've seen that there are different ways to calculate gearing, but does gearing matter? Does it really matter that a company has borrowed a lot of money? The answer is . . . maybe, or may be not – it all depends! There are two factors I'd have to consider before answering the question:

- **Are the company's profits increasing or declining?** The company in my example has to pay at least 6,000 a year interest (10% of 60,000) regardless of its profitability. If its profits increase, interest is an increasingly smaller proportion of its profits, but if they fall, interest could eliminate any profits that the company made.
- **Can the company afford to service and repay the debt?** To do this you have to look at the interest cover and the loan repayment schedule.

A final word of warning about gearing ratios

All the methods use the capital and reserves, so the gearing ratios have the same problems I talked about when discussing net worth. The revaluation of assets and pension fund surpluses and deficits could either increase or decrease the reserves shown on the balance sheet, and goodwill write-offs may have reduced the value of reserves. If you are making comparisons you should:

- **Exclude pension fund surpluses and deficits.** If you feel that the trend indicates that it's prudent to include them, you could calculate two sets of gearing.
- **Exclude the revaluation reserve.** Revaluation of assets is not allowed in some countries, whilst in others it is done for tax reasons.
- **Add back any goodwill previously written off through reserves.** Companies must disclose, in the notes to the reserves, the amount of goodwill that has been written off through reserves. (If you wanted to be technically correct you then have to amortise the goodwill, but don't panic – most people don't bother!)
- **Add back some of the provisions for liabilities and charges.** Some countries only allow provisions to be made once an obligation exists, whereas others may make provisions when the management feel they would be prudent.

However, for most purposes it is just worth bearing in mind that:

- A revaluation will affect most ratios.
- Past acquisitions may affect the ratios. Whether this is important, or not, depends on how much goodwill has been written off through reserves, and whether this has changed during your analysis period.

Interest cover

This is an affordability measure. You know from your own personal experience that it's possible to borrow more money than you can afford. Hardly a week passes when I haven't received an offer for a platinum credit card and £10,000 instant credit. Most of us don't accept these offers because we know that we can't afford it. Companies can also borrow more than they can afford, relying on profit growth in the long term to enable them to repay the loans. The interest cover ratio tells you if they can afford their current level of borrowings by showing you how many times interest can be paid from the available profit. It is simply calculated by dividing the profit before interest by the net interest payable. I'm using the following extract from my example's profit and loss account to calculate interest cover.

Operating profit	Interest is 60%	10,000
Interest	of the company's	(6,000)
Profit before tax	operating profit!	4,000

Now remember I said that ratios *quantify* what you can already see – interest cover is no exception. However, it doesn't express interest as a percentage; it tells you how many times the company could pay the interest bill from its profits by dividing interest into the available profit.

$$\frac{\textit{Profit before interest}}{\textit{Interest payable}} = \frac{10{,}000}{6{,}000} = \mathbf{1.67\ times}$$

It's obvious that the company probably has a problem repaying the loans, unless it either has lots of cash or profits rise. After all, interest is only a percentage of the money that it has borrowed, and at current rates a small percentage. Does this business have any cash, and is it generating any cash? Well, it has 5,000 cash at its year end, had a cash *outflow* before financing on its cash flow statement of 14,500, and increased its loans during the period. This means that it's reliant on profit growth to be able to repay its loans. The only comfort is that the long-term loan is at a fixed rate so the company is only exposed to increases in interest rates on its short-term borrowings.

Interest cover is an important ratio, as it's a common lending covenant. This means that if interest cover drops to a certain level, usually 2.5 times (that means that interest is 40% of the company's profit), the loan has to be renegotiated or even repaid. If you read *The Financial Times*, at the moment it's often referring to companies being in breach of their banking covenants, and having to sell off part of their business to repay their loans. They borrowed money when the global economy was good, but profits have now fallen and they're in breach of covenant.

Now I've calculated interest cover from profit, as this is the normal way it's calculated. However, interest is paid from cash and it can also be useful to look at the cash interest cover using the cash flow statement. I've extracted the relevant numbers from my example's cash flow statement:

Net cash inflow from operating activities	*7,000*
Returns on investment and servicing of finance:	
Interest received	1,000
Interest paid	(7,000)
Net cash outflow from returns on investment and servicing of finance	*(6,000)*

This is even worse! The operational cash flow is the same as the interest paid, although the company still has an interest cover above 1 as it received some interest during the year:

$$\frac{\textit{Operational cash flow}}{\textit{Net interest paid}} = \frac{7{,}000}{6{,}000} = \mathbf{1.17\ times}$$

It wouldn't take much of a fall in profits, or poor working capital control, before the company wouldn't be able to pay the interest out of its operating cash flow! If the long-term loan had been at variable interest rates the company would be even more vulnerable, as it would be exposed to rises in interest rates on all its debt.

High levels of borrowing and poor interest cover are indications of possible future solvency problems. Interest cover is crucial; if you look at the large companies that went into liquidation during the last recession and those currently having difficulties, they were highly geared companies with low interest cover. In fact you probably don't even need to be highly geared, your borrowings could be relatively low, but you could still have poor interest cover. The important question is – can the company afford its current level of debt?

A small complication – capitalising interest

When you're calculating interest cover you need to remember that the interest figure shown on the face of the profit and loss account is the *net* interest figure. I'll show you why this might be important by using a different example:

Operating profit	70,000
Net interest payable	(20,000)
Profit after interest	50,000

There will be a note in the accounts analysing the interest charge:

Interest payable	60,000
Interest receivable	(15,000)
Interest capitalised	(25,000)
Net interest payable	20,000

What is the interest cover? A lot of analysts would say 3.5 times, but is it? You're calculating a ratio because it gives you useful information and you're using interest cover as an affordability measure. Whether interest is charged to fixed assets or the profit and loss account is irrelevant. (That's why interest cover calculated from the cash flow statement is so useful, even though it is still unusual to find it included in any analysis.) Banking covenants are concerned with the *payment* of interest, not where it's charged. You might also be comparing companies having different accounting policies on capitalising interest. This means that you'd have to include the capitalised interest in the interest charge, preparing an adjusted interest cover.

$$\frac{\textit{Profit before interest}}{\textit{Adjusted interest paid}} = \frac{70{,}000}{45{,}000} = \mathbf{1.56\ times}$$

Their interest cover doesn't look quite so good now!

The loan repayment schedule

Now you've discovered that the company in my example is relying on future profit, and cash, growth to repay its loans. It certainly couldn't repay them now. So the next question you have to answer is *when* do the loans have to be repaid. The answer lies in the loan repayment schedule, which is disclosed in the notes to the balance sheet. The note for the company in my example is:

Borrowings are repayable as follows:	
Between one and two years:	
Bank and other loans	45,000
Between two and five years:	
Bank and other loans	15,000
In five years or more:	
Bank and other loans	5,000
	70,000

The company could have to repay all the 45,000 in the next two years, and has to repay 35,000 in two years' time. (I've used could rather than will, as the bank overdraft of 10,000 may not have to be repaid. It is shown as repayable within a year, as this reflects the legal position.) It only has 5,000 cash at its year end, so you need to know whether it is managing to generate cash. If you look at its summarised cash flow statement, things would have to improve over the next two years:

Net cash inflow from operating activities	*7,000*
Net cash outflow from returns on investment and servicing of finance	*(6,000)*
Net cash outflow from taxation	*(1,500)*
Net cash outflow from capital expenditure	*(13,000)*
Equity dividends paid	*(1,000)*
Net cash outflow before financing	*(14,500)*
Net cash inflow from financing	*10,000*
Decrease in cash	*(4,500)*

It is difficult to reach any definite conclusions knowing nothing about the company, and only having one year's cash flow (you'd really want to be looking at trends in cash flow). But if the company's cash flows remain at this level it will experience difficulties in repaying the debt unless it can:

- *Repay existing loans with new loans:* to determine this you'd need to ask yourself whether lenders would view the business as a good risk taking into account things like their relative performance, their market conditions and their interest cover. You'll also find that most companies tell you, in the notes to the accounts, if they have any unused borrowing facilities.
- *Generate sufficient cash to repay the loans:* this doesn't have to come from its operations; it may be able to generate cash by reducing its working capital, or selling some of its assets.
- *Have a share issue:* a number of major companies have managed to have a rights issue, getting more cash from their shareholders by highlighting the alternatives!

Summary of the solvency ratios and analysis

I've introduced you to a number of ratios, and some of the other things you need to consider to assess a company's solvency. I'd now like to summarise how these ratios are calculated, and why you use them.

- **The liquid ratio, the quick ratio, or the acid test**: these are the three names for the ratio that measures a company's *liquidity*. It compares the assets that the company can quickly realise as cash (usually the current assets less stock and debtors falling due in more than a year), with the company's current liabilities. This is a pessimistic view, as you are assuming that all the creditors falling due in a year have to be repaid today. This is only likely to happen if creditors have been waiting so long for payment that they decide to petition to have the company liquidated. The *payment period*, or *creditor days*, is a good indicator of whether the company is having difficulties paying suppliers, as it gives an indication of how long the company takes to pay them. This is usually calculated by dividing the creditors by the company's turnover and multiplying by 365. A more accurate, but less comparative, formula uses cost of sales, rather than turnover, as an approximation to purchases.
- **The current ratio**: this is concerned with short-term solvency, and looks at the relationship between the company's assets that can be realised within a year and the liabilities it has to repay in the next year. The size of the ratio is determined by the nature of the company's business and the interrelationship between the length of time the company takes to convert its materials into cash, and the frequency that its customers buy its products.
- **Net worth**: this tells you if, and by how much, the company's total assets exceed its total liabilities. It is the bottom line on the balance sheet, and is the same as the net assets and the total capital and reserves. In practice, however, you'll have to make a number of adjustments to get a comparable number.
- **Gearing, or leverage**: this measures the relationship of the company's debt to its equity, or capital employed. The most popular gearing ratio is the net debt to equity ratio, which expresses the company's net debt (all loans less cash) as a percentage of its

capital and reserves. You may have to adjust the company's reported capital and reserves to get a comparable measure. Gearing just quantifies how much has been borrowed; to find out if this level of debt is a problem you have to look at the interest cover, the loan repayment schedule and the cash flow statement.

- **Interest cover**: this is an affordability measure that divides profit before interest by the net interest payable. It is an important ratio, as it's a common lending covenant. If interest cover falls to a certain level, usually 2.5 times (that means that interest is 40% of profit), the loan has to be either renegotiated or repaid. A company that has a low interest cover is relying on future profit, and cash, growth to repay its loans. If you're comparing companies with different accounting policies, or are concerned about a possible breach of banking covenant, you'll need to adjust the net interest payable to exclude capitalised interest.

  Interest cover can also be calculated from the cash flow statement, by dividing the operating cash flow by the net interest paid.
- **The loan repayment schedule**: this is a note to the accounts that tells you when the loans have to be repaid, and is very important if the company has a low interest cover. (If they're struggling to pay the interest, which is only a small percentage of the amount they've borrowed, you know they're going to have difficulties repaying their loans.) The loan repayment schedule tells you if they're going to have to repay any loans in the near future.
- **Using cash and the cash flow statement**: the balance sheet identifies how much cash the business has at its year end, and the cash flow statement shows you how much it generated during the year. Looking at the two helps you understand whether the company is likely to have any difficulties repaying its loans on time.

Johnson Matthey's solvency

You've seen how to calculate the ratios from a simple set of accounts. Now I'd like to show you how to calculate them from a real set of accounts. And, as you've probably guessed, it's going to become more complicated. I'll just be calculating the ratios for 2002 using Johnson Matthey's accounts, and will show you the trend when I analyse its accounts in Chapter 14.

I'll follow the same procedure and show you how to measure Johnson Matthey's:

- immediate solvency, or liquidity;
- short-term solvency;
- long- and medium-term solvency.

Immediate solvency/liquidity

This is measured by a ratio called the acid test (which is also called the liquid or the quick ratio), and looks at the relationship between the company's liquid assets and its creditors falling due in a year. I've extracted the relevant lines from Johnson Matthey's 2002 group balance sheet and ticked its liquid assets ...

		Liquid asset?
Current assets		
Stocks	**414.3**	✗
Debtors: due within one year	**345.2**	✓
Debtors: due after more than one year	**108.8**	✗
Short term investments	**16.6**	✓
Cash at bank and in hand	**92.6**	✓
	977.5	
Creditors: Amounts falling due within one year		
Borrowings and finance leases	**(65.8)**	
Precious metal leases	**(131.0)**	
Other creditors	**(359.2)**	
Net current assets	**421.5**	

You'll notice that I've excluded all of its stock, as you can see that some of its precious metals are leased. This means that its liquid assets are debtors falling due in a year, investments and cash – £454.4 million (345.2 +16.6 + 92.6). It has total creditors falling due in a year of £556 million (65.8 + 131.0 + 359.2), so its acid test in 2002 is 0.82:

$$\frac{\textit{Liquid assets}}{\textit{Creditors falling due in a year}} = \frac{454.4}{556.0} = \mathbf{0.82}$$

If all its creditors asked for immediate repayment, Johnson Matthey would be able to pay them 82 pence for every pound it owes. This ratio is really only important if it is taking a long time to pay its creditors. The first place to check is the directors' report, as some companies disclose their creditor days there. Johnson Matthey's directors' report discloses that it takes four days to pay its suppliers:

> **Policy on Payment of Commercial Debts**
>
> The group's policy in relation to the payment of all suppliers (set out in its Group Control Manual, which is distributed to all group operations) is that payment should be made within the credit terms agreed with the supplier. At 31st March 2002, the company's aggregate level of 'creditor days' amounted to 4 days. Creditor days are calculated by dividing the aggregate of the amounts which were owed to trade creditors at the end of the year by the aggregate of the amounts the company was invoiced by suppliers during the year and multiplying by 365 to express the ratio as a number of days.

You won't find this amount of information in every company's directors' report, and you'll find later that it may not be as useful as it appears. So you may have to work it out for yourself, and I'll show you how to do this. It will also be interesting to compare the creditor days calculated from the information in the accounts, with the creditor days based on its purchases during the year.

To do this I need some numbers from the company's 2002 accounts – its turnover, cost of sales and trade creditors. Its turnover was £4,830.1 million, its cost of sales before exceptional items was £4,502.5 million (£4,185.7 million cost of materials + £330.6 million other cost of sales – £13.8 million exceptional items charged to cost of sales), and its trade creditors were £167.5 million at the end of the year.

I'll calculate the creditor days based on both turnover and the cost of sales:

$$\frac{\textit{Trade creditors}}{\textit{Turnover}} \times 365 = \frac{167.5}{4{,}830.1} \times 365 = \mathbf{12.7\ days}$$

$$\frac{\textit{Trade creditors}}{\textit{Cost of sales}} \times 365 = \frac{167.5}{4{,}502.5} \times 365 = \mathbf{13.6\ days}$$

The creditor days calculated from the formula are much higher than the four days reported in the company's directors' report, implying that its purchases are much lower than either the turnover or the cost of sales. Why the difference? In the directors' report creditor days don't have to be the *group's* creditor days, the Companies Act only requires disclosure of the *parent's* creditor days so only some of the transactions will be included.

However, one thing's certain – Johnson Matthey's suppliers aren't waiting too long for their money! Now let's have a look at its short-term solvency.

Short-term solvency

This is measured by the current ratio, which measures the relationship between the company's assets that can be realised within a year and its creditors that may have to be repaid within a year. It's 'within a year' and 'realised' that's important, and this means that you can't always use the total current assets. You've seen that Johnson Matthey has debtors falling due in more than a year, its pension fund repayment. This has to be excluded. Consequently, the current asset figure that would be used in the current ratio is £868.7 million (£977.5 million total current assets – £108.8 million debtors falling due in more than a year).

$$\frac{\textit{Current assets}}{\textit{Creditors falling due in a year}} = \frac{868.7}{556.0} = \mathbf{1.56}$$

Johnson Matthey has £1.56 in realisable current assets for every £1.00 it owes. It doesn't look likely that it will have any short-term solvency problems; now let's see if it could have any problems in the long term.

Long- and medium-term solvency

There's a number of things to consider when looking at its longer-term solvency – its net worth, gearing, interest cover, loan repayment schedule and its cash balances and cash generation.

Net worth

You know that this should be very simple to identify, as it's the capital and reserves found on the bottom line of most UK balance sheets. You're only glancing at this to make sure it's a positive number and that the company's total assets are greater than its total liabilities. Whilst you could do some adjustments to make the numbers internationally comparable, it's probably not worth it, as this is just a rough check. Johnson Matthey is worth £817.6 million, with £813.7 million being funded by its shareholders and £3.9 million being funded by the minority shareholders in some of its subsidiaries.

Gearing

Now you know that there are a number of gearing ratios, and usually you only calculate one of them. But I'm going to calculate all of them so you know you how to calculate them from published accounts. I'll calculate:

- the traditional gearing ratio;
- long-term debt to equity;
- all debt to equity;
- net debt to equity.

Traditional gearing

This shows how much of the invested capital has been borrowed. It expresses the loans as a percentage of the company's capital employed, which is all the loans (the lenders' investment) and the capital and reserves (the shareholders' investment).

First, I'll take the loans. Johnson Matthey had, at the end of March 2002, £65.8 million in loans that are due to be repaid in a year, and £185.8 million due to be repaid in more than a year. So its long-term debt is £185.8 million, and its total debt is £251.6 million.

Now the capital and reserves are shown on the bottom line of the balance sheet, but you've learnt that it's not necessarily that simple – if you want to make some international comparisons you may have to make some adjustments. You may decide that, for the purpose of your analysis, it's unnecessary. But I'll show you how to make the adjustments, just in case you need to make them. So I'll calculate the gearing ratios using two capital and reserve figures – one based on the unadjusted accounts, and an adjusted one.

First, let's look at Johnson Matthey's capital and reserves on its balance sheet:

Capital and reserves	
Called up share capital	218.7
Share premium account	128.2
Capital redemption reserve	4.9
Associates' reserves	(0.2)
Profit and loss account	462.1
Shareholders' funds	813.7
Equity minority interests	3.9
	817.6

Its total shareholders' investment is £817.6 million, with £813.7 million coming from its shareholders and £3.9 million coming from minority interests. But the profit and loss account has been reduced by:

- £98.1 million unspent provisions for liabilities and charges. This cash has not left the business, and you saw in Chapter 8 that different countries have different rules about provisions.
- £46.0 million goodwill has been written off for businesses it acquired before December 1998. This is money that has been invested in the business, and most countries have always shown goodwill as an intangible asset.

It hasn't revalued its properties, so its adjusted capital and reserves is £961.7 million (£817.6 million + £98.1 million + £46.0 million). If the company you're analysing has revalued, you'll have to exclude the revaluation reserve if you're comparing it with companies that haven't revalued their assets.

Consequently, Johnson Matthey's adjusted capital employed is £1,213.3 million (loans of £251.6 million + adjusted capital and reserves of £961.7 million) and its unadjusted capital employed is £1,069.2 million (loans of £251.6 million + unadjusted capital and reserves of £817.6 million).

Now I can calculate its traditional gearing ratios, firstly based on the unadjusted figures:

$$\frac{\textit{Total loans}}{\textit{Unadjusted capital employed}} = \frac{251.6}{1{,}069.2} = \mathbf{23.5\%}$$

I'll now calculate the same ratio using the adjusted capital employed. The gearing falls by almost 3%:

$$\frac{\textit{Total loans}}{\textit{Adjusted capital employed}} = \frac{251.6}{1{,}213.3} = \mathbf{20.7\%}$$

Long-term debt to equity

This is a different approach to the gearing calculation, this time expressing the long-term loans as a percentage of the shareholders' investment in the business. Johnson Matthey has long-term loans of £185.8 million, unadjusted capital and reserves of £817.6 million, and adjusted capital and reserves of £961.7 million.

Using its unadjusted capital and reserves, its long-term debt to equity ratio is 22.7%.

$$\frac{\textit{Long-term loans}}{\textit{Unadjusted capital and reserves}} = \frac{185.8}{817.6} = \mathbf{22.7\%}$$

Using the adjusted capital and reserves, its long-term debt to equity ratio falls to 19.3%:

$$\frac{\textit{Long-term loans}}{\textit{Adjusted capital and reserves}} = \frac{185.8}{961.7} = \mathbf{19.3\%}$$

All debt to equity

This looks at the relationship of the company's total borrowings to the shareholders' investment. Johnson Matthey's total debt is £251.6 million. Using its unadjusted capital and reserves, its all debt to equity ratio is 30.8%:

$$\frac{\textit{Total loans}}{\textit{Unadjusted capital and reserves}} = \frac{251.6}{817.6} = \mathbf{30.8\%}$$

Using the adjusted capital and reserves, its all debt to equity ratio falls to 26.2%:

$$\frac{\textit{Total loans}}{\textit{Adjusted capital and reserves}} = \frac{251.6}{961.7} = \mathbf{26.2\%}$$

Net debt to equity

This is the most widely used definition of gearing and looks at net borrowings as a percentage of the shareholders' investment. At the end of March 2002, Johnson Matthey had cash of £92.6 million, and this is deducted from the total debt to give net debt of £159 million (251.6 – 92.6).

Using its unadjusted capital and reserves, its net debt to equity ratio is 19.4%.

$$\frac{\textit{Total loans – cash}}{\textit{Unadjusted capital and reserves}} = \frac{159.0}{817.6} = \mathbf{19.4\%}$$

Using the adjusted capital and reserves, its net debt to equity ratio falls to 16.5%:

$$\frac{\textit{Total loans – cash}}{\textit{Adjusted capital and reserves}} = \frac{159.0}{961.7} = \mathbf{16.5\%}$$

You have seen that gearing can be calculated in many different ways. Goodwill, revaluations and provisions change the capital and reserves and, whilst it doesn't matter when you're looking at one year in isolation, it can distort the trends shown by your analysis. Consequently, if they have changed significantly during the period you need to adjust the reported figures to have a comparative basis. Once you have a common base, you have to select the most appropriate gearing calculation to use. This is largely determined by the company's capital structure – after all, it would be pointless using a measure based on long-term debt if all the company's borrowings are short term! The net debt to equity ratio usually offers the best basis for comparison.

Johnson Matthey is not highly geared, despite its recent acquisitions. Now it's time to see whether it can afford the debt it has.

Interest cover

This looks at the company's ability to service its debt and you can calculate it from both the profit and loss account and the cash flow statement. I'll start by calculating the interest cover from the profit and loss account, as this is the usual way to calculate it. Here's the relevant extract from Johnson Matthey's profit and loss account:

Profit and loss account extract

	2002 Before exceptional items and goodwill amortisation £ million	2002 Exceptional items and goodwill amortisation £ million	2002 Total £ million
Group operating profit	193.4	(24.9)	168.5
Share of profit in associates – continuing	(0.1)	–	(0.1)
Share of profit in associates – discontinued	–	–	–
Total operating profit	193.3	(24.9)	168.4
Profit on sale/closure of discontinued operations			
Sale of French print business	–	(5.5)	(5.5)
Closure of Metawave Video Systems Ltd	–	(0.1)	(0.1)
Sale of Electronic Materials	–	–	–
Sale of Organic Pigments	–	–	–
Profit on ordinary activities before interest	193.3	(30.5)	162.8
Net interest	(6.1)	–	(6.1)
Profit on ordinary activities before taxation	187.2	(30.5)	156.7

Now your first problem . . . which profit are you going to use? Do you use the profit before interest? But this includes profits on disposals of businesses that just reflect the difference between the cash received and the value of the net assets sold. And it includes profits from associates, which aren't necessarily realised as cash. So perhaps group operating profit is a better measure. But then you have to decide whether you ought to include, or exclude, the exceptional items. To help you decide, let's think for a moment about why you're interested in interest cover. It's an affordability measure, and you're trying to identify if the company is likely to have any difficulties with its banks. Normally you're trying to look at trends, to see if it's getting better or worse. If you're interested in trends you need to exclude the operating exceptional items, as they're 'one-offs'. So on balance, the most appropriate figure to use in a measure showing you the underlying affordability trend is the group operating profit before exceptional items.

Now we've decided on the best profit figure to use, calculating the interest cover is a matter of simple arithmetic:

$$\frac{\textit{Group operating profit before exceptionals}}{\textit{Net interest payable}} = \frac{193.4}{6.1} = \mathbf{31.7\ times}$$

You can see that Johnson Matthey has no problem supporting its current level of borrowings; even if its profit fell by 90% it would still have an interest cover of over three times!

Now let's look at the cash flow statement and see how its cash-based interest cover looks.

Cash flow statement extract

Net cash inflow from operating activities	**224.1**
Dividends received from associates	**0.1**
Returns on investments and servicing of finance	
Interest received	**11.0**
Interest paid	**(15.9)**
Net cash flow from returns on investment and servicing of finance	**(4.9)**

You don't need to calculate the ratio to know there's no problem. But I will still calculate it to show you how it's done. The interest cover rises to almost 46 times!

$$\frac{\textit{Operational cash flow}}{\textit{Net interest paid}} = \frac{224.1}{4.9} = \mathbf{45.7\ times}$$

You'll notice that the net interest *payable* on the profit and loss account is different from the interest *paid* shown on the cash flow statement. Interest is accrued on the profit and loss account, whereas the cash flow statement is only concerned with the interest that is received and paid during the year.

It's clear that Johnson Matthey has no problem affording its current borrowings, and its interest cover indicates that it could support much higher levels of borrowing. Now let's see when its loans have to be repaid.

The loan repayment schedule

The group's loan repayment schedule is disclosed in the notes to the accounts:

19c Maturity of financial liabilities

	2002	2001
	£ million	£ million
In one year or less, or on demand	**88.1**	37.7
In more than one year but not more than two years	**0.7**	1.5
In more than two years but not more than five years	**176.3**	0.9
In more than five years	**9.2**	76.3
	274.3	116.4

£88.1 million might have to be repaid in the next year (remember that bank overdrafts are theoretically repayable on demand, but banks are unlikely to demand repayment unless they have concerns about the business's liquidity). The majority of its loans are repayable in two to five years' time.

Johnson Matthey's cash and cash generation

You've already seen that Johnson Matthey had cash of £92.6 million at the end of March 2002, and had net debt of £159 million. If you look at its cash flow statement in 2002 it had a cash outflow before use of liquid resources and financing of £165.3 million. However, if you exclude the net acquisitions of £145.7 million, as you wouldn't normally expect acquisitions to be fully funded from the year's cash flow, this drops to £19.6 million. It had £237.4 million cash at the start of 2002, and used some of this to finance its acquisitions.

Cash Flow Statement

Net cash inflow from operating activities	**224.1**
Dividends received from associates	**0.1**
Returns on investments and servicing of finance	**(4.9)**
Taxation	**(55.8)**
Capital expenditure and financial investment	**(131.0)**
Acquisitions and disposals	
Acquisitions	**(143.5)**
Disposals	**(2.2)**
Net cash outflow for acquisitions and disposals	**(145.7)**
Equity dividends paid	**(52.1)**
Net cash outflow before use of liquid resources and financing	**(165.3)**

Now you may recall that I mentioned earlier that companies often disclose their unused agreed borrowing facilities in the notes to their accounts. Here's Johnson Matthey's note:

19d Undrawn committed borrowing facilities

	2002	2001
	£ million	£ million
Expiring in one year or less	**20.1**	25.0
Expiring in more than one year but not more than two years	**–**	25.0
Expiring in more than two years	**127.4**	50.0
	147.5	100.0

It has £147.5 million agreed (*committed*) and unused (*undrawn*) borrowing facilities, and most of them are available for more than two years.

What have we learnt?

Well, Johnson Matthey's so solvent it probably wasn't worth measuring it and calculating the ratios. The ratios are measuring what you can already see, and you don't have to calculate every ratio to understand the business's financial performance. In isolation the ratios tell you very little and, in Johnson Matthey's case, the only reason you'd do them is to see if there's any trend in its solvency.

11

Profitability

- **What is the definition of the return on capital employed?** – PBIT – why has this profit been selected?; what is the capital employed?
- **Calculating the return on capital employed**
- **Improving the return on operating capital employed** – improving the profit margins; improving the asset turn
- **The hierarchy of ratios**
- **Summary of the profitability ratios**
- **Johnson Matthey's profitability ratios in 2002** – the return on capital employed; improving its return on operating capital employed; improving profitability; improving the asset utilisation; what have we learnt?

Imagine that you have come into a lot of money. If you suddenly won five million pounds, how would you choose your investments? You'd naturally want a good return, but I wonder how you feel about risk. Would you be prepared to lose all of your money? I thought not, I didn't think you'd want to have to go back to work again! You'd probably compare any return you're offered with the rate that you could get from a bank or building society. For most of us, this would be a 'risk-free rate' (in as much as anything can be risk free). If you had a lot of money, you could probably find a better risk-free rate, but bank interest rates are a reasonable benchmark.

If the risk increased you'd expect the investment to offer a better return. Comparing risk and return is an everyday activity; we do it when we look for jobs (are you in the best paid job available?) in just the same way as when we plan our investments. Most people are risk averse; a small increase in risk means that you'd want to see a substantial increase in the return. Other people aren't, and embark on lifestyles (and investments) that you would find too risky even to contemplate.

When you're looking at a company's financial performance you want to be able to make comparisons, particularly if you're an investor as you have to choose your investments. You want to compare its profitability to the risk-free rate, and to other businesses in the same sector. Any company you choose has to beat the risk-free rate, as investing in a company is never risk free. The investment return you'd find acceptable is determined by two factors: your personal risk profile, and the risk inherent in the company. You would want to see a higher return from a car company than a grocer, as we all have to eat every day but don't have to buy a car every year! The return on capital employed, sometimes called the return on assets, ratio enables you to have a basis for comparing the overall profitability of companies.

It's also important for another reason. During the 1990s some consultants in the USA developed a concept called 'shareholder value'. They 'discovered' that companies add value for their shareholders when their return on capital is greater than their cost of raising the capital. If it costs 10% to finance the business, the return on capital should be greater than 10%! The greater the difference between the return on capital and the cost of capital, the greater the valued added, or destroyed if the return is less than the cost. The consultants believe that this value added is the major determinant of share price movements. So the return on capital is a useful measure for both comparing companies and explaining share price movements.

The return on capital is exactly what it says – it measures return being generated on the capital being used by the company. It usually defines the capital as the total capital invested in the business, regardless of whether it is in the form of equity or debt. This allows you to compare companies with different capital structures, identifying which company is generating the best return overall. (If you were concerned purely with the return for the shareholders, you would calculate another ratio (the return on equity) which is discussed in detail in Chapter 13.)

You will discover that companies can improve their return on capital in a number of different ways, and it is important to understand why the return on capital has changed. You need to understand whether any improvement is a 'one-off', or whether it represents a sustainable growth in profits.

In this chapter I will be looking at the return on capital ratio in detail and showing you how companies can improve it.

What is the definition of the return on capital employed?

It has traditionally been defined as:

$$\frac{\textit{Profit before interest and tax (PBIT)}}{\textit{Capital employed}}$$

However, companies and analysts use slightly different definitions. Companies have a tendency to choose a definition that improves their reported return on capital trend, and analysts tend to use a definition that improves the company's comparability. So although there appears to be a nice simple formula to program into your spreadsheet, it may not be the best definition to use. I have another problem – I'm not sure that one definition of return on capital is enough. I like to do two: one looking at the business's overall return on capital, and another looking at a return on capital based on the company's trading activities.

I'll start by looking at an overall return on capital measure, and then adapt it for the company's trading activities. I mentioned in the last chapter that calculating the capital employed is not as simple as it seems if you want to be able to compare a company's performance over time, and with its competitors. In recent years there have been a number of changes in accounting standards, and now there's the move to harmonise national standards with the international standards. Companies change their accounting policies, they restructure, buy and sell subsidiaries. When you're trying to make comparisons you have to find a way to eliminate, or at least minimise, these differences. This means that you can't necessarily use the profit before interest and tax in the ratio, and may have to make some adjustments to arrive at a comparable capital employed. I'm going to show you how to do this in the next few pages.

PBIT – why has this profit been selected?

First, I'd like to explain why this profit figure has traditionally formed the basis for the return on capital calculation. You know the return on capital is a useful comparative tool that's used to compare a company's performance in two ways:

- **Over time**: you have to use a profit before tax, as the tax rules change from one year to the next. If you're looking at a company's performance over a period of time you have to ignore the factors outside its control.
- **With other companies in the same sector**: you want to be able to compare companies with different capital structures. Now if you think about the profit and loss account for a moment, interest comes out of before-tax profits, whereas dividends are shown after tax. Using profit before interest ensures that you are comparing apples with apples!

But PBIT isn't a perfect profit figure to choose; look at my 'building blocks of profit' model again (Figure 11.1).

Fig. 11.1 The building blocks of profit

Sales
Less

- Operating costs

Operating profit

+/–

- Share of associated undertakings' profits
- Profits, or losses, on sale of fixed assets
- Profits, or losses, on sale of businesses
- Restructuring costs

Should these be included? Most of them are 'one-offs'.

= Prrofit before interest

You can see that operating profit is likely to be the major component of profit before interest, but the other elements could be important in some years, and not in others. I'd just like to review these other components to see if they should be included.

Share of associates' and joint ventures' profits and losses

These are shown immediately after operating profit, and for some businesses they are an important part of their profit. You know that the company only influences, but doesn't control, these investments and the only cash return it will get is the dividends received. The investments are part of the capital employed, as the invested capital is used to finance them, and consequently the profit from those investments should be included in the profit figure used.

Profit, or losses, on sale of assets

As these are shown before tax they are part of the PBIT margin. Now in essence they reflect an under-depreciation, or over-depreciation, of assets. But they're not an ongoing source of profits and including them affects the return on capital, but rarely represents sustainable profits, or losses. They are recognised as one-offs and are shown as exceptional items on the profit and loss account. I don't include them in the profit used in the return on capital employed calculation, as they destroy the comparability of the ratio.

Profit on sale of subsidiaries

Profits, or losses, on disposal of subsidiaries should always be excluded, as they can severely distort comparability of the return on capital.

And there's a few other things you have to consider . . .

Profit from discontinued operations

You know that companies analyse their profit between continuing and discontinued operations. This analysis is useful, as it enables you to understand the company's likely ongoing profitability. If the company has discontinued some of its operations, it's probably sold them. The proceeds from the sale may have been used to repay debt, and reduce the capital invested in the business. (For example, BT stated in its 2002 accounts: 'The 2002 financial year has been dominated by a series of corporate transactions designed to focus and transform the group and reduce its net debt position.' Later in its financial review it disclosed that its debt reduction, from £27.9 billion to £13.7 billion, 'was achieved by our successful rights issue in June 2001, the mmO² demerger, sales of investments and the Yell business and the property sale and leaseback transaction.')

Because the sale of businesses often reduces the capital employed in the business, some analysts ignore the profit from the discontinued operations. However 'discontinued' may not mean disappeared. A discontinued operation is one that has been sold or terminated during the year, or *shortly after the year end*. This is defined as the earlier of:

- three months after the date of the balance sheet;
- the approval date of the financial statements.

This means that the assets and liabilities of the discontinued operations may still be shown on the balance sheet, and included in capital employed. And the sale of the business doesn't necessarily mean that the capital employed has reduced. The company may not have used any, or all, of the sale proceeds to reduce the capital invested in the business. Johnson Matthey sold its Electronics Materials Division to AlliedSignal Inc. in August 1999 for £393.6 million, it repaid some loans and its capital employed fell by £124.3 million. This means that there's no hard and fast rule for handling discontinued operations, and you have to assess each case on its merits.

Not all exceptional items show below operating profit

Most exceptional items are included within the appropriate cost heading, but are disclosed separately. Exceptional items are by definition unusual, and not expected to occur on an ongoing basis. The return on capital employed is intended to be a comparable measure so these should be excluded, as long as you believe the item is truly exceptional. (The recent accounting scandals in the USA have highlighted a tendency for some US companies to classify expenditure as exceptional, knowing that it would then be excluded from analysts' ratios.)

And what about the income from the company's other investments?

And finally there's the problem that the company's other investments have been funded from its invested capital, so shouldn't the income the company receives from them be included in the profit figure? If you're going to be consistent with the number used for capital employed you have to include the income from investments and the interest receivable.

A revised profit figure

As you're using return on capital as a comparability measure, you need to eliminate one-offs. Consequently, the most appropriate figure to use for the calculation of the business's overall return on capital employed would be:

Operating profit – exceptional items + the share of associates' and joint ventures' operating profit + interest receivable and similar income

However, if you were just looking at the return on the business's operating activities you would ignore the return from the business's investments and use:

Operating profit – exceptional items

Now you've found a comparable profit figure, let's move on to look at the capital employed.

What is the capital employed?

The capital employed is the total investment in the business – the lenders' and the shareholders' investment. But you've probably guessed by now that deciding on the figure to use won't be as easy as it sounds! Traditionally the capital employed has been defined as the total assets less current liabilities. This meant that it equals the capital and reserves, all creditors due in more than a year, provisions for liabilities and charges, and minority interests. Now in some situations this may be an acceptable measure to use, and you may choose to use this definition, as it's simple. But unfortunately it isn't always appropriate, and I'd like to explain why.

First, I'll look at the shareholders' investment.

Identifying the shareholders' investment

Unfortunately, you can't always just use the capital and reserves shown on the balance sheet. You have to consider:

- minority interests;
- the appropriate reserve figure to use.

Minority interests

The minority interests should be included, as minority interests are deducted from profit *after* tax and consequently their share of the subsidiaries' profits is included in operating profits.

Reserves

Unfortunately, the published reserves may not be a comparable measure, as they are affected by the company's accounting policy on revaluation and the goodwill that was previously written off through reserves.

- You know that some companies revalue their assets and others don't. In some countries asset values are kept up to date, and in others they aren't. If you want to compare companies with different revaluation policies, or in different countries, you have to exclude the revaluation reserve to make the numbers comparable.

- You've already seen in Chapter 3 that companies can have sizeable amounts of goodwill, arising from acquisitions they made before December 1998, written off through their reserves. This stays charged to the reserves until the company is sold, when it is used to calculate the profit, or loss, on disposal. Most companies overseas have always shown goodwill as an intangible asset, and this is the most logical presentation. Goodwill represents capital paid to acquire the business, and consequently needs to be included in the capital employed.

Consequently the shareholders' investment is:

Adjusted capital and reserves + minority interests

↑

Capital and reserves – revaluation reserve + goodwill previously written off through reserves

And there's another adjustment you'll have to make in the future . . .

Cast your mind back to Chapter 7 and the discussion on pension accounting . . . FRS 17 requires pension fund surpluses and deficits to be shown on the balance sheet. The corresponding movement in the profit and loss account reserve will be disclosed in the note on reserves. This means that the capital and reserves will change with the annual valuation of the company's final salary pension schemes at the company's balance sheet date. The adoption of FRS 17 will mean that the capital and reserves figure will become more volatile. (FRS 17 doesn't have to be fully implemented until 2005, but earlier adoption is encouraged.)

Now you may recall that the International Accounting Standards Board's view is that, in the long term, the valuation gains and losses could offset one another. They recognised that often today's surplus becomes tomorrow's deficit, and vice versa. This may be the approach you'd want to adopt in your analysis. You're trying to look at trends, and want to remove any 'one-offs' from your calculation. So this means that usually you'd want to adjust the capital and reserves for the pension surplus, or deficit. However, if there's an ongoing trend you may feel it's more prudent to include pension fund surpluses, or deficits.

Identifying the loans

If you think about the traditional definition of capital employed it only included the company's long-term debt, as the return on capital was seen as a measure of the return on the long-term capital. However, in recent years company treasurers have become more innovative and will switch from long-term to short-term debt if the rates are more attractive. This short-term debt is shown as part of the current liabilities, but is part of the capital invested in the business.

Some companies and analysts use a net debt figure, deducting cash from the total debt. (Johnson Matthey does this in the ratios shown in its ten-year summary.) Whilst it does simplify the profit figure (it eliminates the need to include interest received), it doesn't always provide a realistic measure of a company's capital employed. The balance sheet is a snapshot, showing the company's cash balance on a certain day. That day often reflects the company's best position, when its cash levels are at their highest. The company has raised loans because it feels that it needed the money to fund its business, and no one likes to pay interest if they don't need to. Companies usually have large cash balances for one of three reasons:

- It's a short-term situation, and the cash will be spent in the near future.
- The cash is locked up somewhere (maybe there are remittance restrictions).
- The company feels that it's prudent to have large cash balances.

Consequently, on balance I think that the cash should not be netted off from the debt in the overall return on capital employed measure. I've included the interest received on cash balances as part of the profit measure, to be consistent in the treatment of investments. However, although all companies need cash to survive, cash isn't one of the company's trading assets and is deducted from the company's operating capital employed.

To summarise, use total debt for the overall return on capital, and net debt for the return on operating capital:

Overall capital:	*Operating capital:*
Short-term debt + long-term debt	*Short-term debt + long-term debt – cash*

A brief word about provisions . . .

Some analysts include provisions as part of the capital employed, arguing that they've already been charged to the profit and loss account but haven't been spent, as they're a paper charge. They argue that logically they should be considered as part of capital employed, as if they hadn't been charged the reserves, and therefore the capital employed, would be greater. (When companies implemented FRS 19 (*Deferred tax*) in 2002, they had to provide for *all* possible deferred tax liabilities, rather than just those they expected to actually occur. This meant that their provisions increased and their reported reserves went down.). But some companies, particularly utilities, have sizeable provisions that affect capital employed, and BT recognised this when it says in its 2002 accounts: 'The group finances its operations primarily by a mixture of issued share capital, retained profits, deferred taxation, long-term loans and short-term loans, principally by issuing commercial paper and medium-term notes.' The change in accounting for deferred tax transferred £1,895 million from the profit and loss account reserve to provisions for liabilities and charges. Needless to say it includes deferred taxation in its own definition of capital employed.

The provisions have reduced the shareholders' funds, no cash has left the business and so, on balance, I think that provisions should be part of the capital employed.

And a final thought – is it appropriate to use the capital employed at the year end?

The profits are earned during the year, and the capital employed is a year end 'snapshot' figure. To be technically accurate you should use an average capital employed figure but if there's been no significant changes during the year, the year end figure will be good enough to show you the trend. However, the average capital employed is the most appropriate measure to use if the company had discontinued any of its operations, as it resolves the problem of whether to include their profit.

A revised overall capital employed figure . . .

Having thought through all the issues, the most appropriate figure to use for the calculation of the business's overall return on capital employed would be:

Adjusted capital and reserves + minority interests + total debt + provisions for liabilities and charges

And one for the company's operating capital employed

And if you were just interested in the return on the business's operating activities you would ignore the business's investments. You would also have to exclude cash, as deposits with up to seven days' notice can be included in cash. This wouldn't strictly reflect the commercial reality, as some cash would have to be available to run the business's operations.

Adjusted capital and reserves + minority interests + total debt + provisions for liabilities and charges – all investments – cash

The two comparable return on capital formulas are . . .

Overall return on capital employed:

$$\frac{\text{Operating profit} - \text{exceptional items} + \text{the share of associates' and joint ventures' operating profit} + \text{interest receivable and similar income}}{\text{Adjusted capital and reserves} + \text{minority interests} + \text{total debt} + \text{provisions for liabilities and charges}}$$

Return on operating capital employed:

$$\frac{\text{Operating profit} - \text{exceptional items}}{\text{Adjusted capital and reserves} + \text{minority interests} + \text{total debt} + \text{provisions for liabilities and charges} - \text{all investments} - \text{cash}}$$

The difference between the two return on capital figures is the company's return on its investments. Now at last I can calculate the return on capital employed using my example.

You'll find it's so simple that I don't have to make any of the adjustments I've discussed, but the situation will be very different when I look at Johnson Matthey!

Calculating the return on capital employed

I'm using the numbers from my example, and have extracted some information from the accounts so that I can show you the appropriate numbers to use in the calculation (Table 11.1).

Table 11.1 Profit and loss account extract:

Turnover	100,000
Cost of sales	(60,000)
Gross profit	40,000
Administration expenses	(20,000)
Distribution costs	(10,000)
Operating profit	10,000
Interest received	1,000
Interest	(7,000)
Profit before tax	4,000

11,000 profit would be used in the overall return on capital calculation, and 10,000 in the return on operating capital employed

I've started the balance sheet extract with cash, so I have all of the relevant numbers for the capital employed figures (Table 11.2).

Table 11.2 Balance sheet extract

Cash	5,000
	40,000
Creditors: amounts falling due in a year:	
Trade creditors	(15,000)
Other creditors	(5,000)
Bank overdraft	(10,000)
	(30,000)
Net current assets	10,000
Total assets less current liabilities	110,000
Creditors: amounts falling due in more than a year:	
Loan (at 10% interest)	(60,000)
Net assets	50,000
Capital and reserves:	
Share capital	20,000
Profit and loss account	30,000
	50,000

The capital employed would be 120,000 in the overall return on capital employed, and 115,000 in the return on operating capital employed, as cash would be excluded.

This means that the company's overall return on long-term capital employed is:

$$\frac{\textit{Operating profit + interest received}}{\textit{Capital employed}} = \frac{11{,}000}{120{,}000} = \mathbf{9.17\%}$$

and the return on operating capital employed is:

$$\frac{\textit{Operating profit}}{\textit{Operating capital employed}} = \frac{10{,}000}{115{,}000} = \mathbf{8.7\%}$$

(If you wanted to use the average capital employed: the opening overall capital employed was 109,000 and the average capital employed 114,500 ((109,000 + 120,000) ÷ 2), an overall return on average capital employed of 9.61%. As the capital employed increased during the year, using an average improves the company's return on capital. I shall calculate the other profitability ratios using the capital employed at the company's year end.)

You now know how to calculate the return on capital, and can see that this company has an overall return on capital of 9.17%, but what does it tell you? It's a figure in isolation, and you have no idea if this figure is good or bad. To understand this you would need to know:

- *What was its return on capital in preceding years?*
- *What is the risk-free rate (for example, building society or money market rates)?*
- *What returns on capital do other companies in the sector get?*
- *What's its cost of capital?*

All ratios need to be looked at in context, as they're meaningless in isolation. At the moment I'm just showing you how to calculate them. In Chapter 14 they'll start to mean something, when I review Johnson Matthey's financial performance over a number of years.

You now understand that:

- Conceptually, the return on capital is a simple ratio, it quantifies the return that the company is earning on the capital it uses. However, you've seen that deciding what should be included in the ratio is more problematic. The profit can be affected by a number of 'one-off' transactions, and the company's accounting policies influence the capital employed shown on the balance sheet.
- The return on operating capital employed is the most important element of the overall return on capital employed.

I'd now like to show you how companies can improve their return on operating capital employed.

Improving the return on operating capital employed

If a company wants to improve its return on operating capital employed it either improves its profitability, or improves its asset utilisation. This is reflected in the two ratios shown in Figure 11.2.

Fig. 11.2 Improving the returns on operating capital employed

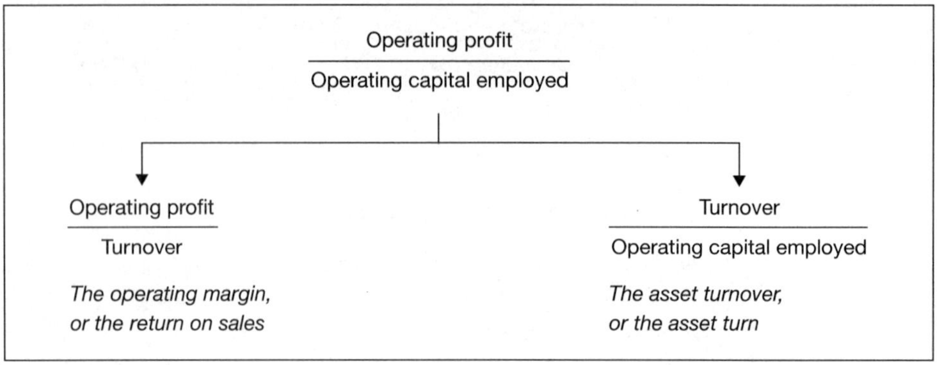

If you can remember junior school arithmetic, you'll see that the return on capital is a straight multiplication of the two subsidiary ratios shown in the figure, as the turnover cancels out to give you the return on capital employed! This means that the return on capital is the multiplication of the operating margin and a ratio known as the asset turn, or the asset turnover. The asset turn tells you how many pounds' worth of sales (or in my example it's pence) are generated for every pound of capital. It is a measure of how efficiently the company is utilising its capital. A fall in this ratio indicates the company is becoming less efficient, requiring more capital for each pound's sales, whereas a rise in the asset turn indicates improved efficiency.

I'll now show you these ratios for the company in my example.

Operating margin:

$$\frac{10{,}000}{100{,}000} \times 100 = \mathbf{10\%}$$

Asset turn:

$$\frac{100{,}000}{115{,}000} = \mathbf{0.87}$$

(or 87p for every £ of capital invested)

And just to check that the arithmetic works . . . 10% × 0.87 = 0.087, or 8.7%.

This company needs to improve its return on operating capital, and it can do this by:

- improving its operating margins; and/or
- using its assets more effectively to generate either more sales from the same assets (and therefore capital employed), or the same sales using fewer assets.

I'll start by considering how it can improve its profit margins.

Improving the profit margins

The operating profit margin, or return on sales, can be analysed into its component parts (Figure 11.3).

Fig. 11.3 The operating profit margin

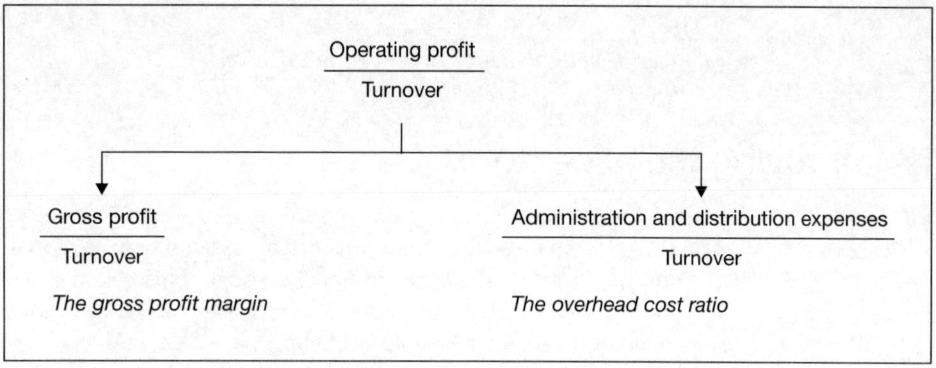

You can see that if the company wants to improve its operating profit margin it increases its gross margin or reduces its overhead cost ratio, as the operating margin is the gross margin minus the overhead cost ratio.

In my example these ratios are:

Gross margin:

$$\frac{40{,}000}{100{,}000} \times 100 = \mathbf{40\%}$$

Overhead cost ratio:

$$\frac{30{,}000}{100{,}000} \times 100 = \mathbf{30\%}$$

And just to check that the arithmetic works . . . 40% – 30% = 10%.

The gross margin isn't always a comparable measure, as different companies may define cost of sales in different ways. So it's always worth checking the definition of cost of sales, before making comparisons between companies.

Improving the gross margin

If a company wants to improve its gross margin, it must reduce costs or grow revenues. It can do this if it:

- increases its prices;
- reduces its cost of sales;
- changes its sales and product mix – if it can increase the proportion of its sales coming from higher-margin activities, its gross profit will improve.

Improving the overhead cost ratio

If a company wants to improve its overhead cost ratio, it must reduce its administration and distribution costs or grow revenues. It can do this if it:

- increases its prices;
- increases its volumes;
- reduces its administration and distribution costs.

Improving the asset turn

The asset turn looks at sales in relation to the capital that is invested in the business. This capital is used to finance the business's assets; consequently, to improve this ratio a company has to improve its asset utilisation. Now I'd like you to think for a moment about the balance sheet, and those assets that are used to generate the business's turnover. They're the business's tangible fixed assets and its working capital. (In some companies you might also include some of their intangible assets, as they're also used to generate turnover. However, not all companies capitalise brands and patents, so it might distort some comparisons.) You'll also have to adjust the working capital, as not all of the debtors and creditors relate to the business's turnover. Some of the debtors and creditors relate to asset purchases and sales. So if you're trying to assess a company's operating performance you have to include just the trade debtors and trade creditors in the operating working capital figure.

You can then analyse the asset turn ratio into its component operational parts (Figure 11.4).

Fig. 11.4 The asset turn ratio

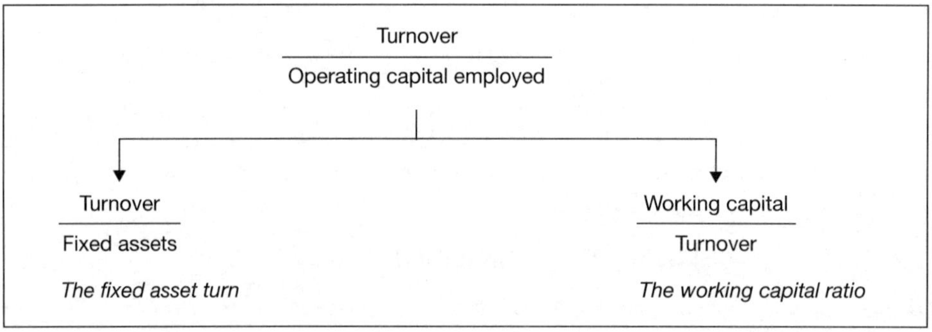

You can see that improving the asset turn is a combination of doing two things: using the fixed assets more effectively, and reducing the company's working capital requirements. You'll also notice that the arithmetical simplicity of the model has now collapsed. This has happened largely because of the way that the ratios are calculated, and partly because of the data that's excluded from the ratios. However, the two ratios do cover the drivers of the company's asset utilisation.

The fixed asset turn identifies how many pounds of sales are generated by every pound invested in fixed assets. If the company wants to improve its profitability, it's investing in fixed assets either because it wants to increase its sales, or because it wants to reduce its costs. Working capital is usually expressed as a percentage of sales showing how many pence (although sometimes it can be pounds) you would have to have tied up in the working capital to generate a pound's worth of sales.

The company, in my example, has 100,000 invested in fixed assets, 10,000 in stocks, 25,000 in trade debtors, and 15,000 in trade creditors. Consequently these ratios are:

Fixed asset turn $\frac{100{,}000}{100{,}000}$ = **1.00** *Working capital* $\frac{20{,}000}{100{,}000}$ = **20%**, or 20p for each £1 of sales

The 20,000 for the working capital has been calculated as follows:

	Stock	10,000
plus	Trade debtors	25,000
less	Trade creditors	15,000
		20,000

Improving the fixed asset turn

The operating fixed assets can be broken down into their component parts:

Tangible assets:
- Land and buildings
- Plant and machinery
- Motor vehicles

Intangible assets (if you've included these as they generate turnover)

If you felt that it was appropriate you could calculate ratios for these:

$$\frac{\textit{Turnover}}{\textit{Land and buildings}} = \textit{Land and buildings turn}$$

$$\frac{\textit{Turnover}}{\textit{Plant and machinery}} = \textit{Plant and machinery turn}$$

$$\frac{\textit{Turnover}}{\textit{Motor vehicles}} = \textit{Motor vehicles turn}$$

$$\frac{\textit{Turnover}}{\textit{Intangible assets}} = \textit{Intangible asset turn}$$

I haven't analysed the tangible fixed assets in my example, so I can't calculate these ratios. Clearly it would be ridiculous to do all of these ratios; you would end up with a lot of facts and no information. You need to identify the type of asset that is helping to generate the sales. So if you were analysing Tesco it may be appropriate to do the land and buildings turn, Corus the plant and machinery turn, P&O the vehicles turn and Allied Domecq the intangible asset turn.

Improving the working capital ratio

The working capital ratio is important, as it is an indicator of management efficiency. An efficient management team would be trying to reduce stocks and debtors, whilst managing their creditors ethically. You now know that the company needs to have twenty pence cash tied up in its working capital for every pound of sales. I can now analyse this in more detail, identifying how many days' stock the company is carrying, how many days' credit it's giving, and how many day's credit it's taking (Figure 11.5).

Fig. 11.5 The working capital ratio

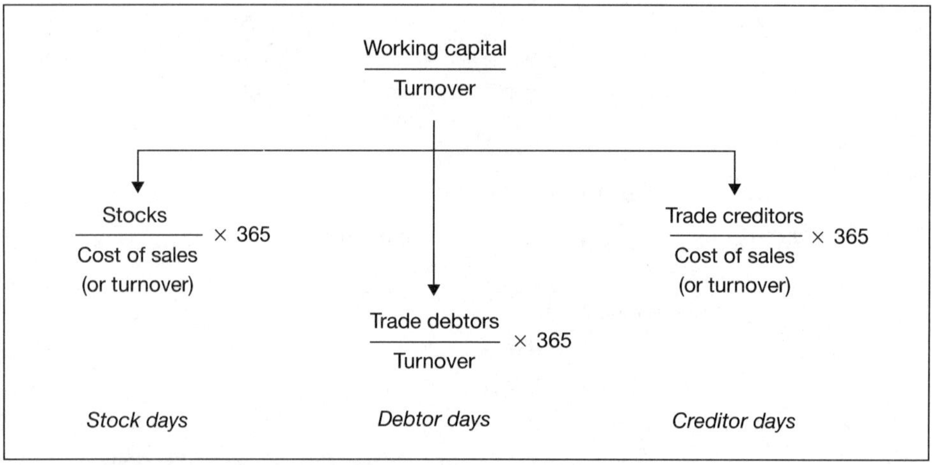

Now let's look at how the company is managing the individual components of working capital; stocks, debtors and creditors.

Stocks

There are two different ways of looking at stocks. Either you calculate how many times a year the company converts its stock into sales (its stock turn), or you calculate how many days' stock the company is carrying (its stock days). They're different ways of measuring the same thing, and you should use the measure you understand and are most familiar with.

Stock turn

Companies often use this measure in their internal management accounts. In retailing, the stocks relate to the merchandise that has been sold in the period. A manufacturer's stocks relate to the materials, labour, and production overheads used in sales. Now you may recall that these figures are not always shown in the published profit and loss account, and you'll find that analysts calculate stock turn (and stock days) using slightly different figures.

Cost of sales is the closest approximation to the materials, labour, and production overheads used in sales. If you're analysing one company, cost of sales would be an appropriate basis for analysing stock. Unfortunately, if you were trying to compare the company with other companies it may not be comparable, as cost of sales means different things to different companies. Most analysts use turnover as the denominator. Even though it is wrong it is consistently wrong, and allows them to make comparisons between companies! However, it creates other problems if you are comparing companies with very different profit margins.

I've calculated stock turn, using both turnover and cost of sales, below:

Turnover based

$$\frac{\textit{Turnover}}{\textit{Stock}}$$

$$\frac{100{,}000}{10{,}000} = \textbf{10 times}$$

Cost of sales based

$$\frac{\textit{Cost of sales}}{\textit{Stock}}$$

$$\frac{60{,}000}{10{,}000} = \textbf{6 times}$$

Based on turnover, the company converts its stock into sales ten times in a year. The higher the stock turn, the more efficient the management.

Stock days

This is the alternative way of looking at stock, and is calculated in a similar way to the way I calculated creditor days in Chapter 10.

Turnover based

$$\frac{\textit{Stock}}{\textit{Turnover}} \times 365$$

$$\frac{10{,}000}{100{,}000} \times 365 = \textbf{36.5 days}$$

Cost of sales based

$$\frac{\textit{Stock}}{\textit{Cost of sales}} \times 365$$

$$\frac{10{,}000}{60{,}000} \times 365 = \textbf{60.8 days}$$

(Remember that I'm multiplying by 365 as I'm using the sales for the year and the stock on a given day.)

You can see how using turnover, rather than the cost of sales, understates stock days and stock turn. As the calculation of stock days is inaccurate, it is important that it is looked at in context. Is the control of stocks improving (the stock days are falling), or does this company have lower stock days than other companies in its sector?

Debtors

Calculating debtor days is very simple:

$$\frac{\textit{Trade debtors}}{\textit{Turnover}} \times 365$$

In our example the company is giving 91.3 days' credit to its customers:

$$\frac{25{,}000}{100{,}000} \times 365 = \textbf{91.3 days}$$

Debtor days is sometimes called the *collection period*.

Creditors

You may recall from Chapter 10 that creditor days is calculated using one of the following formulas:

Sales based

$$\frac{\textit{Trade creditors}}{\textit{Turnover}} \times 365$$

Cost of sales based

$$\frac{\textit{Trade creditors}}{\textit{Cost of sales}} \times 365$$

$$\frac{15{,}000}{100{,}000} \times 365 = \mathbf{54.8\ days}$$

$$\frac{15{,}000}{60{,}000} \times 365 = \mathbf{91.3\ days}$$

Creditor days is sometimes called the *payment period*.

The hierarchy of ratios

I have evolved a hierarchy of ratios, showing how the return on capital employed is determined by its subsidiary ratios (Figure 11.6). If the return on capital changes, you want to know *why* it has changed.

Fig. 11.6 Hierarchy of ratios

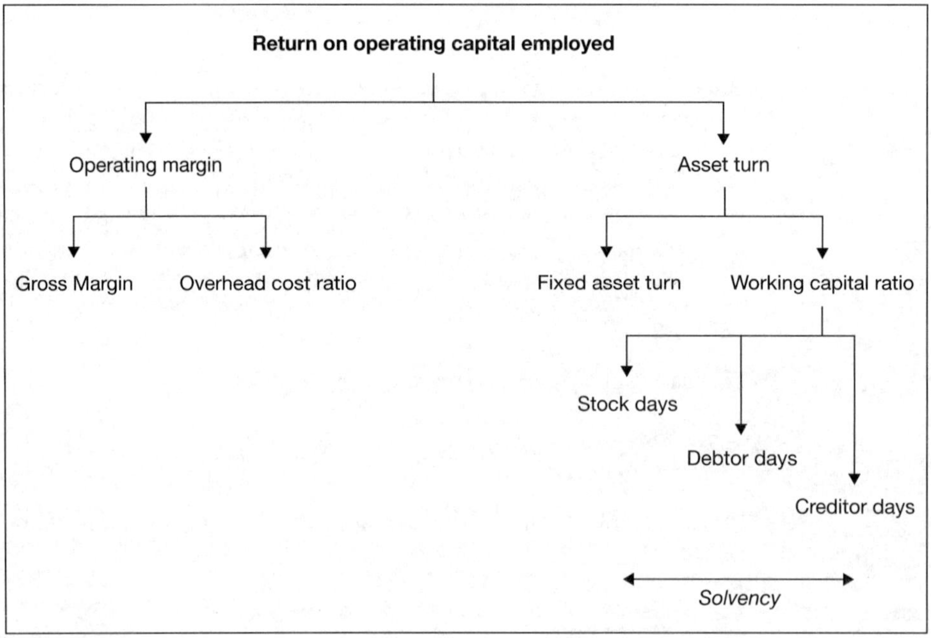

The working capital ratios also affect the business's solvency, and you've seen that high creditor days makes the acid test a very relevant ratio to use. After all, if suppliers have been waiting six months for their money they may feel they've little to lose in asking the courts to liquidate the company!

The hierarchy of ratios identifies the main determinants of the return on operating capital. This hierarchy helps you to identify why the company's profitability has changed, and how effectively the company is utilising its operating assets. This return on operating capital is the driver of the company's overall return on capital employed. Small changes in the subsidiary ratios will have a disproportionate effect on the return on capital, because of the multiplying relationship between the operating margin and the asset turn. You have to identify the changes in these ratios if you want to understand the company's underlying performance. Some changes will generate 'one-off' improvements, whereas others will give ongoing benefits. Companies improve their return on capital through improving the subsidiary ratios by focusing on improving profit margins, utilising their fixed assets more effectively, and minimising their working capital.

You should also understand that improving the return on capital by reducing the working capital has solvency implications. Reducing working capital adversely affects the solvency ratios and both the current ratio and the acid test will fall.

Summary of the profitability ratios

I've introduced you to a hierarchy of profitability ratios, and I'd now like to summarise how these ratios are calculated, and why they're important.

- **The return on capital employed**: this is the most important measure of a company's profitability, but unfortunately it is easier to understand than to calculate. It measures the percentage profit the company is making on the capital that is invested in its business. This return should be greater than the cost of financing the business (its cost of capital), and a risk-free rate. Unfortunately, there is no standard definition, with the only consensus being that the profit used should be a profit before interest and tax. Some analysts exclude all exceptional items, some use operating profit. Defining the capital employed is even more problematic. You can't rely on return on capital figures quoted in company accounts, as they're unlikely to be comparable.

  To illustrate the range of definitions used for the return on capital employed percentages published in the accounts, I'll tell you about how BT, Tesco and Johnson Matthey define their return on in capital employed:
  - BT uses profit before tax, goodwill amortisation and interest on its long-term borrowings. It then compares this to its average capital employed, defining capital employed as total assets, excluding goodwill, less current liabilities, excluding corporate taxes and dividends payable, and provisions other than those for deferred taxation. The year end figures are used for calculating the average, except for its short-term investments and borrowings where it uses the average daily balances.
  - Tesco uses an unspecified profit figure, and divides it by average capital employed excluding net debt.

- Johnson Matthey gives a return on capital figure in its ten-year summary that it calls the 'return on assets'. It is calculated by dividing its operating profit before exceptional items and goodwill amortisation by its average capital employed. It defines its capital employed as the total of capital and reserves, minority interests, goodwill written off through reserves and net debt.

It's clear that there's little agreement about how to calculate the return on capital employed; you have to choose an appropriate, comparable definition. I've suggested that it's useful to have two returns on capital – an overall return on capital and a return on operating capital.

If a company wants to improve its return on capital it has to improve either its profitability or its asset utilisation. The return on capital employed is a multiplication of the profit margin and the asset turn, or asset turnover.

- **The profit margin**: this expresses the profit used in the return on capital employed calculation as a percentage of the company's turnover. Improving the profit margin is a combination of increasing the company's gross margin and decreasing its overhead cost ratio.
- **The asset turn, or the asset turnover**: this tells you how many pounds of sales the company generates for every pound of capital invested in the business. If the number increases, the company is using its assets more effectively. Improving the asset turn is a combination of improving the fixed asset turn and reducing the working capital ratio.
- **The gross margin**: this tells you the profit percentage after deducting the company's cost of sales. It isn't always a comparable measure, as there isn't a standard definition of cost of sales.
- **The overhead cost ratio**: this expresses the administration and distribution expenses as a percentage of turnover. As there aren't standard definitions for either administration or distribution expenses, you should be wary of using this ratio when you're comparing companies with different definitions of cost of sales.
- **The tangible asset turn**: this tells you how many pounds of sales are generated for every pound invested in tangible assets. If the number increases the company is using its tangible assets more effectively.
- **The working capital ratio**: this expresses the stocks, trade debtors, and trade creditors as a percentage of sales. It tells you how many pence the company needs to have tied up in the working capital to fund a pound's sales.
- **Stock turn**: this divides cost of sales, or turnover, by stocks and shows you how many times in the period the company converted its stock into sales. If the number increases it usually means that the company is improving its stock control. However, falling work in progress could mean that the company has had a fall in orders.
- **Stock days**: this gives an approximation to the number of days' stock the company is carrying. You calculate this ratio by dividing stocks by cost of sales, or sales, and multiplying by the number of days in the period. If the number decreases it usually means that the company is improving its stock control (with the proviso above about work in progress).
- **Debtor days, or the collection period**: this tells you how many days' credit the company is giving. You calculate this ratio by dividing debtors by sales, and multiplying

by the number of days in the period. If the number increases it usually means that the company is improving its credit control.

- **Creditor days, or the payment period**: this gives an approximation to the number of days' credit the company is taking. You calculate this ratio by dividing stocks by cost of sales, or sales, and multiplying by the number of days in the period.

Small changes in the subsidiary ratios can have a large effect on the return on capital employed, because of the multiplier effect of the profit margin and the asset turn.

Johnson Matthey's profitability ratios in 2002

I'd now like to show you how to calculate these ratios from published accounts, and it's time to find out a little more about Johnson Matthey. You know that it's solvent – but is it profitable? And if so, is it profitable enough? What drives its profitability? Let's see if we can find out . . .

The return on capital employed

I'll calculate the two return on capital employed ratios I introduced earlier – the overall return on capital employed and the return on operating capital employed, which I'll use to work through the profitability hierarchy.

Overall return on capital employed

First, I have to determine the profit and need some extracts from their 2002 profit and loss account, and the note on interest. An extract from the profit and loss account is shown on page 248.
The profit used in the overall return on capital employed is:

Operating profit – exceptional items + the share of associates' and joint ventures' operating profit + interest receivable and similar income

Johnson Matthey's operating profit before exceptional items is £193.4 million, its share of associates' profits, or actually they're losses, is –£0.1 million and it has £10.9 million interest received. Consequently, the profit used in the overall return on capital employed is £204.2 million. Now I need to identify the appropriate figure for the capital employed based on the following formula:

Adjusted capital and reserves + minority interests + total debt + provisions for liabilities and charges

	2002 Before exceptional items and goodwill amortisation £ million	2002 Exceptional items and goodwill amortisation £ million	2002 Total £ million
Group operating profit	193.4	(24.9)	168.5
Share of profit in associates – continuing	(0.1)	–	(0.1)
Share of profit in associates – discontinued	–	–	–
Total operating profit	193.3	(24.9)	168.4
Profit on sale/closure of discontinued operations			
Sale of French print business	–	(5.5)	(5.5)
Closure of Metawave Video Systems Ltd	–	(0.1)	(0.1)
Sale of Electronic Materials	–	–	–
Sale of Organic Pigments	–	–	–
Profit on ordinary activities before interest	193.3	(30.5)	162.8
Net interest	(6.1)	–	(6.1)
Profit on ordinary activities before taxation	187.2	(30.5)	156.7

Note on interest

	2002 £ million
Interest payable on bank loans and overdrafts	(10.9)
Interest payable on other loans	(6.1)
	(17.0)
Other interest receivable	10.9
Net interest	(6.1)

Johnson Matthey's capital and reserves on its balance sheet is shown below:

Capital and reserves	
Called up share capital	218.7
Share premium account	128.2
Capital redemption reserve	4.9
Associates' reserves	(0.2)
Profit and loss account	462.1
Shareholders' funds	813.7
Equity minority interests	3.9
	817.6

Its published capital and reserves of £813.7 million has to be adjusted to include £46.0 million goodwill written off through reserves. So its adjusted capital and reserves is £859.7 million. Its minority interests are £3.9 million, its provisions for liabilities charges are £98.1 million and its total debt is £251.6 million. Consequently, its capital employed is £1,213.3 million (859.7 + 3.9 + 98.1 + 251.6). Its overall return on capital is 16.8%:

$$\frac{\textit{Profit before exceptional items, interest paid and tax}}{\textit{Adjusted capital employed}} = \frac{204.2}{1{,}213.3} = \mathbf{16.8\%}$$

Return on operating capital employed

This excludes the return from any investments and expresses the operating profit before exceptional items as a percentage of the operating capital employed. Johnson Matthey has a group operating profit of £193.4 million, and its operating capital employed is overall capital employed less any investments and cash:

Adjusted capital and reserves + minority interests + total debt + provisions for liabilities and charges – all investments – cash

This means that its fixed asset investments of £2.7 million, current asset investments of £16.6 million and cash of £92.6 million have to be deducted from the adjusted capital employed of £1,213.3 million. This means that its operating capital employed is £1,101.4 million, and its return on operating capital employed is 17.6%:

$$\frac{\textit{Operating profit before exceptional items}}{\textit{Adjusted operating capital employed}} = \frac{193.4}{1{,}101.4} = \mathbf{17.6\%}$$

Improving its return on operating capital employed

I'll now work through the profitability hierarchy to show you how to calculate the subsidiary ratios from published companies' accounts.

The return on operating capital is a multiplication of two ratios (Figure 11.7).

Fig. 11.7 Return on operating capital

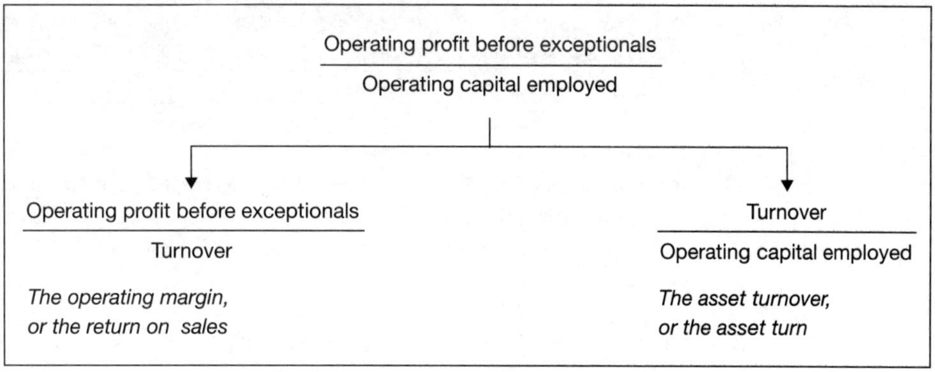

Both the operating margin and the asset turn use turnover, which was £4,830.1 million in 2002.

Operating profit margin

$$\frac{\textit{Operating profit before exceptional items}}{\textit{Turnover}} = \frac{193.4}{4{,}830.1} = \mathbf{4\%}$$

Asset turn

$$\frac{\textit{Turnover}}{\textit{Operating capital employed}} = \frac{4{,}830.1}{1{,}101.4} = \mathbf{4.39\ times}$$

This means that every pound invested in Johnson Matthey's operating capital generates £4.39 turnover, making 4% profit. I can now check my return on operating capital by multiplying the operating margin of 4% by the asset turn of 4.39 times – 17.56%.

Improving profitability

This is a combination of improving the gross margin and the overhead cost ratio. I'll need some more numbers from its profit and loss account to be able to calculate these ratios:

5 Group operating profit after exceptional items and goodwill amortisation

	2002 Continuing operations £ million	2002 Acquisitions £ million	2002 Total continuing operations £ million	2002 Discontinued operations £ million	2002 Total £ million
Group turnover	4,761.6	67.3	4,828.9	1.2	4,830.1
Cost of materials sold	(4,156.8)	(28.3)	(4,185.1)	(0.6)	(4,185.7)
Net revenues	604.8	39. 0	643.8	0.6	644.4
Other cost of sales	(310.1)	(20.0)	(330.1)	(0.5)	(330.6)
Gross profit	294.7	19.0	313.7	0.1	313.8
Distribution costs	(58.4)	(1.4)	(59.8)	(0.2)	(60.0)
Administrative expenses	(78.7)	(6.2)	(84.9)	(0.4)	(85.3)
Group operating profit	157.6	11.4	169.0	(0.5)	168.5

For continuing operations, exceptional credits of £4.6 million (2001 £ nil) are included in cost of materials sold, and exceptional charges of £18.4 million (2001 £0.6 million) are included in other cost of sales, £0.5 million (2001 £ nil) in distribution costs and £2.5 million (2001 £ nil) in administrative expenses. For acquisitions, exceptional charges of £1.3 million (2001 £ nil) are included in administrative expenses.

If you read through the paragraph above you'll find that a lot of exceptional items have been included in the above numbers. This means that the company's gross profit before exceptional items is its total gross profit of £313.8 million less the exceptional credit of £4.6 million plus the exceptional charge of £18.4 million – £327.6 million. Its overheads are the £60 million distribution costs plus the £85.3 million administrative expenses less exceptional costs of £0.5 million, £2.5 million and £1.3 million and less the £6.8 million goodwill amortisation charge (not disclosed above) – £134.2 million. (And just to check that everything's been included – the gross profit before exceptional items of £327.6 million less the overheads before exceptional items of £134.2 million equals the operating profit before exceptional items of £193.4 million.)

Now I can work out the gross margin and the overhead cost ratio.

Gross profit margin

In 2002 Johnson Matthey's gross profit margin is 6.78%:

$$\frac{\textit{Gross profit before exceptional items}}{\textit{Turnover}} = \frac{327.6}{4{,}830.1} = \mathbf{6.78\%}$$

As Johnson Matthey separates out its materials cost from its other cost of sales, I can also identify its margin on materials, or the value it has added, by expressing its net revenues as a percentage of turnover:

$$\frac{\textit{Net revenues}}{\textit{Turnover}} = \frac{644.4}{4{,}830.1} = \mathbf{13.34\%}$$

Johnson Matthey is making 13.34% above the cost of its materials.

Overhead cost ratio

Johnson Matthey's overheads were 2.78% of turnover in 2002:

$$\frac{\textit{Overheads before exceptional items}}{\textit{Turnover}} = \frac{134.2}{4{,}830.1} = \mathbf{2.78\%}$$

Improving the asset utilisation

The arithmetical simplicity of the profitability hierarchy now starts to break down, as the assets are compared to turnover and only those assets and liabilities that relate to turnover are included from this point onwards.

Johnson Matthey can improve its asset utilisation by utilising its tangible assets and working capital more effectively. To calculate the ratios you need to know its 2002 tangible assets and working capital. The tangible assets are taken straight from the balance sheet, £495.1 million. The working capital is the stocks of £414.3 million plus the trade debtors of £303.9 million less the trade creditors of £167.5 million, a total of £550.7 million. (I've extracted the trade debtors and trade creditors numbers from the notes to the accounts.)

The tangible asset turn

Johnson Matthey's tangible asset turn is 9.76 times.

$$\frac{\textit{Turnover}}{\textit{Tangible assets}} = \frac{4{,}830.1}{495.1} = \mathbf{9.76\ times}$$

This means that every pound it invests in tangible assets generates £9.76 sales.

The working capital ratio

Johnson Matthey's working capital ratio is 0.114:

$$\frac{\textit{Working capital}}{\textit{Turnover}} = \frac{550.7}{4{,}830.1} = \mathbf{0.114}$$

This means that, at its current levels of working capital, it needs to find 11.4 pence in cash to fund every pound's worth of sales it makes. This ratio can be very useful if the company you're analysing is planning to expand, as you can use this to see if the company has enough cash to finance its expansion programme at current levels of working capital. I'll show you how, by using Johnson Matthey's cash balance. At the end of 2002 it had £92.6 million cash, and this would be enough to support increased sales of £812.28 million (92.6 ÷ 0.114). Its existing cash balances would support a 16.8% increase in sales. It's just as useful if the company's sales are declining, as you can work out how much cash would be generated from a fall in sales. So if Johnson Matthey's sales fell by 10%, at current levels of working capital, it would generate just over £55.06 million cash (4,830.1 × 0.114) from the reduction in its working capital.

You now know its overall working capital ratio; let's look at its subsidiary ratios by analysing the components of working capital.

Control of stocks

You've seen that there are two different ways of analysing stocks – the stock turn, and stock days. You can also analyse stocks using cost of sales, or turnover, as a comparable measure for companies with similar profit margins. I'll show you how to calculate all four possible combinations, although you'd only ever use one in a financial analysis. The choice is yours!

Stock turn

This shows you how many times in a year the company converts its stock into sales. The higher the number, the more effectively the company is managing its stocks. As I'll also be using cost of sales in some of the ratios, you need to know that Johnson Matthey's cost of sales before exceptional items in 2002 was £4,502.5million.

Turnover based:

$$\frac{\textit{Turnover}}{\textit{Stock}} = \frac{4{,}830.1}{414.3} = \mathbf{11.66\ times}$$

Cost of sales based:

$$\frac{\textit{Cost of sales}}{\textit{Stock}} = \frac{4{,}502.5}{414.3} = \mathbf{10.87\ times}$$

There isn't much difference between using turnover and cost of sales, but this is unusual as it's caused by Johnson Matthey's high materials costs. Now let's have a look at the alternative way of measuring stock control – stock days.

Stock days

This shows you how many days' stock the business is carrying. A low number usually indicates efficient stock control.

Turnover based:

$$\frac{\textit{Stock}}{\textit{Turnover}} \times 365 = \frac{414.3}{4{,}830.1} \times 365 = \mathbf{31.31\ days}$$

Cost of sales based:

$$\frac{\textit{Stock}}{\textit{Cost of sales}} \times 365 = \frac{414.3}{4{,}502.5} \times 365 = \mathbf{33.59\ days}$$

Debtor days, or the collection period

This shows you how long Johnson Matthey's customers take to pay them.

$$\frac{\textit{Trade debtors}}{\textit{Turnover}} \times 365 = \frac{303.9}{4{,}830.1} \times 365 = \mathbf{22.97\ days}$$

Creditor days, or the payment period

This gives an indication of how long Johnson Matthey takes to pay its suppliers. The creditor days calculation can use either turnover or cost of sales, and I'll show you both.

Turnover based:

$$\frac{\textit{Trade creditors}}{\textit{Turnover}} \times 365 = \frac{167.5}{4{,}830.1} \times 365 = 12.66 \text{ days}$$

Cost of sales based:

$$\frac{\textit{Trade creditors}}{\textit{Cost of sales}} \times 365 = \frac{167.5}{4{,}502.5} \times 365 = 13.58 \text{ days}$$

What have we learnt?

To be honest, not much more than we knew already, having looked at the company's financial statements. Its biggest cost is materials, which is what you'd expect in a business whose main material is precious metals. Its return on trading capital employed, 17.5%, is greater than its overall return on capital employed, 16.8% – but that's not surprising given its balance between fixed asset investments and cash and short-term investments. Interest rates are not exciting in 2002. The company's return on capital is driven by asset utilisation rather than operating profits. Again not unusual in a company with a large refinery business, where plants are run throughout the year.

Profitability ratios have to be viewed over a number of years. You really want to know if Johnson Matthey is more, or less, profitable than it was and why its profitability is changing. I'm afraid you'll have to wait until Chapter 14 to discover the trend.

12

Cash management

- **The operating and financial reviews**
- **The cash flow statement** – the operational cash flow; interest cover; cash available for investment; matching funds to applications
- **The loan profile** – the types of loans; the loan repayment schedule
- **Johnson Matthey's cash management** – vulnerability to a fall in receipts; cash interest cover; matching funds to applications; its loan profile; what have we learnt?

There's a close relationship between cash management and solvency, as a company that manages its cash resources effectively is unlikely to have any solvency problems. Consequently, the way that a company manages its cash is crucial to its long-term survival. It has to fund the business in the most efficient way and optimise its use of cash resources. If you want to understand a company's financial performance, its opportunities and its threats you must be able to analyse the way that it is managing cash. To do this you have to look at its:

- operating and financial reviews;
- cash flow statement;
- working capital ratios;
- loan profile.

The operating and financial reviews

These give you useful insights into a company, its opportunities, problems and cash management:

- The operating review identifies the main factors affecting the business's performance and gives a full discussion on the operating results. Because it analyses the business's dynamics and identifies the main risks and uncertainties facing the business, it gives useful insights that are not found elsewhere in the accounts.
- You saw, in Chapter 7, that Johnson Matthey's financial review talked you through the financial statements and identified the main factors for the changes in the business's financial performance. It also talked about some of the risks facing the company and the way that they're managed. There's a lot of information about the company's cash flow management, including:
  - specific information about its operational cash flows and the factors affecting them;
  - its current liquidity, seasonal borrowing requirements, and the maturity profile of its borrowings.

The cash flow statement

Once you have an overview of the company's cash management, you can start to analyse its cash flow during the year in more detail. The cash flow statement shows the year's cash inflows and outflows, and is discussed in detail in Chapter 4. The cash flows are categorised in a way that makes the business's cash movement during the year easy to understand.

I'll use the cash flow statement (Table 12.1) in my example to illustrate the analysis of a cash flow statement. But you'll see that this is a more detailed version than the one in Chapter 9, as I've detailed the operational cash flow, and reconciled it to the operating profit and the net debt.

Table 12.1 Cash flow statement

Operating activities	
Cash received from customers	95,000
Cash paid to suppliers	(35,000)
Cash paid to, and on behalf of, employees	(24,000)
Other cash paid	(29,000)
Net cash inflow from operating activities	*7,000*
Returns on investment and servicing of finance:	
Interest received	1,000
Interest paid	(7,000)
Net cash outflow from returns on investment and servicing of finance	*(6,000)*
Taxation:	
Tax paid	(1,500)
Net cash outflow from taxation	*(1,500)*
Capital expenditure:	
Purchase of fixed assets	(15,000)
Disposal of fixed assets	2,000
Net cash outflow from capital expenditure	*(13,000)*
Equity dividends paid	*(1,000)*
Net cash outflow before financing	*(14,500)*
Financing:	
Issue of ordinary share capital	5,000
Loan	5,000
Net cash inflow from financing	*10,000*
Decrease in cash	*(4,500)*

Notes to the cash flow statement

1. *Reconciliation of operating profit to net cash inflow from operating activities*

Operating profit	10,000
Depreciation	1,000
Increase in stock	(2,000)
Increase in debtors	(5,000)
Increase in creditors	3,000
Net cash inflow from operating activities	7,000

2. *Reconciliation of net cash to movement in net borrowings:*

(Decrease) in cash in the year	(4,500)
Cash (inflow) from borrowings	(5,000)
Movement in net borrowings for the year	(9,500)
Net borrowings at the start of the year	(5,000)
Net borrowings at the end of the year	(14,500)

If you're analysing a cash flow statement it's useful to consider:

- How vulnerable is the company's operational cash flow to a fall in cash receipts?
- What is the cash interest cover?
- What proportion of the investment in fixed assets is being generated from internal sources?
- Is the company matching long-term sources of funds to long-term applications?

The operational cash flow

In my example I've shown both the period's cash receipts and payments for operating items and the note reconciling the operating profit to the operational cash flow. This means that you can see both *what* the cash flows are and *why* they're this amount. I've shown you the receipts and payments, so that I can show you two ways to identify the company's vulnerability to a fall in cash receipts.

First, let's look at the note reconciling the operational cash flow to the operating profit. The current year's trading *will* generate £11,000 (the profit plus the depreciation charge). However, the company has only managed to generate £7,000 because an additional net £4,000 has had to be tied up in the working capital. The increase in stock (£2,000) has been more than covered by the increase in creditors (£3,000), suggesting that the company may either be taking longer to pay its suppliers or has had an increase in its other creditors. (This could happen if capital expenditure increased during the year. If these were real accounts, you would have two years' figures and could check this by looking at the note on creditors and calculating the creditor days.) The big movement in the working capital has come from debtors, which have increased by £5,000. (Again, with two years' figures and the notes, you could see if this meant that customers were taking longer to pay the company, or its sales were expanding.)

So the reconciliation note tells you that the largest increase in working capital has come from the debtors. Now, let's look at the receipts in the cash flow from operating activities. The company's cash receipts were £95,000. The company appears to be vulnerable to a fall in receipts, as it would only take a fall in receipts of 7.4% (7,000 ÷ 95,000) for the company to lose its operational cash flow. Whether this was likely to happen depends on the trends in debtor days. So you know the percentage, but what does this mean in days?

The working capital ratios

I calculated these in the last chapter, using information from the profit and loss account and the balance sheet. These ratios always give you some useful information. The cash flow statement identifies that the additional £4,000 invested in the working capital reduced the company's operating cash flow, and that this has contributed to its cash flow problems. The working capital ratios tell you whether this was because increased business required more working capital, or the management is less efficient in controlling its working capital.

Unfortunately, I can't work this out, as I don't have any comparative figures. However, I can use the debtor days' calculation from the last chapter to find out whether the 7.4% fall in cash receipts is likely to happen.

$$\frac{\textit{Trade debtors}}{\textit{Turnover}} \times 365 = \frac{25{,}000}{100{,}000} \times 365 = \mathbf{91.3\ days}$$

Last year the company's turnover was £100,000, so on average it sold around £274 every day (100,000 ÷ 365 = 273.97). Now I've worked out, using the cash receipts, that a 7.4% reduction in the cash receipts eliminates the operating cash flow of £7,000. Now I can turn this into debtor days. The debtor days would have to increase by over 25 days to lose £7,000 (7,000 ÷ 273.97 = 25.55). This increase in debtor days is probably unlikely.

Interest cover

This can be worked out from the cash flow statement, as well as the profit and loss account. You can see that in my example the company is just covering its interest paid with its operational cash flow and the interest received. Whilst you can see that the company is close to having difficulties with its bank, you can't draw any conclusions from one year's cash flows.

Cash available for investment

This is a useful measure that shows if the company's capital expenditure and acquisitions could be funded from any of the cash generated during the year. You can identify this from the following cash flows:

Net cash flow from operating activities	7,000
Net cash flow from returns on investment and servicing of finance	(7,000)
Net cash flow from taxation	(1,500)
Equity dividends paid	(1,000)
Cash available for investment	(2,500)

As the company's operational cash flow just manages to cover its cash flows from returns on investment and servicing of finance, it is unable to fund anything from the current year's cash flow. Any investment in its business would have to be financed from existing cash balances, external sources, or disposals.

Matching funds to applications

It is important that a company acquires its long-term assets with long-term funds – buying fixed assets with bank overdrafts is risky. The bank can demand repayment at any time, whereas the payback from fixed assets is long term. On the other hand, funding seasonal working capital requirements with overdrafts is a reasonable option. The general rule is that long-term assets should be funded with long-term sources of funds.

The company in my example spent £12,000, net, on its fixed asset purchases, and raised £5,000 from a share issue and £5,000 from long-term loans. The balance of £2,000 was partly funded by using £500 from its cash balance, with the remainder coming from bank overdrafts. This means that £10,500 came from long-term sources and there's a £1,500 'mismatch'. On its own it doesn't appear serious, but it could indicate poor cash management.

The loan profile

Looking at the types of borrowing that a company has can tell you a lot about the way it manages its cash. You'll find information about:

- the types of loans it has;
- when the loans have to be repaid;
- its current maximum agreed level of borrowings;
- its exposure to interest rate movements and how it manages this exposure.

Listed companies usually disclose some of this information in their financial review, and the rest can be found by reading the notes carefully.

The types of loans

Loans can be secured, or unsecured. Whilst it is common for small private companies to have secured borrowings, in the UK it is unusual for large listed companies to have secured loans. When you look at some multinational companies' accounts you may find a small proportion of their borrowings is secured. This tends to be in their overseas subsidiaries, as in some countries there is a legal requirement that all loans are secured. Consequently, if you are looking at a large company's accounts and find that previously all loans were unsecured, but are now secured, you have an indication of its bank's level of confidence, or rather lack of confidence, in the company.

It is worth remembering that not all loans have to be repaid. There are an increasing number of convertible loans, usually in the form of bonds. (These are shown separately on the balance sheet.) These loans give the lender the option, usually on maturity, to receive cash when the loan is repaid, or to convert into shares at a price that was fixed when the bond was issued. If the option price is below the share's current market price, the bondholders would be better off converting into ordinary shares, and then selling the shares if they want the cash. In that situation, it is unlikely that the bondholders would exercise the cash option. But it all hinges on the company's current share price. So if the company has convertible bonds you need to compare the current market price, and its trend, with the option price, as this will give you an indication of whether the company is likely to have to repay the loan.

The loan repayment schedule

You may remember that I showed you the importance of the loan repayment schedule in Chapter 10 when discussing solvency.

You've already seen that the company in my example would have difficulties repaying its loans in the short term – there's insufficient cash being generated in the business to cover its tax bill, let alone repay any loans. But it doesn't have to repay its loans now; all we know at the moment is that it will have to repay them at some time in the future. *When* they have to be repaid is obviously important, and that's why you need to look at the company's loan repayment schedule. If it isn't generating sufficient cash to repay them when they fall due it will have only three alternatives:

- have a share issue to repay its loans – but this is unlikely to be possible in the short term, as it has just had a share issue;
- repay its existing loans with new loans – again unlikely because of its poor interest cover and cash generation;
- sell some assets, or businesses.

Johnson Matthey's cash management

Now you've already discovered that Johnson Matthey is solvent, so you'd expect it to manage its cash well. Let's see if it does . . .

There's a copy of Johnson Matthey's cash flow statement on page 262, so that I can review its cash management in 2002. The improvement in its operating cash flow came from changes in its working capital, which moved from a net cash outflow of £58 million in 2001, to a small cash inflow of £1.9 million in 2002. In 2002 it had significantly increased cash outflows for taxation, capital expenditure and financial investment, and acquisitions. There were also smaller movements in interest (it moved from a net interest-receiving position to a net interest-paying one) and dividends (where the cash payment increased by more than 12%). This meant that its cash outflow before management of liquid resources and financing increased to £165.3 million. Whilst there were small inflows from financing and liquid resources, most of the funding came from the group's cash resources.

Vulnerability to a fall in receipts

In 2002 Johnson Matthey's turnover was £4,830.1 million, which means that if its customers took an extra day to pay, it would lose just over £13.2 million cash (4,830.1 ÷ 365 = 13.233). As its operational cash flow was £224.1 million, its customers would have to take almost 17 more days to pay it before the operational cash flow is eliminated. As they're currently paying in just under 23 days, payment terms would have to increase by over 70%, and it is highly unlikely that this would happen.

Cash interest cover

You may recall from Chapter 10 that Johnson Matthey has no problems affording its interest, as its interest cover is almost 46 times!

$$\frac{\textit{Operational cash flow}}{\textit{Net interest paid}} = \frac{224.1}{4.9} = \mathbf{45.7\ times}$$

Consolidated Cash Flow Statement

Annual Report and Accounts 2002

for the year ended 31st March 2002

	Notes	2002 £ million	2001 £ million
Reconciliation of operating profit to net cash inflow from operating activities			
Operating profit		**168.5**	174.1
Depreciation and amortisation charges		**55.1**	41.1
Profit on disposal of tangible fixed assets and investments		**(1.4)**	(0.7)
(Increase)/decrease in owned stocks		**(83.6)**	15.0
Decrease/(increase) in debtors		**73.9**	(82.0)
Increase in creditors and provisions		**11.6**	9.0
Net cash inflow from operating activities		**224.1**	156.5
Cash Flow Statement			
Net cash inflow from operating activities		**224.1**	156.5
Dividends received from associates		**0.1**	0.1
Returns on investments and servicing of finance	27	**(4.9)**	5.8
Taxation		**(55.8)**	(38.2)
Capital expenditure and financial investment	27	**(131.0)**	(94.7)
Acquisitions and disposals			
Acquisitions	27	**(143.5)**	(6.2)
Disposals	27	**(2.2)**	0.6
Net cash outflow for acquisitions and disposals		**(145.7)**	(5.6)
Equity dividends paid		**(52.1)**	(46.5)
Net cash outflow before use of liquid resources and financing		**(165.3)**	(22.6)
Management of liquid resources	27	**0.2**	157.8
Financing			
Issue and purchase of share capital	27	**(44.1)**	7.9
Increase/(decrease) in borrowings and finance leases	27	**57.5**	(12.1)
Net cash inflow/(outflow) from financing		**13.4**	(4.2)
(Decrease)/increase in cash in the period		**(151.7)**	131.0
Reconciliation of net cash flow to movement in net debt			
(Decrease)/increase in cash in the period		**(151.7)**	131.0
Cash (inflow)/outflow from movement in borrowings and finance leases	28	**(57.5)**	12.1
Cash inflow from term deposits included in liquid resources		**(0.2)**	(157.8)
Change in net funds/debt resulting from cash flows		**(209.4)**	(14.7)
Borrowings acquired with subsidiaries		**(46.8)**	(1.3)
Loan notes issued to acquire subsidiaries		**(40.6)**	–
New finance leases		**(4.3)**	–
Translation difference	28	**2.2**	(9.9)
Movement in net funds/debt in year		**(298.9)**	(25.9)
Net funds at beginning of year	28	**139.9**	165.8
Net (debt)/funds at end of year	28	**(159.0)**	139.9

Now let's consider Johnson Matthey's cash management in more detail.

Matching funds to applications

If you look at Johnson Matthey's cash flow statement, you can group its cash flows into those that are associated with 'revenue' items, reinvestment, and capital restructuring.

Some of its operating cash flow has to be used to pay interest, tax and dividends, and it received some dividends from its associates. I've classified these cash flows as 'revenue' items:

Net cash inflow from operating activities	224.1
Dividends received from associates	0.1
Returns on investments and servicing of finance	(4.9)
Taxation	(55.8)
Equity dividends paid	(52.1)
Operating cash flow available for reinvestment	111.4

So, having taken account of financing costs and tax, Johnson Matthey has £111.4 million of its 2002 operational cash flow available to reinvest in its business. I'll consider the reinvestment in its existing business first. It spent a net £131 million on capital expenditure; so most of its capital expenditure (85%) could be funded from its operating cash flow, with only £19.6 million to be funded from other long-term sources. It also made acquisitions costing a net £145.7 million, so in total it had £165.3 million to fund from long-term sources. It raised £6.1 million from the exercise of share options and a net £57.5 million from loans. The balance, of £101.7 million, was partly funded from the net withdrawal of £0.2 million from its liquid resources and using some of the opening £237.4 million cash balance. Its cash also funded its £50.2 million share buy-back, leaving a cash balance of £85.7 million at the end of 2002. You see this reflected on the cash flow statement when its cash decreased in 2002 by £151.7 million (237.4 – 85.7 = 151.7).

So you can see that Johnson Matthey matched its long-term sources of funds with its long-term expenditure, using its large cash balances to fund part of the expenditure. (You may recall from Chapter 11 that its return on its operating capital was 17.6% – much higher than current interest rates.)

Its loan profile

First, you need to see the type of loans that Johnson Matthey has, and this is disclosed in the notes to its accounts.

18 Borrowings and finance leases

	Group 2002 £ million	Group 2001 £ million
Borrowings and finance leases falling due after more than one year		
Bank and other loans repayable by instalments		
From two to five years	**0.8**	0.4
From one to two years	**0.1**	0.1
Bank and other loans repayable otherwise than by instalments		
6.36% US Dollar Bonds 2006	**70.2**	70.3
Other after five years	**6.0**	6.0
Other from two to five years	**104.6**	–
Finance leases repayable		
After five years	**3.2**	–
From two to five years	**0.7**	0.5
From one to two years	**0.2**	0.4
Borrowings and finance leases falling due after more than one year	**185.8**	77.7

You can see that most of its loans are bank loans largely repayable at the end of their term, and most of the repayments have to be made in two to five years' time. It has one bond, repayable in 2006.

In its financial review it discloses its interest rate risk and liquidity policy, and you'll see that it hasn't used all of its borrowing facilities:

Interest Rate Risk

At 31st March 2002 the group had net borrowings of £159.0 million. This included £70.2 million (US $100 million) of long term fixed rate borrowings in the form of an issue of US dollar bonds, which carry an interest coupon of 6.36%. The remaining 56% of the group's net borrowings are funded on a floating rate basis, mainly in the form of loans under committed bank facilities. A 1% change in all interest rates would have a 0.6% impact on group profit before tax. This is well within the range the board regards as acceptable.

Liquidity Policy

Our policy on funding capacity is to ensure that we always have sufficient long term funding and committed bank facilities in place to meet foreseeable peak borrowing requirements. The group has committed bank facilities of £255 million. Borrowings drawn under these facilities at 31st March 2002 amounted to £107.5 million. The group also has a number of uncommitted facilities and overdraft lines.

Most of its loans don't have fixed interest rates, so it is exposed to interest rate movements with profit before tax changing by 0.6% for every 1% change in interest rates.

What have we learnt?

Johnson Matthey can afford to support higher levels of borrowing, and if expansion, or acquisition, opportunities arise it has additional borrowing facilities in place. It manages its cash in a prudent way, matching funds to applications.

13

The investor's perspective

- **The investment ratios** – earnings per share (eps); dividends per share; the price/earnings (PE) ratio/the multiple; PEGs; the earnings yield; the return on equity; book value, or net asset value, per share; price to book ratio; price to sales; cash flow; EBITDA and enterprise value
- **Shareholder value**
- **Summary** – Valuations based on earnings; dividends; assets; sales; cash; EBITDA; enterprise value; discounted cash; shareholder value-VBM and EVA™
- **Johnson Matthey's investment ratios in 2002** – earnings-based ratios; dividend-based ratios; asset-based ratios; sales-based ratios; cash-based ratios; EBITDA; enterprise value; what have we learnt?

You already know why people invest in shares – they want to make money! No one would invest in a company unless they thought they were going to make money, and preferably more money than they can get from a bank, or a building society. There are two ways to make money from shares – either the price rises and you have a capital gain on your investment that can only be realised when you sell the shares, or you receive dividends. Some shares attract investors looking for growth (capital gain), and others attract those looking for income (dividend payments). You'll find this reflected in some of the ratios that analyse the company's performance from the investor's point of view.

Investors are interested in:

- the return on their investment, and this can be expressed in two different ways:
  - the overall return, the return on equity;
  - the annual return, dividends;
- the stock market's view of the future return on their investment:
  - the price earnings, also called the PE, ratio.

Analysts also use other measures based on assets, sales, cash flow, market value, and shareholder value. Institutional investors use a combination of these to identify whether the share represents a good investment, considering the company's ratios with other companies in its sector.

In this chapter I'll look at the company from the investor's perspective, showing you how to calculate these investment ratios, and tell you what they reveal about the company's performance.

The investment ratios

I'm going to start by introducing you to two other ratios that are published in company accounts – earnings per share and dividends per share, as they are used in some of the other investment ratios.

Earnings per share (eps)

The earnings per share figure is shown at the bottom of listed companies' profit and loss account (I didn't include it in Johnson Matthey's profit and loss account in Chapter 2, as I hadn't told you what it was). It's an important ratio for all investors, and institutional investors are always attracted to companies showing earnings per share growth. In principle it's fairly easy to calculate, as it's the profit attributable to ordinary shareholders divided by the number of shares in issue. So if this profit was £2,000 and there were 10,000 shares in issue, the earnings per share would be 10 pence. If you had only one share in this company, 10 pence of the profit would be yours! You are unlikely to receive all this as dividends, so the immediate cash benefit will probably be less. The retained earnings affects the share price, as long as the market believes that the additional investment will generate increased profits in the future. So the earnings per share influence the two possible returns for investors, as if the earnings per share grow, the dividends and the share price will probably increase as well.

All listed companies have to publish their earnings per share in the accounts. This is calculated on the basis of:

$$\frac{\textit{Profit attributable to ordinary shareholders}}{\textit{Number of ordinary shares in issue}}$$

Let's work out the earnings per share in my example – the relevant extracts from the financial statements are shown below.

Profit and loss account extract:

Profit before tax		4,000
Tax	This is the profit	(2,000)
Profit after tax ←	that is attributable	2,000
Dividends	to the ordinary	(1,000)
Retained profit	shareholders	1,000

(You'll recall that my example is a simple one – there are preference shares or minority interests to be deducted from the profit after tax.)

Balance sheet extract:

Capital and reserves:	There are 20,000	
Share capital (nominal value 1.00 each)	shares in issue at	20,000
Profit and loss account	their year end	30,000
		50,000

Cash flow statement extract:

Financing:	They've had a	
Issue of ordinary share capital	share issue	5,000
Loan	during the year	5,000
Net cash inflow from financing		*10,000*

The share issue complicates the calculation of the number of shares in issue, as the figure used is usually the weighted average number of shares in issue during the year. There are only two exceptions to this:

- A rights issue: this is slightly more complicated, as you have to account for the discount element in the price.
- A change in the company's capital structure that has no corresponding increase in its available resources. (This happens in a share split or a bonus issue.) In this case, the company has to base *all* the earnings per share figures shown in the accounts on the new number of shares, even if the change occurred after its balance sheet date.

If the company had had the share issue three months before its year end, the weighted average number of shares in issue would be 16,250 [(20,000 × 0.25) + (15,000 × 0.75)]. This means that its earnings per share would be:

$$\frac{2{,}000}{16{,}250} = \mathbf{0.123}$$

(If the company's reporting currency was sterling, this would be expressed as 12.3 pence.

There's usually more than one earnings per share . . .

Unfortunately, the calculation of earnings per share is not always this simple, as it's often complicated by:

- **Goodwill amortisation and exceptional items:** these can distort the trends; consequently, most companies also show an *adjusted* earnings per share eliminating the effect of goodwill amortisation and exceptional items.
- **Share options:** the exercise of share options and warrants can reduce the earnings per share in the future, if the number of shares increases without a corresponding improvement in profits. This is referred to as *earnings dilution*. The accounting standard (FRS 14 *Earnings per share*) requires all companies having outstanding share options to publish also a *diluted earnings per share*, including all the outstanding options in the number of shares.

This means that usually you'll find that companies publish a number of earnings per share figures, reflecting different profit figures and numbers of shares. The three earnings per share figures you'll usually find at the bottom of companies' profit and loss accounts are:

- a *basic* earnings per share figure, calculated by dividing the profit attributable to ordinary shareholders by the weighted average number of shares in issue;
- a *diluted* earnings per share figure, calculated by dividing the profit attributable to ordinary shareholders by the weighted average number of shares in issue plus any outstanding share options;
- an *adjusted* earnings per share figure. Companies can show other earnings per share figures, and many show one that is calculated by dividing the profit before exceptional items and goodwill amortisation that is attributable to ordinary shareholders by the weighted average number of shares in issue. This gives you an understanding of the underlying earnings per share and is the earnings figure used by the financial press (see below) to calculate the published ratios.

  Companies may show two adjusted figures – an adjusted basic earnings per share, and an adjusted diluted earnings per share.

And there's going to be more earnings per share figures in the future . . .

If the proposals in the alignment proposal (FRED 26 *Earnings per share*) are accepted you'll find another two earnings per share figures on the profit and loss account. Both the basic and diluted earnings per share will also have to be calculated using the profit from continuing operations. This will give you a measure of sustainable earnings.

And the financial press and analysts use yet another earnings calculation . . .

You've seen that companies show a number of earnings per share figures in their accounts. Whilst presenting multiple earnings per share figures represents a more realistic view of the company's performance, it is a problem for businesses like the *The Financial Times* whose readers would find it confusing to be confronted by a number of different ratios. Consequently, the financial press use a definition of earnings developed by the UK's Society of Investment Professionals (the analysts' professional body). This adjusts for some, but not all, exceptional items, and provides a more comparable basis for measuring a company's performance.

Dividends per share

I know it's unusual in accounting, but this is just what it says it is! It's the dividend that is paid on each of the company's shares. It's usually disclosed in the accounts, but can be simply calculated by dividing the total dividend by the number of shares receiving the dividend.

In my example the company proposes to pay £1,000 in dividends, and had 20,000 shares in issue. (The dividend shown on the profit and loss account is the final proposed dividend – you can see in the cash flow statement that there haven't been any dividends paid during the year.) The dividend per share is calculated by dividing the total dividend by the number of shares receiving the dividend, so the dividend per share is £0.05:

$$\frac{1{,}000}{20{,}000} = \mathbf{0.05}$$

It's worth mentioning that not all companies pay dividends. Microsoft has never paid a dividend and doesn't intend to. It believes that shareholders get a better return if they forgo a cash payment and the money is reinvested in the business. This means that Microsoft's shareholders only get a return if its share price rises, and they have to sell shares if they want any cash.

You now understand the two ratios that are published in the financial statements, and I'll now show you how they're used in other investment ratios. You know that the shareholder will receive £0.05 as a dividend – but is the company being generous, or mean? To find out you look at its *dividend cover*, or the *payout ratio*.

Dividend cover

This is similar to interest cover, and measures how many times the dividend could be paid from the available profits.

$$\frac{\textit{Profit attributable to ordinary shareholders}}{\textit{Dividends}} = \frac{2{,}000}{1{,}000} = \mathbf{2\ times}$$

The payout ratio

This expresses the dividend cover in a different way, identifying the percentage of the available profit that is paid out as dividends:

$$\frac{\textit{Dividends}}{\textit{Profit attributable to ordinary shareholders}} \times 100 = \frac{1{,}000}{2{,}000} = \mathbf{50\%}$$

The company is paying out half of the available profit as dividends. The more the company gives to its shareholders, the less it has available to reinvest in the business. Determining the size of the dividend is a fine balancing act for most companies. They want to pay sufficient to maintain a stable share price, but they need to retain funds for reinvestment. Dividend cover at two times may appear imprudent, but it's not unusual for a UK company to pay this percentage. And, just like salary increases for staff, the decision is largely determined by people's expectations, and what everyone else is paying.

Dividend yield

The dividend yield tells us the percentage cash return on the investment, and can be directly compared with interest rates and other investment opportunities. It expresses the dividend per share as a percentage of the current share price. The dividend yield is calculated using the following formula:

$$\frac{\textit{Dividend per share}}{\textit{Today's share price}} \times 100$$

To calculate the dividend yield for my example, I have to know the market price and it's £2.46. This means that the dividend yield is 2.03%:

$$\frac{0.05}{2.46} = \mathbf{2.03\%}$$

So if you buy the share at the current price, and dividends remain the same, you'd receive a cash return of 2.03% on your investment. I've used the current share price in my example, but if you use the ratios published in the financial press, the share price isn't the same as the cash you would receive if you sold the share, or the price you'd have to pay to buy the share. It is the average of the buy price and the sell price – the 'mid' price. The dividend yield published in the financial press is updated for any subsequent interim results.

The share offers a poor dividend return – I'd be better off keeping my money in a bank. However, it may offer some scope for capital gain. This depends on the company's ability to deliver future profit growth, relative to its sector, and to see the market's view of the share's potential I have to look at another ratio, the *price earnings* ratio.

The price earnings (PE) ratio/the multiple

There are different names for the same thing. *The Financial Times* publishes listed companies' PE ratios, but often talks about their multiples in its articles. The price earnings ratio compares the company's current share price to its reported earnings per share:

$$\frac{\textit{Today's share price}}{\textit{Earnings per share}}$$

Using a share price of £2.46 for the company in my example, it has a PE ratio of 20.

$$\frac{2.46}{0.123} = \mathbf{20}$$

All published PE ratios are updated for interim results. You now know how to calculate the PE ratio, but what does it tell you? The company's share price is 20 times its current earnings. This means that if you buy the shares at today's price of £2.46, and profits remain constant, it will take you 20 years to get your money back and still hold the share. (You'll get your money back from the dividends paid and the capital gain. Both are reflected in the earnings calculation. Dividends are paid out of after-tax profits, and relative retained profits should improve the share price if they're reinvested wisely.)

Although people criticise the stock market for its short-termism, there are very few of us who would be prepared to wait 20 years to get our money back! Most investors are looking for a payback in five to seven years, depending on the investment's risk profile. So if someone is prepared to pay 20 times current earnings, but expects to get their money back in five to seven years, they're expecting profits to rise significantly in the next few years. You're taking a *current* figure, the share price, and comparing it with a *historical* figure, the earnings per share. A high PE ratio usually indicates that the market *expects* profits to grow (although it might just be that the share is expensive). A low PE usually means that the market *expects* profits to fall. You'll notice that I've italicised the word expects – a high PE ratio isn't necessarily 'good'; neither is a low PE a bad sign. It's about the market's expectation, which may or may not be realised.

If the market believes that earnings will grow, and the company has a profits warning, the share price will fall steeply. A share with a high PE is often volatile; small pieces of good news (supporting the market's view) will cause the price to jump. However, any small item of bad news (contradicting the market's view) and the price will plummet.

Now here's another way of looking at PE ratios . . .

Prospective PEs

As the share price reflects expectations of *future* earnings, it is often more appropriate to compare the price to the expected earnings – this is called the *prospective PE.* This uses the estimated earnings per share for the year, rather than the latest published earnings per share. The prospective PE matches the anticipated current earnings with the current price. So if the earnings in my company were expected to double from the reported £0.123 to

£0.246, the prospective PE would be half the PE published in the financial press – 10 times earnings (2.46 ÷ 0.246). You can see that this is probably a more useful measure – the market has already built the anticipated profit growth into the current price. The company may have had a bad year last year and is now expected to recover. This example illustrates that a high PE doesn't necessarily mean that the company is a growth stock; it may simply reflect that the company has had a temporary fall in its profits.

As the prospective PE is based on an individual analyst's view of current earnings, a company's prospective PE will vary from analyst to analyst (although you can get consensus earnings forecasts as you'll discover later). In practice, the historic earnings are also likely to be adjusted, as analysts don't necessarily rely on the published figures. There has sometimes been a tendency for reported earnings per share figures to be 'managed' – after all, directors' bonuses and reported ratios depended on it!

PE relatives

A company's PE ratio should be considered in context, relative to the market and the company's sector. Share prices move with:

- the market as a whole;
- the relative attractiveness of the sector;
- the company's position within the sector;
- the market's view of the company's performance.

The Financial Times publishes sector averages in the Actuaries share indices, and some ratios for the sector. Consequently, it's possible to look at the company's performance relative to its sector by using the following calculation:

$$\frac{\textit{PE ratio of the company}}{\textit{PE ratio of the sector}}$$

Looking at the company's relative performance within the sector gives you an indication of the market's view of the company's relative attractiveness. A company with a PE of 20 looks to have a lot of potential for profit growth, but if the sector average PE is 25, this company is believed to offer less potential for growth than most other companies in its sector.

So PE ratios reflect the market's view of the company's profit growth over the next few years, now let me introduce you to another way of looking at growth – the PEG ratio.

PEGs

The PEG ratio was developed a few years ago by Jim Slater. It is another earnings-based measure that compares the price earnings ratio with the forecasted earnings growth, hence the name PEG (*p*rice *e*arnings to *g*rowth). In my example the prospective price earnings ratio is 10 and the forecasted earnings growth is 100%, as the earnings per share is expected to double from £0.123 to £0.246. This means that the PEG would be 0.1 (10 ÷ 100). A good investment is supposed to have a PEG less than one, as this means that the expected earnings' growth hasn't been fully reflected in the share price. So at last there is something positive to say about the company in my example!

PE ratios are used in the PEG ratio, but there's another way of comparing the price to the earnings – the *earnings yield*.

The earnings yield

The earnings yield is the reciprocal of the PE ratio, and is calculated in the same way as the dividend yield:

$$\frac{\textit{Earnings per share}}{\textit{Today's share price}}$$

in my example the current share price is £2.46 and the company's earnings per share is 0.123, so the earnings yield is 5% (0.123 ÷ 2.46). This means that if you buy the share at the current price, and profits stay the same, you can expect to earn 5% on your money.

The PE ratio and the earnings yield look at the relationship between profit and the current share price. But there is another important relationship, that of profit to the capital that the shareholders have invested in the company – the *return on equity*.

The return on equity

This is an overall measure of the return on the shareholder's investment, looking at the investment in the context of the company's book value. It takes the profit attributable to ordinary shareholders and divides it by the company's share capital and reserves (also referred to as the company's *shareholders' funds* or *equity*):

$$\frac{\textit{Profit attributable to ordinary shareholders}}{\textit{Capital and reserves}}$$

In my example the capital and reserves are £50,000 and the profit attributable to ordinary shareholders is the profit after tax of £2,000, so the return on equity is 4% (2,000 ÷ 50,000). It doesn't sound like a good return on investment, but you would really need to know more information before you could take a view. You would need to know:

- what the returns on equity had been in the past;
- how they compare to their competitors' returns on equity;
- the components of the capital and reserves, and if they've changed. A revaluation of assets would have a detrimental effect on the return on equity, as would a share issue towards the end of the financial year (the additional profits arising from the cash injection wouldn't have had time to be fully reflected in increased profit).

As you can see, the return on equity suffers from the same problems as net worth and the return on capital. However, it is a popular measure, particularly overseas, where shareholders' funds are more comparable. The shareholders' funds also affects the next ratio.

Book value, or net asset value, per share

This tells you the value of the net assets attributable to each share, and is calculated by dividing the capital and reserves by the number of shares in issue:

$$\frac{\textit{Capital and reserves}}{\textit{Number of shares in issue}}$$

In my example this would be £2.50 (50,000 ÷ 20,000). This is often described as indicative of the company's break-up value, but this largely depends on the accuracy of the asset valuations. However, it does give some indication of how much of the share price is underpinned by the company's asset value and how much by its growth prospects. This relationship between the book value and the current price is measured in the *price to book ratio*.

Price to book ratio

This compares the book value, or net assets, per share with the current share price. If you felt that the book value reflected an accurate asset value, this ratio would provide you with an indication of the inherent security of the share. If the net asset value is higher than the market value, shareholders might get their money back if the company is liquidated.

$$\frac{\textit{Today's share price}}{\textit{Net asset value per share}}$$

In my example the current share price is £2.46 and the company's book value per share is 2.50, giving a price to book ratio of 0.984. This means that the market values the company almost 2% below its net book value. Another way to calculate this ratio is to compare the company's value on the stock market (called its *market capitalisation*) with its value to its ordinary shareholders in the accounts. The market capitalisation in my example is £49,200 (20,000 shares in issue × the current share price of £2.46). If I divide it by the £50,000 capital and reserves, I get the same price to book ratio of 0.984. This implies that the share price is underpinned by the company's asset value rather than its growth potential.

Price to sales

To calculate a price to sales ratio, you have to calculate the sales per share. In my example the turnover is £100,000, and the weighted average number of shares in issue is 16,250. This gives sales per share of £6.15 (100,000 ÷ 16,250). As the current share price is £2.46, the price to sales ratio is 0.4 (2.46 ÷ 6.15).

Like all price-based ratios, they're more meaningful if considered relative to the company's sector and are usually quoted as price to sales relative, in the same way as you see PE relatives. They offer a different perspective to earnings and cash-flow-based valuations, and are particularly useful in valuing cyclical stocks. Industries with high fixed costs and high breakeven points are often cyclical stocks, and small changes in their sales can have a dramatic effect on their earnings.

They can also be useful in other situations. Just think about a company adopting a long-term strategy and growing its market share to strengthen its future position. This strategy could have a detrimental effect on its earnings and cash flow in the short term. But this strategy would be evident in its sales per share ratio.

Price to sales should always be considered in the light of at least one other variable – the company's operating margins. A company could have a high price to sales relative because it has the highest operating margin in the sector. This should then work through to enhanced earnings, dividends, and cash flow.

In industries where companies have to have a high investment in research and development, like pharmaceuticals, just comparing operating margins wouldn't help explain differences in the price to sales ratios. There are a number of different ways that you can resolve this problem:

- The charge for research and development could be added back to operating profit.
- The price could be compared to research and development expenditure.
- The price should be considered relative to other businesses in the sector.

Price to sales ratios have a number of advantages:

- Sales are the same in every country, making it a useful measure for cross-border comparisons.
- Sales are easier to predict than earnings and cash flow, as they are more stable and have fewer determining variables.
- They are a very good basis for valuing cyclical businesses, which often have high fixed costs and earnings swings through the economic cycle.

Cash flow

Cash flow measures are generally thought to be better measures than earnings, as they can't be manipulated in the same way. There are two approaches to cash flow used in valuation:

- cash flow per share;
- discounted cash flow.

Cash flow per share

There are a number of different ways of calculating the cash flow per share, and I'll introduce you to:

- the cash that is available for investment;
- the two totally different definitions of free cash flow.

Cash available for reinvestment in the business

This method identifies the cash flow per share before any reinvestment in either the working capital or the fixed assets. This shows the cash that has been generated by the business and is available for reinvestment. To calculate it you would need to take information from the cash flow statement, and use the following formula:

$$\frac{\textit{The net operating cash flow + the cash flow from returns on investment and servicing of finance + the taxation cash flow}}{\textit{Weighted average number of shares}}$$

(You'll notice that dividend payments are not included in this definition, as they are usually determined after the company has decided how much it needs to reinvest in its business.)

The relevant extracts from my example's cash flow statement are:

Net cash inflow from operating activities	*7,000*
Net cash outflow from returns on investment and servicing of finance	*(6,000)*
Net cash outflow from taxation	*(1,500)*

The total cash flow available for reinvestment is then (£500) which when divided by the 16,250 weighted average number of shares in issue gives a cash flow per share of (£0.031). This means that the company has generated insufficient cash during the year to fund any reinvestment in its business.

If you access the Multex global estimates from their own website, or the FT.com website, this is the definition of cash flow per share they use in their analysis.

Free cash flow

I have some really bad news – free cash flow is a term that has two fundamentally different definitions.

- You may recall that Johnson Matthey defined free cash flow in its financial review as the cash flow after interest, tax, dividends, and capital expenditure but before acquisitions and share buy-backs. Companies often use this definition of free cash flow to describe the cash they've generated during the year that they could then spend on acquisitions or buy-backs.
- Now analysts define free cash flow very differently – it's the cash flow that is available to the providers of capital, after any reinvestment in the existing business. So it's the operating cash flow less taxation less capital expenditure and acquisitions and disposals. This is the definition of free cash flow I'll use, as it's the one that you'll come across in analysts' reports. It's also the definition used in the discounted cash flow valuations discussed in the following pages.

This means that analysts define free cash flow as the cash flow that's available for the providers of capital, and companies define it as the cash flow available for acquisitions and capital restructuring. Now I really don't think you could get much further apart! If anyone talks to you about a company's free cash flow, the first thing you have to ask them is how they've defined it!

Here's the relevant extracts from the cash flow statement.

Net cash inflow from operating activities	*7,000*
Net cash outflow from taxation	*(1,500)*
Net cash outflow from capital expenditure	*(13,000)*

The free cash flow is (£7,500), and the free cash flow per share is (£0.462). (The total free cash flow of (£7,500) ÷ 16,250 weighted average shares in issue.) This means that the large capital expenditure prevented the company from being able to fund its obligations to its providers of capital from the cash it generated during the year.

Price to cash flow

This ratio compares the price of the share to the cash flow per share. Different analysts use different cash flows for this ratio, so I'll show you how to calculate it using both the cash available for reinvestment in the business and the free cash flow. You'll see that the company in my example has negative figures, as both their cash flow per share figures are negative.

Based on the cash available for reinvestment in the business

If the company's current share price is £2.46, and the cash flow per share is (£0.031), the price to cash flow is 79.35.

Based on the free cash flow

If the company's current share price is £2.46, and the free cash flow per share is (£0.462), the price to cash flow is (5.32).

Discounted cash flow

Discounted cash flow takes a future value and identifies the original amount you would have had to invest to receive that amount in the future. The best way to show you what I mean is answer the question 'How much would I need to invest today to receive £105, in a year's time, if interest rates were 5%?' It's easy to work out:

$$\frac{105}{1.05} = 100$$

If you wanted to know how much you needed to invest to have £110.25 in two years' time and interest rates are at 5% the answer is the same, as you're getting another year's interest:

$$\frac{110.25}{1.05^2} = 100$$

This £100 is referred to as the *present value* of £110.25 using a *discount rate* of 5%.

This technique is applied to all sorts of investment decisions, and ideally the present value of an investment's cash flows should exceed the original investment. So if you were offered an investment opportunity, with the same risk as putting money on deposit, that guaranteed you £110.25 in two years' time but you were only asked to invest £95, you have a bargain! You are making £5 more than the alternative opportunity. This £5 is referred to as the *net present value*, and is the difference between the present value and the amount you're being asked to invest. As long as the present value is positive, you're doing better than putting the money in a bank; if it's negative, you'd be better off investing in the bank.

So a positive net present value indicates a good investment. However, whether an investment shows a positive net present value depends on two things:

- the accuracy of the predicted future cash flows;
- the discount rate used.

Discounted cash flow is a commonly used way of valuing a company. Theoretically, the value of a company is the present value of its free cash flows in perpetuity. Think about it – this means you have to estimate the company's free cash flows in perpetuity! In practice, however, the company's free cash flows are usually just estimated for a short period, three to five years, and the subsequent cash flows are determined using the growing perpetuity formula:

$$\frac{\textit{Free cash flow in the first year after the forecast period}}{\textit{Weighted average cost of capital – anticipated growth in future cash flows}}$$

Let me explain the formula by sharing a little secret with you – I'm going to live forever! And I think I'm going to need £100,000 a year to support my extravagant lifestyle. I'm trying to work out how much I'd need to invest to guarantee this annual income if interest rates are at 5%. Calculating this is fairly simple:

$$\frac{\textit{Required income}}{\textit{Interest rate}} = \frac{100{,}000}{5\%} = \mathbf{2{,}000{,}000}$$

So I need to have £2 million to support my lifestyle in perpetuity – or do I need a little more? I've heard a nasty rumour about something called inflation. Now if inflation's running at 3%, my real return is only 2% so I think I'd need £5 million . . .

$$\frac{\textit{Required income}}{\textit{Interest rate – inflation}} = \frac{100{,}000}{5\% - 3\%} = \mathbf{5{,}000{,}000}$$

Now it's just a case of substitution . . . The free cash flow replaces my required income, the weighted average cost of capital replaces the interest rate and the anticipated growth replaces inflation!

A small word of caution about the growing perpetuity formula . . .

Whilst everyone uses the growing perpetuity formula, it does have some worrying underlying assumptions:

- The profit margins and asset turns are constant in perpetuity.
- Therefore returns on capital are constant.
- The marginal return on capital is the same as the return on capital.
- Cash growth is constant.

The weighted average cost of capital

Now the formula referred to the weighted average cost of capital – what is it? The weighted average cost of capital (the WACC) simply reflects the cost of financing the company's funds. However, the cost of equity that is used in the WACC isn't the cost of dividends – although this is the cash cost to the business of funding the equity. If you're a shareholder what really matters is the opportunity cost of having money tied up in the business. This opportunity cost comprises three elements:

- The return you expect to get from a risk-free investment, like government bonds.
- The risk of investing in the stock market. (You expect a bigger return from the stock market than the building society.)
- The risk of investing in a specific company. This is measured by the volatility in its share price. (This is reflected in the company's *beta*, which measures the movement in the company's shares when the market as a whole moves by 1%. So if the company's shares move by 3%, the beta would be three. If a company's beta is less than one the share is less volatile, and therefore less risky, than the market as a whole. If its beta is more than one, the share is more volatile and riskier than the market.)

These three elements are brought together in a model, called the *capital asset pricing model*, which calculates the cost of equity as:

The risk-free rate + (the market risk premium × the company's beta)

Over time, the returns on shares have been around 6% higher than the return on long-term government bonds. (I'm ignoring the late 1990s when, to support companies' market values, there didn't appear to be any risk premium for investing in the stock market. Investors seemed to think the stock market was a one-way bet!) Long-term government bond rates are currently averaging around 5% in the UK, so an average cost of equity is just around 11%. Most companies also borrow, so the WACC is just the weighted average cost of the two. To calculate the WACC, the cost of each component of the company's capital employed is weighted by its proportion of the total. But it's not as simple as it looks, as when you're calculating the WACC you have to use the *market value*, rather than the book value, and you have to adjust the interest to reflect its *cost after tax*.

Calculating the weighted average cost of capital

The WACC is the discount rate that is used in discounted cash flow valuations. I'll show you how to calculate it by using the company in my example. First, here's the relevant extracts from the company's balance sheet showing you its loans:

Bank overdraft	10,000
Loan (at 10% interest)	60,000

As these are conventional bank loans, the book value of £70,000 is used. The company's market capitalisation is £49,200 (20,000 shares in issue × the current share price of £2.46). Consequently, the total capital employed is £119,200; 41.28% of the capital is equity, and 58.72% is debt. Now I'll calculate the cost of equity assuming that the company has a beta of 1.2, and the market risk premium is 6%. The cost of equity is 12.2%:

The risk free rate + (the market risk premium × beta)

5% + (6% × 1.2) = 12.2%

I'll assume that the cost of financing all of the debt is 10%, and corporation tax is 30%. Why have I introduced tax rates? It's to make the interest cost comparable with the shareholders' return, which is after tax. The after-tax cost of interest is 7% (10% less the tax benefit of 30%). You'll notice that loans are cheaper than equity, and this isn't just in my example. Loans are currently the cheaper to finance, as interest rates are low.

I can now calculate the company's weighted average cost of capital:

	(41.28% × 12.2%)	+	(58.72% × 7%)	
=	5.04%	+	4.11%	= **9.15%**

Using discounted cash flow valuations . . .

So you now know that the company's free cash flows are estimated for a short period, and the subsequent cash flows are derived from the growing perpetuity model. These are then discounted by the company's cost of capital. A positive net present value shows that the company is achieving a better return than its cost of capital. If the present value of the free cash flows is greater than the market capitalisation less the debt, the company is seen as a 'buy'. If the present value is less than the market capitalisation less the debt it is rated as a 'sell'.

Unfortunately, discounted cash flow valuations can only be prepared within a company, or by analysts, as they'll usually have far more information about the company than is publicly available. They are likely to be the only people who will have access to the detailed information you need to be able to forecast the cash flows. But don't forget – although discounted cash flows appear more precise than other valuation methods, they are equally subjective. They are reliant on the accuracy, and timing, of the forecasted cash flows and the growth rates used in the growing perpetuity formula.

EBITDA and enterprise value

If you read the financial press, you'll find it often refers to EBITDA and enterprise value, so I'd like to tell you what they are. First, I'll tell you about EBITDA.

EBITDA

EBITDA is an acronym for *e*arnings *b*efore *i*nterest, *t*ax, *d*epreciation and *a*mortisation. Although the word 'earnings' is used, it's operating profit that is used to calculate EBITDA. Some companies disclose it in their accounts but it's easy to calculate it yourself, as it's just the operating profit plus depreciation and amortisation. You can find the depreciation and amortisation charge in the notes to the accounts, or it's shown on the cash flow statement in the reconciliation of the operating cash flow to operating profit. I'll use the numbers shown on my example's cash flow statement.

Reconciliation of operating profit to net cash inflow from operating activities

Operating profit	10,000
Depreciation	1,000
Increase in stock	(2,000)
Increase in debtors	(5,000)
Increase in creditors	3,000
Net cash inflow from operating activities	7,000

EBITDA is 11,000 – the operating profit of 10,000 plus depreciation of 1,000

EBITDA is a profit measure that is especially useful when making international comparisons, as the depreciation and amortisation rules vary from one country to another. As depreciation and amortisation are the largest non-cash charges made to operating profit, EBITDA is a cash-related measure indicative of the underlying cash flow from the company's operations. Some analysts also add back provisions, the other major non-cash charge, to more closely align EBITDA with the cash flow.

Now you know about EBITDA, I can introduce you to enterprise value.

Enterprise value

I've already discussed the return on equity and the return on capital employed. Both of these ratios are based on the *original* investment in the company. Enterprise value represents the *market* value of the company's capital employed, using net debt in the calculation.

You have seen, in the price to book ratio, that the shareholders' funds, the equity, may not be the same as the company's value in the stock market. The market value of the company's equity is its market capitalisation – its current share price multiplied by the number of shares in issue. In my example, the market capitalisation is £49,200 (20,000 shares in issue × the current share price of £2.46). This is less than the shareholders' funds of £50,000, as you've already seen that it has a price to book ratio of less than one.

The company also has a bank loan of £60,000, a bank overdraft of £10,000, and cash of £5,000. The net debt is £65,000 and the market capitalisation is £49,200, so the company's enterprise value is £114,200. (If the company's debt is quoted, for example it may have bonds rather than a bank loan, the debt's market value would be used in the calculation.)

Enterprise value is rarely used in isolation, and is usually compared with sales and EBITDA. This means that you might have to adjust the enterprise value to exclude associates, as they're not included in either sales or EBITDA. Consequently, most analysts make an adjustment that eliminates associates from the company's enterprise value.

Fortunately, the company in my example is simple and has the following ratios.

Enterprise value to sales

The company's turnover is £100,000 and consequently its enterprise value to sales ratio is 1.142.

$$\frac{114,200}{100,000} = 1.142$$

My example currently has a market value of £1.14 for every pound of sales it makes.

Enterprise value to EBITDA

With EBITDA of £21,000 the enterprise value to EBITDA is 5.44:

$$\frac{114,200}{21,000} = 5.438$$

The company's value is 5.44 times its EBITDA. This is really the reciprocal of a market based return on capital employed (EBITDA to enterprise value).

Shareholder value

The business cliché of the 1990s was shareholder value. Most people have no idea what this means. Is it measured by profits, earnings, return on capital – or something completely different? Shareholders want the best total return – dividends and capital growth. However, no one seems to know what drives a company's long-term value and what destroys it. The attempt to determine the drivers of shareholder value has become a modern holy grail. A number of different consulting companies think that they have found it. They have developed different 'packages', broadly offering the same solutions.

In 1990 some consultants from McKinsey & Company, Inc. wrote a book called *Valuation*, which introduced the concept of *value-based management* (*VBM*). It started from the premise that a company must generate a better return than its cost of capital, and a company only adds value for its shareholders when it achieves this. They call the difference between the return on capital and the cost of capital *economic profit*, and the value of a business is the original capital invested plus the present value of the economic profit.

This approach has also been adopted by another firm of consultants called Stern Stewart. Their research showed that if a company wants to increase its market value, it has to generate a return greater than its cost of capital. They call the difference between the return on capital and the cost of capital *economic value added*, or *EVA*™. The difference between the capital originally invested in a business and its current market value is called the *market value added*, or *MVA*. Both EVA™ and MVA can be positive or negative, depending on whether the company is adding or destroying value. The link between the two is that a company's market value added is the net present value of all the future EVAs™.

Both approaches are based on the view that the conventional accounting definitions of profit and capital employed are inadequate measures, as they don't reflect the underlying profitability and capital invested in the business. Whilst their approach is broadly similar, their jargon and adjustments are different. This sometimes makes it difficult to appreciate the underlying similarities.

Value-based management is a *process* enabling companies to develop an understanding of how to grow value by developing the systems and structures that enable value growth. It shows companies how to identify the most important elements of growing shareholder value in their organisation (the *value drivers*) and how to calculate the value that is being generated by the business. The financial value drivers are:

- turnover growth;
- operating profit margin;
- required reinvestment:
  - working capital;
  - capital expenditure;
- cost of capital;
- adjusted cash tax charge (they ignore deferred taxation and the effect of interest on the tax charge).

You'll notice that the tax is included in the value drivers, but wouldn't affect a conventional return on capital calculation. That's because shareholder value models don't use a conventional return on capital calculation! They're ultimately concerned with the return to *investors*, which is always after tax. The return on capital is a very different figure from the one you're used to seeing. Firstly, the profit figure is not the same as the reported one. Goodwill amortisation is always added back. But after that, different models make different adjustments . . .

Stern Stewart argue that accounting conventions force companies to charge as costs many things that are in reality investments in the business's future, like research and development and staff training. These should be capitalised and amortised over a three-year period, as they're an investment in future earnings and shouldn't be charged to the profit and loss account in one year. (In practice, analysts only capitalise research and development, as training costs are rarely disclosed.) Operating leases are also capitalised.

I've summarised the differences in Table 13.1.

Table 13.1 Differences between the McKinsey model and the Stern Stewart model

McKinsey model	Stern Stewart model
Profit is called NOPLAT (an acronym for *n*et operating *p*rofit *l*ess *a*djusted *t*axes)	*Profit is called NOPAT* (an acronym for *n*et operating *p*rofit *a*fter *t*ax)
NOPLAT adjustments: ■ Tax on operating profit ■ Goodwill amortisation	**NOPAT adjustments:** ■ Tax on operating profit ■ Goodwill amortisation ■ Unspent provisions ■ Research and development (but there is a charge for the amortisation of research and development) ■ Operating leases
Invested capital is . . . ■ Operating fixed assets ■ Operating current assets (excluding investments) ■ Current liabilities (excluding financing elements – debt and dividends)	**Invested capital is . . .** ■ Operating fixed assets ■ Operating current assets (excluding investments) ■ Current liabilities (excluding financing elements – debt and dividends) ■ Provisions ■ Research and development (net of amortisation) ■ Operating leases

As the definitions are different, the two models will have different surpluses over the cost of capital (usually called the *spread*) and different valuations. However, the principles are the same. Both models are a clever combination, and repackaging, of some old ideas – the profitability hierarchy and discounted cash flow. The profitability hierarchy provides the value drivers, and discounted cash flow the ultimate valuation.

Summary

I've covered many different ways of looking at a business from the investor's point of view, and I'd now like to categorise and summarise them and tell you about some of their advantages and disadvantages.

Earnings based

Ratios that use earnings per share are:

- not internationally comparable;
- improved if the company buys back its shares.

These ratios include:

- **Earnings per share**: this takes the profit available for the ordinary shareholders and divides it by the number of shares in issue. You'll usually find a number of earnings figures in a company's accounts. The *basic* earnings per share divides the profit available for ordinary shareholders by the weighted average number of shares in issue. The *diluted* earnings per share divides the profit available for ordinary shareholders by the weighted average number of shares that would have been in issue if all the share options had been exercised. The *adjusted* earnings per share uses the profit before exceptional items.
- **Price earnings ratios**: there is no need to calculate these as they are published in the financial press. The price earnings ratio is a payback measure telling you how many years it would take you to get your money back if profits remain constant. A high PE ratio may mean that the share is expensive, but usually indicates that the market expects profits to rise. A low PE may mean that the share is cheap, but it usually means that the market expects profits to fall. *Prospective* PEs use the expected earnings per share in the following year, rather than historical earnings per share. A PE *relative* compares the company's PE ratio with the average for its sector.
- **Earnings yield**: this is a different way of looking at the PE ratio, expressing the earnings per share as a percentage of the current share price.
- **PEG**: this compares the prospective price earnings ratio with the expected rate of growth in earnings over the same period. If the PEG is less than one the share may be a good one to buy, as the expected earnings' growth has not been fully reflected in the share price.
- **Return on equity**: this expresses the profit attributable to ordinary shareholders as a percentage of the shareholders' funds.

Dividend based

The ratios using dividends are:

- **Dividend per share**: this is the dividend that is paid on each share and is calculated by dividing the total dividend by the number of shares receiving a dividend.
- **Dividend yield**: this tells you the percentage dividend return if you buy the share at the current price and dividends are the same as the current dividend per share. The dividend yield can be compared to interest rates.
- **Dividend cover**: this tells you how many times the dividend could be paid from the available profit, and is calculated by dividing the profit available to ordinary shareholders by the ordinary dividend. Another way of looking at this is the *payout ratio;* this expresses the dividend as a percentage of the profit available to ordinary shareholders.

Asset based

The main problem with asset-based ratios is that they are based on the book values, which can be very different to the market values. As depreciation and asset valuation differ from one country to another, they are not internationally comparable.

The ratios using assets are:

- **Book value, or net asset, per share**: this tells you the value of each share's investment in the company's net assets, and is calculated by dividing the capital and reserves by the number of shares in issue.
- **Price to book ratio**: this compares the company's share price with the share's book value, and gives an indication of the inherent security of the share. If the price to book ratio is less than one, shareholders should receive some money if the business is liquidated.

Sales based

Sales-based valuations are useful when making international comparisons, and for valuing cyclical businesses. The following ratios use sales:

- **Sales per share**: this divides the turnover by the weighted average number of shares in issue during the year.
- **Price to sales**: this compares the current share price to the sales per share and, like all price-based ratios, is more informative when compared to the sector as a *price to sales relative*. Operating margins should be taken into account when looking at relative price to sales ratios, as investors will be prepared to pay a higher price if the company's operating margins are higher than the sector average.
- **Enterprise value to sales**: this compares the company's market value with its sales.

Cash based

There are a number of different definitions of cash that can be used, the commonest being:

- **The cash available for reinvestment**: this is the net operating cash flow plus the cash flow from returns on investment and servicing of finance, and the cash flow from taxation.
- **Free cash flow**: companies often use a different definition to that used by analysts:
  - Companies define free cash flow as the cash flow after interest, tax, dividends, and capital expenditure. This is the cash that is available for acquisitions and capital restructuring.
  - Analysts define free cash flow as the cash that is available for the providers of capital, so it is the cash after taxation and reinvestment in the business. This definition of free cash flow is used in discounted cash flow valuations.

Cash is a 'clean' measure of performance; it can't be created and is internationally comparable. The ratios using cash are:

- **Cash flow per share**: this takes the chosen cash definition and divides it by the weighted average number of shares in issue during the year.
- **Price to cash flow**: this compares the current share price with the cash flow per share, telling you how many years' cash flow are needed to pay back the current price.

EBITDA

This is an internationally comparable measure that is closely aligned to a company's cash flow. It is calculated by adding the depreciation and amortisation charges back to the company's operating profit. EBITDA is used in the following ratios:

- **EBITDA to sales:** this is a more internationally comparable version of the operating profit margin. Some analysts use the reciprocal of this – sales to EBITDA.
- **Enterprise value to EBITDA:** this compares the company's net market value to EBITDA, telling you how many years' EBITDA are needed to support the company's current value.

Enterprise value

This is the company's market capitalisation and its net debt. The debt is shown at market value if it is traded; otherwise its book value is used. Enterprise value is used in the following ratios:

- **Enterprise value to EBITDA.**
- **Enterprise value to sales:** this compares the enterprise value to the turnover, and tells you how many years' sales are reflected in the company's net market value.

Discounted cash flow

In theory, the value of a company is the present value of its free cash flows in perpetuity, using the company's weighted average cost of capital as the discount rate. This means that theoretically the company's free cash flows should be estimated in perpetuity. However, in practice the company's free cash flows are usually only estimated for a short period, three to five years, and the subsequent cash flows are determined using the growing perpetuity formula. Unfortunately, this means that the majority of the company's value is derived from the growing perpetuity formula, and the formula's underlying assumptions are questionable.

Shareholder value, VBM, and EVA™

These are all variants of the same underlying principle – a company's value only differs from the value of the original capital invested to the extent of the present value of the difference between its return on capital and its cost of capital. These models represent a process for understanding and growing value and are a combination of net present value and the hierarchy of profitability.

The return on capital used in shareholder value models is different from that used in conventional financial analysis. The profit will be after adjusted cash taxes, and before goodwill amortisation. EVA™ valuations also add back any provisions that have been charged to profit but not spent, operating leases, and research and development. Operating leases are depreciated in the same way as other fixed assets, and research and development is amortised over three years. The invested capital is the operating capital employed with EVA™ valuations also including operating leased assets (net of depreciation), research and development (net of amortisation), and provisions. This means that different models will give different business values.

Johnson Matthey's investment ratios in 2002

I'd now like to show you how to calculate most of these ratios for a real company, and it's time to find out a little more about Johnson Matthey. You know that it's solvent and profitable – but is this reflected in its investment ratios? Let's see if we can find out.

Earnings-based ratios

Earnings per share

I'll start with its earnings per share, as you don't have to work it out – it's always shown at the bottom of the profit and loss account. Johnson Matthey shows four earnings per share figures:

		2002 Before exceptional items and goodwill amortisation	2002 Total
Earnings per ordinary share	*Notes*		
		pence	pence
Basic	9	60.4	49.0
Diluted	9	59.7	48.5
Dividend per ordinary share	8	24.6	24.6

You can see that its exceptional items reduced its earnings per share and if all its share options had been exercised, the earnings per share would have fallen slightly.

(Johnson Matthey also shows its dividend per share at the bottom of its profit and loss account, but not all companies do this. You may have to find it in its five-year summary or in the note about dividends – this analyses the dividend payment between the interim dividend and the final dividend).

Neither of these earnings per share figures is used in the calculation of the published PE ratio, as the earnings figure used in the financial press uses the earnings definition used by the Society of Investment Professionals. It's very difficult to work this out yourself, as you have to consider the tax effect of the exceptional items. I'll use the earnings before exceptional items and goodwill amortisation to calculate the PE ratio and the earnings yield.

Price earnings ratio

Because the share price used in this ratio is a 'current' one, I'll be using Johnson Matthey's share price when I started to write this chapter – 870 pence. Using this, Johnson Matthey's PE ratio is 14.4:

$$\frac{\textit{Current share price}}{\textit{Earnings per share}} = \frac{870.0}{60.4} = \mathbf{14.4}$$

Prospective PE

You can find consensus earnings figures on the FT.com website, and the median consensus for Johnson Matthey's earnings per share for the year ending March 2003 is currently 63.03 pence, with a high estimate of 72.47 pence and a low estimate of 58.87 pence. This means that the 'bullish' analysts predict that underlying earnings per share will grow by almost 20%, the 'bearish' analysts predict it will fall by 2.5%, and on average the company's earnings per share are expected to grow by 4.4%. Just a little difference!

I'll use the median estimate to calculate the prospective PE:

$$\frac{\textit{Current share price}}{\textit{Earnings per share}} = \frac{870.00}{63.03} = \mathbf{13.8}$$

PE relative

The Chemical sector's PE is 10.9, giving Johnson Matthey a PE relative of 1.32:

$$\frac{\textit{Company's PE ratio}}{\textit{Sector's PE ratio}} = \frac{14.4}{10.9} = \mathbf{1.32}$$

This implies that Johnson Matthey is expected to have 32% more earnings growth than the sector as a whole. You can also work out the prospective PE ratio relative to the sector. The Chemicals sector is expected to have a PE ratio of 10.1 in 2003, giving Johnson Matthey a prospective PE relative of 1.37:

$$\frac{\textit{Company's prospective PE ratio}}{\textit{Sector's prospective PE ratio}} = \frac{13.8}{10.1} = \mathbf{1.37}$$

This implies that Johnson Matthey's earnings growth is expected to continue to be greater than its sector average.

Earnings yield

This is the reciprocal of the PE ratio, expressing earnings as a percentage of the current price:

$$\frac{\textit{Earnings per share}}{\textit{Current share price}} = \frac{60.4}{870.0} = \mathbf{6.9\%}$$

Johnson Matthey's earnings are 6.9% of its current share price.

PEG ratio

Johnson Matthey's earnings' growth is already fully reflected in its share price, as its prospective PE ratio is over three times its expected earnings' growth rate:

$$\frac{\textit{Prospective PE ratio}}{\textit{Expected earnings' growth rate}} = \frac{13.8}{4.4} = \mathbf{3.14}$$

Return on equity

This shows the return on the shareholders' funds. Now you've learnt by now that, if you want to make comparisons, you have to adjust the shareholders' funds for any goodwill previously written off through reserves, provisions and, if appropriate, revaluation. The published shareholders' funds are £813.7 million:

Capital and reserves	
Called up share capital	218.7
Share premium account	128.2
Capital redemption reserve	4.9
Associates' reserves	(0.2)
Profit and loss account	462.1
Shareholders' funds	813.7
Equity minority interests	3.9
	817.6

However, the company's profit and loss account has been reduced by:

- £98.1 million unspent provisions for liabilities and charges. This cash has not left the business, and you saw in Chapter 8 that different countries have different rules about provisions.
- £46.0 million goodwill has been written off for businesses the company acquired before December 1998. This is money that has been invested in the business, and most countries have always shown goodwill as an intangible asset.

The company hasn't revalued its properties, so its adjusted capital and reserves is £957.8 million (£813.7 million + £98.1 million + £46.0 million). If the company you're analysing has revalued, you'll also have to exclude the revaluation reserve if you're comparing it with companies that haven't revalued their assets. I'll work out four return on equity figures using profit attributable to shareholders before and after exceptional items, and the company's published and adjusted equity figures. Its profit attributable to shareholders before exceptional items was £131.5 million, after exceptional items it fell to £106.8 million. (You'd normally only calculate one return on equity ratio, but I want to show you the four possibilities.)

$$\frac{\textit{Profit attributable to shareholders}}{\textit{Shareholders' funds}} = \frac{106.8}{813.7} = \mathbf{13.1\%}$$

$$\frac{\textit{Profit before exceptional items}}{\textit{Shareholders' funds}} = \frac{131.5}{813.7} = \mathbf{16.2\%}$$

$$\frac{\textit{Profit attributable to shareholders}}{\textit{Adjusted shareholders' funds}} = \frac{106.8}{957.8} = \mathbf{11.2\%}$$

$$\frac{\textit{Profit before exceptional items}}{\textit{Adjusted shareholders' funds}} = \frac{131.5}{957.8} = \mathbf{13.7\%}$$

The last return on equity, using profit before exceptional items and adjusted shareholders' funds, is a comparable measure showing Johnson Matthey's underlying return on equity.

Dividend-based ratios

Dividend yield

If you bought Johnson Matthey's shares at their current price, and dividends were unchanged, you would receive just over 2.8% of your investment as dividends:

$$\frac{\textit{Dividend per share}}{\textit{Current share price}} = \frac{24.6}{870.0} = \mathbf{2.83\%}$$

Dividend cover

Johnson Matthey's dividends were £53.2 million, and it could pay its dividend twice out of the profit after exceptional items:

Before exceptional items:

$$\frac{\textit{Profit attributable to ordinary shareholders}}{\textit{Dividends}} = \frac{131.5}{53.2} = \mathbf{2.5\ times}$$

After exceptional items:

$$\frac{\textit{Profit attributable to ordinary shareholders}}{\textit{Dividends}} = \frac{106.8}{53.2} = \mathbf{2.0\ times}$$

Asset-based ratios

Unless the asset values are kept up to date, these have limited relevance. However, I'll show you how to work them out.

Book value, or net asset, per share

Johnson Matthey had 218,695,663 shares in issue at the end of March 2002. (For this ratio you use the shares in issue at the year end, as you're comparing it with the shareholders' funds at the year end.) Consequently, each share had £3.72 asset value.

$$\frac{\textit{Shareholders' funds}}{\textit{Number of shares in issue}} = \frac{813.7}{218.7} = \mathbf{3.72}$$

Price to book ratio

This shows you that its share is trading at 2.34 times its book value:

$$\frac{\textit{Current share price}}{\textit{Net asset value per share}} = \frac{870}{372} = \mathbf{2.34}$$

This may reflect that its assets are undervalued on the books, which they are, and/ or that the share price is largely underpinned by an expectation of profit growth, and you've seen that the market does expect its profits to grow.

Sales-based ratios

Johnson Matthey's 2002 turnover was £4,830.1 million.

Sales per share

During 2002 the weighted average number of shares in issue was 217,829,287. (This is used to calculate the sales per share, as the turnover is generated throughout the year.) Consequently Johnson Matthey had £22.17 sales per share.

$$\frac{\textit{Turnover}}{\textit{Number of shares}} = \frac{4{,}830.1}{217.83} = \mathbf{£22.17 \text{ or } 2{,}217 \text{ pence}}$$

Price to sales

$$\frac{\textit{Current share price}}{\textit{Sales per share}} = \frac{870}{2{,}217} = \mathbf{0.39}$$

Their price to sales ratio is low because the turnover figure is so high because of the high precious metal value.

Cash-based ratios

The cash available for reinvestment

This is derived from the cash flow statement, and is a net operating cash flow after returns on investment and taxation. Here's the relevant extract from Johnson Matthey's cash flow statement:

	£ million
Net cash inflow from operating activities	224.1
Returns on investments and servicing of finance	(4.9)
Taxation	(55.8)
Cash available for reinvestment	**163.4**

Free cash flow

I'll use the definition of free cash flow that you'll find in analysts' reports. This is the cash flow that's available for the providers of capital, so it's the operating cash flow less taxation less capital expenditure and acquisitions and disposals. Here are the relevant extracts from Johnson Matthey's cash flow statement:

	£ million
Net cash inflow from operating activities	224.1
Taxation	(55.8)
Capital expenditure and financial investment	(131.0)
Acquisitions and disposals	(145.7)
Free cash flow	**(108.4)**

Johnson Matthey's free cash flow is negative in 2002, following its acquisitions and disposals. You've seen, in the earlier chapters, that this level of expenditure is unusual. Its free cash flow before acquisitions and disposals is £37.3 million.

Cash flow per share

I'll show you how to calculate both cash flow per share figures, starting with the cash available for reinvestment. They both use the weighted average number of shares in issue, as the cash is generated throughout the year:

Cash available for reinvestment:

$$\frac{\textit{Cash available for reinvestment}}{\textit{Number of shares}} = \frac{163.4}{217.83} = \mathbf{£0.75}$$

Free cash flow per share:

$$\frac{\textit{Free cash flow}}{\textit{Number of shares}} = \frac{(108.4)}{217.83} = \textbf{£(0.5)}$$

Price to cash flow

This doesn't usually use the free cash flow, so I'll base it on the cash available for reinvestment.

$$\frac{\textit{Current share price}}{\textit{Cash flow per share}} = \frac{870}{75} = \textbf{11.6}$$

Johnson Matthey's share is trading at 11.6 times its cash flow.

EBITDA

This is usually based on operating profit before exceptional items, as analysts are concerned about a company's underlying profitability. Johnson Matthey's operating profit before exceptional items was £193.4 million in 2002. (This is also known as its EBIT.) Its depreciation and amortisation charge was £55.1 million, so its 2002 EBITDA is £248.5 million:

	£ million
Operating profit before exceptional items	193.4
Depreciation and amortisation	55.1
EBITDA	**248.5**

This is used in a number of ratios, including EBITDA to sales.

EBITDA to sales

Johnson Matthey's 2002 turnover was £4,830.1 million, and its EBITDA to sales ratio was 5.14%.

$$\frac{\textit{EBITDA}}{\textit{Turnover}} = \frac{248.5}{4{,}830.1} = \textbf{5.14\%}$$

Sales to EBITDA

You'll often see this in analysts' reports, and it's simple to calculate, as it's the reciprocal of EBITDA to sales.

$$\frac{\textit{Turnover}}{\textit{EBITDA}} = \frac{4{,}830.1}{248.5} = \mathbf{19.44}$$

Johnson Matthey turned its EBITDA into sales 19.44 times in 2002.

Enterprise value

This is Johnson Matthey's market capitalisation and its net debt. Its market capitalisation was £1,910 million, and its net debt was £159 million, giving an enterprise value of £2,069 million. (I've used the book value of its debt; strictly speaking, I should have used the market value of its US$ bond. This would add another £0.5 million to its enterprise value, but will make no difference to the ratios below. I've ignored it, as it's irrelevant for the ratios below. But in other companies it may be important, you'll find the market values disclosed in the notes to the accounts under 'fair values of financial instruments'.)

Enterprise value to EBITDA

$$\frac{\textit{Enterprise value}}{\textit{EBITDA}} = \frac{2{,}069}{248.5} = \mathbf{8.33}$$

Johnson Matthey's market value is 8.33 times its EBITDA.

Enterprise value to sales

$$\frac{\textit{Enterprise value}}{\textit{Turnover}} = \frac{2{,}069.0}{4{,}830.1} = \mathbf{0.43}$$

Johnson Matthey's market value is 0.43 times its turnover.

What have we learnt?

As I've just looked at 2002, we've only learnt a limited amount about how investors see Johnson Matthey. But we have discovered that it's a growth share rather than an income share, as its dividend yield is low. The market expects its profit to grow faster than the sector average, and this expectation is already built into its share price as it has a PEG ratio of 3.14. In 2002 it generated cash for reinvestment, but this was insufficient to pay for its net acquisitions during the year.

14

Johnson Matthey

- **Starting the analysis . . .**
- **Johnson Matthey's ten-year summary** – a few comments on the company's ten-year summary; a few questions
- **Johnson Matthey's 2002 operating review** – a few comments on the company's operating review; a few more questions
- **Johnson Matthey's financial statements** – initial observations on the three years' financial statements
- **Analysing Johnson Matthey's financial performance 2000–2** – profitability; investment potential

I'm now going to analyse Johnson Matthey's performance over the last three years. Normally I prefer to analyse companies over five years, but I've shortened the analysis period as Johnson Matthey's business has changed significantly since 1998:

- Until February 1998 a lot of its ceramics and coatings business operated through a joint venture called Cookson Matthey Ceramics. On 6 February it bought Cookson's share of the business.
- On 17 August 1999, it sold its electronic materials division.

Some of electronic materials' profits are shown as discontinued in 2000, but I have adjusted for this to show the underlying trend over the last three years.

Starting the analysis . . .

I always start a financial analysis in the same way, by understanding where the company has come from. It's even more important when you're analysing over a relatively short period, like three years. So I start with the company's financial summary, and Johnson Matthey's shows its financial performance over the last ten years, instead of the normal five.

Once I have this context, I'll read through the financial and operating reviews as this gives me more information about divisional performance and the risks and opportunities facing its business. I then read through the rest of the accounts to get some more information about the business, and follow up any questions I may have. Once I've done this I can decide what I want to analyse, and what ratios I'll need to calculate. (I know I've shown you how to do all of them in the earlier chapters, but I don't ever use them all.)

Consequently, in this chapter you'll find:

- Johnson Matthey's ten-year summary;
- its operating review (its financial review is shown in full in Chapter 7);
- a summary of its accounts for their financial years 2000–2;
- the ratios I plan to use, and why I plan to use them;
- ratio analysis and commentary for its financial years 2000–2.

Johnson Matthey's ten-year summary

Ten Year Record

	1993 £ million	1994 £ million	1995 £ million	1996 £ million	1997 £ million
Turnover					
Parent and subsidiaries	1,853.7	1,955.0	2,177.8	2,528.9	2,423.2
Share of joint ventures	–	–	97.1	156.7	156.9
Total	1,853.7	1,955.0	2,274.9	2,685.6	2,580.1
Operating profit before exceptional items and goodwill amortisation	71.6	81.6	100.4	111.0	116.3
Goodwill amortisation	–	–	–	–	–
Exceptional items	–	–	–	–	–
Total operating profit	71.6	81.6	100.4	111.0	116.3
Other exceptional items	3.7	(11.7)	(0.7)	–	–
Profit before interest	75.3	69.9	99.7	111.0	116.3
Net interest	(1.5)	(4.6)	(4.3)	(8.8)	(8.0)
Profit before taxation	73.8	65.3	95.4	102.2	108.3
Taxation	(25.6)	(23.1)	(34.3)	(34.3)	(33.0)
Profit after taxation	48.2	42.2	61.1	67.9	75.3
Equity minority interests	(0.3)	(0.2)	(1.0)	(1.7)	(1.2)
Profit attributable to shareholders	47.9	42.0	60.1	66.2	74.1
Dividends	(19.1)	(21.8)	(25.9)	(31.4)	(33.6)
Profit retained	28.8	20.2	34.2	34.8	40.5
Earnings per ordinary share (graph 2)	25.5p	22.0p	30.9p	32.5p	34.2p
Earnings per ordinary share before exceptional items and goodwill amortisation (graph 1)	24.2p	25.8p	31.2p	32.5p	34.2p
Dividend per ordinary share (graph 3)	10.3p	11.4p	13.5p	14.5p	15.5p
Summary Balance Sheet					
Assets employed:					
Goodwill	–	–	–	–	–
Tangible fixed assets	263.1	281.1	256.1	321.7	337.7
Fixed assets investments/joint ventures/associates	1.1	1.1	70.9	100.4	84.2
Stocks	155.0	153.6	153.2	196.6	184.7
Debtors and short term investments	185.7	207.2	190.9	232.2	252.6
Other creditors and provisions	(242.3)	(254.2)	(223.4)	(304.0)	(291.1)
	362.6	388.8	447.7	546.9	568.1
Financed by:					
Net borrowings and finance leases/(cash)	90.6	76.1	102.4	134.2	143.7
Retained earnings	80.8	116.9	151.6	99.8	107.4
Share capital, share premium and capital redemption	190.3	194.4	195.7	313.6	316.8
Equity minority interests	0.9	1.4	(2.0)	(0.7)	0.2
Capital employed	362.6	388.8	447.7	546.9	568.1
Cumulative goodwill taken directly to reserves	49.6	50.5	57.5	150.3	156.3
Return on assets (Operating profit before exceptional items and goodwill amortisation/average capital employed and cumulative goodwill taken directly to reserves)	20.2%	19.2%	21.3%	18.5%	16.4%

2001 and prior years have been restated to reflect the changes in accounting policies. The earnings per ordinary share for 1995 and prior years have been adjusted for the bonus element in the 1 for 8 rights issue made on 19th September 1995.

1998 £ million	1999 £ million	2000 £ million	2001 £ million	2002 £ million
3,138.8	3,385.4	3,866.0	5,903.7	4,830.1
128.8	–	–	–	–
3,267.6	3,385.4	3,866.0	5,903.7	4,830.1
139.2	147.1	146.2	175.0	193.3
–	–	(0.2)	(0.3)	(6.8)
(4.5)	(1.9)	(9.8)	(0.6)	(18.1)
134.7	145.2	136.2	174.1	168.4
4.4	8.8	23.4	1.1	(5.6)
139.1	154.0	159.6	175.2	162.8
(9.0)	(15.9)	(2.4)	5.3	(6.1)
130.1	138.1	157.2	180.5	156.7
(28.5)	(35.1)	(47.3)	(54.2)	(50.2)
101.6	103.0	109.9	126.3	106.5
(0.3)	0.7	(0.2)	(0.6)	0.3
101.3	103.7	109.7	125.7	106.8
(38.7)	(41.3)	(44.3)	(51.3)	(53.2)
62.6	62.4	65.4	74.4	53.6
46.7p	47.8p	50.5p	57.3p	49.0p
42.8p	42.8p	46.6p	57.2p	60.4p
17.8p	19.0p	20.3p	23.3p	24.6p
–	4.2	5.1	8.6	182.6
461.5	480.2	311.3	386.8	495.1
4.2	1.8	1.0	1.0	2.7
244.8	243.7	253.2	278.8	414.3
381.1	439.6	447.7	536.0	470.6
(409.9)	(419.6)	(455.0)	(539.8)	(588.7)
681.7	749.9	563.3	671.4	976.6
225.1	221.6	(165.8)	(139.9)	159.0
130.9	200.1	386.8	461.0	461.9
319.6	322.4	337.8	345.7	351.8
6.1	5.8	4.5	4.6	3.9
681.7	749.9	563.3	671.4	976.6
171.4	171.4	46.0	46.0	46.0
17.6%	16.6%	19.1%	26.4%	22.2%

1 Earnings Per Share Before Exceptional Items and Goodwill Amortisation

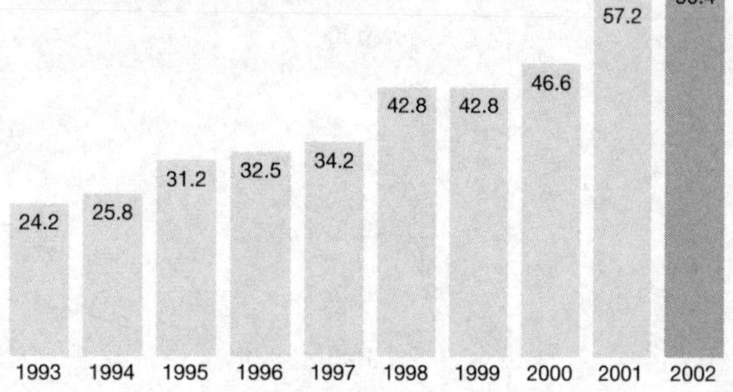

2 Earnings Per Share

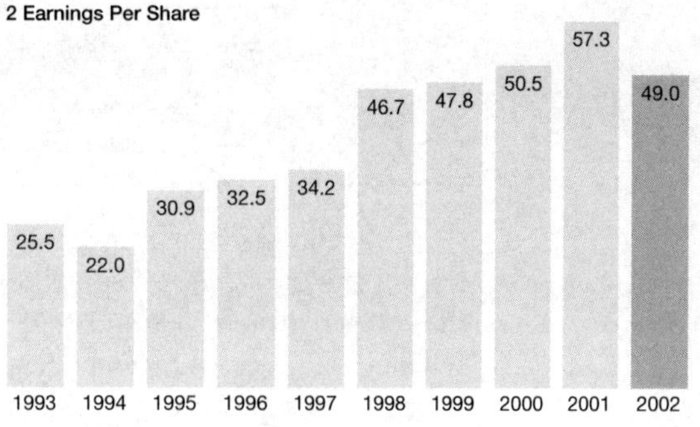

3 Dividends Per Share

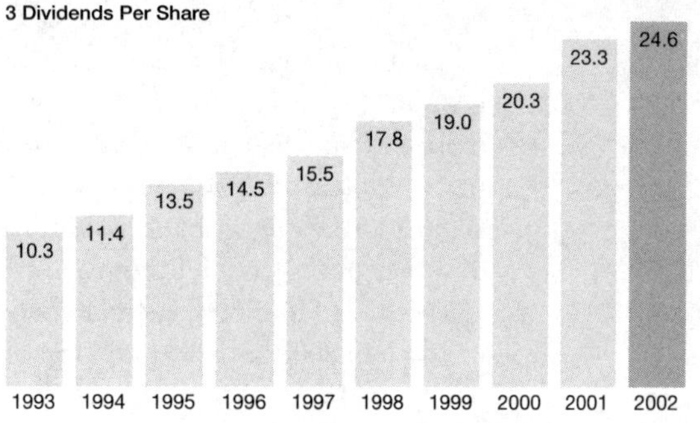

A few comments on the company's ten-year summary

You can clearly see that both the group's turnover, and its underlying operating profits, have grown steadily in the last ten years (Figure 14.1).

Fig. 14.1 Ten-year turnover and operating profit

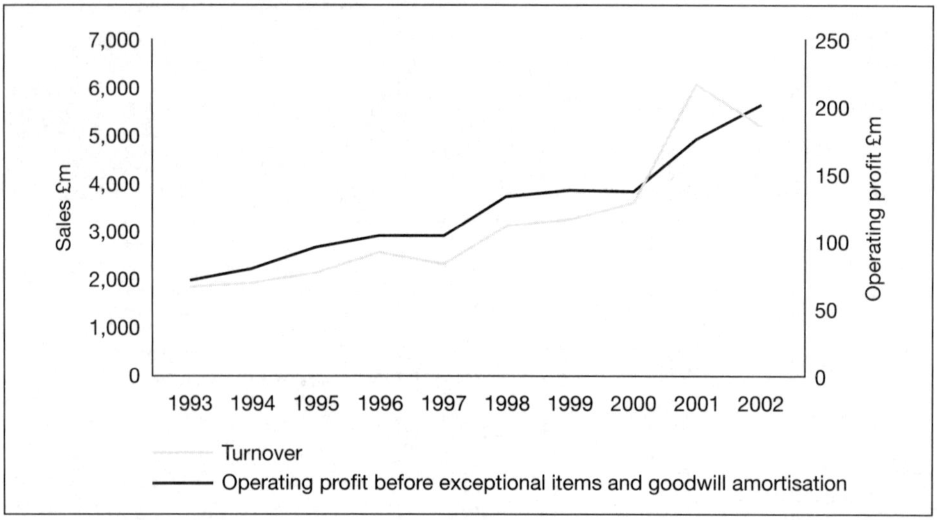

However, in the last four years turnover growth hasn't been steady, rising by 14% between 1999 and 2000 (despite the sale of its electronic materials division), then rising by almost 53% between 2000 and 2001, and falling by 18% in 2002. This may well be the result of changes in precious metal prices, and must be checked before preparing any ratios.

Operating profit fell by just under 1% between 1999 and 2000, and rose by almost 20% in 2001 and 10.5% in 2002.

The company has always been able to afford its loans, as interest charges have never been a large proportion of its profit.

It made major acquisitions in 1996 and 2002, and another significant acquisition in 1998. (I'm picking this up from the movement in goodwill, shown before 1999 under the capital employed line as taken through reserves, and after 1999 on the balance sheet.) This may partly explain the significant changes in tangible assets during this period. The earlier acquisitions were probably part of the electronic materials division, as the goodwill written off through reserves fell from £171.4 million to £46 million when the division was sold.

The sale of its electronic materials division left it with considerable cash balances (it had net cash in 2000 and 2001 and was a net interest receiver in 2001). These cash balances fell following the 2002 acquisitions, which were probably also partly financed with loans.

A few questions . . .

Looking at the company's ten-year summary has raised questions about:

- the effect of precious metal prices on turnover;

- how much of the changes in tangible assets arose from acquisitions, and how much from capital expenditure.

Now let's have a look at its operating review.

Johnson Matthey's 2002 operating review

Catalysts & Chemicals

Catalysts & Chemicals Division produced a very strong performance with operating profit 17% up on 2000/01 at £94.7 million. The division consists of the group's Catalytic Systems, Chemicals and Fuel Cells businesses.

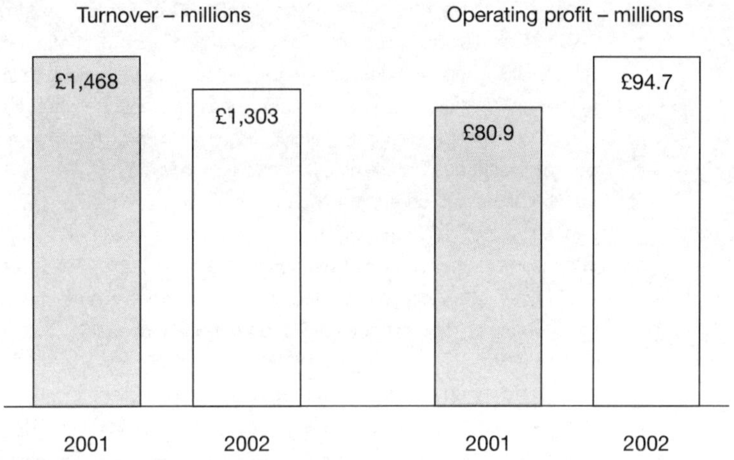

Catalytic Systems

Catalytic Systems, which includes Johnson Matthey's global car catalyst, heavy duty diesel and stationary source emission control businesses, had another strong year. In North America, sales of new vehicles fell and catalyst volumes declined in our fiscal year. Our business performed well in this more difficult market, benefiting from the introduction of new technology. There was growth in the heavy duty diesel retrofit market during the year and we made gains in market share. The well publicised problems of the US power industry led to increased investment in small turbine generating capacity and growth in the market for catalysts for this application.

In Europe, vehicle sales fell slightly in our fiscal year. Our recent investment in new manufacturing technology has brought the opportunity to develop new, more advanced products with cost effective manufacturing routes. Customer acceptance of these innovations resulted in growth in our market share. As a result the European region's sales were well up on prior year. The new manufacturing facility, opened last year in Royston, UK, increased its output throughout the year. There was also a considerable increase in demand for catalysts made in South Africa. As a result we have expanded our plant near Johannesburg.

The investment programme to replace our manufacturing capacity with our new production technology, which allows more accurate control of materials and greater flexibility of product design is nearing completion. Production lines incorporating the new technology have now been installed at all of our plants around the world. During the year we completed our ninth manufacturing facility in Shanghai, China. This new plant was opened in June 2001 and is entirely based on our new technology.

Chemicals

The Chemicals business had a good year achieving growth in both revenues and profits in the face of mixed market conditions.

The platinum group metal (pgm) refining business performed very well benefiting from strong demand, particularly from primary producers. However, the catalyst and chemical products businesses were affected by a downturn in some of the end markets that they serve. Two novel polymer fibre technologies, resulting from our investment in Oy Smoptech AB in Finland, were commercialised during the year and offer good prospects for growth: Smopex® a range of customised metal scavengers to aid recovery of precious metals and FibreCat® an anchoring technology for homogeneous catalysts. The year also saw the launch of Johnson Matthey Catalytic Services, a new business offering fee based contract development and optimisation of catalytic processes.

The expansion and upgrading of pgm refining facilities on both sides of the Atlantic continues apace. New smelting technology has been installed in the UK that further improves Johnson Matthey's competitive advantage in insoluble metals refining. An innovative technology for catalyst recovery using a patented processing technique has been developed in collaboration with Chematur AB and will be launched later this year under the trade name Aquacat®.

The Research Chemicals business achieved excellent results with good growth in the Alfa Aesar catalogue business and a strong contribution from the acquisition of Avocado Research Chemicals in February 2002. Avocado, based in Heysham, UK, is a leader in the manufacture and supply of organic compounds for use in research laboratories. Its well established catalogue predominantly serves customers in the fine chemical and pharmaceutical industries as well as in contract and academic research.

Fuel Cells

The Fuel Cells business continues to make excellent progress working in close collaboration with key customers to improve the performance and durability and to reduce the cost of fuel cell components. Early commercial fuel cell products have started to become available for premium back up power and portable applications, and we expect that by the middle of this decade joint efforts with customers will produce commercial products for an increasing number of premium markets in the small stationary sector. At the same time our automotive customers will be producing small fleets of vehicles to validate this new technology in the field. This will lead to mass-produced products for the transport sector at the end of this decade and into the next.

Our worldclass R&D and testing facilities at Sonning Common, UK have achieved dramatic improvements in the performance of our fuel cell products. These advances are placing us in a strong position to command a significant share of this new market as it reaches commercialisation. Work was completed during the year on a new plant for testing and developing fuel processors at West Whiteland, USA. The year also saw good progress on the first phase of our investment in a dedicated Membrane Electrode Assembly (MEA) manufacturing facility at Swindon, UK.

Research and Development

In Catalytic Systems we continue to invest in research and development and in testing capacity to match our regenerated manufacturing base and retain market leadership. During the year R&D activities have centred on improved three way catalysts for petrol vehicles and the development of products for lean burn engines, especially diesels. Heavy duty diesel engines are a focus for regulation in the coming years and we are investing in R&D to facilitate technical partnerships with the engine makers. R&D programmes in the Chemicals business continue to deliver new products and technologies to customers and more efficient processes at our plants. During the year these efforts resulted in the launch of new ranges of platinum group metal heterogeneous selective oxidation catalysts and highly active platinum on carbon catalysts for a wide variety of hydrogenation and other reactions. The business' ligand library continues to grow and a novel palladium based homogeneous catalyst has been developed in anticipation of increased demand for catalysts to carry out difficult coupling reactions.

Precious Metals

Precious Metals Division's operating profits were 3% down on last year at £55.9 million.

Trading conditions for the division's global platinum group metal (pgm) trading and marketing business proved less favourable as prices declined from the exceptional levels of recent years. However, demand for platinum and for fabricated pgm products continued to grow.

Platinum

Platinum and palladium prices fell sharply in the first half of 2001/02 from the highs seen in January 2001. The prospect of a global economic slowdown, the liquidation of long positions held by speculators and, in the case of palladium, a sharp fall in consumer demand, saw prices reach their low points in October. Thereafter the prices of both metals enjoyed a modest recovery as economic sentiment improved in the USA and Russian palladium sales were curtailed.

Although negative market sentiment undermined the price of platinum, the metal's fundamentals remained strong with demand outstripping supply. Autocatalyst demand increased as the market share of diesel engine cars, which use platinum based catalysts, grew significantly and new tougher legislation came into force in Europe. Although jewellery demand declined in the USA and Japan as consumer spending fell, the market in China once again displayed remarkable growth. Industrial demand grew modestly overall, with increased use in glassmaking, petroleum refining and dental alloys, partly offset by weaker demand for coating computer disks, as manufacturers cut production and inventory levels.

The palladium market moved into surplus during the year, with falling demand from all the main consuming sectors. Auto manufacturers continued to thrift palladium on autocatalysts and to shift back to platinum based catalysts for gasoline engines, while demand from dental alloy producers and electronic component manufacturers was affected by aggressive substitution away from palladium and a slump in demand for electronic goods.

The average price of platinum for the year was $503 per oz, 13% lower than in 2000/01. The average price of palladium was also lower at $473 per oz, down 39% in the same period. This decline in prices and the thin trading conditions experienced for much of the year reduced the profits of the division's marketing and trading operations from the record levels enjoyed in 2000/01.

Despite the difficult economic climate for our traditional products, profits from the division's pgm manufacturing activities in the UK and USA increased again this year. Our industry leading metallurgical expertise, combined with our capabilities in precision forming and machining, further strengthened our technological advantage in key sectors. New product introductions were well received by our customers and, additionally, generated revenue from technology licensing in selected markets. Our medical components business, based in the USA, had another good year with continued growth of base and precious metal components for surgical devices.

Gold and Silver

Johnson Matthey's gold and silver refineries located in Salt Lake City (USA), Brampton (Canada), Royston (UK), Melbourne (Australia) and Hong Kong enjoyed mixed fortunes. With world gold production unchanged, the market for primary gold refining continued to be very competitive but an improvement in the gold price in the second half of the year contributed to an increase in secondary refining. The performance of our Royston operation was impacted by high metal holdings at the start of the year as the refinery was reorganised to improve processing efficiency. The rationalisation of our Canadian business was completed during the year and the benefits of exiting low margin activities contributed to a further growth in profits. From 11th September onwards a series of gold price spikes stimulated dishoarding throughout the Asia region, which benefited the refineries in Hong Kong and Australia. In addition, the Hong Kong refinery achieved Good Delivery accreditation for its gold bars in August and Brampton was awarded similar status for its silver bars in December 2001.

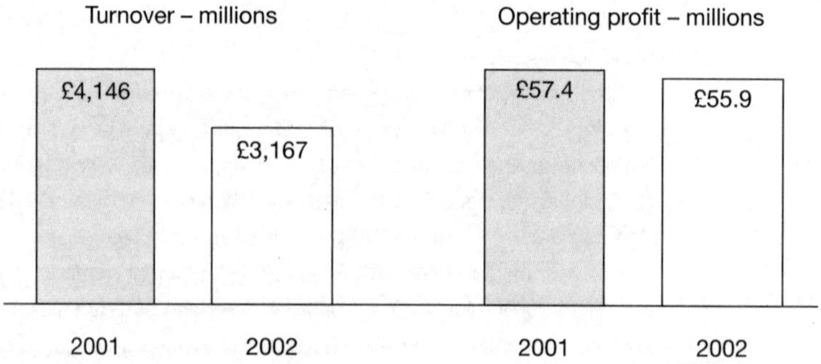

Research and Development

The division's research and development programmes are focused on two main areas. Fundamental work is being undertaken on the performance of catalysts for ammonia oxidation that is designed to improve conversion efficiencies whilst minimising the production of unwanted by-products, which act as greenhouse gases. Secondly, our US based medical components business is actively developing new products for use in cardiovascular devices. These utilise the unique characteristics of platinum group metal alloys and the super-elastic properties of nitinol. In support of this growing area, a new development cell is being established at our Pennsylvania facility, which will further reduce response times to customer requests for new medical products.

Colours & Coatings

Colours & Coatings Division's operating profits were 21% down on last year at £25.5 million as the result of intense margin pressure and difficult market conditions, particularly in the third quarter.

The Colours & Coatings Division is one of the world's leading suppliers of inorganic colours and the associated frits, glazes and enamels by which they are applied to a wide range of substrates.

The division serves a number of markets including automotive, glass, tile, sanitaryware, tableware, plastics, inks and surface coatings. The division is organised into three sectors reflecting its major markets: Structural Ceramics, which combines the Tile, Sanitaryware and Zircon businesses; Glass, which serves the automotive glass, architectural glass and glass packaging markets; and Speciality Coatings, which serves the tableware, plastics and surface coatings industries.

2001/02 saw the completion of expansion projects to serve growth markets in the tile and glass businesses. These are already delivering benefits. However, the sharp decline in the tableware market necessitated a review of the division's UK business, which will result in the closure of its Meir facility by early 2003. This has led to an exceptional charge of £24 million in the year. This rationalisation will result in savings of £3 million in 2002/03 and £7 million per annum from 2003/04 and should be cash positive following the sale of assets.

Structural Ceramics

The Structural Ceramics sector achieved modest sales growth despite a considerable softening of its market during the second half. However, while the business is well protected in a downturn by having some of the lowest unit costs in the industry, margin pressure was intense, particularly in the frit and zircon businesses, and operating profits fell slightly from last year's record levels. Work has been completed on the construction of a new highly automated frit manufacturing facility in Spain and the first kilns are now operational. A new frit plant in Brazil is nearing completion and will be operational early in 2002/03. The Brazilian facility will be the first to produce high quality, gas fired frits in the country and will provide both higher product quality and lower production costs. Asian markets slowed during 2001/02, but there was good growth in Eastern Europe. Products currently made by Structural Ceramics on the Meir site will be transferred to Spain and Italy.

Glass

The Glass sector performed well in the face of very difficult market conditions. Sales grew slightly and operating profits were similar to last year. The completion during the year of the business' £4 million expansion programme at the Glass masterplant in Maastricht enabled it to achieve record output of glass enamels. While both the European and North American markets for automotive black obscuration enamels were slower than in previous years, the business saw good growth in sales of conductive silver pastes. Consolidation of suppliers to the US market place is offering good opportunities to win new business. The business has a strong pipeline of new products and is conducting research into related market niches.

Speciality Coatings

The newly formed Speciality Coatings sector combines the division's Tableware and Pigments and Dispersions businesses. Its activities remain organised on market facing lines to serve the needs of the tableware, plastics and surface coatings industries. Sales and profits in the Tableware business fell sharply during the year as its market continued to contract, especially in the UK. The closure of the Meir facility will reduce Tableware's cost base significantly, yet will not significantly impact sales as most production will be relocated to other plants. The business also sold its decal printing facility in Limoges to local management in September as part of a reduction in its global capacity. Outside the UK and US, tableware sales increased slightly. Two important new colour ranges were launched during the year, targeted at the needs of porcelain and stoneware producers, and a new screen printing gold was also introduced to the market. Investment in the decorative gold facility in Royston has progressed well, delivering both a new range of products and environmental benefits. The Pigments and Dispersions business had a difficult year, with a small decline in sales in tough markets. Sales grew in Asia and the USA. Cadmium and transparent iron oxide margins were under pressure, but there was good growth in the Colourplex®, Micraflo® and Timbasol® product groups.

Research and Development

Research for the Colours & Coatings Division is based at the Johnson Matthey Technology Centre and at the division's main European facilities. Research activities include fundamental studies into the base chemistry of the businesses' core products as well as new product development.

The introduction of new products and new application effects is an important part of the division's strategy for growth. Its customer markets are fashion driven and so development programmes are closely linked to the need to develop innovative new ways of using colours and to match changing consumer tastes.

Increasing environmental requirements are also leading to the development of heavy metal free ranges for all product areas and an increased focus on recyclability. There is also an increasing focus on new process development as well as new product development. New milling and drying technologies are reducing costs in zircon and glass. UV drying technology is reducing printing times and costs in decal, while a new gelling process has improved our liquid gold products. Good progress is being made on reducing process costs in colour production.

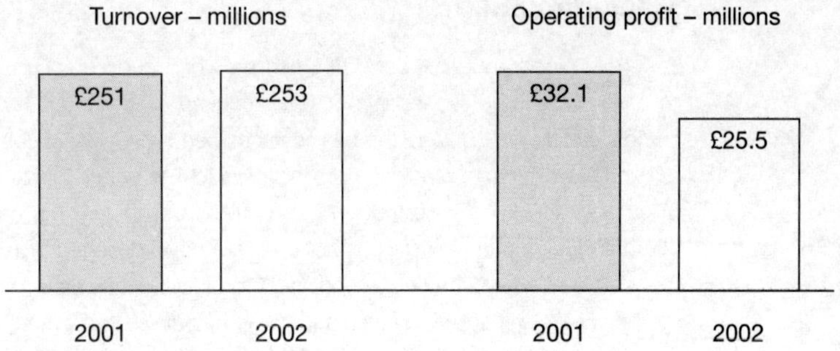

Pharmaceutical Materials

Pharmaceutical Materials Division performed very well in 2001/02 with operating profits 74% up at £31.3 million.

Pharmaceutical Materials was created as a separate division in 2001 following the acquisition of Pharm-Eco Laboratories, Inc. and Meconic plc.

During the fiscal year 2001/02, Johnson Matthey acquired Pharm-Eco Laboratories, Inc. and Meconic plc, the parent company of Macfarlan Smith. These acquisitions, along with Johnson Matthey's long established active pharmaceutical ingredient (API) manufacturing business in West Deptford, USA, enable the newly formed Pharmaceutical Materials Division to provide the pharmaceutical industry with chemical synthesis, process development and manufacturing services throughout the entire life cycle of both proprietary and generic drugs. In addition, Macfarlan Smith provides Pharmaceutical Materials with a European base and offers major opportunities for cross selling and collaboration in development of new products for both the European and American markets, especially in the field of controlled drugs.

West Deptford

The division's West Deptford facility manufactures a range of small to medium volume, high value active pharmaceutical ingredients, mainly metal based and controlled substances. These products comprise ingredients used in both generic and proprietary drugs, including the platinum anticancer drugs cisplatin and carboplatin and the powerful painkillers fentanyl and hydromorphone. In 2001/02 sales at West Deptford increased 12% over the prior year despite a drop in revenues from platinum pharmaceuticals resulting from the termination of patent protection on cisplatin. Most of this growth occurred in the second half of the year when the business received regulatory approval for three new products, all of which were developed for new customers and were launched in early calendar year 2002. In support of these and other new products, a major expansion of manufacturing and laboratory facilities on the site is nearing completion with plant validation and commissioning early in fiscal year 2002/03. This expansion will immediately increase plant capacity by up to 40% and includes space for additional reactors as well as the necessary laboratories to support further growth.

Macfarlan Smith

Based in Edinburgh, UK, Macfarlan Smith is a world leader in the manufacture and marketing of controlled drugs. Johnson Matthey acquired Meconic plc, Macfarlan Smith's parent company in July 2001, and the business has performed well in Johnson Matthey's first nine months of ownership. Macfarlan Smith's product line of bulk opiates such as codeine, morphine and dihydrocodeine yielded good sales, and those of specialist opiates, several of which are being used in new applications or in novel dosage forms, showed excellent sales growth. Other established non-controlled products such as Bitrex™, an extremely bitter substance added to many household and garden products to prevent accidental poisoning, and galantamine, used in the treatment of Alzheimer's disease, also performed strongly. Late in the year, Macfarlan Smith completed a new manufacturing plant on its Edinburgh site. This facility was constructed to manufacture key specialist opiate and other controlled drug products and contains space for additional capacity to support expected growth in these products.

Pharm-Eco

Pharm-Eco Laboratories, Inc., based near Boston, USA, was acquired by Johnson Matthey in April 2001. Pharm-Eco is a leading provider of contract chemistry services to the pharmaceutical industry, including medicinal chemistry, process development and the manufacturing of drugs in the early and middle phases of their development cycle. Outsourcing of chemistry services by both small and large drug companies is a growing trend, and Pharm-Eco made excellent progress in all segments of its business during the year. Major new contracts were obtained in the areas of medicinal chemistry, as well as the small scale manufacture of products for use in clinical trials. Pharm-Eco has also expanded its activities in analytical chemistry services and by adding specialised equipment to perform process hazard assessments for customers. The business' sales grew well throughout the year with particularly strong growth in the second half of 2001/02. In support of this, a long term programme of installing additional laboratories and manufacturing capacity has been initiated at Pharm-Eco's principal site in Devens, Massachusetts. Employee numbers have grown by 33% from the time of acquisition.

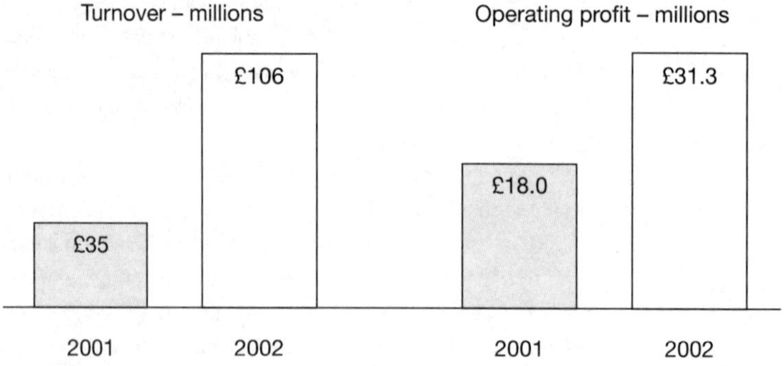

Research and Development

Pharmaceutical Materials Division's research and development activities are primarily focused on developing manufacturing processes for active pharmaceutical ingredients. At West Deptford and Macfarlan Smith, the development of novel manufacturing and analytical methods for new products provides a steady pipeline of products for these businesses. Collaboration between the research and development groups at West Deptford and Macfarlan Smith is enabling the development of common products and implementation of the most efficient manufacturing processes within the two businesses. Macfarlan Smith has particularly strong extraction technology that complements West Deptford's strength in drug synthesis. This provides opportunities for synergies through the sharing of production technology and expertise. Pharm-Eco provides synthesis and process development services for drugs in pre-clinical and the early to middle phases of clinical trials. The ultimate success of any drug in these stages of clinical development is uncertain. However, Pharm-Eco's experience in product development and scale-up places Johnson Matthey in a strong position to manufacture commercial quantities for Pharm-Eco's clients should their products obtain regulatory approval.

A few comments on the company's operating review

The first thing that comes across is technical innovation, both in products and processes, stemming from a need to innovate to maintain its business's profitability. The second general point is that it can only grow its sales through product innovation and competitive pricing, as otherwise it is reliant on its end users to stimulate consumer demand and respond to changes in consumer tastes. In essence the future success of its business is underpinned by its ability to stay ahead of the game.

All the profit figures shown in the operating review are continuing operating profits before exceptional items and central costs.

When you read the divisional reviews you find:

- **Catalysts & Chemicals:** this is the biggest contributor to the group's profits, accounting for almost 46% of it. This division's 17% increase in profits drove the increase in the group's operating profit, as the total group's continuing profits rose by just under 11% (from £175.1 million to £193.8 million). The division has three separate businesses:
  - *Catalytic Systems:* this has had a major capital expenditure programme, installing new manufacturing capacity in all of its plants worldwide. This gives it more accurate materials' control, and greater product design flexibility. Its automotive business appears vulnerable to new vehicle sales and emission control legislation. In response to this it has grown its market share of retro-fit heavy duty catalysts, and its new technology has enabled it to grow its market share within the new vehicle market. (Improving control of precious metals must have the effect of reducing costs, and greater design flexibility is bound to be attractive to car companies.) This division has also benefited from the problems in the US power industry, where there's been an increased demand for catalysts for small turbine generation.

- *Chemicals:* the businesses in the chemicals division are affected by different factors. The pgm refining business is exposed to the demand from primary producers, and the recovery part of the business to recovery costs and platinum prices. Its response to this has been to develop a technological advantage – installing new smelting technology and patent protected recovery technology. The catalyst and chemicals business faces a common business risk – end-user demand. Its response is to develop new technologies, and diversify to offer contract services.
- *Fuel Cells:* this business is still in its infancy, with the first commercial products just being launched for backup power and portable applications in 'premium' (I assume that means expensive) markets. The car companies have only just started to test small vehicle fleets. As this is a potentially large market offering considerable future profit opportunities, Johnson Matthey needs to remain the leading player in fuel cell development. You wouldn't expect to see details of any developments in its operating review, but it does talk about 'dramatic improvements' in its fuel cell products.

■ **Precious Metals**: in 2002 this division provided almost 66% of the group's continuing turnover, and 27% of its profits. Its profits were 3% down on 2001. It is organised into two divisions:
- *Platinum:* there are two different businesses within the platinum business unit. The trading and marketing business's profits appear exposed to price movements, as its profits fell following the 13% fall in platinum prices and the 39% fall in palladium prices, whereas the fabrication business is exposed to changes in end-user demand, and Johnson Matthey's response is its usual one of improving its technological advantage.
- *Gold and silver:* the refinery business is exposed to price movements, and it has been trying to improve profitability by improving processing efficiency and moving out of low-margin products.

■ **Colours & Coatings**: this division is the smallest contributor to the group's continuing operating profits, 12% of the total, with its operating profits falling in 2002. The division appears to operate in more competitive markets and is exposed to pressure on prices, and most of its technical innovations are focused on improving manufacturing efficiencies and reducing costs (although it's also addressing environmental concerns through its recycling developments). Only two of its businesses appear to be growth businesses – glass and tile. The division is organised into three market-focused businesses:
- *Structural Ceramics:* this market could be difficult in 2003 as it 'softened' during the second half of 2002. However, Johnson Matthey should be well placed in a downturn, as it has the lowest unit costs in the industry. The closure of the factory in Meir, Stoke on Trent, should reduce its operating costs and minimise margin erosion. New investments have been made overseas in highly automated plants, and are focused on reducing manufacturing costs and improving quality.
- *Glass:* whilst this is one of the division's growth markets, it appears that there were mixed market conditions in 2002. Johnson Matthey is developing new products and looking for niche applications.
- *Speciality Coatings:* this has two separate businesses – tableware and pigments and

dispersions. The contraction of the total tableware market, particularly in the UK, meant that the profits and sales fell. It's probably unlikely that this market will improve in the short to medium term, and success in these markets will depend on their ability to cut costs and respond to changes in consumer tastes. The closure of the Meir plant is expected to save £3 million in 2003, and £7 million from 2004. This should benefit both the tableware and structural ceramics businesses. The pigments and dispersion business is also trading in 'tough markets', where future success depends on patented product innovation and cost reduction.

- **Pharmaceutical Materials**: this division's 74% increase in profits could well have arisen from the acquisition of Pharm-Eco and Macfarlan Smith during 2002. Although this is a new division, it contributed 15% to the group's total profit. It appears to have considerable growth opportunities, as all three businesses have expanded their capacity in the last year. These businesses operate in niche markets providing materials and services to pharmaceutical companies. There are three businesses in the pharmaceutical division:
  - *West Deptford:* sales increased by 12%, with the regulatory approval for three new products in the second half of the year more than offsetting the expiry of an existing patent. Manufacturing capacity has been increased by more than 40% to support planned growth. The product pipeline will be an important factor for the continued success of this business.
  - *Macfarlan Smith:* this is primarily involved in manufacturing and marketing controlled drugs, and has recently installed a new manufacturing plant to cope with expected increase in demand for these products.
  - *Pharm-Eco:* its markets are also expected to expand, as more pharmaceutical companies outsource chemistry services, and consequently a long-term capital expenditure programme has been initiated.

To summarise: all Johnson Matthey's businesses face one common risk – a fall in end user demand that it can't affect directly through its own sales activities. It is trying to minimise this risk by:

- being technically innovative, both in products and processes – in some markets the focus is on product development, and in other, more competitive, markets the focus appears to be on process development and cost reduction;
- diversifying into niche growth markets, like pharmaceuticals, where it can use its unique skills.

A few more questions

Looking at its operating review has raised questions about:

- the effect of precious metal prices on turnover;
- how much of the improvements in the Pharmaceutical Materials Division's profits came from acquisitions, and how much from its existing business.

Johnson Matthey's financial statements

Now it's time to look at Johnson Matthey's financial statements over the last three years. Its profit and loss account holds few surprises, as most of it was shown in the ten-year summary. However, you'll notice that I've presented it in a different way from that shown in its accounts, as I've shown all the profit figures before exceptional items and the profit from discontinued operations below the profit and loss account (Table 14.1).

Table 14.1 Profit and loss accounts

	2000 £m	2001 £m	2002 £m
Turnover – continuing business	3,769.0	5,899.5	4,828.9
Turnover – total business	3,866.0	5,903.7	4,830.1
Cost of materials sold	(3,304.7)	(5,330.6)	(4,185.7)
Net revenues	561.3	573.1	644.4
Other cost of sales	(295.2)	(265.6)	(330.6)
Gross profit	266.1	307.5	313.8
Administration expenses	(68.8)	(75.6)	(85.3)
Distribution costs	(61.1)	(57.8)	(60.0)
Operating profit – after exceptional items	136.2	174.1	168.5
Share of associates' profits			(0.1)
Profit (loss) on sale of subsidiaries	22.3	1.1	(5.6)
Profit on sale of surplus properties	1.1		
Profit before interest	159.6	175.2	162.8
Interest received	13.0	17.7	10.9
Interest paid	(15.4)	(12.4)	(17.0)
Profit before tax	157.2	180.5	156.7
Tax	(47.3)	(54.2)	(50.2)
Profit after tax	109.9	126.3	106.5
Minority Interests	(0.2)	(0.6)	0.3
Profit attributable to ordinary shareholders	109.7	125.7	106.8
Ordinary dividend	(44.3)	(51.3)	(53.2)
Retained profit	65.4	74.4	53.6
Earnings per share (pence):			
Reported	50.5	57.3	49.0
Adjusted for exceptional items and goodwill amortisation	46.6	57.2	60.4
Dividend per share (pence)	20.3	23.3	24.6
Additional profit and loss information:			
Operating profit – continuing operations before exceptional items	146.5	174.9	193.9
Operating profit – continuing business after exceptional items	136.5	174.0	169.0
Operating profit – before exceptional items	146.2	175.0	193.4
Discontinued operations operating profit	(0.3)	0.1	(0.5)
Profit before tax, goodwill amortisation and exceptional items	143.8	180.3	187.2
Profit after tax before goodwill amortisation and exceptional items	101.4	126.2	131.2
Profit attributable to ordinary shareholders before goodwill amortisation and exceptional items	101.2	125.6	131.5

The balance sheets (Table 14.2) show more information than those in Johnson Matthey's accounts, as I've extracted trade debtors and trade creditors from the notes to the accounts.

Table 14.2 Balance sheets

	2000 £m	2001 £m	2002 £m
Fixed assets:			
Tangible assets	311.3	386.8	495.1
Intangible assets	5.1	8.6	182.6
Investments	1.0	1.0	2.7
	317.4	396.4	680.4
Current assets:			
Stocks	253.2	278.8	414.3
Debtors due in a year[1]	333.5	416.2	345.2
Debtors due in more than a year	97.9	103.9	108.8
Investments and short-term deposits	16.3	15.9	16.6
Cash at bank and in hand	282.0	237.4	92.6
Total	982.9	1,052.2	977.5
Creditors: amounts due in a year:			
Bank loans and overdrafts	(46.2)	(19.8)	(65.8)
Precious metal leases	(60.6)	(91.8)	(131.0)
Trade creditors	(139.6)	(145.3)	(167.5)
Other creditors	(176.0)	(222.5)	(191.7)
Total	(422.4)	(479.4)	(556.0)
Net current assets	560.5	572.8	421.5
Total assets less current liabilities	877.9	969.2	1,101.9
Creditors: amounts due in more than a year:			
Loans	(70.0)	(77.7)	(185.8)
Other creditors	(0.2)	(1.0)	(0.4)
	(70.2)	(78.7)	(186.2)
Provisions for liabilities and charges:			
Deferred tax	(44.4)	(49.7)	(66.1)
Other provisions	(34.2)	(29.5)	(32.0)
	(78.6)	(79.2)	(98.1)
	729.1	**811.3**	**817.6**
Capital and reserves:			
Share capital	221.1	222.5	218.7
Share premium	116.7	123.2	128.2
Profit and loss account	386.9	461.0	462.1
Associated undertakings' reserves	(0.1)		(0.2)
Capital redemption reserve			4.9
Shareholders' funds	724.6	806.7	813.7
Minority interests	4.5	4.6	3.9
	729.1	**811.3**	**817.6**
[1] Includes trade debtors of	265.0	357.5	303.9

I've shown the gross cash flows on the cash flow statement (Table 14.3) and the reconciliation to operating profit (Table 14.4).

Table 14.3 Cash flow statements

	2000 £m	2001 £m	2002 £m
Net cash flow from operating activities	130.3	156.5	224.1
Dividends received from associated undertakings	*0.1*	*0.1*	*0.1*
Returns on investment and servicing of finance			
Interest received	13.1	18.0	11.0
Interest paid	(15.6)	(12.0)	(15.9)
Dividends paid to minority interests		0.2	
Net cash flow from returns on investment and servicing of finance	(2.5)	5.8	(4.9)
Taxation	*(33.5)*	*(38.2)*	*(55.8)*
Capital expenditure and financial investment			
Purchase of fixed assets	(74.1)	(98.8)	(134.1)
Purchase of long-term investments	(0.2)	(0.1)	(1.0)
Finance lease to an associate	(0.5)		
Disposal of investments	2.8	3.3	3.5
Capital repayment of finance lease to an associate	0.1		
Disposal of fixed assets	6.2	0.9	0.6
Net cash flow from capital expenditure and financial investment	*(65.7)*	*(94.7)*	*(131.0)*
Acquisitions and disposals			
Purchase of businesses (net of cash and cash equivalents)	(2.9)	(6.2)	(143.5)
Investment in and loans to associated undertakings			
Disposal of businesses	393.7	0.6	(2.2)
Sale of shares in associated undertaking			
Net cash flow from acquisitions and disposals	*390.8*	*(5.6)*	*(145.7)*
Equity dividends paid	*(42.2)*	*(46.5)*	*(52.1)*
Net cash flow before management of liquid resources	*377.3*	*(22.6)*	*(165.3)*
Management of liquid resources	*(169.8)*	*157.8*	*0.2*
Net cash flow before financing	*207.5*	*135.2*	*(165.1)*
Financing			
Issue of ordinary share capital	15.7	7.9	6.1
Capital element of finance lease rentals	(0.3)	(0.4)	(0.2)
Repayment of money loans	(163.4)	(11.7)	(45.7)
Increase in other borrowings			103.4
Purchase of own shares	(7.7)		(50.2)
Net cash flow from financing	*(155.7)*	*(4.2)*	*13.4*
Increase/(Decrease) in cash	***51.8***	***131.0***	***(151.7)***

Table 14.4 Reconciliation of operating profit to cash flow from operating activities

	2000 £m	2001 £m	2002 £m
Operating profit	136.2	174.1	168.5
Depreciation	46.6	41.1	55.1
Loss/(profit) on sale of fixed assets	(0.9)	(0.7)	(1.4)
Future cash generated from this year's operations	181.9	214.5	222.2
Decrease/(increase) in stocks	(26.7)	15.0	(83.6)
Decrease/(increase) in debtors	(77.2)	(82.0)	73.9
Increase/(decrease) in creditors and provisions	52.3	9.0	11.6
Net cash flow from operating activities	*130.3*	*156.5*	*224.1*

Initial observations on the three years' financial statements

The changes in turnover do appear to be explained by precious metal prices, as there is a very different trend when you look at net revenues (Figure 14.2).

Fig. 14.2 Turnover and net revenue

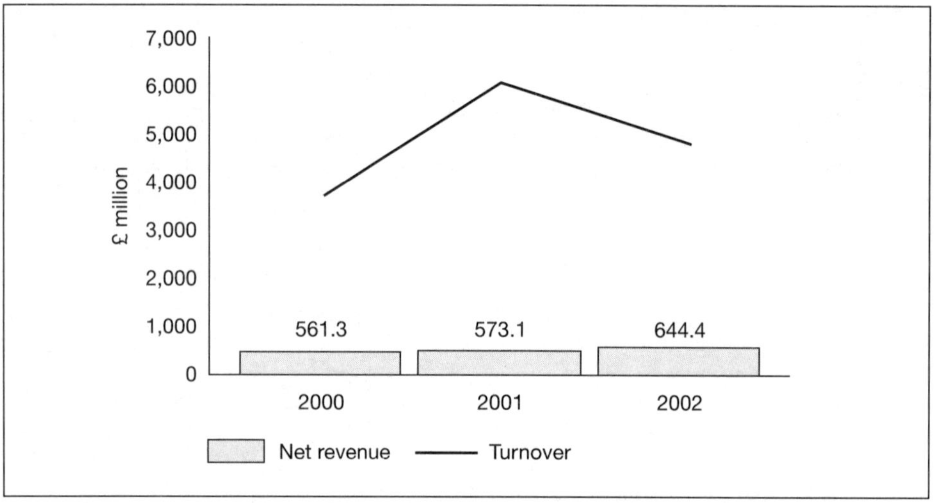

But if you remember the financial review, shown in Chapter 7, the company has a table that shows its sales excluding precious metals for each division (Table 14.5).

Table 14.5 Sales excluding previous metals for each division

	Sales excluding Precious Metals		Return on Sales	
	2001 £ million	**2002 £ million**	2001 %	**2002 %**
Catalysts & Chemicals	535	**597**	15.1	**15.9**
Precious Metals	162	**143**	35.5	**39.1**
Colours & Coatings	246	**251**	13.1	**10.2**
Pharmaceutical Materials	30	**101**	60.2	**30.9**
Discontinued	4	**1**	n/m	**n/m**
	977	**1,093**	17.9	**17.7**

(The financial review usually contains any additional information that's necessary for you to understand how the business is performing.)

Johnson Matthey is bound to pass through precious metal price changes to its customers, and so this sales figure is probably a better reflection of the group's trading performance. Now let's look at a comparison of turnover, sales and net revenue over the three-year period using the information shown in its financial reviews (Figure 14.3).

The difference between sales and net revenue is the other materials used in sales, and these grew significantly between 2000 and 2001.

The group's underlying profit (operating profit before exceptional items) has grown steadily throughout the period. In Figure 14.4 I've compared it to sales.

Fig. 14.3 Turnover, sales and net revenues

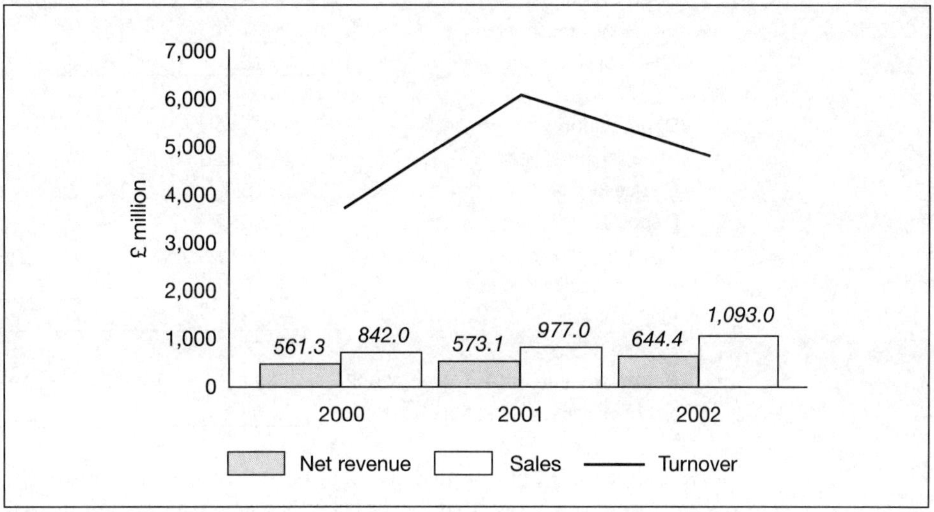

Fig. 14.4 Sales and operating profit

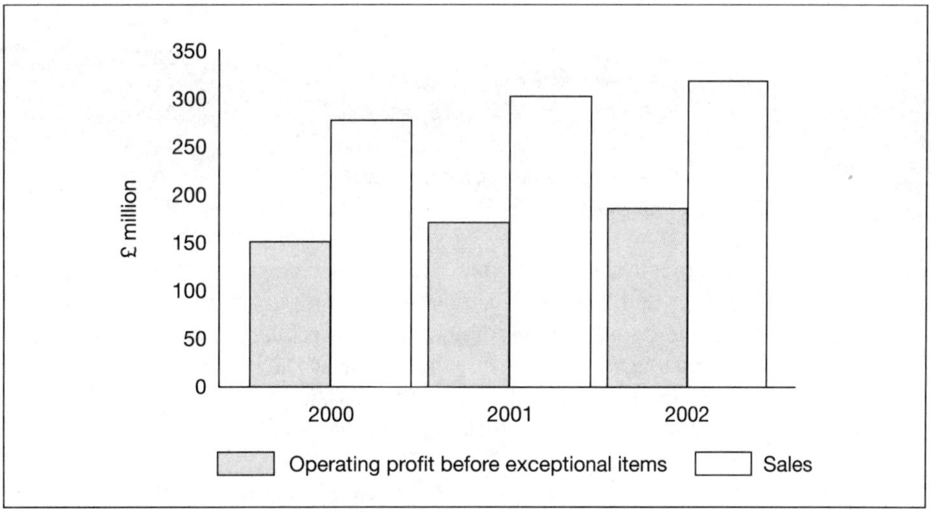

Now let's move on to look at its balance sheet. The large increase in tangible assets in 2002 is largely explained by capital expenditure and partly by acquisitions, as you can see in the group's tangible asset note:

	Freehold land & buildings £ million	Long & short leasehold £ million	Plant & machinery £ million	Total £ million
Cost				
At beginning of year	140.2	12.7	519.4	672.3
Purchases	13.4	0.9	119.5	133.8
Acquisitions	19.9	–	23.1	43.0
Disposals	(1.1)	–	(25.9)	(27.0)
Disposal of subsidiary	(1.0)	–	(1.6)	(2.6)
Exchange adjustments	(1.3)	(0.1)	(5.6)	(7.0)
At end of year	170.1	13.5	628.9	812.5
Depreciation				
At beginning of year	41.4	5.1	239.0	285.5
Charge for the year	5.2	0.7	42.4	48.3
Disposals	(0.1)	–	(13.1)	(13.2)
Disposal of subsidiary	(0.2)	–	(0.7)	(0.9)
Exchange adjustments	(0.3)	–	(2.0)	(2.3)
At end of year	46.0	5.8	265.6	317.4
Net book value at 31st March 2002	**124.1**	**7.7**	**363.3**	**495.1**
Net book value at 31st March 2001	98.8	7.6	280.4	386.8

Stock has increased out of proportion to both turnover and net revenue, and the note on the group's stocks shows that this has largely come from a major increase in precious metal work in progress:

	Group	
	2002 £ million	2001 £ million
Raw materials and consumables	**47.7**	49.0
Work in progress – precious metals	**240.1**	120.3
– other	**28.6**	17.7
Finished goods and goods for resale	**97.9**	91.8
Total stocks	**414.3**	278.8

The financial review commented on the increase in stocks: 'Inventories rose significantly at year end, part of which should be temporary, as metal holdings have been increased during the major upgrading of the pgm refinery at Royston.' It appears the company was taking longer to process the metal during the upgrade. The real increase in the volume of stock held is likely to be larger than its value increase, as precious metal prices fell during 2002. The increase in stocks is significant, as it reduced the company's operating cash flow by £83.6 million.

The two things that stand out from reading the cash flow statement are 2002's relatively high expenditures on both fixed assets and acquisitions. Having read the operating review you now know where it was spent. The capital expenditure is largely on new plant and equipment, where the company has been investing heavily in new processes to improve manufacturing performance to give it a competitive advantage. The acquisitions were in the

Pharmaceutical Materials Division (Meconic and Pharm-Eco) and Catalysts & Chemicals (Avocado Research Chemicals and Oy Smoptech).

Now let's review my earlier questions to see if I now have the information to answer the questions arising from the company's ten-year summary and the operational review. The questions were:

- What was the effect of precious metal prices on turnover? *You now understand that the big swings in turnover were caused by precious metal prices, as its net revenues grew by only 2.1% between 2000 and 2001, and by 12.4% between 2001 and 2002.*
- How much of the changes in tangible assets arose from acquisitions, and how much from capital expenditure? *You've now seen the company's cash flow statement, which showed you how much cash it had spent buying fixed assets, and the tangible asset note that analysed the assets between its purchases and those acquired with acquisitions. So you now know that most of the increase came from the purchase of fixed assets.*
- How much of the improvements in the Pharmaceutical Materials Division's profits came from acquisitions, and how much from its existing business?

This is explained in its note on acquisitions where it discloses the effect of the acquisitions on the financial statements. It's worth looking at this note as it shows you the assets and liabilities it acquired, how they were financed, and how the acquisitions affected both the profit and loss account and the cash flow statement. I'll take Meconic as an example. When Johnson Matthey acquired it, it acquired a business with net liabilities including £20.6 million borrowings due within a year. (You can see the details of the assets and liabilities it acquired in Chapter 3.) Since its acquisition Meconic contributed £10.4 million to the net cash inflow from operating activities, paid £0.3 million returns on investments and servicing of finance, paid £0.3 million of tax and £4.6 million for capital expenditure and financial investment. This means that it contributed a net £5.2 million to the group's cash flow. (It's always worth reading this note, as some companies are acquired for their cash generation and may have a larger effect on cash flow than on profits.)

Now let's look at how acquisitions affected the Pharmaceutical Materials Division's profit in 2002:

	Macfarlan Smith (Meconic) £ million	Pharm-Eco Laboratories £ million	Total acquisitions £ million	Pharmaceutical division £ million	Acquisitions as a % of the total
Turnover	54.5	11.7	66.2	105.5	62.7%
Operating profit	10.0	1.9	11.9	31.3	38.0%

You can see that its acquisitions made a bigger contribution to the division's turnover than its profit. The divisional profits are shown before exceptional costs (you may recall that £1.3 million of the group's exceptional costs were rationalisation costs at Meconic), so without the acquisitions the Pharmaceutical Materials Division's profit would have been £19.4 million (31.3 – 11.9). As the division's profits were £18 million in 2001, the profits from its existing business increased by 7.8%.

Now I've answered all of my questions, so it's time to move on to do some ratio analysis.

Analysing Johnson Matthey's financial performance 2000–2

It's now time to start the analysis and the first question is – what do I want to analyse? You should now have a reasonable understanding of Johnson Matthey's business. You've seen how it has changed over the last ten years, identified the key drivers of its performance in its operating review, and looked at its financial statements for the last three years. When you analyse a business's performance you're interested in its:

- **Solvency**: can it repay the money it owes on time? This is normally the first place you start. Now you've looked at Johnson Matthey's accounts, I think you already know the answer to that question . . . it's a resounding 'YES'. You don't have to work out any ratios to know that its business would have to undergo a fundamental change (like the transition from GEC to Marconi) before it would experience difficulties repaying on time. This means that doing ratios proving this would largely be a waste of time. If you're like me you'll have a spreadsheet that does them automatically, but it's pointless calculating them unless they're going to tell you something. However, many of the companies you'll analyse will not have Johnson Matthey's financial strength and you'll undoubtedly have to calculate these ratios.
- **Cash management**: this links with solvency, as it explores how the company is managing its cash. You've already seen Johnson Matthey's cash flow statements and know that it manages its cash effectively. Measuring this would give us no additional information.
- **Profitability**: is the business profitable? Is its profitability improving or declining? Why is it changing?
- **Attractiveness to investors**: does Johnson Matthey represent a good investment? Are investors' expectations unrealistic?

As solvency and cash management aren't an issue in Johnson Matthey, I'll start by looking at its profitability.

Profitability

First, I'll look at its return on capital employed ratios. This means that I have to identify the profit figures and the capital employed figures I'm going to use. So let's look at the company's profit. I'm analysing the business over three years, so if I want to look at its underlying profitability I'll have to use profit before exceptional items. For the return on operating capital employed I'll use its operating profit before exceptional items and for the overall return on capital employed I'll add the income from its investments to this figure.

	2000	**2001**	**2002**
	£m	£m	£m
Operating profit before exceptional items	*146.2*	*175.0*	*193.4*
Share of associate's profits	0.0	0.0	(0.1)
Interest received	13.0	17.7	10.9
Profit for overall capital employed	*159.2*	*192.7*	*204.2*

Now let's identify the capital employed – I'm going to use an adjusted capital employed including provisions for liabilities and charges and goodwill written off through reserves.

	2000	2001	2002
	£m	£m	£m
Shareholders' funds	724.6	806.7	813.7
Minority interests	4.5	4.6	3.9
Long-term loans	70.0	77.7	185.8
Short-term loans	46.2	19.8	65.8
Capital employed	*845.3*	*908.8*	*1,069.2*
Goodwill written off through reserves	46.0	46.0	46.0
Provisions for liabilities and charges	78.6	79.2	98.1
Adjusted capital employed	*969.9*	*1,034.0*	*1,213.3*

Now let's find the operating capital employed:

	2000	2001	2002
	£m	£m	£m
Adjusted capital employed	969.9	1,034.0	1,213.3
Long-term investments	(1.0)	(1.0)	(2.7)
Short-term investments	(16.3)	(15.9)	(16.6)
Cash	(282.0)	(237.4)	(92.6)
Adjusted operating capital employed	670.6	779.7	1,101.4

Return on capital employed ratios

First, I'll calculate the overall return on capital employed and then the return on operating capital employed:

Overall return on capital employed

	2000	2001	2002
Overall return on capital employed	16.4%	18.6%	16.8%

You can see that the return on overall capital employed improved in 2001, as the growth in profits was greater than the growth in capital employed. Unfortunately, this reversed in 2002, when the increase in the capital employed was greater than the increase in profits.

Return on operating capital employed

	2000	2001	2002
Return on operating capital employed	21.8%	22.4%	17.6%

You can see the same trend, but with less growth between 2000 and 2001, and a greater decline between 2001 and 2002.

Now I need to find out why the return on operating capital employed has fallen. I think it's largely because of falling asset utilisation, but let's see if I'm right. As this is the driver of the overall return on capital, and is the only return that can be analysed in detail, I'll use the return on operating capital to work through the operating profitability hierarchy.

Profit margin

	2000	2001	2002
Operating margin before exceptional items	3.78%	2.96%	4.00%

Now you may remember that at the start of this section I told you that you were entering the world of the amateur detective. I'd like you to think for a moment about why Johnson Matthey's operating margin is likely to have fallen in 2001 . . . You're right – increased precious metal prices fed straight through to turnover. I can check this by stripping out the precious metals and using the sales numbers I showed you earlier:

	2000	2001	2002
Profit	146.2	175.0	193.4
Sales excluding precious metals	841.0	977.0	1,093.0
Return on sales	17.4%	17.9%	17.7%

Now this shows a different story; the return on sales has been reasonably stable with the best percentage return in 2001, and a slight fall in 2002. Now let's see if we can find out *why* some of the company's profitability ratios fell.

Profitability analysis

First, I'd like to rewrite the company's profit and loss accounts for the last three years:

	2000	2001	2002
Turnover	3,866.0	5,903.7	4,830.1
Precious metals	(3,024.0)	(4,926.7)	(3,737.1)
Sales excluding precious metals	842.0	977.0	1,093.0
Other material costs net of exceptional items	(280.7)	(403.9)	(444.0)
Net revenues	561.3	573.1	649.0
Other cost of sales net of exceptional items	(290.3)	(265.0)	(321.4)
Gross profit	271.0	308.1	327.6
Overheads before exceptional costs	(124.8)	(133.1)	(134.2)
Operating profit before exceptional items	146.2	175.0	193.4

As I want to use operating profit before exceptional items, these numbers are different from those shown in the earlier profit and loss account. And it may not be perfect, as I had to decide which materials benefited from the exceptional credit of £4.6 million, and I chose 'other materials'.

Now let's look at Johnson Matthey's gross margin and overhead cost ratios over the period.

Gross margin

	2000	2001	2002
Gross margin before exceptional items	7.01%	5.22%	6.78%

I've calculated this ratio using the company's turnover, the standard definition, and you'll see that there's a fall in 2001 again. Let see what the trend looks like when I exclude precious metals and base it on sales:

	2000	2001	2002
Sales based gross margin	32.19%	31.54%	29.97%

This shows that its underlying gross margin has been falling over the period.

Overhead cost ratio

I've calculated the overhead cost ratio based on sales and you can see that it has fallen steadily over the period, as the increase in overheads has been less than the increase in sales:

	2000	2001	2002
Sales based overhead cost ratio	14.82%	13.62%	12.28%

The operating margin fell in 2002 because the improvement in the overhead cost ratio was insufficient to cover the fall in gross margin.

If you think back to Chapter 9, I showed you that the three commonest reasons for changes in profitability were changes in price, mix and volumes. In its operating review Johnson Matthey told us that some of its businesses, mainly in the Colours and Coatings Division, had been under 'margin pressure'. Some of its businesses were experiencing falling volumes, but most were growth businesses. Operating profits can fall in a growth business in the short term when the business moves up a fixed cost 'step', but the analysis suggests that any problem lies in its gross margin. So that would only leave higher 'other' material prices, or changes in the product or business mix. There's no information about product mix in the financial statements, only business mix in the segmental analysis. So let's see what this tells us.

Segmental analysis

I've used the note shown in Chapter 7 and its equivalent in the 2000 accounts to look at how the business mix has changed in the period. First, I'll show you how the balance of sales in the company's continuing businesses (so this excludes precious metals and their discontinued businesses) has changed (Figure 14.5).

Fig. 14.5 Divisional contribution to sales

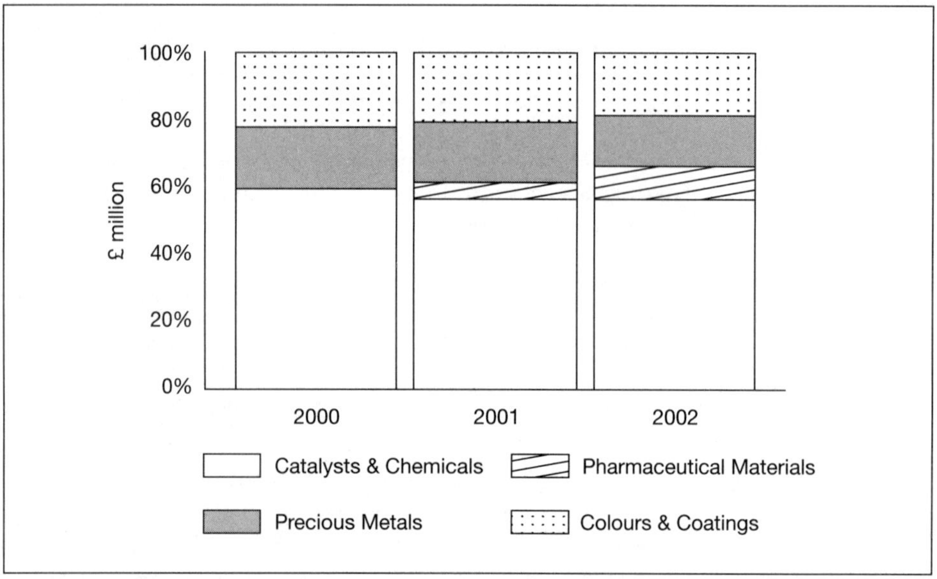

I've presented the information in a different order to that found in the notes, placing Pharmaceutical Materials next to Catalysts & Chemicals, as it was part of this division in 2000. The Precious Metals contribution seems to follow metal prices – it's more important when prices are high.

Now let's look at the company's return on sales; this is effectively the divisional underlying operating margin, as precious metals are stripped out, there's no allocation of its central costs and it's based on its continuing business (Figure 14.6).

The return on sales in Precious Metals is the highest in the group in 2002. It fell in 2001, when prices were at their highest. Colours & Coatings improved in 2001, then fell back to 10.2% in 2002. However, unless its markets become even more difficult, its margin should improve slightly in 2003, as costs fall following the reduction in capacity. (This should reduce its fixed costs and breakeven points and it disclosed that costs are expected to reduce by £3 million in 2003.) Catalysts & Chemicals had its highest return on sales in 2000, 17.2%, which fell in 2000 to 15.1% and recovered slightly in 2002 to 15.9%. The Pharmaceutical Materials Division's return on sales fell in 2002, but should rise in 2003 if the expected sales growth materialises and the rationalisation benefits work through.

Fig. 14.6 Return on sales

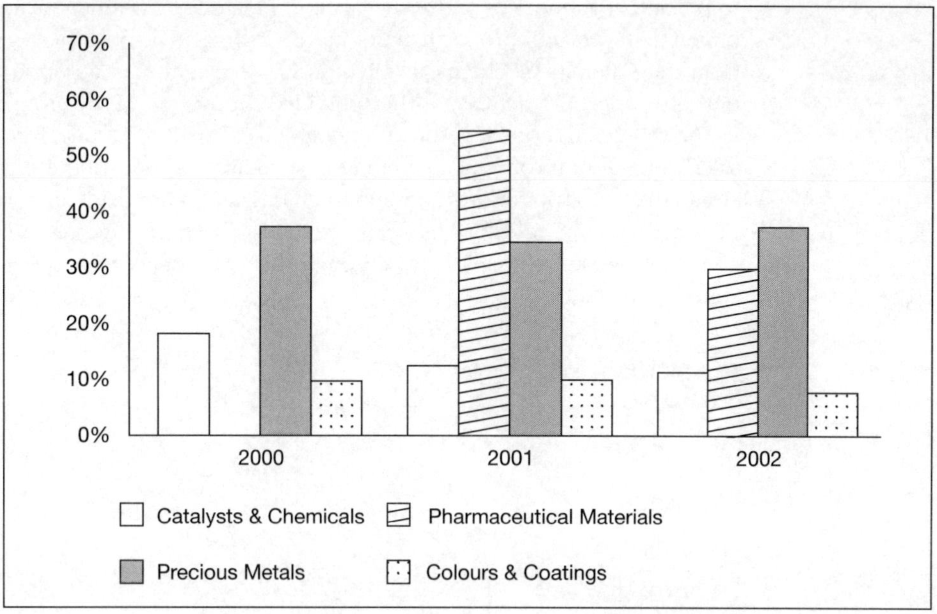

Now I'll show you how the return on sales affected the divisional contribution to the group's continuing profits (Figure 14.7).

Fig. 14.7 Divisional contribution to profit

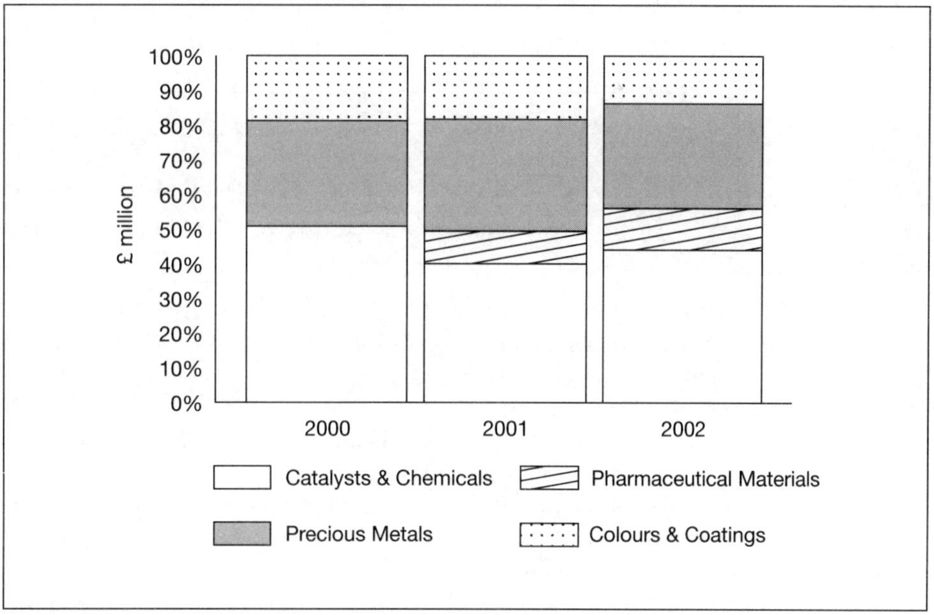

This follows some of the trends identified earlier; Precious Metals' performance is linked to precious metal prices and Pharmaceutical Materials currently provides a larger contribution to the group's profits than Colours & Coatings. The percentage of the group's profit from the Catalysts & Chemicals Division has declined in the period, as the other businesses' profits have increased (they provided almost 54% of the group's profits in 2000).

The segmental note also shows a geographical analysis of turnover (unfortunately not sales), operating profit and operating assets based on where the products are made. It shows that most of the turnover and operating assets are made in Europe, whereas most of the operating profit is made in America. Operating margins differ widely in the company's geographic markets, although this may reflect the different mix of products sold (Figure 14.8).

Fig. 14.8 Operating margins

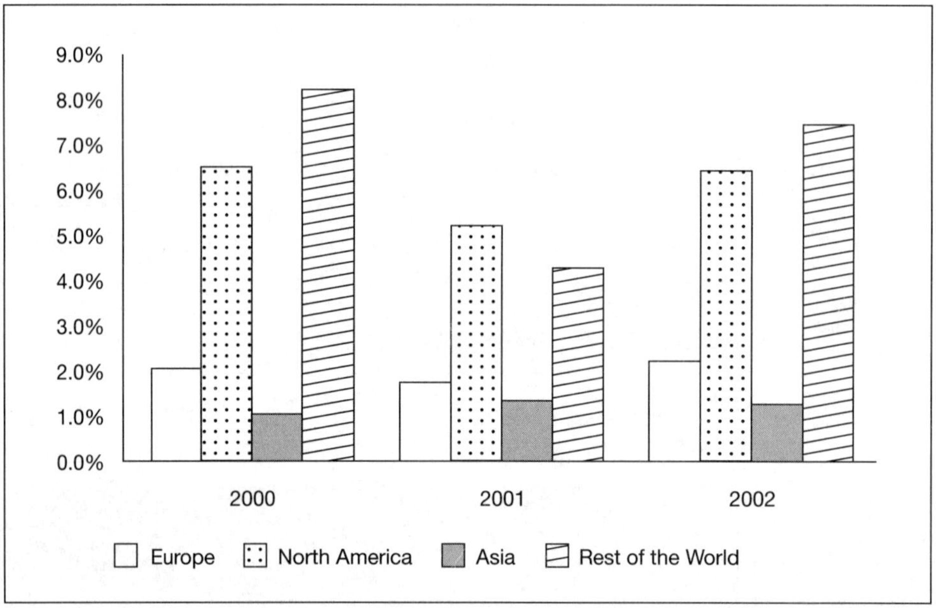

You can clearly see that the geographical business balance also has a significant effect on the group's operating margin. This also affects its return on operating assets – just look at the different returns on operating assets in its divisions (Figure 14.9) and in the different regions (Figure 14.10).

When you look at the segmental information, you can clearly see that small changes in the business mix, or the geographical mix, will have a considerable effect on both the operating margin and the return on operating capital employed. Consequently, it's a reasonable assumption that the changed mix in the period has had an important effect on the group's reported profitability.

Fig. 14.9 Divisional return on operating assets

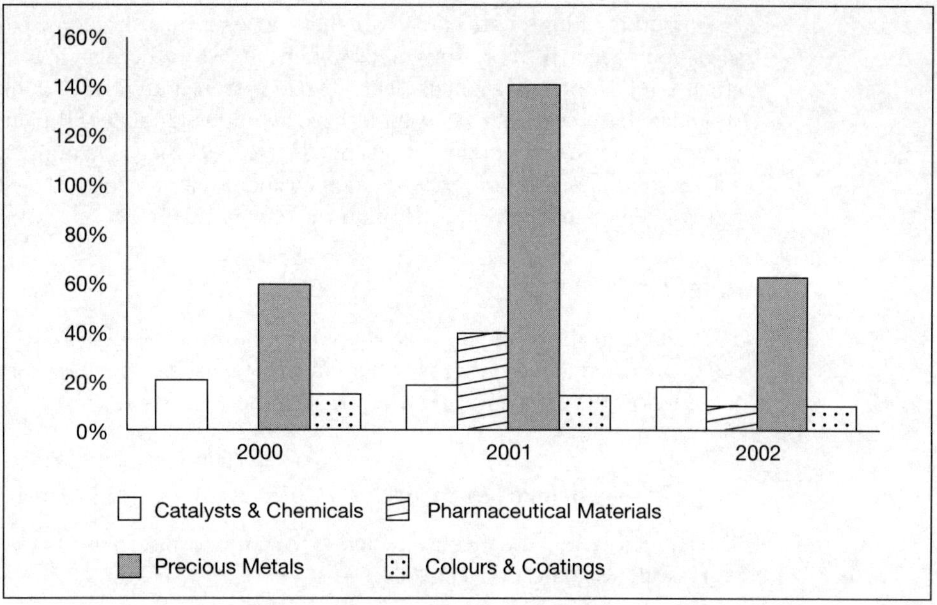

Fig. 14.10 Geographic return on operating assets

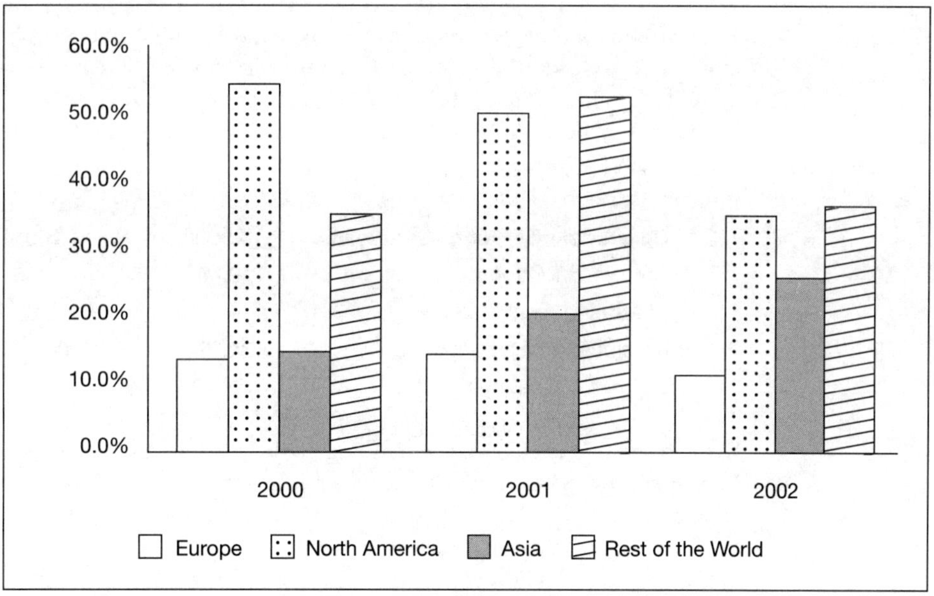

I'd like to now consider Johnson Matthey's asset utilisation, starting with its asset turnover.

Asset utilisation analysis

The first thing I have to decide is whether the asset turn should be based on turnover or sales. You've seen how precious metal values can distort the analysis, but some of the assets are affected by precious metals. Tangible fixed assets aren't, and I think that their analysis should be based on sales as I want to have an understanding of the underlying asset utilisation. However, the working capital needs to reflect the value of precious metals, as this will be an integral part of the stock, debtor and creditor values. That still leaves the asset turn and I'll calculate this using both turnover and sales.

Asset turn

The asset turn shows me how many pounds of turnover, or sales, are generated for every pound invested in the business. When turnover is used as the basis for the calculation the ratios follow the usual inverted 'v', with 2001 the best year:

	2000	**2001**	**2002**
Asset turn (turnover based)	5.76 times	7.57 times	4.39 times

When precious metal values are excluded from the turnover, the asset turn has fallen each year – with a significant fall in 2002.

	2000	**2001**	**2002**
Asset turn (sales based)	1.26 times	1.25 times	0.99 times

The divisional and geographic mix once again has a significant effect on Johnson Matthey's ratios, and I've used the segmental analysis to calculate a divisional asset turn. I've based both of the calculations on turnover, as a sales figure is only given in its divisional analysis. Unfortunately I couldn't graph them for you unless I used a different scale for their Precious Metals Division . . .

Divisional operating asset turn	**2000**	**2001**	**2002**
Catalysts & Chemicals	2.45	3.55	2.92
Pharmaceutical Materials		0.89	0.39
Precious Metals	34.92	106.85	38.63
Colours & Coatings	1.42	1.30	1.26

You can see that the Pharmaceutical Materials Division has the lowest asset turn (but the best operating margin), which has fallen in 2002 following the acquisitions. (You would expect some decline, as all the acquisitions' assets are included, whereas the sales are just those made after the businesses were acquired.)

You should now know some possible reasons for the changes in 2002, particularly if you consider the fixed asset component of the operating capital employed:

- Catalysts & Chemicals has installed new technology in all of its plants to improve process efficiency. This was a recent improvement and, whilst it has led to some increase in sales, its main effect has been to reduce costs by improving the company's precious metal control.

- Pharmaceutical Materials has been increasing its capacity to cope with anticipated growth in 2003 and beyond.
- You've seen that the Precious Metals Division has two different businesses. The trading and marketing business would generate high sales from low operating assets. This part of the division's sales and profits is driven by precious metal prices. When they're high, like 2001, they do very well – but with a low asset base. The other part of its business is the refinery business, where it has been reinvesting.
- Colours & Coatings faced two problems in 2002 – excess capacity, and price pressure in a number of its markets. Its response was to close its factory at Meir and to invest in new factories and processes that would reduce its cost base. These actions may improve its profitability at the expense of its asset turn (particularly tangible asset turn). However, in the long run, being the lowest-cost manufacturer will increase its sales when there is an upturn in its markets. At the moment it probably protects it from falling any further.

I'm hoping that you're now starting to see how you can bring all the strands of information together to understand where a business has come from, where it is now, and where it's going in the future. I'm only making deductions, but they appear to be sensible ones in the context of the information available. They certainly provide you with a lot of questions you'd like to ask Johnson Matthey . . .

The geographical asset turn shows the differences you'd expect having seen the turnover and return on operating asset graphs:

Geographic operating asset turn	**2000**	**2001**	**2002**
Europe	6.7	9.8	5.3
North America	8.3	10.0	5.2
Asia	15.6	16.7	19.6
Rest of the World	4.3	13.0	4.7

Now its time to analyse the asset turn in more detail, starting with the tangible fixed asset turn.

Tangible fixed asset turn

Johnson Matthey's tangible asset values are not affected by precious metal prices, so it's more relevant to compare them to sales rather than turnover. This ratio tells you how many pounds of sales are generated for every pound invested in tangible assets, and you can see that it's declined steadily in the period.

	2000	**2001**	**2002**
Sales based tangible asset turn	2.70	2.53	2.21

There are a number of possible explanations for the decline:

- The sales are for the total year and the tangible assets have only recently been installed, so have yet to affect this ratio.
- The capital expenditure was justified by cost reduction rather than sales growth.
- The fixed assets aren't being used effectively.

You've already read about how stock increased during the major upgrading of the pgm refinery at Royston. That must have been very close to the end of the financial year, otherwise it wouldn't have affected stock levels. You've also read about how much of the new process technology has been designed to reduce costs. And finally the Pharmaceutical Materials Division has been increasing capacity for 2003 onwards. So, on balance, the first two options are more likely.

So now you know that the company's fixed asset turn has fallen, and you've identified some likely reasons for the fall. Let's move on to consider its control of working capital.

Working capital control

Now I'm going to move back to using turnover, as the working capital value should mirror precious metal prices, albeit February and March prices rather than the average price that's reflected in turnover.

Working capital ratio

This looks at stocks, trade debtors and trade creditors in relationship to turnover. It tells you how many pence Johnson Matthey needs to fund a pound's sales, and can also be expressed as a percentage.

	2000	**2001**	**2002**
Working capital ratio	0.10	0.08	0.11

You can see that working capital declined in 2001, when presumably funding high precious metal values was expensive. You already know that work in progress increased, and the reason for it. Let's see if that was the sole reason for the increase in working capital.

Analysing the components of working capital

I've based all of the working capital ratios on turnover, rather than cost of sales, as the company's relatively small gross margin shouldn't affect the trend.

Stock days

	2000	**2001**	**2002**
Stock days (using turnover)	23.91	17.24	31.31

You can see that stock days declined dramatically in 2001, but in 2002 were significantly above 2000.

Debtor days

	2000	**2001**	**2002**
Debtor days	25.02	22.10	22.97

Debtor days fell in 2002, and have moved up slightly in 2002. A change this small could be explained by the changes in the business mix.

Creditor days

	2000	2001	2002
Creditor days (using turnover)	13.18	8.98	12.66

Creditors appeared to have been paid faster in 2001, and this is supported by the information in the directors' report where the company discloses that its creditor days 'amounted to 3 days'. (This compares with the disclosure of six days in 2000 and four days in 2002.) Probably no one wanted to be exposed to 2001's high and volatile metal prices.

You now understand that the deterioration in Johnson Matthey's working capital ratio arose from the increase in stocks which, we saw earlier, arose from an increase in its precious metal work in progress.

Profitability summary

Now let's summarise what we've discovered about Johnson Matthey's profitability . . .

Both its overall return on capital employed and the return on operating capital employed peaked in 2001 and declined in 2002.

When I analysed its profitability the return on sales was at its highest in 2001, when the improvement in the overhead cost ratio offset the decline in gross margins. Gross margins have declined throughout the period. It's probable that most of these changes arose from changes in business and geographic mix, as the composition of the group's turnover has changed significantly over the period, and margins are very different across its businesses and regions. The development of the Pharmaceutical Materials Division should improve its profitability, as it has a high return on sales.

The sales-based asset turn has declined over the last three years, and most of this can be explained by the declining fixed asset turn. This means that the company's capital expenditure has not led to increased sales in the short term. However, this isn't surprising as, apart from the Pharmaceutical Materials Division, most of its capital expenditure in 2002 was concerned with process improvement and cost reduction. This should work through in improved profitability and sales growth, or maintenance, in the medium term.

The increase in work in progress in 2002 affected most of the profitability ratios. The financial review identified that most of the increase arose from the upgrading of a refinery, and this is supported when you look at creditors, which have not moved in proportion to stock. If stock days could have been maintained at the same level as 2000 the capital employed would have reduced significantly. (I've ignored 2001, as it appeared to be an exceptional year for working capital control, probably as a result of high metal prices.) Twenty-four days stock would have reduced stocks to £317.6 million (turnover of 4,830.1 × $^{24}/_{365}$). This would have reduced capital employed by £96.7 million (2002 stock of 414.3 – 317.6) to £1,004.7 million (operating capital employed of 1,101.4 – 96.7). This would have increased the company's return on operating capital employed from 17.6% to 19.2%.

Investment potential

Any investor buying shares is hoping to make money. They're only going to do this if the share prices rises and they receive some dividends. I've used the company's closing share price at the end of its financial year to calculate its capital gain during the years and added this to the dividend payment:

	2000	2001	2002
Capital gain	£2.505	£2.830	£0.460
Dividend	£0.203	£0.233	£0.246
Total shareholder return per share	£2.708	£3.063	£0.706

Unusually for the market in this period, the shareholders have made a capital gain every year. Now you've already learnt that the current share price already incorporates the market's view about a company's *future* performance. Analysts will have extrapolated this from its past performance using information they have gleaned about Johnson Matthey's business plans. They're interested in identifying trends in:

- **Sales**: you know that this drives some costs and working capital, and consequently affects cash flow. Sales may also affect fixed costs and tangible assets if the company is trading close to its capacity limit.
- **Operating profits**: this is the most important element in the profit and loss account, as it's the only sustainable source of earnings.
- **EBITDA**: this just adjusts operating profit to make it more comparable across companies. It's also indicative of the cash that should be generated from the company's trading activities.
- **Dividends and dividend cover**: this affects both the investors' return and the retained profits. If the company has a low level of retained profit, it will have to raise funds to finance any planned expansion programme.
- **Cash flow**: cash can be used to finance the business's expansion, or it could be returned to investors.

All of these drive the company's share price and consequently its enterprise value. In Chapter 13 I showed you the ratios analysts use to assess companies' investment potential. Most of these compare one of the elements I've listed above to the share price. The recent falls, and volatility, in the stock market have made historical analysis of little value; consequently, I'd like to adopt a slightly different approach in looking at Johnson Matthey's investment potential. I'm going to look at:

- how these key factors have changed in the last three years;
- where analysts expect them to move in the next three years.

So let's see how Johnson Matthey's ratios have changed over the last three years . . .

The last three years

Sales and sales per share

I'll start by looking at sales as this drives profits, EBITDA and cash flow. Analysts use turnover, rather than sales, so the sales per share ratio follows a rather predictable pattern:

	2000	**2001**	**2002**
Issued shares – millions	221.1	222.5	218.7
Sales per share	£17.49	£26.53	£22.09

Operating profit and EBITDA

Operating profit and EBITDA have increased steadily in the three years. (However, EBITDA as a percentage of turnover fell in 2001, as the increase in turnover arose from precious metal prices that were passed straight through to customers.)

	2000	**2001**	**2002**
Operating profit – before exceptional items	£146.2m	£175.0m	£193.4m
EBITDA – before exceptional items	£192.8m	£216.1m	£248.5m
EBITDA to sales	5.0%	3.7%	5.1%

This growth is reflected in the underlying earnings per share.

Earnings per share

	2000	**2001**	**2002**
Basic earnings per share (pence)	50.5	57.3	49.0
Before exceptional items and goodwill amortisation (pence)	46.6	57.2	60.4

Return on equity

The underlying return on equity (profit before exceptional items as a percentage of adjusted equity) has also improved during the period.

2000	**2001**	**2002**
11.92%	13.48%	13.73%

Cash flow and cash flow per share

The improvement in profits has worked through into the cash available for reinvestment in the business, which has grown steadily in the period:

	2000	2001	2002
Cash available for reinvestment – £ million	94.3	124.1	163.4
Cash available for reinvestment per share	£0.43	£0.56	£0.75

However, the high level of reinvestment in the business has meant that the free cash flow has declined in the period, although the 2000 figure is abnormally high because of the cash received from the disposal of the Electronic Materials Division:

	2000	2001	2002
Free cash flow – £ million	421.9	18.0	(108.4)
Free cash flow per share	£1.91	£0.08	(£0.50)

Dividends and dividend cover

	2000	2001	2002
Dividend per share (pence)	20.3	23.3	24.6
Dividend cover (before exceptional items)	2.2	2.4	2.5
Dividend cover after exceptional items	2.5	2.5	2.0

The next three years?

Now I'd like to show you the median analysts' view of Johnson Matthey's performance in the next three years, and I'll start with turnover (Figure 14.11). The years 2000–2 are Johnson Matthey's reported numbers and the subsequent years (marked E) are the median analysts' estimates.

Fig. 14.11 Turnover

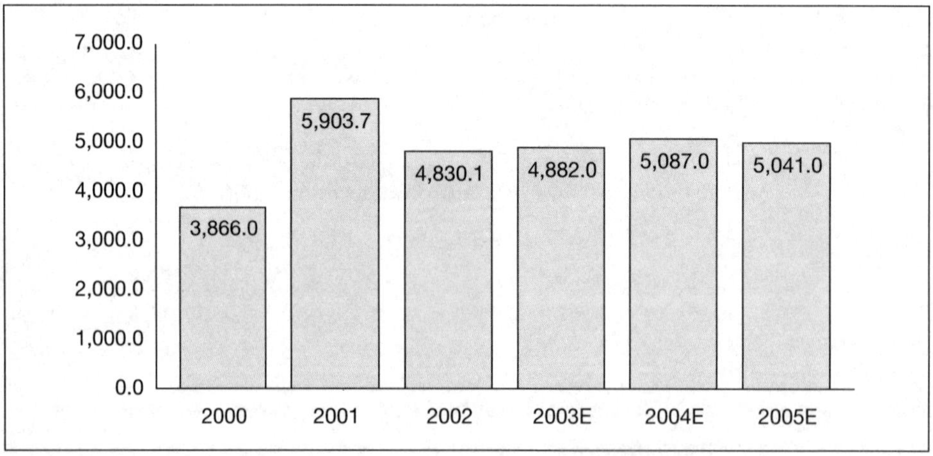

You can see that analysts are predicting a modest growth in Johnson Matthey's turnover in the next three years. Operating profit and EBITDA are not expected to grow significantly in 2003 (3.2% operating profit growth and 6.1% growth in EBITDA), but are expected to show much greater growth in 2004 and 2005 (Figure 14.12). However, the average forecasted growth in operating profit over the next three years (9.8%) is very similar to the actual growth over the last three years (9.9%). (I've calculated the percentages using the growth from 1999 to 2002.)

Fig. 14.12 Operating profit and EBITDA

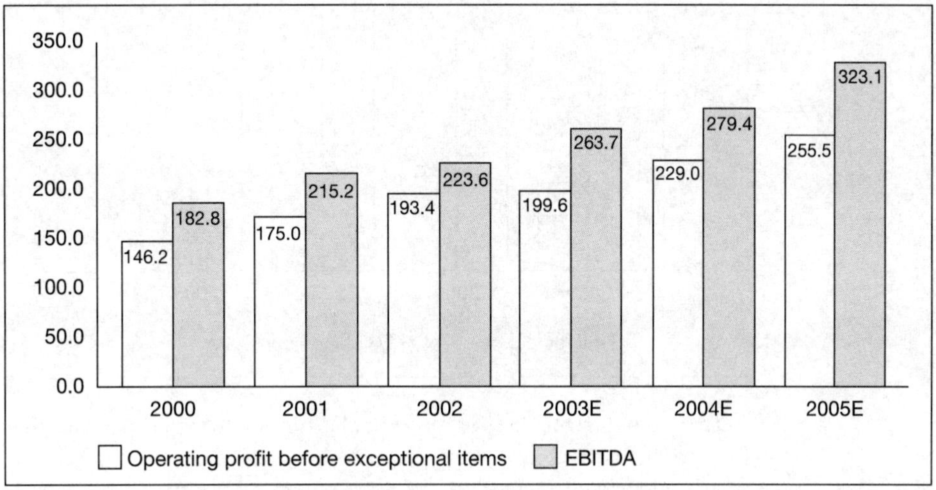

Analysts expect Johnson Matthey's cash flow available for reinvestment to continue to grow over the next three years, although not as fast as it has grown in the last three years (Figure 14.13).

Fig. 14.13 Cash flow

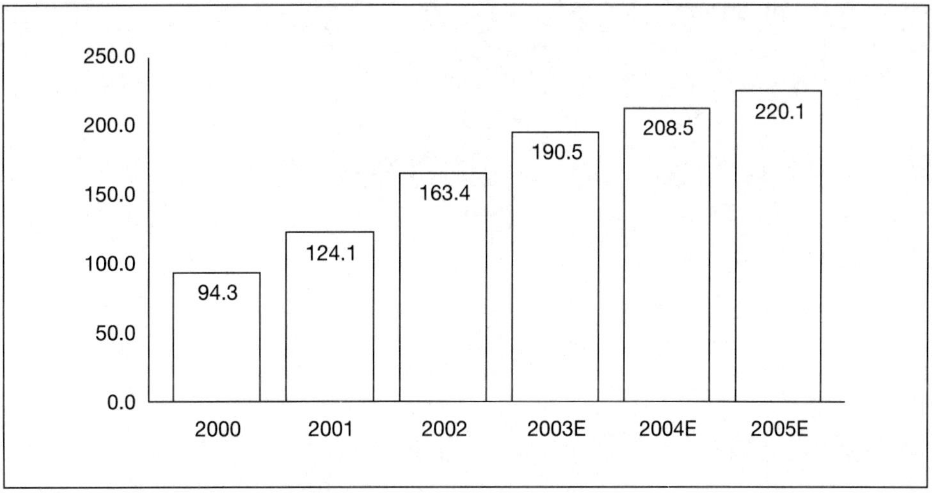

This is then reflected in earnings and dividends per share, both of which are expected to grow at a slower rate over the next three years than they have over the last three years (Figure 14.14).

Fig. 14.14 Earnings and dividend per share

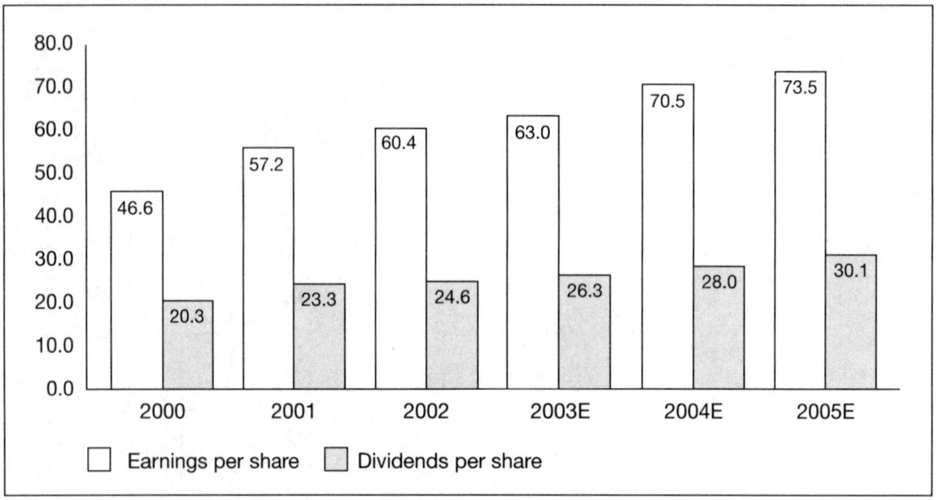

These are the estimates of Johnson Matthey's future performance that are underpinning its current share price. None of these estimates appears overly optimistic in the context of our detailed analysis of its last three years, and our observation of its last ten years. It's even possible, all things being equal, that Johnson Matthey will exceed the market's expectations and that its shares are undervalued.

PART 3

How can I use my analysis?

15

How can I use my analysis?

In the first part of this book you learnt about the information that you could find in the accounts, and in the second part you learnt how to analyse and interpret the data. This final part of the book shows you how to use your analytical and interpretative skills. There are three main areas where you're most likely to use financial analysis:

- analysing suppliers' accounts;
- analysing customers' accounts;
- analysing competitors' accounts.

It's also possible that you could be asked to help the group identify an acquisition prospect.

In this part of the book I'll show you how to assess their businesses, and how financial analysis can address your key concerns. Once you add financial understanding to your existing knowledge about your suppliers, customers and competitors, you'll have a comprehensive understanding of their company's position in the marketplace. This section shows you how to undertake a financial analysis, and once you've acquired this important skill you'll have a real understanding of your company's strengths and weaknesses, and of the threats and opportunities facing it.

This section of the book shows you how to apply your knowledge. It looks at each application and identifies:

- the important questions you need to answer;
- the ratios that will help you answer these questions.

Each chapter shows you how to approach the analysis, and the most appropriate ratios to use.

16

Suppliers' accounts

- **The first decision . . . which accounts to use**
- **First steps**
- **Relevant ratios –** solvency; can the supplier finance the order; profitability
- **The importance of your order**
- **Summary**

The viability of suppliers is essential for any company's long-term survival. No one wants to squeeze a good supplier so hard on price and payment terms that it faces liquidation. This means that understanding your suppliers' financial performance is an integral part of the supply relationship. You need to understand your suppliers' businesses, if you want to protect your own business.

When you're analysing suppliers' accounts you're trying to answer a number of questions:

- *Will they be able to deliver the order if we give it to them?*
- *Have we got a good deal?*
- *What's the strength of our negotiating position?*

If you look at the first question, you'll see that there are two parts to it, and financial analysis can only help you with one of them:

- The first element concerns the supplier's manufacturing ability. It's asking the question 'Will they be able to deliver the right quality product, on time?' Unfortunately, no amount of financial analysis can answer this question.
- The second part is concerned with the supplier's financial viability, and this is where financial analysis helps. You want your suppliers to be successful.

If you want to assess their financial viability, you can look at the three elements of the deal:

- *The price:* whilst you want your suppliers to be successful, you don't want their success to be at the expense of your business. It's a supply partnership where both parties should win. You have to reassure yourself that your suppliers aren't ripping you off, but are generating sufficient profits to continue to be your suppliers in the future. It's a balance, and your ability to influence your suppliers' business depends on how important you are to them and on the level of competition.
- *Stock levels:* your suppliers may have agreed to carry stock for you, or have agreed a consignment stock arrangement that will reduce your working capital requirements, with the effect of increasing theirs. Can they afford to do this?
- *Credit terms:* do you have the same credit terms as their other customers? If you're paying faster, have you got a better price?

The third concern raises the question of how important you are to them. You will have a completely different negotiating position if you are 1% of their business than if you are 20%. Your analysis could show you that they need your business much more than you need them!

In this chapter I'll address these concerns and show you the relevant ratios to use when assessing your suppliers' financial performance.

The first decision . . . which accounts to use

You may find that your supplier is part of a large group. This means that you have to decide whether you want to use the individual company's accounts or the group accounts. If it's a very small part of a large group, you may feel that the group accounts would be inappropriate. If it is registered in the UK you will be able to get its accounts from Companies

House, but if it is based overseas it will be more difficult, and in some countries impossible, to get a private company's accounts. There are two problems you'll have if you choose to use the individual company's accounts:

- They'll be more out of date. Private companies in the UK must file their accounts within ten months of their year end. Most companies file on the last possible day, so private companies' accounts aren't as up to date as those available from listed companies.
- They'll be less detailed, particularly if they're a smaller company. (If you want to know the information you'll find in smaller companies' accounts, I tell you about it in Chapter 20.)

But you may need to look at the individual company's accounts anyway, particularly if you have concerns about its solvency. Being part of a group doesn't necessarily mean that the group will extend financial support. You may remember that in October 2002 the American power company TXU decided to protect the group's credit rating by selling its European business, TXU Europe. It cut off all financial support to its cash-strapped European subsidiary, which was then unable to pay its suppliers in full. Fortunately, at the eleventh hour, and in just five days, most of the British part of the business, supplying electricity to 5.25 million customers mainly in the old Eastern and Norweb regions, was sold to Powergen (owned by Germany's E.on).

The individual company's accounts may be out of date, but more relevant. However, don't forget that the group accounts will give you some useful information about different businesses in the note on segmental information. The sales, profit and operating assets are analysed between the different businesses in this note.

First steps

The first steps are always the same:

1. Look at the company's five year summary; this shows you how it has performed over the last five years and should give you an instant feel for the business's performance.
2. Next go to the operating review, as this will explain how it has performed in the last year and the main threats and opportunities facing its businesses.
3. Then read the financial review – this will reiterate some of the information in the operating review, but will also disclose information about the risks facing the business, the way the business is funded, and its cash management.
4. By now you should understand where the business has come from, and how it performed last year. So the next step is to look at the financial statements, reading the notes for any extra information you need. It's always worth reading the segmental analysis note, as this shows you which part of the group has the best returns.
5. By now you should know what you want to measure and what ratios you'd like to use. The ratios I've detailed below are the ones you're most likely to want to calculate, but the ratios you use should really be determined by what you've found when you looked at the accounts.

So let's have a look at the ratios that will help you analyse your supplier's financial performance . . .

Relevant ratios

Most of the ratios have some relevance in the analysis of suppliers' accounts, but I've selected the ones that are particularly useful. I'll start by considering their solvency, as you're bound to be interested in whether they're likely to be around in the future.

Solvency

Your first concern is whether your suppliers can deliver the goods on time. You'll already have assessed their operational performance, now it's time to assess their financial performance. If they are going to deliver on time, they ought to pay their suppliers on time and repay bank loans when they're due. The solvency ratios should be useful as they help you to identify whether your suppliers have:

- current, or potential, problems with their suppliers and banks;
- the ability to absorb any increase in their working capital.

I'll start by showing you how to see if they may have potential problems with their suppliers, and then look at potential problems with their banks. You know that suppliers are always concerned with how long they have to wait to be paid, and this is measured by their creditor days.

Creditor days

You may find creditor days in the directors' report (you probably remember that Johnson Matthey disclosed in its directors' report that the parent paid its suppliers in four days). If it isn't disclosed there, you'll have to calculate it from the accounts. Creditor days is calculated using the following formula:

$$\frac{\textit{Trade creditors}}{\textit{Purchases/Cost of sales}} \times 365$$

If you're calculating creditor days, the first thing that you have to decide is whether to use turnover, purchases (if you have this) or cost of sales. As you're trying to assess the possible risk of dealing with a specific supplier, you can use purchases (for suppliers using a Format 2 presentation of their profit and loss account) or a cost of sales-based calculation (if they use a Format 1 presentation of their profit and loss account). This calculation would show creditor days that more nearly reflected the actual payment period.

It's important to see if the company's experiencing difficulties paying its own suppliers. If your supplier is always 'on stop' it is unlikely to be able to meet your delivery deadlines, so creditor days is a good indicator of its probable supplier relationships.

Now you can move on to consider their banking relationships.

Interest cover

I think that this is one of the most important ratios, as it identifies whether the company can afford its current level of debt. I usually start with the profit-based measure, as this may be a banking covenant, using the following formula:

$$\frac{\textit{Profit before interest}}{\textit{Net interest payable}}$$

A company with a low interest cover, below three times, can't afford to have falls in profits or rising interest rates. It's also relying on future profit growth to repay its loans, and may be close to a loan covenant. A low interest cover also indicates that it is unlikely to be able to increase its working capital, as this would probably have to be financed and additional loan finance is unlikely to be available. Banks are reluctant to lend to companies with low interest cover, as the company has problems affording its existing debt, let alone any additional debt. On the other hand, a company with a high interest cover, over seven times, would find no difficulty supporting, and obtaining, additional loans.

You could double-check the company's ability to afford its loans by calculating the cash based interest cover:

$$\frac{\textit{Operational cash flow}}{\textit{Net interest paid}}$$

Now if you felt that the company could be under pressure from suppliers, or asked to repay its loans immediately, it's worth checking its acid test.

The acid test

This looks at the relationship of the company's liquid assets, those it can rapidly convert into cash, to its current liabilities. So it tells you whether the company could repay all its creditors if it's asked to do so. As usually companies don't have to repay their current liabilities immediately, it's only worth doing this ratio if you think that the company has a problem.

$$\frac{\textit{Liquid assets}}{\textit{Creditors falling due within a year}}$$

Before you calculate this ratio you have to determine the company's liquid assets. They're largely determined by the nature of the business, but in a manufacturing company they are likely to be debtors receivable within a year, short-term deposits and cash. You'll find that most companies are unable to repay all of their short-term liabilities out of liquid assets, as they're not expecting to have to repay them all immediately. The most important thing to identify is the trend. Is the business becoming more, or less, liquid and why? Could liquidity be a problem when they come to finance your order?

The current ratio

This ratio measures the company's ability to repay short-term liabilities with its short-term assets:

$$\frac{\textit{Current assets}}{\textit{Creditors falling due within a year}}$$

The size of the 'ideal' current ratio varies from one industry to another. It depends on the length of the company's 'conversion' cycle, and the frequency of the purchasing decision. The longer it takes the company to turn its raw materials back into cash, the larger the current ratio. You've seen that businesses like Tesco don't have enough current assets to pay their short-term creditors. The buying decision is made daily, and their customers pay them long before they have to pay their suppliers. Unfortunately, your suppliers are rarely in the same position as grocers! If they have insufficient current assets to meet their short-term liabilities, they may have to sell fixed assets to repay their creditors. This means that the likelihood of the short-term liabilities having to be repaid is critical. So far you've looked at immediate and short-term solvency, but banking relationships will also depend on the company's ability to repay loans on time, so it may be worth looking at the company's loan repayment schedule, cash balance and cash generation.

The loan repayment schedule

This shows you *when* its loans have to be repaid. If the company has to repay its loans in the next two years, it's useful to look at the company's cash and cash generation to see if your supplier is likely to be able to repay them from its existing resources.

Cash and cash generation

The balance sheet shows you how much cash the business has at its year end, and the cash flow statement shows you how much it generated during the year. It's useful to see how much cash the company could use from this year's cash flow to repay its loans. You can do this by totalling the following cash flows:

Net cash flow from operating activities
Net cash flow from returns on investment and servicing of finance
Net cash flow from taxation
Net cash flow from capital expenditure and financial investment

(I've selected these cash flows, as the company needs some cash to reinvest in its business, and has to pay tax and interest. Acquisitions and dividends are discretionary.)

The total of these cash flows is the amount the business could have repaid from the current year's cash flow. If you look at this over a number of years, you can calculate an average cash flow and see whether it is increasing, or decreasing. You should now know how much cash the business has, how much it generates each year, and whether it's likely to be enough to repay its loans. If it isn't, the company may have difficulties repaying its loans unless it can:

- *Repay existing loans with new loans:* to determine this you'd need to ask yourself whether lenders would view the business as a good risk. You should consider things like its relative performance, its market conditions and its interest cover. You can also take into account its unused borrowing facilities.
- *Generate sufficient cash to repay the loans:* this doesn't have to come from its operations. Companies can generate cash by reducing their working capital, or selling some of their assets.
- *Have a share issue:* a number of major companies have managed to have a rights issue, getting more cash from their shareholders by highlighting the alternatives!

Can the supplier finance the order?

If you're giving a supplier a large order, you should check that it will be able to find sufficient finance to be able to deliver the goods. If you're giving it a £1 million order it has to fund the working capital requirements. There are two ways of approximating the cash needed to fund the order:

- use its working capital ratio;
- calculate the order's specific working capital.

The working capital ratio

This is simply calculated:

$$\frac{\textit{Stock + trade debtors + trade creditors}}{\textit{Turnover}}$$

This tells you how many pence the supplier will need to have tied up in the working capital to fund a pound's worth of sales, based on its current business mix. So if its working capital ratio is 0.3, it needs to have 30 pence in its working capital for every pound of sales. This means that if you give it the £1 million order it will either have to find £300,000 to fund the order, or reduce its working capital requirements. (If it reduced its stock and debtors days and increased its creditor days, it could use the same amount of working capital to fund the increased sales.) If the company is listed, you could look at its undrawn committed borrowing facilities to see if it could raise the cash, and calculate the subsidiary working capital ratios to see if there's room for improvement. All of the working capital ratios are very useful as:

- They are a measure of management efficiency – an efficient management team would be minimising its investment in working capital.
- You can see if the company could fund an increase in its sales from its existing resources. If you add the cash shown on the balance sheet to the undrawn committed borrowing facilities, you have the total cash currently available to the company. If you divide this by

the working capital ratio, you discover the sales that can be supported from the current available funds. So if a company has £0.2 million cash at its year end, and £1.4 million undrawn committed facilities, it has £1.6 million funds available. If it needed 20 pence invested in its working capital to fund a pound's sales, its available funds would support extra sales of £8 million (£1.6 million ÷ 0.2).

- Stock days and debtor days affect your supplier's relationships with its customers. If the supplier has been reducing its finished goods stocks and debtors, you may have difficulty convincing it to carry your stock, or to offer you extended credit terms. You could find that its average debtor days is 72, and you pay in 45 days. You're paying faster than its average customer, so perhaps there's some scope for discussions on price.

So I think it's useful to use the following ratios:

- Total stock days (or you could calculate stock turn if you prefer):

$$\frac{\textit{Stocks}}{\textit{Cost of sales (or turnover as appropriate)}} \times 365$$

- Work in progress days, as this also gives you some idea of manufacturing times:

$$\frac{\textit{Work in progress}}{\textit{Cost of sales (or turnover as appropriate)}} \times 365$$

- Finished goods stock days, as this also indicates whether it is likely to be willing to carry your stock:

$$\frac{\textit{Finished goods stocks}}{\textit{Cost of sales (or turnover as appropriate)}} \times 365$$

- Debtor days:

$$\frac{\textit{Trade debtors}}{\textit{Turnover}} \times 365$$

- Creditor days:

$$\frac{\textit{Trade creditors}}{\textit{Cost of sales (or purchases as appropriate)}} \times 365$$

The specific working capital requirements of the order

The working capital ratio is a good approximation for the order's working capital requirement if your order will be on the same terms as the rest of the company's business. If it isn't you may have to adjust the working capital accordingly. However, if you have the information, or are prepared to make some assumptions, you can work out how much cash the supplier will need to finance your order. You'd need to know, or assume, the:

- materials cost percentage;
- length of the production cycle (the lead time is a good approximation for this);
- labour cost percentage;
- overhead cost percentage;
- probable profit margin on the order.

If you have an 'open book' relationship with your suppliers (where they give you a breakdown of their costs and cost structure), you would have this information. Otherwise you will have to deduce this, and may decide that you have to make so many assumptions that the current working capital ratio would give you a good enough guide to the cash requirements. However, I'll show you how to calculate the working capital requirements using Example 16.1.

EXAMPLE 16.1

A supplier is offered an order for £1 million, with payment 60 days after delivery. The lead time for delivery is two months. The supplier has told you that its cost, and profit, structure is:

- Materials are 50% of the total cost.
- Labour is 30% of the total cost.
- Overheads are 20% of the total cost.
- The profit margin is 5% of sales.

You have calculated the following ratios from the company's accounts:

- raw materials stock days – 30 days;
- finished goods stock days – 15 days;
- creditor days – 50 days.

This means that the profit and loss account for the order would be:

Turnover	1,000,000
Material costs	475,000
Staff costs	285,000
Overheads	190,000
Profit	50,000

To complete the order the supplier has to fund the working capital. It has to hold the stock and wait the agreed credit period, and this would be offset by the credit it receives from its own suppliers. So let's work out how much it'll need.

Stock

The supplier has to fund the three components of stock: raw materials, work in progress, and finished goods. You just use a variant of the stock days formula to find out how much it has to finance:

Cash required to fund raw materials stocks, based on 30 days stock:

$$\frac{30}{365} \times 475{,}000 \quad = 39{,}041$$

I'm only including the materials costs at this stage, as the other costs are only incurred once it starts to manufacture the product.

Cash required to fund its work in progress, based on the two months' lead time for delivery:

$$\frac{60}{365} \times 950{,}000 \quad = 156{,}164$$

(I've assumed that all of the costs begin to be incurred as the product is manufactured, and consequently I've based this calculation on the total costs, rather than the materials cost.)

Cash required to fund the finished goods stock – based on 15 days stock:

$$\frac{15}{365} \times 950{,}000 \quad = 39{,}041$$

The total cash that will be tied up in stock is £234,246.

Debtors and creditors

The cash required to finance the credit terms will be:

$$\frac{60}{365} \times 950{,}000 \quad = 156{,}164$$

(I've used the costs in this calculation, not the sales, as the company doesn't have to fund the profit, only the costs.)

This will be offset by the credit that the supplier is able to get from his suppliers:

$$\frac{50}{365} \times 950{,}000 \quad = 130{,}137$$

Total working capital requirement

The supplier will have to finance £260,273:

£234,246 (stock) + £156,164 (debtors) – £130,137 (creditors) = £260,273.

You know the company's cash position, and its unused borrowing facilities. Could it raise another £260,000 to satisfy your order? If not, could it reduce its working capital requirements for the rest of its business? The last thing you would want to do is to give a supplier an order that would cripple its business!

Profitability

Companies always have a dilemma when dealing with their suppliers. They want them to be profitable, as in the long run they'll only survive if they're profitable. But you don't want them to be too profitable, as that might mean that they are ripping you off! When you're looking at suppliers' accounts you're interested in the trends in both the operating profit margin and the return on capital employed.

Operating profit margin, or return on sales

You want your suppliers to have an acceptable operating profit margin, but you don't want them to be too profitable at your expense! This means that you need to calculate their profit margin over a number of years to see if it has changed, and if it has, why it has changed. The operating margin is simple to calculate:

$$\frac{\textit{Operating profit}}{\textit{Turnover}}$$

If their margin has changed, you should think about what may have caused it to change. I discussed the possible reasons in detail in Chapter 8, but the changes in profit margins usually arise from changes in:

- *Volumes:* once the company's sales are above breakeven, anything above variable costs is pure profit. Small changes in sales can lead to a large change in profits, and therefore profit margins.
- *Price:* this is both the selling price and the price that the company pays for its costs. You're particularly interested if cost reduction has improved profits. The company could have used different, cheaper materials, or perhaps its staff costs or overheads have reduced. You should be able to see this by looking at its costs, and don't forget staff numbers and total staff costs are always disclosed in the notes to the accounts. If your supplier has improved its overall profitability through cost reduction, perhaps you'd like a share of the improvement and there's some scope for a price reduction?
- *Mix:* this could be product mix, business mix, or market mix.

Your supplier should give you some clues about the reason for the change in its operational review and the note on segmental analysis.

Return on operating capital employed

If you think about it, customers can have a large impact on their suppliers' return on operating capital. The price you negotiate affects their profitability; your stockholding requirements and credit terms affect their asset utilisation. You know that to add 'shareholder value' they need a return on capital that's greater than their cost of capital. So you're interested in their return on capital and why it's changed. The return on operating capital employed is calculated using the following formula:

$$\frac{\textit{Operating profit}}{\textit{Operating capital employed}}$$

If return on capital has changed over the period, why has it changed? You've already looked at their operating profit margin ... if that doesn't explain the difference, the explanation lies in their asset utilisation.

Asset utilisation

This is reflected in the asset turn ratio:

$$\frac{\textit{Turnover}}{\textit{Operating capital employed}}$$

You know that this is a combination of two things, their utilisation of tangible assets and their control of working capital. You've already looked at their working capital, so that only leaves their tangible asset turn. You calculate it using the formula below:

$$\frac{\textit{Turnover}}{\textit{Tangible fixed assets}}$$

There are three reasons why you can have changes in tangible asset turns:

- The assets are being used more, or less, effectively. Perhaps they're now used continuously, instead of on two shifts – or vice versa.
- The composition of the tangible assets could have changed. Perhaps they now rent properties, whereas they previously owned them. This will be disclosed in the notes.
- The asset's value has changed following an acquisition, or a major capital expenditure programme, or disposals. This would be shown in the cash flow statement and disclosed in the note on tangible assets.

You've already calculated the working capital ratios when you've considered the supplier's ability to finance the order, so you should now understand what has driven any changes in its working capital.

The importance of your order

If you want to know the strength of your negotiating position you have to know how important your business is to your supplier. What percentage is your business of its total turnover? (It's at this point that it's useful to have the individual company's accounts. Your order may be totally irrelevant to the group, but could be 20% of the individual company's business.) If you are a large customer you have a strong negotiating position, but often can't afford to drive too hard a bargain, as you could determine the company's future. If you negotiate price reductions and extended credit terms you affect both its profitability and solvency. You could be responsible for the company being liquidated – or force the group's parent to close, or sell, your supplier. If you have a key supplier in financial difficulties, and you're one of its key customers, you have a strategic dilemma. Should you continue to negotiate hard, or should you structure the negotiation to help the supplier? It's often cheaper to pay a better price than to find an alternative supplier. Being a large customer is a two-edged sword, and with power come responsibilities!

Summary

Financial analysis is an integral part of the sourcing decision. Before you place a large order, you should ascertain the financial viability of the supplier and how your order will affect its business. Sometimes companies are liquidated because they are expanding too fast. They have no difficulty getting the orders, but they just can't get the cash to fund them!

Financial analysis is not just important in vetting suppliers; it can also play a useful role in the negotiating process. It helps you to identify your best negotiating position, and use it effectively.

17

Customers' accounts

- **The first decision . . . which accounts to use**
- **First steps**
- **Relevant ratios** – solvency; profitability
- **Summary**

If you want to develop a close relationship with your customers it is essential that you understand their business. You have to appreciate their business's strengths and weaknesses if you would like to understand the opportunities and threats facing your business. Clients' accounts are a useful addition to your normal market intelligence as they will quantify the success, or otherwise, of their marketing activities, and clarify some of the threats and opportunities facing their, and consequently your, business.

When you're looking at your clients' businesses you're usually interested in discovering:

- *Will they be able to pay us on time?*
- *Will they be in business next year?*
- *Is there any potential for increasing our sales?*
- *What is the best way to structure the sales negotiation?*

Financial analysis helps you address some of these concerns, and gives you useful information for your sales negotiations. If you read through your customers' accounts, and analyse them, you'll understand:

- where they sell their products:
  - the sales in each division;
  - the sales in different countries and regions;
- which parts of their business have the potential for real sales growth;
- where they're making their profits:
  - the profits of each division;
  - the profits made in different countries and regions;
- where their profits have grown, or fallen;
- their cost structure;
- where they make the best return on their operating assets;
- the other companies in the group, as they could represent sales opportunities;
- the parts of the business they intend to develop in the future.

The accounts don't just contain financial information; the operating review, shown in listed companies' accounts, also discloses the key factors that influence their businesses' performance. It should disclose the factors, and the trends, underlying the company's performance, and any factors that are expected to impact on the company's future performance. It will tell you about any industrial, or environmental, changes expected to affect the company's results. This includes new product developments, acquisitions, disposals, changes in its market conditions, and market share. The financial review discusses the business's risks and how it manages them, the effect of exchange rates, its turnover and margins. Reading the accounts will give you an understanding of how your clients see their performance and their focus for the future. It often provides you with a starting point for a more detailed discussion with your clients. For example, if you are selling capital equipment, you will be able to see your customers' current level of capital expenditure and some indication of their likely future spend.

The first decision . . . which accounts to use

You may find that your customer is part of a large group. This means that you have to decide whether you want to use its individual company's accounts or the group accounts. If it's a very small part of a large group, you may feel that the group accounts would be inappropriate. If it is registered in the UK you will be able to get its accounts from Companies House, but if it is based overseas it will be more difficult, and in some countries impossible, to get a private company's accounts. There are two problems you'll have if you choose to use the individual company's accounts:

- They'll be more out of date. Private companies in the UK must file their accounts within ten months of their year end. Most companies file on the last possible day, so private companies' accounts aren't as up to date as those available from listed companies.
- They'll be less detailed, particularly if they're a smaller company. (If you want to know the information you'll find in smaller companies' accounts, I tell you about it in Chapter 20.)

But you may need to look at the individual company's accounts anyway, particularly if you have concerns about its solvency. Being part of a group doesn't necessarily mean that the group will extend financial support.

The individual company's accounts may be out of date, but more relevant. However, don't forget that the group accounts will give you some useful information about different businesses in the note on segmental information. The sales, profit and operating assets are analysed between the different businesses in this note.

First steps

The first steps are always the same:

1. Look at the company's five-year summary; this shows you how it has performed over the last five years and should give you an instant feel for the business's performance.
2. Next go to the operating review, as this will explain how it has performed in the last year and the main threats and opportunities facing its businesses.
3. Then read the financial review – this will reiterate some of the information in the operating review, but will also disclose information about the risks facing the business, the way the business is funded, and its cash management.
4. By now you should understand where the business has come from, and how it performed last year. So the next step is to look at the financial statements, reading the notes for any extra information you need. It's always worth reading the segmental analysis note, as this shows you which part of the group has the best returns.

5. By now you should know what you want to measure and what ratios you'd like to use. The ratios I've detailed below are the ones you're most likely to want to calculate, but the ratios you use should really be determined by what you've found when you looked at the accounts.

So let's have a look at the ratios that will help you analyse your customers' financial performance.

Relevant ratios

I'll start by considering your customer's solvency, as one of your first concerns is whether the company will be able to pay your invoices. So let's see if it can, and whether it is likely to continue trading in the future . . .

Solvency

The solvency ratios are useful as they help you to identify whether your customer has:

- current, or potential, problems with its other suppliers and banks;
- sufficient financial strength to grow its business.

I'll start with potential problems with suppliers, and then move on to consider problems with banks. Ideally you'd do this analysis *before* granting your customer credit, as it could be giving you the order because it is 'on stop' with its existing suppliers. You're concerned with how long you'll have to wait to be paid, and this is measured by creditor days.

Creditor days

You may find creditor days in the directors' report, if your client is listed on the stock market (you probably remember that Johnson Matthey disclosed in its directors' report that the parent paid their suppliers in four days). If it isn't disclosed there, you'll have to calculate it from the accounts. Creditor days is calculated using the following formula:

$$\frac{\textit{Trade creditors}}{\textit{Turnover/Cost of sales}} \times 365$$

If you're calculating creditor days, the first thing that you have to decide is whether to use turnover, purchases (if you have this) or cost of sales. As you're trying to assess the possible risk of dealing with a specific customer, you can use purchases (if your customer follows the Format 2 presentation in its profit and loss account) or a cost of sales-based calculation (if it uses a Format 1 presentation of its profit and loss account). This calculation would show creditor days that more nearly reflected its actual payment period. This can be a useful ratio for existing clients, as well as new ones. It tells you their average payment period, and you can compare this with the time they're taking to pay you.

Now you can move on to consider their banking relationships.

Interest cover

You know that banks sometimes withdraw their support, and force a company into receivership. The last thing that you'd want is to be an unsecured creditor in a business that's in receivership – you're right towards the end of the payment queue and the chances of being paid are remote. This is why interest cover is important; it's a common banking covenant that identifies whether the company can afford its current level of debt. It's quickly calculated by using the following formula:

$$\frac{\textit{Profit before interest}}{\textit{Net interest payable}}$$

A company with a low interest cover, below three times, is exposed to falls in profits and rising interest rates. It's also relying on future profit growth to repay its loans, and may be close to a loan covenant. Banking relationships become increasingly difficult as the interest cover approaches three, and if it falls to two and a half times your client may be asked to repay its loans.

Now you could double-check the company's ability to afford its loans by calculating cash-based interest cover:

$$\frac{\textit{Operational cash flow}}{\textit{Net interest paid}}$$

There's another clue about banking relationships – the company's *committed undrawn borrowing facility*, disclosed in the notes to listed companies' accounts. If banks are prepared to commit themselves to give the company additional funds, they are confident in the company and its future.

Now if you felt that the company could be under pressure from suppliers, or asked to repay its loans immediately, it's worth checking its acid test.

The acid test

Customers will try to extend payment terms if they have a liquidity problem, so the acid test is a useful ratio. It looks at the relationship of the customer's liquid assets, those it can rapidly convert into cash, to its current liabilities. So it tells you whether the company could repay all its creditors if it's asked to do so. As companies usually don't have to repay their current liabilities immediately, it's only worth doing this ratio if you think that the company has a problem.

$$\frac{\textit{Liquid assets}}{\textit{Creditors falling due within a year}}$$

Before you calculate this ratio you have to identify the company's liquid assets. They're largely determined by the nature of its business, but they are likely to comprise debtors receivable within a year, short-term deposits and cash. You'll find that most companies are unable to repay all of their short-term liabilities out of liquid assets, as they're not expecting to have to repay them all immediately.

The current ratio

I'd use this ratio, rather than the acid test, if you felt that it's unlikely that your customer is going to have to repay all its short-term liabilities immediately. It measures the company's ability to repay short-term liabilities with its short-term assets:

$$\frac{\textit{Current assets}}{\textit{Creditors falling due within a year}}$$

The size of the 'ideal' current ratio varies from one industry to another. It depends on the length of the company's 'conversion' cycle, and the frequency of the purchasing decision. The longer it takes the company to turn its raw materials back into cash, the larger the current ratio. You've seen that businesses like Tesco don't have enough current assets to pay their short-term creditors. The buying decision is made daily, and their customers pay them long before they have to pay their suppliers. So if you're selling to retailers you may find relatively low current ratios.

So far you've looked at immediate and short-term solvency, but banking relationships will also depend on the company's ability to repay loans on time, so it may be worth looking at the company's loan repayment schedule, cash balance and cash generation.

The loan repayment schedule

This shows you *when* their loans have to be repaid. If your customer has to repay its loans in the next two years, it's useful to look at the company's cash and cash generation to see if it is likely to be able to repay them from its existing resources.

Cash and cash generation

The balance sheet shows you how much cash the business has at its year end, and the cash flow statement shows you how much it generated during the year. It's useful to see how much cash the company could use from this year's cash flow to repay its loans. You can do this by totalling the following cash flows:

Net cash flow from operating activities
Net cash flow from returns on investment and servicing of finance
Net cash flow from taxation
Net cash flow from capital expenditure and financial investment

(I've selected these cash flows, as the company needs some cash to reinvest in its business, and has to pay tax and interest. Acquisitions and dividends are discretionary.)

The total of these cash flows is the amount the business could have repaid from the current year's cash flow. If you look at this over a number of years, you can calculate an average cash flow and see whether it is increasing, or decreasing. You should now know how much cash the business has, how much it generates each year, and whether it's likely to be enough to repay its loans. If it isn't, your customer may have difficulties repaying its loans unless it can:

- *Repay existing loans with new loans:* to determine this you'd need to ask yourself whether lenders would view the business as a good risk. You should consider things like its relative performance, its market conditions and its interest cover. You can also take into account its unused borrowing facilities.
- *Generate sufficient cash to repay the loans:* this doesn't have to come from its operations. Companies can generate cash by reducing their working capital, or selling some of their assets.
- *Have a share issue:* a number of major companies have managed to have a rights issue, getting more cash from their shareholders by highlighting the alternatives!

Profitability

You've looked at your customer's solvency, now let's look at its profitability. Does it have any growth potential? Are its sales increasing or decreasing? If you look at its profit and loss account you'll see the trends in its turnover and profits.

Operating profit margin, or return on sales

The operating margin is simple to calculate:

$$\frac{\textit{Operating profit}}{\textit{Turnover}}$$

If the margin has changed, you should think about what may have caused it to change. I discussed the possible reasons in detail in Chapter 8, but the changes in profit margins usually arise from changes in:

- *Volumes*: once the company's sales are above breakeven, anything above variable costs is pure profit. Small changes in sales can lead to a large change in profits, and therefore profit margins.
- *Price*: this covers both its selling price and the price your customer pays for its own costs.
- *Mix*: this could be product mix, business mix, or market mix.

Your customer's accounts should give you some clues about the reason for any change in the operational review and the note on segmental analysis.

If your client is focusing on improving its operating profitability, and you are selling its revenue items, it will probably be looking for price reductions in the next negotiation. (This would be particularly relevant if your product was one of its major costs. If it can negotiate a 5% reduction on something that is 40% of their its cost, it will have a significant improvement in its profits!)

If your customer is part of a large group, you may only be selling to a specific part of their business. In this case you'll find that the segmental analysis, usually the first note in the accounts, is a useful part of your analysis.

Segmental analysis

This shows you what's happening in the part of the business you're selling to, and how this compares to the rest of the group's results. Groups tend to focus their investment and energies on the part of their business that is generating the best return, or with the best prospects. You can work out the operating margin, and the return on capital for the group's various businesses. Any division that is under-performing is likely to be sold, or closed down, whereas any division that is performing well will be developed and strengthened. You can also see which parts of the group are receiving most of the investment (their operating assets will be increasing), and those that are being used as cash cows (their operating assets will be decreasing).

Return on operating capital employed

Every business has to have an acceptable return on its capital. If it wants to add value for its shareholders, it has to have a return on capital that's greater than its cost of capital. So you're interested in its return on capital and why it's changed. The return on operating capital employed is calculated using the following formula:

$$\frac{\textit{Operating profit}}{\textit{Operating capital employed}}$$

If the return on operating capital has changed over the period, why has it changed? You've already looked at the business's operating profit margin . . . if that doesn't explain the difference, the explanation lies in its asset utilisation.

Asset utilisation

This is reflected in the asset turn ratio:

$$\frac{\textit{Turnover}}{\textit{Operating capital employed}}$$

You know that this is a combination of two things, its utilisation of tangible assets and control of working capital. Let's consider its tangible asset turn first. You calculate it using the formula below:

$$\frac{\textit{Turnover}}{\textit{Tangible fixed assets}}$$

There are three reasons why the tangible asset turn may have changed:

- The assets are being used more, or less, effectively. Perhaps they're now used continuously, instead of on two shifts – or vice versa.
- The composition of the tangible assets could have changed. Perhaps the company now rents properties, whereas it previously owned them. This will be disclosed in the notes.
- The asset's value has changed following an acquisition, or a major capital expenditure programme, or disposals. This would be shown in the cash flow statement and disclosed in the note on tangible assets.

The tangible asset turn is particularly interesting if you're selling your customer capital items. If it is trying to use its fixed assets more effectively, you could have a sales opportunity. Perhaps you have a machine, or tooling, that can extend its asset life, or speed up production.

The next thing to consider is their working capital, starting with the working capital ratio:

$$\frac{\textit{Working capital}}{\textit{Turnover}}$$

All of the working capital ratios are very useful as:

- They measure management efficiency – an efficient management team would be minimising its investment in working capital.
- You can see if the company could fund an increase in its sales from its existing resources. If you add the cash shown on the balance sheet to the undrawn committed borrowing facilities, you have the total cash currently available to the company. If you divide this by the working capital ratio, you discover the sales that can be supported from the current available funds. So if a company has £0.2 million cash at its year end, and £1.4 million undrawn committed facilities, it has £1.6 million funds available. If it needed 20 pence invested in its working capital to fund a pound's sales, its available funds would support extra sales of £8 million (£1.6 million ÷ 0.2).
- You can use the stock days and creditor days to prepare for your negotiation with the client. If you found that the company's creditor days were longer than your current payment terms, your customer is paying you faster than its other suppliers. The company's buyer will probably try to extend your payment terms in the negotiation, unless you're prepared to offer a prompt payment discount. If the company is trying to reduce its stocks, they will be looking for an improvement in lead times and may be asking you to carry part of its stock. Perhaps you should consider a consignment stock arrangement?

So I think it's useful to use the following ratios:

- Total stock days (or you could calculate stock turn if you prefer):

$$\frac{\textit{Stocks}}{\textit{Cost of sales (or turnover as appropriate)}} \times 365$$

- Debtor days:

$$\frac{\textit{Trade debtors}}{\textit{Turnover}} \times 365$$

- Creditor days:

$$\frac{\textit{Trade creditors}}{\textit{Cost of sales (or turnover as appropriate)}} \times 365$$

Summary

Financial analysis is a useful tool for anyone involved in sales. It gives you a wealth of additional information and can be used as a guide to future negotiations. If you use financial analysis in conjunction with your market intelligence you should be able to turn your customer's threats into your business opportunities!

18

Competitors' accounts

- **The first decision . . . which accounts to use**
- **First steps**
- **Relevant ratios –** solvency; profitability
- **Summary**

Curiosity is a human trait. We are always intrigued by our competitors' financial performance and want to know whether they're performing better, or worse, than we are. We see their marketing activities, have some idea about their commercial strategies, and want to know how this translates into their financial performance. Are their marketing activities more, or less, successful than ours? This will be reflected in their profitability and the way investors feel about their business.

If you're looking at your competitors you're usually interested in three things:

- *Solvency:* you're concerned with the answers to questions like . . . Will they be able to continue trading? Do they have enough cash to support an aggressive discounting policy?
- *Relative profitability:* you're interested in identifying the most profitable company in the sector and why they're the most profitable.
- *Relative investment potential:* you're interested in how the stock market views the company and whether its share price indicates that the market feels that it has better, or worse, profit growth prospects.

Financial analysis helps you address these concerns. It shows you whether competitors' marketing activities are successful, whether they are likely to survive, and their perceived investment potential.

The first decision . . . which accounts to use

You may find that you only compete with the company in one of its markets, or you only compete with one company in a large group. This means that you have to decide whether you want to use the individual company's accounts or the group accounts. If the competing company is a very small part of a large group, you may feel that the group accounts would be inappropriate. If it is registered in the UK you will be able to get its accounts from Companies House, but if it is based overseas it will be more difficult, and in some countries impossible, to get a private company's accounts. There are two problems you'll have if you choose to use the individual company's accounts:

- They'll be more out of date. Private companies in the UK must file their accounts within ten months of their year end. Most companies file on the last possible day, so private companies' accounts aren't as up to date as those available from listed companies.
- They'll be less detailed, particularly if they're a smaller company. (If you want to know the information you'll find in smaller companies' accounts, I tell you about it in Chapter 20.)

But you may need to look at the individual company's accounts anyway, particularly if you have concerns about its solvency. Being part of a group doesn't necessarily mean that the group will extend financial support. You may remember that in October 2002 the American power company TXU decided to protect the group's credit rating by selling the British part of its European business, TXU Europe. It cut off all financial support to its cash-strapped European subsidiary, which was then unable to pay its suppliers in full. Fortunately, at the eleventh hour, and in just five days, most of the British part of the business, supplying electricity to 5.25 million customers mainly in the old Eastern and Norweb regions, was sold to Powergen (owned by Germany's E.on).

The individual company's accounts may be out of date, but more relevant. However, don't forget that the group accounts will give you some useful information about different businesses in the note on segmental information. The sales, profit and operating assets are analysed between the different businesses in this note.

First steps

The first steps are always the same:

1. Look at the company's five-year summary; this shows you how the business has performed over the last five years and should give you an instant feel for its performance.
2. Next go to the operating review, as this will explain how it has performed in the last year and the main threats and opportunities facing its businesses.
3. Then read the financial review – this will reiterate some of the information in the operating review, but will also disclose information about the risks facing the business, the way the business is funded, and its cash management.
4. By now you should understand where the business has come from, and how it performed last year. So the next step is to look at the financial statements, reading the notes for any extra information you need. It's always worth reading the segmental analysis note, as this shows you which part of the group has the best returns.
5. By now you should know what you want to measure and what ratios you'd like to use. The ratios I've detailed below are the ones you're most likely to want to calculate, but the ratios you use should really be determined by what you've found when you looked at the accounts.

So let's have a look at the ratios that will help you compare your competitors' financial performance with your own.

Relevant ratios

I'll start by considering their solvency, as you're bound to be interested in whether they're likely to continue trading in the future.

Solvency

The solvency ratios should be useful as they help you to identify whether the company has:

- Current, or potential, problems with its suppliers and banks.
- Sufficient financial strength to support a price-led market penetration programme. You

know that any reduction in price requires a disproportionate increase in volume to maintain profits at current levels and, unless the product is very price sensitive, reducing prices usually leads to falling profits. This means that any company engaging in marketing activities driving prices down needs a strong balance sheet to survive and realise the future benefits of increased market share.

- The ability to absorb an increase in the working capital. Many manufacturers are under pressure to carry their customer's stock and extend debtor days. If the company has solvency problems, it is unlikely to be able to respond to these requests.

I'll start with potential problems with suppliers, and then move on to consider problems with banks. You know that suppliers are concerned with how long they have to wait to be paid, and this is measured by creditor days.

Creditor days

You may find creditor days in the directors' report (you probably remember that Johnson Matthey disclosed in its directors' report that parent paid its suppliers in four days). If it isn't disclosed there, you'll have to calculate it from the accounts. Creditor days is calculated using the following formula:

$$\frac{\textit{Trade creditors}}{\textit{Turnover/Cost of sales}} \times 365$$

If you're calculating creditor days the first thing that you have to decide is whether to use turnover or cost of sales. Generally, turnover is a more comparable basis, if the companies' definitions of cost of sales are different. However, it's only comparable if the companies have similar operating margins. As long as there is no real differences in profitability, turnover is an acceptable base – at least you'd be consistently wrong!

It's important to see if the company's experiencing difficulties paying its suppliers. If it's always 'on stop' it is unlikely to be able to meet delivery deadlines, so creditor days is a good measure of likely supplier relationships.

Now you can move on to consider its banking relationships.

Interest cover

I always look at interest cover, as it identifies if the company can afford its current level of debt. I usually start with the profit-based measure, as this may be a banking covenant. It's quickly calculated by using the following formula:

$$\frac{\textit{Profit before interest}}{\textit{Net interest payable}}$$

A company with a low interest cover, below three times, is exposed to falls in profits and rising interest rates. It's also relying on future profit growth to repay its loans, and may be close to a loan covenant. This means that it is unlikely to want to reduce its prices, as it needs profits to increase, not fall. A low interest cover also indicates that it is unlikely to be able to increase its working capital, as this would have to be financed and loan finance is unlikely to be available. Banks are reluctant to lend to companies with low interest cover, as the company has problems affording its existing debt, let alone any additional debt. On the other hand, a company with a high interest cover, over seven times, would find no difficulty supporting, and obtaining, additional loans.

Now you could double-check the company's ability to afford its loans by calculating cash-based interest cover:

$$\frac{\textit{Operational cash flow}}{\textit{Net interest paid}}$$

There's another clue about banking relationships – the company's *committed undrawn borrowing facility*, disclosed in the notes to the accounts. If banks are prepared to commit themselves to give the company additional funds they must be confident in the company and its future. If the company is close to its agreed borrowing level, it will be reluctant to carry customers' stock, or give extended credit terms.

Now if you felt that the company could be under pressure from suppliers, or asked to repay its loans immediately, it's worth checking its acid test.

The acid test

This looks at the relationship of the company's liquid assets, those it can rapidly convert into cash, to its current liabilities. So it tells you whether the company could repay all its creditors if it's asked to do so. As usually companies don't have to repay their current liabilities immediately, it's only worth doing this ratio if you think that the company has a problem.

$$\frac{\textit{Liquid assets}}{\textit{Creditors falling due within a year}}$$

Before you calculate this ratio you have to determine the company's liquid assets. They're largely determined by the nature of the business, but in a manufacturing company they are likely to be debtors receivable within a year, short-term deposits and cash. You'll find that most companies are unable to repay all of their short-term liabilities out of liquid assets, as they're not expecting to have to repay them all immediately.

So far you've looked at immediate solvency, but banking relationships will also depend on the company's ability to repay loans on time, so it may be worth looking at the company's loan repayment schedule, cash balance and cash generation.

The loan repayment schedule

We all know that loans have to be repaid, and the loan repayment schedule shows you *when* they have to be repaid. If the company has to repay its loans in the next two years, it's useful to look at the company's cash and cash generation.

Cash and cash generation

The balance sheet shows you how much cash the business has at its year end, and the cash flow statement shows you how much it generated during the year. It's useful to see how much cash the company could use from this year's cash flow to repay its loans. You can do this by totalling the following cash flows:

Net cash flow from operating activities
Net cash flow from returns on investment and servicing of finance
Net cash flow from taxation
Net cash flow from capital expenditure and financial investment

(I've selected these cash flows, as the company needs some cash to reinvest in its business, and has to pay tax and interest. Acquisitions and dividends are discretionary.)

The total of these cash flows is the amount the business could have repaid from the current year's cash flow. If you look at this over a number of years you can calculate an average cash flow and see whether it is increasing, or decreasing. You should now know how much cash the business has, how much it generates each year and whether it is enough. If it isn't the company may have difficulties repaying its loans unless it can:

- *Repay existing loans with new loans:* to determine this you'd need to ask yourself whether lenders would view the business as a good risk taking into account things like its relative performance, its market conditions and its interest cover. You can also take into account its unused borrowing facilities.
- *Generate sufficient cash to repay the loans:* this doesn't have to come from its operations. Companies can generate cash by reducing their working capital, or selling some of their assets.
- *Have a share issue:* a number of major companies have managed to have a rights issue, getting more cash from their shareholders by highlighting the alternatives!

Profitability

You're probably familiar with your competitor's prices, and have a fair idea of its service levels. Now let's find out how this translates into profitability. Is it more, or less, profitable than your company? To answer this you need to look at the two measures of profitability – operating profit margins and the return on capital.

Operating margins, or return on sales

Are its operating margins similar to yours? It's simple enough to find out, as all you have to do is to calculate the operating margin:

$$\frac{\textit{Operating profit}}{\textit{Turnover}}$$

If its operating margin is different, why is it different? I usually expect, over a period of time, to find similar operating margins within the same industry. There are a number of reasons why the margins may be different. Perhaps patented new products allow one company to charge higher prices, or one company has a larger market share. (If you want to review how this affects profitability, you'll need to read Chapter 9 and the discussion of fixed and variable costs and breakeven analysis.) Its costs could be different – maybe it is manufacturing abroad. The notes to the profit and loss account will tell you how many people the company employs and its total staff costs. (However you'll need to read these carefully if there's a lot of part-time staff, as some companies disclose total employees whereas others disclose full-time equivalents.)

If a similar competitor in the same market has a very different operating margin, it may have:

- identified a new market – this gives it only a short-term advantage, as competitors rapidly enter a new profitable market;
- developed a new manufacturing process, or a different method of distribution – again this gives only a short-term advantage, as competitors will copy it unless it has been patent protected;
- engaged in creative accounting – I've a very simple rule: *If it looks too good to be true, it probably is!*

You'd be really concerned about the first two, although it's difficult to keep new developments secret for very long so you may have already heard about them. Careful reading of the notes to the accounts would help to verify, or eliminate, the creative accounting option. And if your competitor is engaged in creative accounting, *why* is it doing it? You don't fool any one for long, as the cash soon runs out.

If its margin is different, you should think about why it's different. I discussed the reasons in detail in Chapter 9, but the difference usually arises from differences in:

- *volumes*: once the company's sales are above breakeven, anything above variable costs is pure profit;
- *price*: this is both its selling price and the price that your compeitor pays for its own costs;
- *mix*: this could be product mix, business mix, or market mix.

Return on capital employed

You know that this is important, as it also affects 'shareholder value' and the investors' perception of the company. It's probably worth working through the main ratios in the profitability hierarchy, as some of the subsidiary ratios can give you some useful insights into your competitor's business.

When looking at competitors' accounts, I'm interested in looking at the return on operating capital employed, as this is where you'll find the effects of their sales and marketing activities. Is their return on capital better, or worse, than other companies in the industry? To find out you need to use the following formula:

$$\frac{\textit{Operating profit}}{\textit{Operating capital employed}}$$

If it's different, why is it different? You've already looked at their operating profit margin ... if that doesn't explain the difference, the explanation lies in their asset utilisation.

Asset utilisation

This is reflected in the asset turn ratio:

$$\frac{\textit{Turnover}}{\textit{Operating capital employed}}$$

You know that this is a combination of two things, its utilisation of tangible assets and control of working capital. Let's consider tangible asset turn first. You calculate it using the formula below:

$$\frac{\textit{Turnover}}{\textit{Tangible fixed assets}}$$

Differences in tangible asset turns could arise for three reasons:

- The assets are being used more effectively; perhaps they're used continuously, instead of on two shifts.
- The composition of the tangible assets could be different. Perhaps one company rents properties and the other owns them – the assets will be analysed in the notes.
- The assets' value is very low. This could happen if they're very old (check the note on tangible assets), or if the assets are leased on operating leases (check the note on operating leases).

The next thing to consider is working capital, starting with the working capital ratio:

$$\frac{\textit{Working capital}}{\textit{Turnover}}$$

All of the working capital ratios are very useful as:

- They measure management efficiency – an efficient management team would be minimising its investment in working capital.
- You can see if the company could fund an increase in its sales from its existing resources. If you add the cash shown on the balance sheet to the undrawn committed borrowing facilities, you have the total cash currently available to the company. If you divide this by the working capital ratio, you discover the sales that can be supported from the current available funds. So if a company has £0.2 million cash at its year end, and £1.4 million undrawn committed facilities, it has £1.6 million funds available. If it needed 20 pence

invested in its working capital to fund a pound's sales, its available funds would support extra sales of £8 million (£1.6 million ÷ 0.2).

- Stock days and debtor days affect your competitors' relationships with their customers. And I'd like to suggest that it would be useful if you calculated a few more ratios. It's useful to analyse stock in its component parts, working out stock days for raw material stock, work in progress and finished goods stock. If your competitors are carrying more raw material stock, they may be in a better position to cope with rush orders and shorter delivery times. A difference in the work in progress may reflect a difference in manufacturing times, which will work through into lead times. A difference in finished goods stock may reflect their willingness, or otherwise, to carry stocks for their customers. Debtor days gives an indication of their credit terms with customers, in the same way that creditor days does with their suppliers.

So I think it's useful to use the following ratios:

- Total stock days (or you could calculate stock turn if you prefer):

$$\frac{\textit{Stocks}}{\textit{Cost of sales (or turnover as appropriate)}} \times 365$$

- Raw material stock days:

$$\frac{\textit{Raw material stocks}}{\textit{Cost of sales (or turnover as appropriate)}} \times 365$$

- Work in progress days:

$$\frac{\textit{Work in progress}}{\textit{Cost of sales (or turnover as appropriate)}} \times 365$$

- Finished goods stock days:

$$\frac{\textit{Finished goods stocks}}{\textit{Cost of sales (or turnover as appropriate)}} \times 365$$

- Debtor days:

$$\frac{\textit{Trade debtors}}{\textit{Turnover}} \times 365$$

- Creditor days:

$$\frac{\textit{Trade creditors}}{\textit{Cost of sales (or turnover as appropriate)}} \times 365$$

The investor's perspective

You may be surprised to find this is important when you're analysing a competitor's business, and it's really only worth doing if the competitor is listed. I've included it because if your competitor is listed, the market has a view about its future profitability, and this view is reflected in its current share price. The company's market capitalisation (the number of shares in issue × the current share price) reflects the market's view of a company's *future* profitability. This is reflected in the price earnings ratio.

PE ratio

This is published in the financial press and is calculated by dividing the current share price by the earnings per share. A PE ratio between five and seven usually indicates that the market expects no real growth in the company's earnings. These shares tend to have relatively high dividend yields, approximating to interest rates (as this would be the alternative opportunity if you felt that there was no opportunity for a capital gain). A high PE indicates that the markets believe that profits will grow, or the share is expensive. You're really interested in your competitor's PE ratio relative to your own, and the rest of your sector. A higher PE relative indicates that the stock market believes that their profits will grow faster than other companies in the same industry.

The market's view is indicative, but it's not perfect. It's possible that a company's growth prospects aren't fairly reflected in its PE ratio, as share prices can be influenced by all sort of extraneous factors. The market prefers some chief executives to others. The board's presentation of its future plans may have been unconvincing; after all, the stock market is the same as any other market – it's full of people! Personal relationships are crucial. A company's shares can under-perform the market, in the short term, because some leading analysts don't like, or trust, the board. The market is not always right – remember that every time a share changes hands both parties believe they have made the right decision!

Other things can affect the share price, like the company's gearing. This affects the company's share price, and its return on equity, in different ways at different stages in the economic cycle. In a highly geared company, shareholders will fare badly in a recession and well in a recovery. Interest has to be paid regardless of profits, whereas dividends can be reduced. When sales and profits increase, a highly geared company can reward its shareholders, as the increased profit is spread amongst relatively fewer shares.

Thinking about the investors' perception of the company is useful, as they're the other funding option available to the company. Loans may currently be the cheapest form of finance, but they're not the only one.

Summary

Financial analysis can give you some useful insights into your competitors' business. You can measure the success of their marketing, identify potential problems facing their business, and see how they could respond to their customers. It gives you a rounded view of your competitors' performance.

19

Identifying a company's acquisition potential

- **Relevant ratios** – return on capital employed; operating profit margins, or return on sales; asset utilisation
- **Post-acquisition profitability**
- **Cash management and the cash flow statement** – operational cash flow; dividends received from associates and joint ventures; returns on investment and servicing of finance; taxation; capital expenditure and financial investment; equity dividends paid; cash flow before management of liquid resources; free cash flow
- **Company valuation** – asset-based valuation; profit-based valuations
- **Summary**

Acquisitive companies usually want to enhance their profitability, and they can achieve this in a number of different ways. An acquisition could:

- improve their market share;
- give economies of scale;
- improve their product range;
- improve their cash position and cash flow.

If you're acquiring companies in the same industry you tend to benefit from economies of scale and increased market share. It may be the cheapest way to improve your product range and improve your technology. (Companies that have a technological advantage and better products are often takeover targets, particularly if their processes and products are patent protected. Although if the stock market has already recognised their potential, they may prove too expensive to acquire.)

Other companies become acquisitive because they want to diversify, particularly if they're a single product company that is vulnerable to market changes. They may want to move out of declining industries into expanding ones, or feel that a diverse company offers better protection against the vagaries of the economic cycle.

This all sounds simple and very obvious, but many companies are less profitable after an acquisition than they were before. So what makes some companies more successful with acquisitions than others? The successful predators all seem to have similar criteria, and there appear to be five 'golden rules'.

- *Firstly, they buy businesses they understand.* They avoid glamorous acquisitions. They often either stay within their own sector, or integrate vertically – buying into suppliers or customers. Any diversification outside of their existing business is in a mature established market producing everyday products. They don't buy companies with sophisticated technologies operating in emerging markets – the risks are too great and are often unquantifiable.
- *Secondly, the business must have the potential to be cash generative.* Most successful predators like the acquisition to generate significant amounts of cash in the first year. The cash could be generated in a variety of ways:
  - The business could be inherently cash generating, allowing the predator to use it as a 'cash cow' – stripping cash from the subsidiary through dividend payments.
  - The company may have subsidiaries that could be sold off to generate cash. You'll often find that this leaves the remaining business more profitable without its subsidiaries than it was with them. Five minus two can equal seven!
  - The company may have under-utilised assets that could be sold. If the acquired company has prime commercial property that is undervalued in its accounts and not reflected in its share price, it is vulnerable to 'asset stripping'. This tends to be more common when there are rising property prices and shortages of good commercial property.
  - The company could be badly managed. If it has more cash tied up in working capital than other companies in the industry, the introduction of proper stock and credit control procedures would rapidly generate cash.

- *Thirdly, the acquired company is 'asset backed'.* In other words, its asset value is greater than its market value. This means that the predator is less exposed to losing money on the acquisition, as long as it can realise the asset values.
- *Fourthly, the company is often performing relatively poorly.* Companies that are performing well will always be more expensive to buy. The ideal takeover target is one that's performing badly at the moment, and has already started to rationalise its business, but it's too early for the effects of their rationalisation programme to show in its financial statements. If the market's uncertain whether its strategy is working, it will still be relatively cheap and the predator will appear to turn the company around. Once the predator has improved the company's profits, it could even be sold at a later date. A poorly performing business with good asset backing is always attractive, as it provides a number of options for the future.
- *And finally they are pessimists, not optimists.* They always look at what can go wrong, rather than what may go right.

In summary, successful predators are risk averse. They tend to buy companies that are undervalued by the market because of their current poor performance, and always avoid exposure to technical risks. Their acquisitions are cash generative, or at worst potentially cash generative once the business's underlying performance has improved. Their asset backing gives them greater security, as any under-utilised assets can always be sold to generate cash.

If you're a manager, you're unlikely to be involved in identifying acquisitions for diversification programmes. But you may become involved in acquiring competitors, particularly smaller competitors who are niche players in your marketplace. They may, or may not, be looking to sell their business. You use your market information in conjunction with some financial analysis to identify a company's acquisition potential. If you take a leaf out of the successful predator's book, you're looking for companies that have:

- relatively poor financial performance;
- the potential to generate cash;
- an asset value greater than their market value.

In this chapter I'll show you how you can use financial analysis to identify a company's acquisition potential, and ensure that it meets the above criteria. I'll show you the ratios to use, and introduce you to the way that your company will eventually determine the price it's prepared to pay to acquire the business.

Relevant ratios

You can see that you're looking for a business where there is scope to improve the profitability, so the profitability ratios are the obvious place for the analysis to start. The company's return on capital employed is crucial, as it gives an indication of both the underlying profitability and the company's future cash generation potential.

Return on capital employed

This is the only application where you're interested in the overall return on capital employed as well as the return on operating capital employed. There could be two reasons why the company may be under-performing its sector:

- Its investments could be a larger proportion of its capital employed and are yielding a poorer return.
- Its return on operating capital employed is lower than the rest of its sector's.

You should start by looking at the company's overall return on capital employed, seeing how it has changed over the period and how it compares to your own. It's calculated using the following formula:

$$\frac{\textit{Operating profit} - \textit{exceptional items} + \textit{the share of associates' and joint ventures' operating profit} + \textit{interest receivable and similar income}}{\textit{Adjusted capital and reserves} + \textit{minority interests} + \textit{total debt} + \textit{provisions for liabilities and charges}}$$

(If you're unsure about which numbers to include, and why, I discuss this in detail in Chapter 11.)

You can then compare this to its return on operating capital employed:

$$\frac{\textit{Operating profit} - \textit{exceptional items}}{\textit{Adjusted capital and reserves} + \textit{minority interests} + \textit{total debt} + \textit{provisions for liabilities and charges} - \textit{all investments} - \textit{cash}}$$

Now you're usually primarily interested in the company's trading performance, so you need to look at the hierarchy of profitability ratios to see what is driving the company's return on operating capital employed. Any changes, or differences, in its return on operating capital employed will have arisen from either its profitability, or asset utilisation. I'll start by looking at the operating margin.

Operating profit margin, or return on sales

The operating margin is simple to calculate:

$$\frac{\textit{Operating profit}}{\textit{Turnover}}$$

You'll probably want to look at this before exceptional items to understand the underlying trend in operating margins.

If the company's margin has changed, or is different from your own, you should think about what may cause this. I discussed the possible reasons in detail in Chapter 9, but profit margins are usually affected by differences in:

- *Volumes*: once the company's sales are above breakeven, anything above variable costs is pure profit. Small changes in sales can lead to large changes in profits, and consequently the company's profit margins.
- *Price*: this is both the selling price and the price that the company pays for its costs. You may already know about its relative selling prices, so your prime interest is likely to be differences in costs, to see if there's any scope for improving its profitability by reducing costs. You should be able to see this by looking at its costs on the profit and loss account, and don't forget staff numbers and total staff costs are always disclosed in the notes to the accounts. The note on segmental analysis usually discloses the central costs that aren't attributable to any business. (These are the costs that are likely to disappear after you've bought the business.)
- *Mix*: this could be product mix, business mix, or market mix. The segmental information note could be useful here, as it analyses profits between different businesses and also geographically. This is useful information, as it could be that the company is strong in markets where you are weak, or vice versa. It also shows you whether the target company would be a good fit with your own.

You should also find some clues about the reason for any changes in the margins in the company's operational review. Then you'll be able to make some informed guesses about why its margin has changed and why it's different to your own.

If its operating margins don't explain any changes, or differences, in its return on operating capital, the explanation lies in its asset utilisation.

Asset utilisation

This is reflected in its asset turn ratio:

$$\frac{\textit{Turnover}}{\textit{Operating capital employed}}$$

If this has changed you need to know why it's changed. You know that this is a combination of two things, utilisation of tangible assets and control of working capital. The asset turn is probably less important than its two constituent ratios; the tangible asset turn and the working capital ratios. I'll start with the tangible asset turn, and you calculate it using the formula below:

$$\frac{\textit{Turnover}}{\textit{Tangible fixed assets}}$$

This is a useful measure that helps you identify if the company's assets are being used effectively. If it used to generate £5.00 of sales for every pound invested in tangible assets and is now only managing to generate £3.00, it may have excess capacity. You could either use this capacity, or you could sell off the assets and generate cash. If the tangible asset turn has changed in the period, or is different to your own, you need to think about why, and there are three possible reasons:

- The assets are being used more, or less, effectively. Perhaps they're used continuously, instead of on two shifts – or vice versa.
- The composition of the tangible assets could have changed. Perhaps the company now rents properties, whereas it previously owned them. This will be disclosed in the notes.
- The asset's value could have changed following an acquisition, or a major capital expenditure programme, or disposals. This would be shown in the cash flow statement and disclosed in the note on tangible assets.

You're also interested in the condition of the company's assets, as this would influence whether you could sell them and how much you'd realise. Unfortunately, you have only a few clues about the state of the assets in the accounts. The cash flow statement would tell you the company's capital expenditure in recent years. As a general rule you would expect a company to be investing at a rate greater than the depreciation charge. Depreciation is based on historical costs and historical technologies. Whilst this does vary from one industry to another, you would expect a company's expenditure to have to exceed the depreciation charge just to stand still. If the company's spending less than its depreciation charge, the business has been run as a cash cow. You can find an indication of the age of the assets by looking at the note to the fixed assets in the accounts. This will show the cost, the depreciation to date and the book value. If the book value is 20% of the cost, and the assets are 80% through their lives, they're probably old. The note on depreciation in the accounting policies will disclose the asset lives, so you may get a feel for how old. But you're never going to get an accurate view on the company's assets' lives, as you'll face two big problems:

- The calculation is distorted by recent capital expenditure, and even if you take this into account your analysis won't be accurate.
- The bands given for the asset lives may be so broad (for example, 3–20 years) that it is impossible to calculate the age of the assets.

The next thing to consider is control of working capital, starting with the working capital ratio:

$$\frac{\textit{Working capital}}{\textit{Turnover}}$$

All of the working capital ratios are very useful as they:

- measure management efficiency, as an efficient management team would be minimising its investment in working capital;
- identify if there's an opportunity to generate cash by reducing the company's investment in working capital;
- identify whether its return on operating capital could be improved, as reducing working capital will also improve this ratio.

As you're likely to be looking at a potential acquisition in a similar business, you can compare its working capital ratios to your own company's to see if it is more, or less, efficient. It's then useful to analyse the components of the target's working capital using the following ratios:

- Total stock days (or you could calculate stock turn if you prefer):

$$\frac{\textit{Stocks}}{\textit{Cost of sales (or turnover as appropriate)}} \times 365$$

- Work in progress days, as this also gives you some idea of manufacturing times and you will be interested in whether it takes longer to produce the goods than your company:

$$\frac{\textit{Work in progress}}{\textit{Cost of sales (or turnover as appropriate)}} \times 365$$

- Finished goods stock days:

$$\frac{\textit{Finished goods stocks}}{\textit{Cost of sales (or turnover as appropriate)}} \times 365$$

  (But you need to remember that high finished goods stock isn't necessarily indicative of poor stock control. It may reflect the company's trading relationships, as it could be holding stocks for its customers.)

- Debtor days:

$$\frac{\textit{Trade debtors}}{\textit{Turnover}} \times 365$$

- Creditor days:

$$\frac{\textit{Trade creditors}}{\textit{Cost of sales (or turnover as appropriate)}} \times 365$$

  Debtor and creditor days will be important as they may reflect, in part, the company's relationships with its customers and suppliers.

Once you've worked out the company's ratios, and compared them with your own and with other companies in the sector, you can then start to see its acquisition potential.

Post-acquisition profitability

You've identified the company's relative profitability over the past few years, now it's time to think about its likely profitability if you owned it.

Only operating profit offers long-term sustainable profits, and this is the place to start. You would expect operating profits to improve after the acquisition. The company will be absorbed into your infrastructure, and costs should reduce as many of the central costs disappear. If you have spare capacity, you may be able to close some of its offices and factories and relocate the business to your sites. As a larger business you'll have more purchasing power, and many of your external costs should reduce. But it won't all be good news. You can't expect to maintain all its sales after you've acquired it. It will probably have some customers who prefer to do business with it because they don't want to do business with your company! You should expect to lose a proportion of its sales. If you know the marketplace, and the customer base, you should be able to make a reasonable estimate of a post-acquisition turnover.

Once you've considered all of these factors you should be able to use the current level of profit to extrapolate a post-acquisition profit, taking into account any likely cost savings that should arise following the acquisition.

Next you move on to look at the likely capital employed. If the target company had industry average tangible asset turns, what would its tangible asset value be? And if you amalgamated some of its facilities with your own, by how much would its tangible asset value fall? If it had similar working capital ratios to your own, or the industry average, how much would it have tied up in its working capital? You could run through a number of different scenarios to develop a likely operating capital employed figure.

You then have to do some sensitivity analysis, remembering that successful predators are risk averse, and what can go wrong usually does. What would be the effect on profitability of losing another 10% of the sales, or of only achieving 50% of the planned cost reduction, or only 50% of the planned reduction in working capital? You'll have to generate a number of profit projections, giving each a probability of occurrence.

Cash management and the cash flow statement

The cash flow statement is an important document as it reveals the company's potential to generate cash. However, if you're considering a small private company you would have to prepare a cash flow statement yourself, as they don't have to publish one.

Operational cash flow

You should start by looking at the operational cash flow, as this is the most important cash flow in any business. You can divide it into two parts, the cash flows that will arise from its sales during the year and the cash flows from working capital. Why the split? You want to be able to eliminate the effect of any changes in the business's working capital, as this could arise from management inefficiencies. You've discovered in earlier chapters that if you take the operating profit, add back depreciation, losses on sale of assets, deduct any profits on sale of assets and the utilisation of provisions, you identify the cash flow from sales. This is unlikely to be the same as the total cash flow from operating activities, as the operating cash flow is also affected by changes in working capital requirements. Ideally you're looking for a company with a strong cash flow from sales, reduced by an increasing investment in working capital. This could arise from either poor management or expansion;

either way it would only be a short-term problem, and the company offers opportunities for future cash generation. Once you've made this 'split' between the two sorts of operating cash flows you could then identify the company's future cash flow by using your revised probable profit and working capital requirements.

Dividends received from associates and joint ventures

This shows the cash received from associates and joint ventures and should be compared to the profit shown in the profit and loss account. Sometimes you'll find that these investments could be making losses, but are still paying attractive dividends. These are the cash flows that would be lost if you decided to sell these investments after you acquired the company.

Returns on investment and servicing of finance

So far I've focused on the importance of the company's profits to the acquisition decision. Unfortunately you don't just buy profits and cash flow, you also buy assets and liabilities. If the company has a lot of debt, you're acquiring it too. You may even have to repay the loans as soon as you acquire the company, as some loans have a covenant requiring immediate repayment if the company is acquired. If you buy the company you take over its debts, and consequently you'll be interested in its ability to service its debts out of its current cash flow. Cash-based interest cover is important, as if it's having difficulties with its bank it may be more likely to accept a low offer. You'll also need to look at a future cash interest cover – you may well acquire the company by increasing your loans (particularly at the moment when it's a cheap form of finance). Will the acquired company make a cash contribution to your business after it's paid the interest on its own loans and your acquisition finance?

Taxation

If you're successful in improving the company's profitability, you'll have to pay more tax on the increased profits.

Capital expenditure and financial investment

Ideally the business should be self-funding, with its cash flow after tax, interest and dividends covering any capital expenditure. You'd really need some idea of the state of its current fixed assets before you could see if this was likely, but you've already seen that it's difficult to get this information from the accounts. The only way to be certain is to see them, and you're only likely to see them once the negotiations have started and if it's a friendly bid.

Equity dividends paid

You're not just interested in the company's ability to pay interest; you'll also want to receive some dividends from it if you acquire it.

Cash flow before management of liquid resources

Ideally you would want the company to have a positive cash flow, or at least a potentially positive cash flow, before the management of liquid resources. You'd hope that this, when combined with its existing cash balance, would be enough to repay its loans when they fall due.

You have seen how the cash flow statement can help you to identify the company's ability to generate cash. Before I move on to look at company valuation I'd like to remind you about the valuation free cash flow I discussed in Chapter 13.

Free cash flow

This is the cash flow that is usually used in company valuations, as it's the cash flow that is available to the providers of capital, after any reinvestment in the existing business. So it's the operating cash flow less taxation, capital expenditure, and acquisitions and disposals. This tells you how much cash is available for servicing and repaying the company's debt, and for the company's investors.

You've now considered the potential acquisition's profitability and its cash generation; I'd now like to look at how the company might be valued, and consequently how an offer price is determined.

Company valuation

It's probably unlikely that you'll be involved in determining the acquisition's price, but if you've helped to identify the acquisition's potential, you're bound to be interested in how the final price is determined. Companies use a combination of four different bases for valuing potential investments:

- assets;
- profits;
- cash;
- dividends

The first three are appropriate for valuing acquisitions; a valuation based on dividends is only relevant when you have a small stake in a company. (It's useful when you are looking at the potential return on your investment and comparing it with the price of the share.)

Asset-based valuation

This looks at the net worth of the company and is a useful starting point in company valuation. You know that the net worth is the bottom line of a typical UK balance sheet, and tells you the value of the company's net assets based on its current accounting policies.

Many UK companies don't revalue their assets, so the asset's book value may be much lower than their market value. You may remember that Johnson Matthey showed its properties at depreciated historical cost, and consequently the net worth shown on its balance sheet understates the value of its tangible assets. If you wanted to know what the company's assets are really worth you would have to find answers to the following questions:

- *Land and buildings:*
  - Are they owned or leased?
  - How long does the lease have to run?
  - Have they been revalued?
- *Plant and machinery:*
  - Has the company been replacing its machinery?
  - How old is the equipment?
- *Other fixed assets:*
  - What are they?
  - How have they been valued?
- *Stock:*
  - What is it?
  - Are the stock days higher than the industry average? (This could be a sign of inefficiency, or the company has obsolete stock that has not been written off, or its trading relationships with its customers require it to offer consignment stock.)
- *Debtors:*
  - What is included?
    ... trade debtors?
    ... other debtors?
    ... prepayments?
    ... debtors due in more than a year?
  - Are its debtor days higher than the industry average? (This could be a reflection of management inefficiency, or it may be that the company has not been writing off its bad debts, or its trading relationships with its customers require it to offer longer payment terms.)
- *Creditors:*
  - What is included?
  - How much is debt?
  - Is it secured?
  - On what?
  - What is the repayment schedule?

You wouldn't be able to find the answers to all of these in the accounts, so you'd probably have to guess some of them. This means that you'd have your view of what the company's assets are worth, but someone else may well have a different view. However, all you've discovered is what the business's assets are worth – not what the *company* is worth. Remember you're buying assets, profits and cash.

Profit-based valuations

There are two different ways of approaching a valuation based on profits:

- return on capital;
- price earnings ratio.

Return on capital

Every company wants to improve its return on capital employed, so the last thing that they would want is to make an acquisition that reduces it. This means that the return on capital is likely to be one of the key acquisition criteria, and it can also be used to value a company. When I've talked about the return on capital in other parts of the book I've always used a pre-tax profit, as I've used it as a comparative measure. However, if you're considering buying another company you would normally look at its after-tax profits, as you're concerned about the tax effect of the acquisition and how it will effect your earnings line.

This means that most companies use an after-tax return on capital employed, applying a target return on capital percentage to the profits of the potential acquisition to determine a price band. I'll illustrate this approach in Example 19.1

EXAMPLE 19.1

A company expects all its businesses to have a post-tax return on capital of 10%. It is considering acquiring a company that is currently averaging £500,000 after-tax profits. However, its analysis has indicated that profits can be increased to £600,000 following the acquisition. The return on capital can be used to value the company based on both its current and anticipated profits:

Based on current profits:

$$\frac{£500,000}{10\%} = £5,000,000$$

This would form the basis for the original offer.

Based on anticipated future profits:

$$\frac{£600,000}{10\%} = £6,000,000$$

This would be the maximum price that the company is prepared to pay.

The PE ratio

This is the other profit-based valuation method. It uses the PE ratios of quoted companies and applies them to the potential acquisition. It is often a useful guide to the price that the business's current owners expect to receive from the sale of the company.

Using the PE ratio also involves judgement, as you have to identify similar companies with similar growth prospects to provide the benchmark. (The growth prospects are important, as these are reflected in the price and therefore the PE ratio.)

Continuing with my example 19.1, if a similar company had a PE ratio of 14 the owners might expect to receive at least 14 times current earnings, i.e. £7,000,000. However, this exceeds the maximum amount suggested by the return on capital criterion. This means that the company's owners may well expect to receive more for the business than your company is prepared to pay.

Discounted free cash flow valuation

You know that, theoretically, the value of any company is the present value of its valuation free cash flows in perpetuity. If you want to value a business using discounted cash flow, you estimate its free cash flows for a short period, three to five years, and discount them by your weighted average cost of capital. You then have to calculate its value in the subsequent years (called its terminal, or continuing, value) and this is calculated using the growing perpetuity formula:

$$\frac{\textit{Free cash flow in the first year after the forecast period}}{\textit{Weighted average cost of capital} - \textit{anticipated growth in future cash flows}}$$

Whilst discounted cash flow valuations appear precise, they're no more accurate than any other valuation method, as they're based on the same forecasts. The terminal value usually represents most of the company's value, and the growing perpetuity formula is based on some unrealistic assumptions.

Summary

Companies attempt to buy other companies for a variety of reasons that usually have more to do with long-term strategic gains than short-term profit enhancement.

However, irrespective of the reason for the acquisition, a structured analysis of a company's past and current financial performance provides valuable information for both the selection and negotiating process. Whilst many of the ratios are the same as those used in other contexts, they enable you to assess a company's acquisition potential. A company's net worth, its ability to generate cash and profits, will be reflected in the price that someone is prepared to pay. There are three main valuation techniques, and in practice they are all used to produce a range of prices based on different assumptions.

20

The availability of accounts

- **The format of the accounts filed at Companies House** – small private companies' accounts; medium-sized private companies' accounts

In the UK accounts are readily available for all companies. Suppliers and customers will normally give you their accounts, but often the accounts they provide aren't the ones you'd like to see. If they're part of a large group they'll usually give you the group accounts. However, you may prefer to analyse the individual company's accounts, rather than the group accounts, as the group's accounts may not reflect the same risks as those facing the company you're interested in. It's possible that the subsidiary company you're dealing with is viable, but the group has financial difficulties. Alternatively, the group may be viable and the subsidiary isn't and will shortly be sold, or closed. (Remember TXU Europe?) By looking at the two you would have a greater understanding of the company and its commercial opportunities and threats.

Accounts are available from three sources:

- **The company itself**: most listed companies will send potential investors a copy of their accounts.
- **Financial Times Annual Report Service**: this is a free service for FT readers, and the accounts are usually sent the next working day, unless new accounts are expected shortly, when they are sent on publication. Not all companies offer their accounts through this service and you can spot those that do as they have ♣ next to their name. To order accounts, you should ring 020 8391 6000 or fax 020 8391 9520. You can also order them from the FT.com website.
- **Companies House**: all companies must file their accounts at Companies House, which has offices in Birmingham, Cardiff, Edinburgh, Leeds, London and Manchester. Its internet address is www.companies-house.co.gov.uk, and it will email you the company's accounts (currently costing £4.00 a copy, but there's a minimum credit or debit card charge of £5.00) and/or the company's annual return. A company's annual return includes:
  - the address of its registered office;
  - details of its company secretary and directors;
  - a summary of its share capital;
  - a list of members and any changes in members since its last annual return.

  This also costs £4.00, but you can have both the accounts and the annual report for £5.00. It's also possible to buy a microfiche, which isn't currently available online, usually containing the company's accounts and annual returns for the last three years.

  You can also contact them at one of their offices, or by telephone (+44 0870 3333636), or you can fax them on 029 20 380517.

The format of the accounts filed at Companies House

The accounts that are filed at Companies House may not be as detailed as the ones I've shown you earlier. Small and medium-sized private companies can opt to file *modified* accounts, whereas large private companies and public companies must file their full accounts. The modified accounts filed by smaller companies are a summarised version of the accounts prepared for their shareholders. (This is designed to help them by ensuring that smaller companies don't have to show the general public information that could be harmful to their business.) These modified accounts don't allow you to do a full financial analysis, as you don't have any information about small companies' profitability.

In Chapter 1, I told you about the changing accounting requirements for smaller companies, and the emergence of two sets of accounting practice. Large companies have to comply with increasingly detailed accounting rules and disclosure requirements, whereas smaller private companies comply with a shorter, restricted set of rules that reduce the disclosures in their accounts. This is reflected in the accounts filed at Companies House for small and medium-sized private companies (I gave you a definition of these in Chapter 1). In its full accounts a small private company can choose to use a shorter format for the balance sheet, combining many items shown separately by larger companies. They can then file an even shorter version of this balance sheet, reducing the detailed disclosures even further.

Small private companies' accounts

A small company must file:

- **A modified balance sheet:** there's an example in Figure 20.1 where you'll see that it only shows the totals for each balance sheet category. This is less detailed than the balance sheet prepared for its shareholders, which you may be able to get from the company, but usually only if it's one of your customers or suppliers.
- **Notes to the accounts disclosing:**
  - accounting policies;
  - debtors falling due in more than a year;
  - creditors falling due within a year;
  - creditors falling due in more than a year;
  - authorised and allotted share capital;
  - details of any shares allotted during the year;
  - analysis of the cost and depreciation of fixed assets (only for the major categories that are disclosed in the abbreviated balance sheet);
  - details of its indebtedness;
  - the basis of converting foreign exchange into sterling;
  - comparative numbers for the previous year.

You can see from Figure 20.1 that whilst small companies disclose some information about their assets they give you very little information about their liabilities.

Medium-sized private companies' accounts

There are fewer exemptions for medium-sized companies, who have to file:

- a directors' report;
- a full balance sheet;
- a modified profit and loss account, which starts with gross profit, and consequently it doesn't disclose the company's turnover or cost of sales.

Fig. 20.1 The presentation of a small company's modified balance sheet filed at Companies House

Fixed assets
- Intangible assets
- Tangible assets
- Investments

Current assets
- Stocks
- Debtors
- Investments
- Cash at bank and in hand
- Prepayments and accrued income

Creditors: amounts falling due within a year

Net current assets

Total assets less current liabilities

Creditors: amounts falling due after more than a year

Provisions for liabilities and charges

Accruals and deferred income

Capital and Reserves
- Called-up share capital
- Share premium account
- Revaluation reserve
- Other reserves
- Profit and loss account

Index